PRIVATE LAW AND BUILDING SAFETY

This collection of essays explores the real-world problem of building safety through the lens of private law.

High profile building failures including the fire at Grenfell Tower, London, England and the collapse of Champlain Towers South, Florida, USA have exposed widespread building safety failures globally. In this book, international experts deploy a variety of different private law perspectives ranging through torts, contract and real property law, to examine building safety failures across the UK, USA, Australia, Singapore, New Zealand, Italy and Canada. The book offers policymakers, practitioners and scholars ground-breaking consideration of this vital yet under-considered aspect of the building safety crisis, along with new and valuable insights into the nature, limits and utility of private law.

The book shows that private law can be part of the solution to – as well as being part of the cause of – the building safety crisis. Consideration is given to existing legislative and judicial responses to the crisis, offering guidance as to how statutory regimes addressing the building safety problem (such as the Building Safety Act 2022) can best be understood and developed. A central lesson is the need to take an integrated, coherent approach, within and beyond private law. The book also illustrates that an understanding of the causes of, and responses to, the building safety crisis is vital to any theory of private law: private law is unable to fulfil its distinctive and crucial role of ordering our relations, one to another, if we adopt an unduly limited view of the reasons and resources available to it.

The book results from a joint research project by the Faculty of Law at the University of Oxford and Melbourne Law School at the University of Melbourne.

Volume 56 in the series Hart Studies in Private Law

Hart Studies in Private Law

This monograph series brings together in one place two types of book: works which examine in-depth the fundamental doctrines and principles of private law, and works which engage with the theoretical underpinnings of private law. The series thus aims to contribute to ever-evolving debates about the nature of private law such as problems of classification and taxonomy, remedies, the relationship with public law and the boundaries of private law generally.

The series includes, but is not confined to, works on contract, tort, unjust enrichment, equity, property and the conflict of laws, welcoming work which intersects with other fields of study to enable a deeper understanding of private law theory and practice.

Private Law and Building Safety

Edited by
Matthew Bell
Susan Bright
Ben McFarlane
and
Andrew Robertson

•HART•
OXFORD • LONDON • NEW YORK • NEW DELHI • SYDNEY

HART PUBLISHING

Bloomsbury Publishing Plc

Kemp House, Chawley Park, Cumnor Hill, Oxford, OX2 9PH, UK

1385 Broadway, New York, NY 10018, USA

Bloomsbury Publishing Ireland Limited, 29 Earlsfort Terrace, Dublin 2, D02 AY28, Ireland

HART PUBLISHING, the Hart/Stag logo, BLOOMSBURY and the Diana logo are trademarks of Bloomsbury Publishing Plc

First published in Great Britain 2025

A catalogue record for this book is available from the British Library.

A catalogue record for this book is available from the Library of Congress.

Library of Congress Control Number: 2025934345

ISBN: HB: 978-1-50997-660-7
ePDF: 978-1-50997-662-1
ePub: 978-1-50997-661-4

Typeset by Compuscript Ltd, Shannon

For product safety related questions contact productsafety@bloomsbury.com

To find out more about our authors and books visit www.hartpublishing.co.uk. Here you will find extracts, author information, details of forthcoming events and the option to sign up for our newsletters.

CONTENTS

LIST OF CONTRIBUTORS

Matthew Bell is an Associate Professor of Law at the University of Melbourne.

Susan Bright is Professor of Land Law at the University of Oxford and a Fellow of New College, Oxford.

Fabiana Bettini is a Lecturer in Property Law at University College London.

Marco Cappelletti is a Tutorial Fellow in Law at Worcester College, Oxford.

Erika Chamberlain is a Professor of Law at the University of Western Ontario.

Simone Degeling is a Professor of Law at the University of New South Wales.

Jodi Gardner is a Professor of Law and holds the Brian Coote Chair in Private Law at the University of Auckland.

Nicholas J McBride is a Fellow of Pembroke College, Cambridge.

Ben McFarlane is Professor of English Law at the University of Oxford and a Fellow of St John's College, Oxford.

Evan C McKenzie is a Professor of Political Science and affiliated member of the law faculty at the University of Illinois Chicago.

Jonathan Morgan is Professor of English Law at the University of Cambridge and a Fellow of Corpus Christi College, Cambridge.

Donal Nolan is Professor of Private Law at the University of Oxford and a Fellow of Worcester College, Oxford.

Andrew Robertson is a Professor of Law at the University of Melbourne.

David Sawtell is a Barrister at 39 Essex Chambers in London and a Bye-Fellow of Peterhouse, Cambridge.

Edward SW Ti is an Associate Professor of Law at Singapore Management University.

TABLE OF CASES

Aotearoa New Zealand

Australia

Canada

European Union

Italy

Singapore

United Kingdom

United States of America

TABLE OF LEGISLATION

Aotearoa New Zealand

Australia

Canada

European Union

France

Italy

Singapore

United Kingdom

United States of America

Introduction

As will immediately be evident from reading the chapters in this book, the research project that led to its publication was undertaken in the shadow of building-related catastrophes. None of these calamities is more prominent than the cladding-fuelled fire at Grenfell Tower in London on 14 June 2017. It claimed the lives of 72 people and has, in various ways, affected the lives of millions in the years that followed.

Disbelief was widely expressed after the Grenfell Tower fire that such a building failure could occur, especially in one of the most affluent areas of London, the city from which so much of the common law has spread across the world. This shock was a significant motivation for this research project, investigating the extent to which private law norms have contributed to the 'problem' of the building safety crisis and might be part of its 'solution'.

In 2019, we were fortunate to receive funding for this investigation from a collaborative research programme, sponsored by Allan Myers AC KC, linking our respective law faculties at the University of Oxford and the University of Melbourne. Given the lack of previous work on the nexus between private law and building safety, we were immediately faced with the challenge of how best to define the scope of the investigation. Soon after came the additional challenge of the COVID-19 pandemic. We continued to discuss how we could best take the project forward and, once travel became possible again in 2022, we began to plan in earnest for symposia through which the project could harness the benefit of diverse expert views.

Those symposia occurred during 2023: in February hosted by Oxford and in August hosted by Melbourne. Both were held in the 'dual delivery' mode of in-person and online, allowing participation by colleagues across a wide range of time zones. The first symposium aimed to engage private law scholars, practitioners and policymakers with the nature of the building safety 'problem' and then to explore together areas for detailed consideration. We then settled upon a set of topics which were worked up and presented at the Melbourne symposium.

The chapters you have before you are the result of this collaboration. We believe that they examine, in an innovative and granular manner, the relationship between private law and building safety, and reveal the light that each of these fields can shed on the other.

As the chapters draw on a number of different jurisdictions, it is perhaps also useful in this introduction to draw attention to some points of terminology. In chapter one, for example, we use the general term 'apartment owner' to refer to a party with a right to possession of a distinct unit in a multi-occupied residential block. As we note there, it is a peculiarity of the property law regime in England

and Wales that such an apartment owner will almost always hold a lease, that, at the time of its initial grant, conferred a right to possession of that unit for, perhaps, 99, 125 or even 999 years. This contrasts with the different types of 'condominium' and strata title regimes typical of other jurisdictions which provide for individual unit ownership within a building that is co-owned and governed by the unit holders. These jurisdictions include: Italy (as discussed by Fabiana Bettini and Marco Cappelletti in chapter two), Florida (as discussed by Evan McKenzie in chapter three), Singapore (as discussed by Edward Ti in chapter four) and Canada (as discussed by Erika Chamberlain in chapter five). Whilst it is of course important to be sensitive to the variations in the regimes from one jurisdiction to the next, the issues with which this book is concerned are sufficiently general to allow meaningful comparisons to be made.

The significance of the building safety crisis, across the several jurisdictions considered in this book, has led to unusually rapid legislative responses. A number of the chapters, for example, examine the UK's Building Safety Act 2022 and the radical changes it has made to parts of private law. As discussed by David Sawtell in chapter eight, much will depend on how judges interpret such legislation; the Court of Appeal heard an appeal from the decision in the *Triathlon* case[1] in March 2025.

To keep abreast of the evolution of this area, bearing in mind that this book is limited to dealing in detail only with the legal position on 1 October 2024, it may be useful to point readers to the Housing After Grenfell blog (https://blogs.law.ox.ac.uk/housing-after-grenfell-blog/). Hosted by the Faculty of Law at the University of Oxford, it will continue to provide posts dealing with changes in the law as jurisdictions across the world grapple with the ongoing building safety crisis.

Finally, we thank all of our contributors for their incredible diligence and unfailing courtesy in working with us. We extend that thanks to all participants at the two symposia and the many other colleagues who have taken an interest in the project, including through collaboration via the project's online page on the University of Melbourne's 'Canvas' platform. We hope that this book conveys the intellectual and collegial pleasure it has been for all of us to work together in this exploration.

We pay our particular thanks to:

- The colleagues who presented at the symposia (in addition to the four of us):
  - Oxford: Nicole Johnston, Donal Nolan, David Sawtell, Michael Teys, Stephen Todd and Gareth Wilson.
  - Melbourne: Fabiana Bettini, Marco Cappelletti, Erika Chamberlain, Simone Degeling, Jodi Gardner, Nicholas McBride, Evan McKenzie, Jonathan Morgan, Donal Nolan, David Sawtell, Edward Ti and Edward Willis.

[1] *Triathlon Homes LLP v Stratford Village Development Partnership* [2024] UKFTT 26 (PC) ('*Triathlon*').

- Asang Wankhede for providing research and logistic support for the Oxford symposium.
- St John's College, Oxford for hosting the Oxford symposium and New College, Oxford for hosting the post-symposium dinner.
- Pinsent Masons for hosting the Melbourne symposium.
- The many supporters of the project at our respective faculties including the research administration, information technology and conference support teams.
- Kirsty Wilson as manager of the Melbourne Law School Academic Research Service and Aidan Mansfield as our research assistant and styles and citation editor.
- The team at Hart Publishing for their support, skill, diligence and collegiality throughout the process of producing this book.

In undertaking this project and writing this book, we have been acutely aware that it is far from a purely abstract exercise. The way in which buildings are planned, constructed, maintained and occupied directly impacts upon the homes and livelihoods of millions of people in our subject jurisdictions (and beyond), and we all have a vital stake in those activities resulting in buildings that keep us safe. We hope this book may make at least a small contribution, not only to avoiding high-profile catastrophes such as the Grenfell Tower fire, but more broadly in striking an effective balance between the self-interest that often underpins the enforcement of private law rights, and the need in a cohesive society for high-quality yet affordable places in which to live and work.

Matthew Bell, Susan Bright, Ben McFarlane and Andrew Robertson
March 2025

1

Private Law and Building Safety: Problems and Promises

MATTHEW BELL, SUSAN BRIGHT, BEN McFARLANE AND ANDREW ROBERTSON*

I. Introduction and Overview

The Grenfell Tower Inquiry, chaired by Sir Martin Moore-Bick, published its Phase 2 (and final) report on 4 September 2024.[1] Over several years, the Inquiry had examined the causes and impact of a fire that broke out in a 24-storey residential tower block in west London in the early hours of 14 June 2017. The fire, fuelled by combustible building materials that had been installed when the Tower was refurbished, utterly devastated the building and caused the deaths of 72 people.

As the Inquiry has documented, and partly as a result as the horrifying images of the fire seen around the world, Grenfell Tower has become emblematic of a global building safety crisis and the risks faced by residents of multi-occupied residential buildings. The Inquiry cautioned against blame for the disaster being ascribed to a narrow set of causes, finding that

> the fire at Grenfell Tower was the culmination of decades of failure by central government and other bodies in positions of responsibility in the construction industry to look carefully into the danger of incorporating combustible materials into the external walls of high-rise residential buildings and to act on the information available to them.[2]

In other words, a number of very serious failures, from government, public bodies and commercial actors, had placed the occupiers of the building in an extremely vulnerable position, allowing a fire beginning in a fourth-floor flat to have such devastating consequences. It took the tragedy at Grenfell Tower to expose the widespread use of combustible materials on high-rise buildings. In many jurisdictions

* We are grateful for the very helpful comments made by contributors to this volume and by symposia participants, as well as by John Mee. All opinions and errors are our own.

[1] Grenfell Tower Inquiry, *Phase 2 Report of the Public Inquiry into the Fire at Grenfell Tower on 14 June 2017* (London, HMSO, 2024).

[2] ibid vol 1, 9.

around the world, thousands of apartment blocks still have life-critical safety defects, due to not only the use of flammable materials but also other construction defects revealed by post-Grenfell investigations. Making these buildings safe to live in should be a priority, but remediation has been slow and for many blocks has not even begun. Apartment owners and residents, who are not to blame for the problem, need redress: they want the building fixed, but also do not want (and should not be required) to pay for the faults of others. Other disasters, such as the collapse at Surfside in Miami which led to 98 deaths and is discussed by Evan McKenzie in his chapter, highlight the challenges faced by owners in maintaining buildings.[3]

The purpose of this book is to explore the interaction between private law and building safety. We recognise that the condition of private law is neither the chief problem contributing to the building safety crisis, nor the best way of addressing that crisis. Given the very broad range of failures identified by the Grenfell Tower Inquiry, for example, a wholesale re-evaluation of the behaviours of government, public bodies and commercial actors is required; as noted by Nicholas McBride in his chapter, this may require addressing still broader factors which lie behind such failures.[4]

The collaborative research project that has led to this book was motivated by the relative lack of sustained, critical consideration of the role of private law in the responses to the building safety crisis. We therefore brought together experts from jurisdictions across the world to meet, across symposia hosted in Oxford and Melbourne, to discuss different aspects of, and perspectives on, private law and building safety.[5] This chapter sets out why we think both that an examination of private law is a necessary step in enhancing building safety, and that an understanding of the causes of, and responses to, the building safety crisis is vital to anyone with an interest in private law.

The central lesson of this chapter – and, we would argue, of the book – is the need to take an integrated, coherent approach. This is true both within and beyond private law. The building safety crisis demonstrates the need to understand the practical incentives for, and legal responsibilities of, parties in a position to prevent or remedy building defects. In its application to multi-occupied blocks consisting of residential units, such as Grenfell Tower and Surfside, the crisis reveals the impact of the content of property law on the duties arising in other parts of private law, such as contract and torts. The crisis also reveals problems that extend beyond building safety. It shows, for example, the pressing need for reform of the leasehold system[6] that has long characterised apartment ownership in England and

[3] EC McKenzie, 'The Surfside Condominium Collapse: What Lessons Have Been Learned?', this volume, ch 3.

[4] NJ McBride, 'Private Law in the Ruins', this volume, ch 10.

[5] The research project leading to this book is described in further detail in the introduction at pp 1–3.

[6] The nature of this system is discussed briefly in the Introduction to the book, and is examined in more detail in section III.A below, as well as in F Bettini and M Cappelletti, 'Tackling Building Safety through Private Law: A Comparative Analysis', this volume, ch 2.

Wales, as well as the need for careful consideration of the duties of condominium associations and similar organisations in other jurisdictions.[7] As one of us has argued elsewhere,[8] the building safety crisis represents a 'property moment': a juncture when an urgent need for reform makes clear that even well-established property rules are not permanent, and that the state has a key, ongoing role in developing property law.

Indeed, we will also argue that legislative responses to the building safety crisis – particularly, but not only,[9] the UK's Building Safety Act 2022 (BSA 2022) – suggest that we are in a wider 'private law moment', where radical state intervention demonstrates how familiar private law structures can be used to achieve particular policy aims. The flexibility shown by those structures presents an important challenge to some influential theories, which argue that the form of a private law claim provides inherent limits on the type of reasons which can justify such claims.[10] We will argue that the recent legislative interventions, although often far-reaching,[11] should not be castigated as a departure from fundamental tenets of private law, but rather be seen to draw on a breadth of resources and ideas already available within private law. A theory of private law, we argue, ought to be capable of accommodating the variety of concepts that can be brought to bear within the standard private law structure of one party making an assertion based on a duty or liability of another.[12] The variety, we argue, provides the flexibility that allows not only property law, but private law more generally, to be 'resilient',[13] in the sense both of adapting to change and continuing to command the general support of society. It is wholly understandable that those whose lives have been affected by the carelessness or dishonesty of others should look to private law, both as a means for redress and as a vehicle for preventing future problems. Private law is unable to fulfil its distinctive and crucial role of ordering our relations, one to another, if we adopt an unduly limited view of the reasons and resources available to it. Indeed, as noted

[7] See the discussion in McKenzie (n 3).

[8] S Bright, 'Resilient High-Rise Property? Grenfell Tower and Beyond' (2023) 8 *Journal of Law Property and Society* 9, 13.

[9] See too the Australian Capital Territory's Property Developers Act 2024.

[10] Most notably EJ Weinrib, *The Idea of Private Law* (Cambridge, MA, Harvard University Press, 1995); EJ Weinrib, *Reciprocal Freedom: Private Law and Public Right* (Oxford, Oxford University Press, 2022).

[11] As shown, for example, in D Sawtell, 'Rationalising Associate Liability under the Building Safety Act 2022', this volume, ch 8.

[12] See eg A Robertson, 'Justifying Liabilities and Duties' in S Degeling, M Crawford and N Tiverios (eds), *Justifying Private Rights* (Oxford, Hart Publishing, 2020) 201, 203; B McFarlane, 'Equitable Estoppel and Restitution as Interstitial Causes of Action' in S Bray, P Miller and H Smith (eds), *Interstitial Private Law* (Oxford, Oxford University Press, 2024).

[13] For discussions of the concept of 'resilience' in the context of property law, see eg E van der Sijde, 'What Can (South African) Property Lawyers Learn from Resilience Thinking? An Exploratory Note on the Aftermath of the Covid-19 Pandemic' in Z Boggenpoel et al (eds) *Property and Pandemics: Property Responses to Covid-19* (Cape Town, Juta, 2021); L Fox O'Mahony and M Roark, *Squatting and the State: Resilient Property in an Age of Crisis* (Cambridge, Cambridge University Press, 2022) 225; Bright (n 8).

by Nicholas McBride in his chapter,[14] preserving its own legitimacy amongst those it governs is itself an important task of private law, as no system of private law can function effectively if it is not generally accepted as legitimate. In short, if we want things to stay as they are (or have been) – if citizens are likely to continue to have a disposition to engage with the law,[15] and property rights, and private law more generally, are to continue to have a prominent role in promoting people's safety and autonomy – then some things do need to change.

In section II of this chapter, we explain the sense in which various building safety issues can be seen as private law problems. In section III, we turn to some problems of constituent parts of private law and how they have impeded private law's effectiveness in preventing building safety defects, and in delivering effective remedies where such defects occur. In section III, we also discuss how some of the legislative responses to the recent high-profile disasters, whilst containing surprising departures from core ideas commonly associated with private law, also build on some concepts inherent in parts of private law. Our essential question throughout is whether private law should be added to the list of institutions that have failed those affected by the building safety crisis. In section IV, we conclude by considering the promise, and limitations, of private law in the wider building safety context.

II. Building Safety: A Private Law Problem

In this section, we will first show that building safety can be understood as a private law problem from the perspectives of both redress and prevention, before briefly considering two building safety examples demonstrating the salience of private law in practice. We start with a simple and relatively uncontroversial understanding of private law as consisting of those substantive rules and principles which define the rights that legal parties hold, and can enforce, one against another. As Professor Andrew Burrows (now Lord Burrows JSC) has observed: 'English private law is best viewed as concerned with the rights which, one against another, people are able to realize in courts.'[16] We accept this as true of both English private law, and private law more generally, with two caveats. First, rights, whilst realisable in court, can of course play an important role in shaping parties' conduct and

[14] See, further, N McBride, *The Humanity of Private Law, Part I: Explanation* (Oxford, Hart Publishing, 2019) ch 6.

[15] See M Harding, 'Equity and the Rule of Law' (2016) 132 *LQR* 278, drawing on the analysis of John Gardner (J Gardner, 'The Supposed Formality of the Rule of Law' in *Law as a Leap of Faith* (Oxford, Oxford University Press, 2012) ch 8) to argue that the existence of such a disposition is important to a 'modal' conception of the rule of law, which sees the rule of law as a 'measure of the fitness of law as a technique for subjecting human conduct to the governance of rules and rulings in the pursuit of the panoply of purposes that law has'.

[16] A Burrows (ed), *English Private Law*, 3rd edn (Oxford, Oxford University Press, 2013) ix.

in facilitating transactions without needing, in fact, to be thus realised.[17] Second, the term 'rights' should be understood broadly. To use Hohfeldian terms,[18] those rights do not consist only of claim-rights (where A's duty to B correlates to a claim-right that B has against A) but also include, for example, powers (where A's liability to B correlates to a power that B has against A) and immunities (where A's lack of a power in relation to B correlates to an immunity that B has in relation to A).[19]

Powers, we argue, are particularly important for three reasons. First, because the redress sought by B in private law can include a recognition of a liability of A arising as a result of A's breach of duty to B (such as a liability to compensate B), and also the enforcement of a primary liability: one which recognises that B has the power to make a claim against A which does not depend on a prior breach of duty by A.[20] Second, as made clear by some significant private law scholarship,[21] powers may be held by a court (or other tribunal) with a power to make orders, and so do not only exist as between the two parties such as A and B. So, for example, one way of understanding the situation in which A is vicariously liable to B for a tort committed by A's employee is as follows: B has a power to make a claim against A, which in turn triggers a power of the court to make an order requiring A to make payment to B. Third, and linked to this point, is another that has recently attracted more attention in analyses of private law.[22] Where A is under a duty, there may be cases in which, even though A's duty does not correlate to a claim-right of B, B will nonetheless have a power, against A, to enforce A's duty, or to make a claim for some form of redress as a result of A's breach of that duty.[23] One context in which this point matters, for example, is where A is under a 'standalone'

[17] This point was famously emphasised in H Hart, *The Concept of Law*, 3rd edn (Oxford, Clarendon Press, 2012) ch 3.

[18] W Hohfeld, 'Some Fundamental Legal Conceptions as Applied in Judicial Reasoning' (1913–14) 23 *Yale Law Journal* 16.

[19] An immunity relevant to the building safety context arises where a limitation period operates to deny A the power to bring a claim against B, thus giving B an immunity in relation to A. For discussion of the importance of limitation periods in this context, see section III.B.

[20] For the use of the term 'primary liability', see eg Robertson (n 12) 203; B McFarlane, 'Equitable Estoppel and Restitution as Interstitial Causes of Action' in Bray, Miller and Smith (n 12). See too S Smith, 'Duties, Liabilities, and Damages' (2012) 125 *Harvard Law Review* 1727.

[21] See eg S Smith, Rights, Wrongs, and Injustices: The Structure of Remedial Law (Oxford, Oxford University Press, 2019); J Goldberg and B Zipursky, *Recognizing Wrongs* (Cambridge, MA, Harvard University Press, 2020).

[22] See eg T Liau, *Standing in Private Law* (Oxford, Oxford University Press, 2023) and note too B Zipursky, 'Rights, Wrongs and Recourse in the Law of Torts' (1998) 51 *Vanderbilt Law Review* 1 and 'Substantive Standing, Civil Recourse, and Corrective Justice' (2011) 39 *Florida State University Law Review* 299.

[23] For example, drawing on L Smith, 'Unjust Enrichment, Property, and the Structure of Trusts' (2000) 11 *LQR* 412, Liau (n 22, ch 8) argues that the personal claim allowed in *Re Diplock* [1948] Ch 465 (CA), [1951] AC 251 (HL) is best seen as one which consisted of the claimant next of kin enforcing a duty of the defendant charities which was owed not to the next of kin themselves but rather to the executors of the deceased estate.

or 'undirected' duty:[24] one that does not correlate to a claim-right of another party, and thus escapes the conventional bilateral understanding of private law duties. In such a case, it still may be possible for the law to allow specific parties, including B, a power to enforce A's duty, or to make a claim for some form of redress as a result of A's breach of that duty.[25]

It is true that Hohfeld's basic scheme of legal relations does not focus specifically on remedies and so, as generally understood, does not directly account for powers of a court or other tribunal to make orders. It is also true that the basic scheme, as it focuses on duties that correlate to claim-rights, may also require some adjustment to account for 'standalone' or 'undirected' duties. This does not mean, however, that these well-established aspects of legal practice need to be seen as illegitimate, or beyond the scope of private law. Rather, we argue, they are important tools which private law can use in its distinctive role of ordering parties' relations and protecting crucial interests, whilst also maintaining its own legitimacy.

A. Redress

When safety issues are exposed in a particular building, it is likely that the immediate desire of an affected owner is to have the defect rectified, without having to bear the cost. That is certainly the case, for example, for apartment owners in those multi-occupied residential blocks that were revealed, following the Grenfell Tower fire, to have unsafe cladding. Such adversely affected parties may therefore often think to seek redress through private law causes of action, such as breach of contract or negligence, which depend on the existence of a specific claim-right that the specific claimant holds, or held, against the specific defendant. As we will see, however, there are often insurmountable obstacles, both substantive and procedural, to establishing liability through these familiar private law routes.

One could therefore argue that building safety is *not* a private law problem: there are many instances of loss inflicted by one person on another for which private law provides no remedy.[26] There are, nonetheless, at least three related senses in which building safety *can* be understood as a private law problem.

[24] See P Miller and A Gold, 'Fiduciary Governance' (2015–16) 57 *William & Mary Law Review* 513, 554–55, drawing on R Perry, 'Correlativity' (2009) 28 *Law & Philosophy* 537, 537, for use of the term 'standalone duty' to refer to 'duties that do not imply a correlative claim right that is enjoyed and may be asserted by a right holder in her personal capacity'. See L Smith, *The Law of Loyalty* (Oxford, Oxford University Press, 2023) ch 8, s I and ch 9, s II for the use of the term 'undirected duty' to refer to the same concept.

[25] A clear example, given by Miller and Gold (n 24) are the duties owed by a trustee of a charitable trust. In England, for example, powers to enforce those duties are held not only by the Attorney-General, but also by 'any person interested': see Charities Act 2011, s 115, discussed by H Jing, 'Enforcing Charitable Trusts: A Study on the English Necessary Interest Rule (2022) 42 *Legal Studies* 228.

[26] See eg Edelman J in *Mallonland Pty Ltd v Advanta Seeds Pty Ltd* [2024] HCA 25 [71]. See too R Stevens, *Torts and Rights* (Oxford, Oxford University Press, 2007) ch 3, referring not only to *Murphy v Brentwood* [1991] 1 AC 398 (HL) but also, for example, to the three House of Lords decisions in *Mogul*

First, building safety remains a private law problem if we believe that private law *should* provide redress: if it should be possible for B – a party affected by a building safety deficiency – to initiate, at B's choosing, a claim against A, a party who owes a duty to B, or is under a liability to B, in relation to that deficiency or its consequences. It is certainly important in this context to note that the rhetoric used by some of those affected by the building safety crisis, and by policymakers when framing responses to it, is often informed by terms and intuitions derived from private law. For example, one complaint of owners of apartments affected by dangerous cladding has been that: 'We were sold homes that should have been safe. You have more protection buying a toaster.'[27]

As far as prevention is concerned, the 'should have been safe' aspect could refer to failures by public bodies, including the government and its agencies, to perform their regulatory functions,[28] or to breach of standalone or undirected duties imposed by, for example, building regulations. The 'should have been' may, however, refer to private law duties, such as the contractual duty of a developer to a purchaser to provide a building reasonably fit for human habitation, duties imposed by the law of torts on building professionals to downstream owners, or statutory duties imposed on a builder and owed to anyone later acquiring a property right in the building.[29] The reference to the protection available when buying a toaster suggests a focus on liability, rather than prevention, with such liability possibly depending on a defendant having breached a duty owed to the purchaser.

The fact that those affected by building safety issues look to private law can be seen as a reflection of the fact that those who design and construct buildings *should* be responsible to downstream owners and occupants because those architects, engineers and builders are best placed to ensure building safety. In a broad sense, those professionals can be understood to be responsible for the safety of the buildings they produce. In that sense, those who are adversely affected by unsafe buildings may be understood to have been wronged by building professionals whose careless work has caused the buildings to be unsafe. Moreover, the imposition of liability on the part of manufacturers of goods to ultimate consumers, particularly with respect to safety issues, is a commonplace consumer protection measure. The intuition of apartment owners, therefore, that some form of private law redress should be available, cannot simply be dismissed as misguided. In fact, it is a sign of the success of a system of private law if citizens have a disposition to engage with it,[30] and to expect it to assist where they have suffered a significant setback in relation to their enjoyment of their property rights.

Steamship Co v McGregor Gow & Co [1892] AC 25 (HL); *Bradford v Pickles* [1895] AC 587 (HL); and *Allen v Flood* [1898] AC 1 (HL).

[27] End Our Cladding Scandal, X @EOCS_Official, 9 April 2022.

[28] Such failures were confirmed by the Grenfell Tower Inquiry *Phase 2 Report* (n 1): see text at n 2 above.

[29] See Defective Premises Act 1972 (UK), s 1.

[30] See text at n 15 above.

Similarly, some of the rhetoric employed by members of the UK government prior to the passing of the BSA 2022 is at least consistent with private law ideas. A January 2022 statement of the minister sponsoring the legislation, for example, refers to developers who had done 'the right thing'[31] by paying for remediation of buildings with fire safety defects, and later parliamentary answers also set out the government's position that 'those responsible for historical building safety defects must pay to put them right'.[32] Of course, such aims could be met using means other than private law: in the United Kingdom, for example, before its focus turned to the BSA 2022, the government asked developers for 'voluntary' contributions to a £4 billion fund to be used for remedying unsafe cladding on buildings between 11 and 18 metres in height, stating that its procurement and planning powers would be used to favour contributors over non-contributors.[33]

Nonetheless, a private law model, whereby particular claimants are allowed to bring claims against particular defendants in relation to specific safety risks, is certainly one means of pursuing the aim of rectifying building safety defects without requiring apartment owners to bear the cost. A number of the reforms made by the BSA 2022 employ such a model, as does recent legislation in the Australian state of New South Wales which creates a statutory duty of care to protect homeowners against economic loss.[34] As shown in Jonathan Morgan's chapter,[35] any legislature seeking to respond to the crisis needs to draw lessons from the law of torts when designing forms of redress: the BSA 2022, passed in haste, has left much of that thinking to the judges who will interpret its broadly phrased terms.[36] Moreover, it is notable that, in exerting its pressure on developers, the government in the end asked them to sign up to a contract to undertake and contribute to particular remediation work, making use of a classic private law form to evidence and clarify a legally binding commitment. At the very least then, the response to the building safety crisis shows the truth of Ernest Weinrib's observation that private law

> is a pervasive phenomenon of our social life, a silent but ubiquitous participant in our most common transactions. It regulates the property we own and use, the injuries we inflict or avoid inflicting, the contracts we make or break. It is the public repository of our most deeply embedded intuitions about justice and personal responsibility.[37]

[31] HC Deb, 10 January 2022, vol 706, cols 285 and 300.

[32] See eg answer given by M Jones, on behalf of the Department for Levelling Up, Housing and Communities, on 20 July 2022 (UIN 34866).

[33] Department for Levelling Up, Housing and Communities, 'Letter to Residential Property Developer Industry', 10 January 2022. See discussion in S Bright and B McFarlane, 'Private Law Failings and Policy Development Following the Grenfell Tower Fire' in J Gardner et al (eds) *Politics, Policy and Private Law*, vol 1 (Oxford, Hart Publishing, 2023).

[34] Design and Building Practitioners Act 2020 (NSW).

[35] J Morgan, 'Tort as a Tool of Government Policy: Section 38 of the Building Act 1984: Sleeping Beauty Awakes?', this volume, ch 7.

[36] See eg Sawtell (n 11, 219ff) considering how a tribunal might approach its powers, under the BSA 2022 ss 124 and 130, to make remediation contribution orders and building liability orders, where 'it considers it just and equitable to do so'.

[37] Weinrib, *The Idea of Private Law* (n 10) 1.

Second, building safety is a private law problem if the nature and structure of the private rights it affords have contributed in some way to the current crisis. This seems to be true in at least three different ways. First, as Weinrib notes, private law 'regulates the property we own and use' and we will see in section III.A how the different property law structures used to regulate multi-occupied residential blocks have complicated remediation of building defects and, in their misaligned incentives, have also contributed to the existence of those defects.[38] Second, it is important to consider whether the scope and content of tort claims available to later purchasers of defective residential buildings – a matter that varies in significant ways across different jurisdictions – has had any impact on the crisis. Certainly, as shown by Donal Nolan's chapter,[39] questions of building safety have been central to the development of key parts of the law of torts, as shown by cases such as *Anns v Merton London Borough Council*,[40] *Murphy v Brentwood District Council*,[41] *Brookfield Multiplex Ltd v Owners' Corporation 61288*[42] and *Winnipeg Condominium Corporation No 36 v Bird Construction Co*.[43] The third aspect is that private law offers parties various means of structuring their relationships, including by creating new legal entities, such as companies. There is a risk that the way in which those structures are used, for example by developers, building professionals and condominium associations,[44] may increase the chances of building safety defects occurring, and may impede redress for such defects.[45] For example, as David Sawtell notes in his chapter, it is not uncommon for a developer to set up a special-purpose vehicle to carry out a particular building project.[46] This vehicle may then be the party identified by standard private law rules as the holder of duties, or as subject to liabilities. However, if under-capitalised, or even dissolved after the completion of the project, that entity will be unable to provide adequate redress.[47] Similarly, it may be that the interposition of corporate entities

[38] As will be seen in section III.A, and in Bettini and Cappelletti's chapter (n 6), this is particularly true in England and Wales, given its leasehold regime, but, as shown in McKenzie's chapter (n 3), can also be the case where condominium associations have ownership of a multi-occupied residential building.

[39] D Nolan, 'Defective Premises and Economic Loss: A Problem Best to Legislation?', this volume, ch 6.

[40] *Anns v Merton London Borough Council* [1978] AC 728 (HL) ('*Anns*').

[41] *Murphy v Brentwood District Council* [1991] 1 AC 398 (HL) ('*Murphy*').

[42] *Brookfield Multiplex Ltd v Owners' Corporation 61288* [2014] HCA 36, (2014) 254 CLR 185.

[43] *Winnipeg Condominium Corporation No 36 v Bird Construction Co* [1995] 1 SCR 85 ('*Winnipeg Condominium*') (SCC). This case is the subject of Erika Chamberlain's chapter in this volume: 'Building Safety in Canada: Has *Winnipeg Condominium* Had an Impact?' (ch 5).

[44] See McKenzie's chapter (n 3) for discussion of how the Surfside collapse exposed weaknesses in the legal duties and practical operation of the boards of condominium associations in Florida.

[45] There may be, for example, difficulties in applying mental elements of torts or other civil wrongs to a company: for discussion, see eg E Bant (ed), *The Culpable Corporate Mind* (Oxford, Hart Publishing, 2023).

[46] Sawtell (n 11) 217.

[47] As Sawtell (ibid) notes, for example, apartment owners in *Rendlesham Estates plc v Barr Ltd* [2014] EWHC 3968 (TCC) who had bought their apartments off-plan had contractual claims against the developer, but those claims were 'effectively worthless' as the developer had very few resources of its own and went into administration.

has an effect in diluting the sense of responsibility which particular individuals feel when carrying out work, or discharging roles, related to the construction or maintenance of a building. McBride details in his chapter the shocking lack of responsibility shown by directors and employees of companies supplying the highly flammable insulation used in the refurbishment of Grenfell Tower, and this may be linked to parties' misguided belief that their duties, as directors or employees, are simply to maximise the profits of their company. Similarly, there is a risk that directors of condominium associations may be too passive in carrying out their role: McKenzie shows in his chapter that changes have been proposed to ensure that directors serving on boards of condominium associations are more active in ensuring that buildings are inspected regularly.[48] Similarly, legislation recently passed in the Australian Capital Territory[49] aims to place personal responsibility on directors of construction companies where this is necessary to ensure that such directors properly carry out their roles in ensuring that the companies comply with building regulations. This legislation has attracted controversy.[50] Moreover, as Sawtell shows, the provisions of the BSA 2022 dealing with liability of 'associated' companies are radical in looking beyond the legally distinct status of separate companies.[51] Nonetheless, such steps may be necessary to ensure that the rules of one part of private law (eg corporate law) do not interfere with the aims of other parts of private law, such as the need to protect apartment owners in their enjoyment of their property.

Third, building safety is a private law problem if the building safety crisis means that private law fails to deliver on some of the promises that it makes to its subjects. Whatever justification is preferred for core private law rights such as bodily integrity or property rights in one's home, such reasons are clearly not fulfilled where a person's life is cut short, and are not fully given effect to if ownership of one's home becomes a burden that reduces, rather than promotes, a person's autonomy. The frustration and, in some cases, anguish of owners who, as a result of the building safety crisis, find themselves trapped in apartments they cannot sell or mortgage is related, in some part, to a failure to fulfil the promise, particularly associated with acquisition of a valuable property right in one's home, of independence and autonomy.[52] Indeed, for such people, their property right has had the opposite effect, drastically limiting their life choices and imposing heavy financial burdens

[48] See eg the changes proposed by the Florida State Bar Association Select Task Force.

[49] Property Developers Act 2024 (ACT).

[50] See eg the objections made by the Property Council of Australia to the Bill which led to the Property Developers Act 2024 (ACT), available at https://www.propertycouncil.com.au/media-releases/developer-licence-bill-will-cripple-housing-and-investment.

[51] Sawtell (n 11).

[52] For a view that sees the promotion of autonomy as central to the general nature and purpose of property law, see eg H Dagan, *A Liberal Theory of Property* (Cambridge, Cambridge University Press, 2021). For the particular importance of the home, see eg L Fox, *Conceptualising Home* (Oxford, Hart Publishing, 2007).

in meeting the costs of both interim safety measures, such as waking watches, and remediation of building defects.[53]

B. Prevention

In the common law world, the law of obligations is primarily focused on questions of liability. The common law is articulated and developed through judgments, and judgments in contract, torts and related areas are primarily focused on whether liability should or should not be imposed in particular circumstances.[54] As thus articulated, the law primarily consists of 'backward-looking attributions of liability' rather than 'forward looking legislation or regulation'.[55] When we think of private law responses to building safety problems, therefore, we tend to focus attention on potential avenues of liability and potential remedies. Preventing the problems in the first place may be perceived to be the distinct job of 'regulation', flowing from 'top-down' guidance or the state's policy prescriptions.

Undoubtedly, regulation in this sense has a central role. Peter Apps, in his acclaimed *Show Me the Bodies: How We Let Grenfell Happen*, observed that the fire

> tells us something about how we are governed, and the priority our political and economic system places on human life – especially when those lives are likely to be poor, immigrant and from ethnic minority backgrounds. Grenfell was the result of a series of choices, the sum of state neglect and corporate wrongdoing across a variety of areas, the epicentre of myriad defects in our social fabric.[56]

Certainly, as made clear by its Phase 2 report, the Grenfell Tower Inquiry has revealed serious failings in the UK regulatory system,[57] which had already been described as 'not fit for purpose' in the 2018 Hackitt Review of Building Regulations and Fire Safety.[58] As illustrated in Edward Ti's chapter, in a jurisdiction such as Singapore where state regulation has imposed, and effectively enforced, higher standards, building failure appears less common.[59] It is a key aim of this book to highlight, however, that this preventative work is not only done through the

[53] See eg Bright (n 8) 13–14, discussing the 'heart-breaking personal tragedies' of leaseholders in unsafe residential blocks, as collected by the End Our Cladding Scandal campaign group.

[54] Robertson (n 12) 203.

[55] JCP Goldberg and BC Zipursky, 'Seeing Tort Law From the Internal Point of View: Holmes and Hart on Legal Duties' (2006) 75 *Fordham Law Review* 1563, 1588.

[56] P Apps, *Show Me the Bodies: How We Let Grenfell Happen* (London, Oneworld, 2022) 3. Similar critiques have been offered in respect of other building-related disasters, including, in relation to the February 2023 earthquakes in Turkey and Syria: B Hubbard et al, 'Why One Upscale Apartment Building Became a Death Trap' *New York Times* (11 May 2023) www.nytimes.com/interactive/2023/05/11/world/europe/turkey-earthquake-apartment-building-collapse.html.

[57] See Grenfell Tower Inquiry, *Phase 2 Report* (n 1), Part 2.

[58] J Hackitt, 'Building a Safer Future: Independent Review of Regulations and Fire Safety: Final Report' (HMSO 2018) Cm 9607 11.

[59] ESW Ti, 'The Role of Private Law in Promoting Building Safety: The Case of Singapore', this volume, ch 4.

'regulatory law' of legislated standards directly enforced by state and public agencies, but is also carried out through private law.

First, as we will see in section III.B, duties assumed by the parties through contractual arrangements can be seen as part of the regulatory environment, even though they have a classic private law form. Second, and linked to this, preventative work is done through the recognition and creation of private law duties. In establishing such duties, the common law does tell people how to behave and people do, at least to some extent, act on the basis of those directives for reasons that can be unrelated to the sanctions or incentives the law provides.[60] Certainly, the prospective impact of private law duties has been taken into account by both judges and legislatures in shaping the law. In response to the Surfside collapse, for example, the US state of Florida was quick to pass legislation making it mandatory for 30-year-old high-rise buildings to be inspected for structural soundness, and the inspection is to be repeated every 10 years.[61] As discussed by Evan McKenzie in his chapter, a failure to complete the required structural integrity study exposes officers or members of the condominium board to liability, for breach of fiduciary duty, to any individual unit owner. A classic private law form is thus used to enforce an essentially regulatory duty,[62] with the twist that it is not possible for the principals (the unit owners), even if acting unanimously, to waive the underlying duty.[63]

In the building safety context, judges have considered the incentive effects of private law rules not only on defendants, but also on claimants. In *Winnipeg Condominium*,[64] for example, in justifying the recognition of a duty of care on builders in relation to the economic loss suffered by a subsequent purchaser in repairing dangerous defects, LaForest J in the Supreme Court of Canada expressly noted the perverse incentives that would be created if a building owner were to have a claim only if and when a dangerous defect actually caused physical harm: 'Maintaining a bar against recoverability for the cost of repair of dangerous defects provides no incentive for plaintiffs to mitigate potential losses and tends to encourage economically inefficient behaviour.'[65]

As Erika Chamberlain notes in her chapter, this reasoning 'stresses the preventive function of allowing recovery for the costs of repairing dangerous defects'.[66] As Chamberlain there concludes, even if, in the specific case of defects posing a 'real and substantial danger',[67] private law only provides a small additional incentive

[60] See eg H Hart, *The Concept of Law*, 3rd edn (Oxford, Clarendon Press, 2012) ch 3; SA Smith, 'The Normativity of Private Law' (2011) 31 *OJLS* 215.

[61] Florida State Legislature, Senate Bill 4-D: Building Safety (2022) 269.

[62] See too the duty of condominium associations to maintain sufficient reserves so that necessary repairs can be promptly carried out, as discussed in McKenzie's chapter (n 3) 84.

[63] Note too that the legislation provides that condominium associations are prevented from waiving unit owners' obligations to contribute to reserved funds: see ibid 96.

[64] *Winnipeg Condominium* [1995] 1 SCR 85.

[65] ibid [37].

[66] Chamberlain (n 43) 134.

[67] As Chamberlain notes, ibid, 'recovery pursuant to *Winnipeg Condominium* is limited to defects that pose a "real and substantial danger"': [1995] 1 SCR 85 [21].

to an owner in any case motivated to act, the imposition of duties and liabilities on builders can have an impact on building safety, and private law is thus 'part of a complex system of regulation and standards enforcement that promotes harm prevention and responsibility for safe construction'.[68] Nolan argues in his chapter that legislation, rather than judicial development, is the proper means to give effect to a policy-motivated decision to allow non-contractual liability for carelessly caused economic loss.[69] As shown by the UK's Defective Premises Act 1972 (DPA 1972), or recent legislation in the Australian state of New South Wales that creates a statutory duty of care to protect building owners against economic loss,[70] an aim of preventing careless building work may be given effect to by using private law forms, and by working with concepts already familiar to private law.

Third, legislation may influence behaviour not by imposing specific duties, but rather through the direct imposition of liability in particular circumstances, or by granting power to courts to impose such liability.[71] The recognition of a liability does not carry quite the same normative effect as the imposition of a duty, but of course the possibility of incurring a liability can, by itself, be an important influence on parties' behaviour. Where legislation imposes such liabilities, it invokes private law as persons affected are given powers to sue those responsible, and existing private law principles may be utilised in quantifying and shaping the remedies that are granted.[72] The usefulness of such mechanisms in prospectively shaping parties' behaviour may, however, be limited where judges are given seemingly broad discretions to impose liability. Under a number of provisions of the BSA 2022, for example, a court may impose a liability where 'it is just and equitable to do so'.[73] As Sawtell argues in his chapter, there is a strong case for judges relying on existing principles of private law when exercising such a discretion to allocate liability; certainly, unless and until *some* principles are applied, it will be impossible for parties to use the prospect of such liability to regulate their behaviour in any tailored way.[74]

This shows that the liability-imposing and behaviour-regulating roles of private law can come apart: this is perhaps clearest when the law is changed with retrospective effect. As Nolan notes in his chapter, the need to avoid such retrospectivity is a powerful argument in favour of legislative, rather than judicial, development of the law. However, where the policy needs are perceived to be greatest, then, if

[68] Chamberlain (n 43) section VI.

[69] Nolan (n 39).

[70] Design and Building Practitioners Act 2020 (NSW) pt 4. See, further, Morgan (n 35) 187; Nolan (n 39) 174–5.

[71] The same applies where the liability is developed wholly by judges, rather than by legislation: see eg Robertson (n 12) 217–18, discussing *Royal Bank of Scotland v Etridge (No 2)* [2001] UKHL 44; [2002] 2 AC 773, where Lord Nicholls set out in detail the steps that banks must take in order to avoid the risk of having a security granted by a guarantor set aside as a result of undue influence or misrepresentation exercised by another party on that guarantor.

[72] See eg the remediation contribution order introduced by the BSA 2022, s 124.

[73] See eg BSA 2022, ss 124(1) and 130(1).

[74] Sawtell (n 11) 226.

a jurisdiction's constitution permits, even legislation may operate retrospectively, as is shown by parts of the BSA 2022.[75] Its extension of limitation periods in cases of a past breach of a then-existing duty under the DPA 1972 is retrospective when it revives a cause of action that had previously been extinguished, but is at least consistent with the fact that the conduct was prohibited when undertaken. In contrast, as Fabiana Bettini and Marco Cappelletti note in their chapter, the retrospective imposition of associate liability (allowing, for example, a related company to be liable for a breach by a different company) cannot be justified as deterrence, given that, at the point in time when the act now giving rising to redress occurred, the liability did not exist.[76] Rather, such liability must instead depend on the perceived justice of promoting, for example, 'the compensation of victims and the spreading of losses'.[77] Such concerns, of course, are already evidenced in important parts of private law, such as the recognition of vicarious liability.[78]

C. Practice: Two Examples

i. The Lacrosse Building Fire

The direct cause of the cladding-fuelled fire at the 23-storey Lacrosse Building in Melbourne, Australia, in November 2014 was the failure by an occupant of an apartment on level 8 to fully extinguish a cigarette he had been smoking on the balcony of his apartment. Flames made their way via an air-conditioning pipe into the highly combustible polyethylene core of the aluminium composite material (ACM) cladding which covered the building and, within minutes, a fire spread vertically across several floors.[79] Sprinkler systems within the building (there were none on the balconies) worked better than their specifications required and the fire was brought under control within about half an hour of the first response by the Melbourne Metropolitan Fire Brigade. In stark contrast with the later Grenfell Tower fire, all the building's occupants – some 460 in total – were safely evacuated.[80]

[75] See too Design and Building Practitioners Act 2020 (NSW) pt 4, which operates to impose a statutory duty on a person who carries out construction work to exercise reasonable care to avoid economic loss caused by defective construction work and applies (via its sch 1 cl 5) to work carried out before the Act was passed on 10 June 2020, if the economic loss first became apparent within 10 years before that passage.

[76] Bettini and Cappelletti (n 6) 55.

[77] ibid 56.

[78] See eg M Cappelletti, 'A Pluralist View of Vicarious Liability in Tort' (2024) 140 *LQR* 61.

[79] Woodward J summarised his findings about the origin and spread of the Lacrosse fire in *Owners Corporation No 1 of PS613436T v LU Simon Builders Pty Ltd* [2019] VCAT 286 ('*PS613436T*') [222], including that it was not possible to determine when in the sequence of events (involving not only a table, but other materials on the balcony, including two vacuum cleaners) the 'direct flame impingement' upon the ACM panels occurred.

[80] Compiled from: *PS613436T* [2019] VCAT 286 [1]–[2]; [11]; [195]–[222]; [241]; Metropolitan Fire Brigade, *Post Incident Analysis Report: Lacrosse Docklands* (Melbourne, 2015) 4, 11, 13; G Genco, *Lacrosse Building Fire 673 La Trobe Street, Docklands on 25 November 2014* (City of Melbourne, 2015)

The role of private law in allocating liability can primarily be seen in the claim brought for economic loss arising from the need to rectify the combustible cladding: this ran to more than A$12 million.[81] There were 211 claimants, including three 'Owners Corporations' and more than 200 individual apartment owners.[82] None of these parties had a direct contract with the builder of the apartments (indeed, the Owners Corporations did not exist when the building was under construction). The claim was made in the Victorian Civil and Administrative Tribunal (VCAT). The essence of the claim was that the highly-combustible ACM cladding should not have been used, and that a building with such cladding should not have been certified as safe by the building surveyor, architect and fire engineer.

Woodward J's initial ruling revealed the complex interfaces within private law, especially where (as here) the applicable private law norms have statutory as well as common law elements. The builder bore what amounted to strict liability to the owners for the consequences of installing the ACM on the building. The cause of action leading to this liability was for breach of contract, but this standard common law form was overlaid by statute, which not only set out a series of warranties deemed to be 'part of every domestic building contract' (including fitness for purpose and the need to comply with the Building Code of Australia), but also extended the benefit of those warranties beyond the directly contracting parties to the apartment owners and the Owners Corporations.[83] The relevant legislation, the Victorian Domestic Building Contracts Act 1995, thus played a role similar to the UK's DPA 1972 in empowering subsequent owners to enforce contractual warranties as if they were parties to those contracts.

Woodward J found, however, that, whilst the installation of the ACM cladding meant that the builder had breached its strict contractual duties, it was reasonable for the builder to have relied upon the duty of skill and care owed to it by the building surveyor, architect and fire engineer under each of those consultants' respective consultancy agreements. Each of them had breached that obligation, in various ways relating to their failure to prevent the specification, installation and occupancy of the building with such cladding. The eventual result was that the builder was liable to the owners for around A$12 million, but was practically insulated from all but 3 per cent of that liability as a result of the carelessness of its consultants.[84] As 'concurrent wrongdoers' under the Victorian statutory scheme

2, 12–13; Victorian Building Authority, *VBA External Wall Cladding Audit: Report* (Melbourne, 2016); Lawrence Reddaway, 'Lacrosse Docklands Fire – Lessons to be Re-learned?' (2015) *50 Building Dispute Practitioners Society News* 10.

[81] *PS613436T* [2019] VCAT 286 [3], [7].

[82] ibid [4].

[83] ibid [7], [282]–[292]. The statutory warranties are imposed by s 8 of the Domestic Building Contracts Act 1995 (Vic) and extended to subsequent owners under s 9 of that Act.

[84] The primary judgment on appeal was *Tanah Merah Vic Pty Ltd v Owners' Corporation No 1 of PS631436T* [2021] VSCA 72; in *Tanah Merah Vic Pty Ltd v Owners' Corporation No 1 of PS613436T [No 2]* [2021] VSCA 122, the Court adjusted slightly the proportionate liability percentages that had been ascribed at trial to the Building Surveyor and Fire Engineer (at [21]).

for 'proportionate liability',[85] the remainder of the liability rested with those consultants (and, ultimately, their respective insurers).[86]

The Lacrosse decisions show the central role that private law norms can play in relation to building safety issues, and how their common law underpinnings are modified – often radically – by statutory overlays. The practical difficulties faced by the claimants, however, were significant. Although the VCAT was established in 1998 as a part of reforms to the tribunal system, intended to encourage the use of simpler, less formal procedures, as noted by Geoff Hanmer, the trial before Woodward J

> ran for 22 days, involved five QCs, five juniors and an army of instructing solicitors, paralegals and expert witnesses. There were 91 volumes of documents tendered as evidence. Legal costs almost certainly exceeded A$2 million, or more than 15 per cent of the damages sought.[87]

ii. The Grenfell Tower Fire

As in the Lacrosse fire three years earlier, the presence of highly combustible ACM cladding at the Grenfell Tower in west London meant that a fire which started in one part of a tower block (in this case in a fourth-floor flat, as a result of an electrical fault in a large fridge-freezer) had disastrous consequences. Unlike at Lacrosse, however, the fire at Grenfell resulted in dozens of deaths and injuries. The cladding had been installed as part of a refurbishment of the building, completed in 2016, mere months before the fire.

As a further contrast to the Lacrosse example, there is as yet no decided case ruling directly on private law liabilities arising from the Grenfell Tower fire.[88] Nonetheless, a sense of the complexity of the private law relationships involved in the refurbishment may be gleaned from the following extract from a statement by the Grenfell Tower Inquiry when releasing its Stage 2 report in September 2024:

> [T]he simple truth is that the deaths that occurred were all avoidable and that those who lived in the tower were badly failed … by those who were responsible for ensuring the safety of the building and its occupants. They include the government, the Tenant Management Organisation, the Royal Borough of Kensington and Chelsea, those who manufactured and supplied the materials used in the refurbishment, those who

[85] Wrongs Act 1958 (Vic), pt IVAA.

[86] *PS613436T* [2019] VCAT 286 [7].

[87] G Hanmer, 'Lacrosse Fire Ruling Sends Shudders Through Building Industry Consultants and Governments' (Housing After Grenfell, 11 April 2019), https://www.law.ox.ac.uk/housing-after-grenfell/blog/2019/04/lacrosse-fire-ruling-sends-shudders-through-building-industry.

[88] Settlements have been reached in some litigation and further claims may still be made: see eg P Apps, 'Grenfell Cladding Manufacturer Agrees $74m Settlement with Shareholders for 'False and Misleading' Statements' *Inside Housing* (18 May 2023) https://www.insidehousing.co.uk/news/grenfell-cladding-manufacturer-agrees-74m-settlement-with-shareholders-for-false-and-misleading-statements-81514.

> certified their suitability for use on high-rise residential buildings, the architect, Studio E, the principal contractor, Rydon Maintenance Ltd, and some of its sub-contractors, in particular, Harley Curtain Wall Ltd and its successor Harley Facades Ltd, some of the consultants, in particular the fire engineer, Exova Warringtonfire Ltd, the local authority's building control department and the London Fire Brigade. Not all of them bear the same degree of responsibility for the eventual disaster, but, as our reports show, all contributed to it in one way or another, in most cases through incompetence but in some cases through dishonesty and greed.[89]

These relationships were characterized by Counsel to the Inquiry as a 'Web of Blame'.[90] A diagram illustrating this 'web', widely published following the close of the Inquiry's hearings in 2022, purported to show the interactions between the primary parties to the refurbishment contracts (government housing agencies, contractors, architects, subcontractors, suppliers), regulators (many of which were private bodies) and consultants.[91]

Despite its complexity, the diagram in fact only scratched the surface of the legal relationships involved in the refurbishment process. It did not attempt to capture duties and liabilities arising under statute or in tort, nor did it mention property rights – in this case, mostly leases – held by many of the residents directly affected by the building failures. Moreover, the diagram included corporate entities, such as Kingspan and Arconic, which have further internal structures and employees and agents whose misconduct may expose them, as well as the companies, to criminal sanctions or private law claims.[92]

Finally, it is worth keeping in mind that the refurbishment of Grenfell Tower was a relatively straightforward building project.[93] The financial consequences of the project's failure have, however, been estimated at £1.2 billion, some 100 times its project cost and 4,000 times greater than the savings achieved via 'value engineering' in replacing the cladding initially specified with the cheaper, combustible material.[94]

[89] Grenfell Tower Inquiry, 'Statement by Sir Martin Moore-Bick on Publication of the Phase 2 Report' (4 September 2024).

[90] Grenfell Tower Inquiry, 'Counsel to the Inquiry's Closing Statement' (10 November 2022), https://www.grenfelltowerinquiry.org.uk/evidence/counsel-inquirys-closing-presentation.

[91] The diagram was included in the Closing Statement (ibid). The Royal Borough of Kensington and Chelsea (RBKC) is the freehold owner of the land, including the Tower, and its Tenant Management Organisation (TMO) managed the building for it. Fourteen apartments in the tower were held on long leases, whereas others were rented to social housing tenants: Grenfell Tower Inquiry, *Phase 1 Report: Report of the Public Inquiry into the Fire at Grenfell Tower on 14 June 2017* (HC 2019, 49) [3.6].

[92] Note eg BSA 2022, ss 147–51 imposing liability in relation to the supply and marketing of certain types of defective construction products.

[93] The revised budget for the Grenfell Tower refurbishment was around £8.4m (see eg evidence of David Gibson to the Inquiry, 15 October 2020: transcript p 23).

[94] See R Booth, 'Cost of Grenfell Tower Disaster Soars to Nearly £1.2bn' *The Guardian* (31 July 2023) https://www.theguardian.com/uk-news/2023/jul/30/grenfell-tower-disaster-cost-soars.

III. Problems with Private Law

In section II, we saw that private law has a role to play in addressing the building safety crisis. In this section, we examine how the building safety crisis has exposed some broader problems, or tensions, within private law as it is theorised and practised throughout the common law world. For the purposes of exposition, we adopt an orthodox classification, looking in turn at property law, contract law and the law of torts. However, as noted in section I, an integrated approach is essential so it must be remembered that, in the building safety context as elsewhere, these different parts of private law are closely interrelated, and are made up of legislation as well as judge-made law.

A. Property

Property law is primarily a facilitative system, an example of what Hart referred to as 'power-conferring' laws which 'provide individuals with facilities for realising their wishes … to create structures … of rights and duties'.[95] In particular, property law provides for the creation and transfer of property rights, and for internal governance arrangements when there is fragmented ownership.[96]

One of the characteristic features of a property right is its effect on third parties: B's acquisition of a property right from A, for example, means that particular duties are now owed to B not only by A but also, prima facie, by all other parties. The 'right to exclude', for example – often said to be a key element of ownership of a physical thing[97] – correlates to the duties which, prima facie, all other parties owe to an owner not to interfere, deliberately or carelessly, with that physical thing.[98] As a breach of such a duty will constitute a tort, there is clearly a very close relationship between property law and the law of torts.

In the building safety context, for example, a key question in the law of torts, prominent in the chapters by Chamberlain, Nolan and Ti, is when, if ever, a party can be liable for carelessly causing pure economic loss. In this context, what counts as 'pure' economic loss is dependent on the prior allocation of property rights.[99] If, for example, D's carelessness consists of damaging a physical thing, and C has a legal property right in relation to that thing,[100] C will generally have a straightforward claim against D, including for economic loss consequential on that damage.

[95] Hart (n 60) 61.

[96] See eg G Alexander, 'Governance Property' (2012) 160 *University of Pennsylvania Law Review* 1854; H Dagan, *A Liberal Theory of Property* (Cambridge, Cambridge University Press, 2021) ch 4.

[97] See eg T Merrill, 'Property and the Right to Exclude' (1998) 77 *Nebraska Law Review* 730.

[98] See eg S Douglas and B McFarlane, 'Defining Property Rights' in J Penner and H Smith (eds), *Philosophical Foundations of Property Law* (Oxford, Oxford University Press, 2013).

[99] As noted by Edelman J in *Mallonland Pty Ltd v Advanta Seeds Pty Ltd* [2024] HCA 25 [85].

[100] Where C's property right is an equitable one, C's loss will be purely economic loss even if it results from damage to the physical thing: see eg *Leigh and Sillivan Ltd v Aliakmon Shipping Co Ltd* [1986]

In contrast, if C has no legal property right in the thing, any loss C suffers as a result of D's interference will be 'pure' economic loss, thus placing C in a quite different position when it comes to making a claim against D.[101]

It would, of course, be a mistake to think that only parties with property rights are affected by building safety issues: many occupiers of residential buildings, not least minor children, will have permission to occupy (a licence) without having a property right in their home. Moreover, as illustrated by the facts in *Winnipeg Condominium*,[102] which involved stone cladding falling from the ninth floor of the building to the street below, passers-by can also be exposed to safety risks. The UK's Building Regulations, for example, aim to secure the 'health, safety, welfare and convenience of persons in or about buildings and others who may be affected by buildings',[103] and such persons clearly include those without property rights in the buildings.

Nonetheless, one of the crucial questions in private law is as to standing: a means is needed to identify parties to whom a duty is owed, and parties who can enforce a liability. Through its relatively clear rules of acquisition, property law provides a simple means, often enlisted by the common law of torts,[104] as well as by legislation, to identify those with standing. The UK's DPA 1972, for example, includes as parties to whom duties under the Act are owed 'every person who acquires an interest (whether legal or equitable) in the dwelling'.[105] Similarly, as we have already seen in section II.C.i, Victoria's Domestic Building Contracts Act offers rights to sue for breach of its statutory warranties not only to the building owner who was a party to the contract, but also to 'any person who is the owner for the time being of the building or land in respect of which the building work was carried out under the contract'.[106]

It should not be thought, however, that the acquisition of a property right is relevant only to the claims a party may bring: it can also be relevant to the duties, liabilities or responsibilities of that party. The responsibilities a legal system places on owners of particular property may be relevant not only to imposing a liability, but also to denying a claim such a party might otherwise have. This can be seen in an important interaction between property law and contract law, which forms a crucial starting point in many systems' rules on building safety. The 'caveat emptor'

AC 785 and *Shell UK Ltd v Total UK Ltd* [2011] QB 86 (CA). In the latter case, recovery of the pure economic loss was, surprisingly, allowed in the tort of negligence.

[101] See eg *Cattle v Stockton Waterworks Co* (1875) LR 10 QB 453.

[102] *Winnipeg Condominium* [1995] 1 SCR 85.

[103] Building Act 1984, s 1(1)(a).

[104] See eg *Hunter v Canary Wharf Ltd* [1997] AC 665 (HL), limiting the right to sue in private nuisance to parties with a property right in the affected land.

[105] DPA 1972, s 1(1)(b).

[106] Domestic Building Contracts Act 1995 (Vic), s 9. See, similarly, Building Act 2004 (ACT), s 88; Home Building Act 1989 (NSW), s 18B; Building Act 1993 (NT), s 54B; Queensland Building and Construction Commission Act 1991 (Qld), sch 1B ss 20–26; Building Work Contractors Act 1995 (SA), s 32; Residential Building Work Contracts and Dispute Resolution Act 2016 (Tas), ss 23–29. There is no directly equivalent warranty scheme in Western Australia.

principle, applied to those taking a conveyance of a legal estate in land, means that, as a default position, no contractual promises are made by the vendor to the purchaser as to the quality and condition of the land, including any buildings on it. In contrast, such warranties are implied into a contract for the sale of goods.[107] Part of the justification of the 'caveat emptor' principle must be that a purchaser of an estate in land has a responsibility to satisfy themselves of the condition of the land: given the expense and significance of such a transaction, it is reasonable to expect that thorough checks are undertaken. The entrenchment of this principle provides one reason why, in the words of the End Our Cladding Scandal complaint cited in section I, a party acquiring a long lease of an apartment may well see themselves as having 'less protection than a purchaser of a toaster'.

As Honoré noted in his survey of the significance of the concept of 'ownership' in different legal systems,[108] the incidents of ownership can include duties, liabilities and responsibilities, not just rights and powers. This is particularly important in relation to building safety, where those with control of a building, often afforded to them by a property right, owe duties in relation to the physical safety of occupiers, visitors and even trespassers.[109] The possibility of ownership carrying obligations also informed part of the UK government's initial response to the building safety crisis, an assertion that 'building owners should do the right thing'[110] by bearing the costs of remediating buildings with dangerous cladding. Any suggestion that an owner of a multi-occupied residential building was under a *legal* duty to individual apartment owners in that building was, however, difficult to square with the reality of English property law.

As explained in Bettini and Cappelletti's chapter,[111] the usual position in England and Wales is that the owner of a multi-occupied residential block, the party holding the freehold of the land on which it stands, will be a landlord, and thus will have no current right to possession of the individual apartments. An 'owner' of an apartment, who will have generally paid a large sum, supported by a mortgage, to acquire their property rights in that apartment will almost always be a leaseholder,[112] with a lease that had an initial term of, perhaps, 99, 125 or even 999 years. The reason behind this now-standard arrangement is that the leasehold form gives apartment owners the security of knowing that the owners of neighbouring apartments will be under ongoing positive duties to maintain the condition of their apartments and that a successor in title to the landlord will

[107] See eg Sale of Goods Act 1979 (E&W), s 14; Goods Act 1958 (Vic), s 17.

[108] A Honoré, 'Ownership' in A Guest (ed) *Oxford Essays in Jurisprudence* (Oxford, Oxford University Press, 1961).

[109] For the position in England, see Occupiers' Liability Acts of 1957 and 1984.

[110] See eg HC Deb, 10 January 2022, vol 706, cols 285 and 300.

[111] See eg the discussion in Bettini and Cappelletti (n 6) s II.A.

[112] They need not hold that lease directly from the freehold owner, as there may be intermediate parties, for example where the freehold owner enters into a long lease with intermediate landlords. See eg S Blandy, 'Legal Frameworks for Multi-owned Housing in England and Wales: Owners' Experiences' in S Blandy et al (eds) *Multi-owned Housing: Law, Power and Practice* (Abingdon, Routledge, 2016).

similarly have some ongoing positive obligations to maintain common areas of the building.[113] The leasehold form also provides a means of imposing on apartment owners an ongoing duty to pay a service charge to contribute to such maintenance as well as to some repairs of the building. A significant part of the economic value of the landlord's interest is the income produced from ground rents receivable, permission fees, insurance commissions, service charges payable by the leaseholders and sums received through lease extensions.[114] This value is most attractive to passive investors, who clearly lack the everyday links to the building which are associated with 'ownership'. This means that, economically speaking, the owner of the building will have little to gain from making repairs. As a result, the general position is that, even if the owner of the building has a direct relationship with the apartment owners, the owner will not have agreed to assume a duty to remedy all safety defects in the building. As a result, as shown by Bettini and Cappelletti, English property law, in contrast to its Italian counterpart, does not always impose an obligation to remediate inherent defects on building owners.[115] Indeed, a standard term of leases of apartments is that, if repairs are carried out, the landlord can pass the costs onto the leaseholders: 'The landlord decides whether to act, sets the pace of the work, selects the standard of remediation works, and yet passes on all of the costs to the leaseholders.'[116]

So, whilst the general notion of 'ownership' may suggest that a party, an owner, should have both the legal power to see that repairs are carried out, and the factual ability to benefit economically from such repairs, English property law prevents there being any such party in relation to a multi-occupied residential block. As has been pointed out by one of us,[117] and as clearly shown by Bettini and Cappelletti in their chapter, such a fragmented system of ownership has important implications for building safety. The essential difficulty is that it removes the basis of some of the private law rules which nonetheless apply. For example, the 'caveat emptor' principle governs the rights of a party acquiring a pre-existing leasehold interest, but in practice it will be impossible for such a party to determine the safety and habitability of their apartment, as this will depend on the condition not only of common areas of the building, but of other apartments, and of the structure of the building as a whole.[118] Leaseholders of apartments in blocks in need of remediation

[113] See the Landlord and Tenant (Covenants) Act 1995. For the inability of a positive covenant entered into between freehold owners to bind successors in title of the covenantor, see eg *Rhone v Stephens* [1994] 2 AC 310. For proposed reform of that rule in England and Wales, see eg Law Commission, *Making Land Work: Easements, Covenants and Profits à Prendre* (Law Com No 327, 2011).

[114] See eg M Davey, 'The Regulation of Long Residential Leases' in E Cooke (ed) *Modern Studies in Property Law*, vol 3 (Oxford, Hart Publishing, 2005) 203, 206.

[115] Bettini and Cappelletti (n 6) 47.

[116] Bright (n 8) 16. See too S Bright, 'Time to Revisit Whether Leaseholders Have to Pay?' *Housing After Grenfell* (26 July 2024), https://blogs.law.ox.ac.uk/housing-after-grenfell-blog/blog-post/2024/07/time-revisit-whether-leaseholders-have-pay.

[117] Bright (n 8) 24.

[118] See eg Lewison LJ in *The Mayor and Commonality of the Citizens of the City of London v Leaseholders of Great Arthur House* [2021] EWCA Civ 431 [50]: 'it cannot be supposed that the purchaser of a single

thus find themselves in an impossible position: if no work is undertaken, and the defects remain, their legal power to charge or sell their leasehold – a key aspect of their 'ownership' of the apartment – will be entirely illusory.[119] On the other hand, if work is undertaken, each leaseholder will, under the terms of its lease, be faced with a huge bill. This is how, as noted in section II.A, private law's promise of autonomy, to be gained through holding an expensively acquired property right, proves hollow, as their leasehold becomes a burden.

The parody of ownership that English common law offers to a leaseholder of an apartment in a multi-occupied residential block was a source of concern long before the current building safety crisis. The legislative introduction of a commonhold system in 2002 offered a new solution to the difficult coordination problem of structuring the rights of such parties.[120] However, the system was, in practice, a failure, with hardly any uptake,[121] partly because mortgage providers were wary of a new system, which departed from well-established conveyancing practice. As noted in section I, it may be, however, that the greater prominence afforded to the plight of leaseholders as a result of the building safety crisis, coupled with increasing publicity about soaring leaseholder costs, will provide a 'property moment'. This may lead the UK Parliament to adopt recent Law Commission proposals[122] to invigorate the commonhold system, and also encourage legal practitioners and mortgage lenders to make those reforms work in practice. Certainly, the condominium-style systems prominent elsewhere in the world, and discussed in the chapters by Bettini and Cappelletti (Italy) and McKenzie (Florida), offer individual unit owners a set of rights that come closer to the ideal of 'ownership', as well as a more structured way of coordinating those rights.

In England, the deplorable position of leaseholders has already led to significant legislative intervention. The BSA 2022 has gone as far as retrospectively altering the property rights of landlords, by barring landlords of at least some multi-occupied residential blocks,[123] in certain situations,[124] from enforcing the

flat in a large block would commission a structural survey of the whole building before committing himself to acquiring a long lease'.

[119] See eg Bright and McFarlane (n 33) 129, explaining that, following government advice as to potential building safety defects, mortgage lenders required surveyors to sign a Form EWS-1 (which came into use in December 2019) to confirm whether any cladding on the building complied with safety requirements. The result is that, until remediation occurs, apartments in such buildings cannot, in practice, be sold other than at a discount to cash buyers.

[120] Commonhold and Leasehold Reform Act 2002.

[121] See Law Commission, *Reinvigorating Commonhold: The Alternative to Leasehold Ownership* (Law Com No 394, 2020) paras 2.29–2.46.

[122] ibid.

[123] The provisions in BSA 2022, sch 8 apply only to a 'relevant building'. The general definition given for this term in s 117(2), subject to the exceptions in s 117(3), is a 'self-contained building, or self-contained part of a building, in England that contains at least two dwellings and (a) is at least 11 metres high; or (b) has at least 5 storeys'.

[124] The provisions are complex and are set out in BSA 2022, sch 8. For discussion, see Bright (n 8) 35–41.

terms of a lease allowing them to recover remediation costs from leaseholders.[125] As Bettini and Cappelletti note, statutory intervention in the leaseholder–landlord relationship is far from unusual,[126] and shows that the parties are not entirely free to set the content of their mutual rights and duties: contractually agreed terms may be adjusted and augmented by statute. Long leases are designed to endure through successive ownership and, by virtue of privity of estate, the initially agreed rights and duties will also bind successors in title of both the landlord and the leaseholder. The longevity and proprietary nature of leases, the economic significance of an apartment purchase, and the importance of the safety and security of home explain why there has been much regulation of the landlord–leaseholder relationship.[127] Indeed, the landlord's rights are significantly limited by statutory provisions that confer on a leaseholder, if certain conditions are met, powers to extend the length of the lease, or even to acquire the freehold interest.[128] The European Court of Human Rights rejected a claim that these enfranchisement powers are inconsistent with protection of the freeholder's property rights under Article 1 of Protocol 1 to the European Convention on Human Rights.[129] It seems the potential of a similar challenge to the BSA 2022 provisions which invalidate landlords' rights to recover remediation costs was uppermost in the minds of the drafters of that legislation. As a result, the level of protection given to leaseholders varies according to a number of different factors, in an attempt to show the proportionate nature of the intervention.[130]

Notwithstanding the stark interference with the property rights of landlords, part of the motivation for the legislative action may be a policy informed by some intuitions familiar to private law. It is the parties ultimately at fault who should bear the cost of the repairs and this would not happen if landlords could simply pass those costs on to individual leaseholders, who would face obvious practical difficulties in suing third parties, with whom they have no contract, for such economic loss. Whilst the scheme for preventing the enforcement of leasehold service charges is complex, some key distinctions are made. The focus is on the position of the landlord, and of the leaseholder, but these are evaluated separately, and there is no requirement that the relevant factors must apply to both of those parties. It is clear, therefore, that the demand of (at least one view of) corrective

[125] BSA 2022, sch 8. We use the term 'property right' here to refer to the right given to the landlord under the terms of the lease, as that right is capable of binding not only the original leaseholder, but also assignees of the leaseholder: it is also capable of being enforced not only by the original landlord, but also by assignees from the landlord.

[126] Such intervention in shorter leases can include, for example, rent controls and the provision of at least some security of tenure: see eg the Rent Act 1977, as applied in eg *Street v Mountford* [1985] AC 809 (HL); or the imposition of repairing duties on the landlord, see eg Landlord and Tenant Act 1985, s 11.

[127] See eg M Davey, 'The Regulation of Long Residential Leases' in Cooke (n 114) 203.

[128] See Leasehold Reform Act 1967 and now the Leasehold and Freehold Reform Act 2024.

[129] *James v UK* (1986) 8 EHRR 123. It is understood by the authors that new human rights challenges are being brought by landlords in relation to changes to lease extension and enfranchisement made by the Leasehold and Freehold Reform Act 2024.

[130] See BSA 2022, sch 8 as discussed by Bright (n 8) 9, 38.

justice, that the relevant reasons affecting the parties' private law position must 'embrace both parties as correlatively situated',[131] is not satisfied. For example, on the side of the landlord, paragraph 2 of schedule 8 specifies that no charge is payable by the leaseholder in respect of remedying a defect if the landlord 'is responsible for the relevant defect' or 'is associated with a person responsible for a relevant defect'.[132] The concept of responsibility applied here does not require any breach of duty by the landlord, and certainly not a breach of a duty owed to the leaseholder. In fact, a landlord is responsible for a relevant defect if, for example, it undertook or commissioned works relating to the defect:[133] no fault is required. Equally, paragraph 2 can apply even if the landlord does not have a contractual claim against a third party which it can use to recover the remediation costs. Clearly, this provision looks just to the position of the landlord: the essential idea is that if the landlord can be seen as the developer of the block, or sufficiently closely related to the developer, all leaseholders are protected from a service charge aiming to recover remediation costs.[134]

If paragraph 2 does not apply, then protection from such service charge enforcement depends, in part, on the position of the leaseholder: it is reserved for 'qualifying' leaseholders. Whilst the relevant section is not clearly drafted, its aim is that a leaseholder qualifies either if their lease relates to their principal home, or if they own no more than three dwellings in the United Kingdom.[135] If the leaseholder does thus qualify, they will be completely protected from use of the service charge to recover remediation costs if the landlord, at the relevant time, met the 'contribution condition'.[136] This condition depends on the net worth[137] of the 'landlord group', which includes the landlord and any person associated with it. It is striking to see how both the perceived wealth of the leaseholder and, separately, of the landlord, and parties associated with it – a paradigm example of a factor which relates to one party only, and does not bear on their correlative relationship with another – is being used so directly as a reason justifying a specific private law outcome.

It should be noted that the factors used in schedule 8 do not go to the question of recognising a duty, or imposing a liability, but rather to what might be seen as a defence: is there a good reason to prevent a landlord enforcing its right, under the terms of the lease, against a leaseholder? This is important as even proponents

[131] E Weinrib, 'The Normative Structuralism of Corrective Justice' in H Dagan and B Zipursky (eds), *Research Handbook on Private Law Theory* (Cheltenham, Edward Elgar, 2020) 484, 485.

[132] For discussion of the significance of such 'associated parties' rules in the BSA 2022, see text at n 182 below and also Sawtell's chapter (n 11).

[133] BSA 2022, sch 8, para 2(3).

[134] See Bright (n 8) 35.

[135] BSA 2022, s 119: see Explanatory Notes to the Building Safety Act, pt 5 para 940.

[136] BSA 2022, sch 8, para 3(1).

[137] BSA 2022, sch 8, para 3(2). The 'contribution condition' is met if the 'landlord group's net worth at the qualifying time was more than N × £2,000,000', where N is the number of relevant buildings (see s 117) of which a member of the landlord group was a landlord at the qualifying time. The 'qualifying time' is defined by s 119(2)(d) as the beginning of 14 February 2022.

of a narrowly focused corrective justice account of private law are prepared to relax the requirements of correlativity of reasons in relation to such defences.[138] Nonetheless, the schedule 8 provisions can perhaps be seen as analogous to some doctrines that can give rise to duties and liabilities. For example, various rules of private law aim to ensure that the economic burden of discharging a duty falls on the 'correct' party, even where more than one party is initially liable. The restitutionary claims available to a guarantor against the party primarily liable,[139] or to a party whose action discharges a duty for which another party is primarily liable,[140] may be seen to serve such a purpose.[141] Similarly, where a number of different parties are jointly and severally liable for a tort, the aim of promoting full compensation for the claimant is met in some systems by allowing the claimant full recovery against any of those liable, leaving those parties to make claims against each other in order to adjust the practical burden of meeting that liability.[142]

One difficulty with applying such parallels to remediation costs was the absence of an initial duty to carry out the work. A leaseholder of an individual apartment would not be under a duty to carry out such work on other parts of the building, and the terms of the lease, as noted above,[143] were unlikely to impose a duty on the landlord to carry out such works. One of the reforms of the BSA 2022 has an impact here: under section 84, in relation to occupied buildings at least 18 metres or seven storeys high, a duty is placed on 'accountable persons' to prevent building safety risks materializing 'as regards the part of the building for which they are responsible'. 'Accountable persons' are defined by section 72 and, whilst the provisions are complex, the term includes a 'person who holds a legal estate in possession in any part of the common parts'. Just as legislation such as the DPA 1972 uses the location of property rights to determine parties to whom a duty is owed, so can property rights be crucial to imposing a duty. However, the duty under section 84 seems to be a standalone, or undirected, one, as, whilst providing some forms of accountability,[144] the statute does not attempt to specify any party to whom the duty is owed.

This aspect of the section 84 duty raises a wider question as to the enforcement of duties and liabilities arising in respect of building safety. This might be thought of primarily as a question for contract and torts – for the law of obligations rather than the law of property. However, this misses a crucial point in relation to multi-occupied residential property. The fragmentation of ownership, as seen in the

[138] See eg R Stevens, 'Defenses' in A Gold et al (eds), *The Oxford Handbook of the New Private Law* (Oxford, Oxford University Press, 2021) 529, 535–37.

[139] See eg *Alexander v Vane* (1836) 1 M & W 511, 150 ER 537.

[140] See eg *Gebhardt v Saunders* [1892] 2 QB 452.

[141] See eg R Stevens, *The Laws of Restitution* (Oxford, Oxford University Press, 2023) ch 9.

[142] See eg Civil Liability (Contribution) Act 1978 (UK). Note the Victorian legislation on proportionate contribution, as applied in the Lacrosse fire litigation discussed in section II.C.i, adopts a different approach.

[143] Text at nn 114–116.

[144] See BSA 2022, s 98 which sets out accountability to the Building Safety Regulator, who has a duty to enforce Part 4 of the BSA, which includes s 84.

current English system, makes it impossible to identify a single party to whom the duties are owed, and who can enforce the liabilities. This means that leaseholders can be powerless to enforce duties, and thus to direct the action of those providing work in connection with building. As Simone Degeling and Jodi Gardner make clear in their chapter, leaseholders can face great practical difficulties in enforcing liabilities in the event of a breach of duty.[145] As one of us has noted, 'many of these procedural issues are likely to be less challenging in a condominium-based system'.[146] It is notable that arguments for reform of the English system have tended to focus on the internal management of multi-occupied residential property, and the balance of rights as between individual leaseholders and landlords.[147] However, a clear lesson of the building safety crisis is that the current structure of property rights is unhelpful in its external impact. The existence of a single legal entity, such as a condominium association or strata title company, is significant not only because it can be under duties to apartment owners, but also because it is a clearly identified party to which private law duties can be owed, and which can enforce private law liabilities.

B. Contract

Like property law, contract law can also be seen as facilitative: it empowers parties to create a set of rights and obligations that help to realise their shared aspirations. Indeed, whereas parties' choices as to the property rights they create are limited by the numerus clausus principle – to count as a property right, with distinctive third-party effect, the content of the right created must fall within one of the existing types of property right[148] – there is no such general restriction on the content of contractual rights. As a result, contracts are sometimes seen as a form of private legislation.[149] Further, based as it is on the parties' mutual agreement, contract law can be seen as central to a conception of private law that focuses on the parties' bilateral relations, where the reasons that justify one party's duty to another apply simultaneously to both duty-holder and duty-bearer.

However, this does not mean that contractual arrangements should always be seen as purely private affairs. First, duties assumed by the parties through contractual arrangements form part of the regulatory environment. Setting safety standards is, for example, one role of complex construction contracts. Indeed, Vandenbergh argues that contracts between private parties make an important contribution to

[145] S Degeling and J Gardner, 'Procedural Challenges and Opportunities for Leaseholders', this volume, ch 9.
[146] Bright (n 8) 31.
[147] See eg Law Commission, *Reinvigorating Commonhold: The Alternative to Leasehold Ownership* (Law Com No 394, 2020) ch 1.
[148] See eg B McFarlane, 'The Numerus Clausus Principle and Covenants Relating to Land' in S Bright (ed), *Modern Studies in Property Law*, vol 6 (Oxford, Hart Publishing, 2011).
[149] See eg Hart (n 60) 40.

the regulatory state by affecting who pays for regulatory requirements and how incentives operate.[150] The regulatory role played by private contracts can also be seen where duties are implied or imposed by law, as is the case with residential building contracts. The common law as it applies to construction standards-setting is broadly similar across the jurisdictions considered in this book.[151] It generally allows parties to agree to certain standards and will imply baseline terms as to workmanship and materials in the absence of express terms. These implied terms rest upon finding the appropriate application in the circumstances of the principles that the materials provided will be of good quality and reasonably fit for their intended purpose, and the works on completion will also be reasonably fit for their intended purpose.[152] In an important interaction between principles of property law and of contract law, noted in section III.A, the particular contractual relationship of vendor and purchaser of an interest in land is one in which standard implications of contractual terms are not made, due to the operation, in common law jurisdictions, of 'caveat emptor'.

There are a number of aspects of classical contract law that limit its utility to parties affected by the building safety crisis. Legislation has attempted to deal with some of these difficulties. First, there is the temporal problem faced by later purchasers of all or part of a building, who will generally have no direct contractual relationship with the developer. This is addressed in part by legislation such as the UK's DPA 1972 which imposes duties with a content modelled on implied contractual duties of habitability, but stipulates that the same duties are also owed to third parties with whom the defendant has no contractual relationship.[153]

Second, linked to the first difficulty, is the fact that the later purchaser has no control over the content of the agreement between the developer and the builder, and other professionals providing work and services. This is also true for individual leaseholders where refurbishment work is undertaken of common parts of a building by means of a contract entered into between a freeholder and professionals. The DPA 1972 addresses this issue in what might be seen as a significant interference with freedom of contract. The duties owed by those providing work in connection with the provision of the dwelling, or maintenance of an existing

[150] M Vandenbergh, 'The Private Life of Public Law' (2005) 105 *Columbia Law Review* 2029, 2033.

[151] For discussion of the position in Italy, a civil law jurisdiction, see Bettini and Cappelletti (n 6).

[152] In *Barton v Stiff* [2006] VSC 307, for example, Hargrave J noted (at [16]) these implied terms as applying both at common law and under s 8 of the Domestic Building Contracts Act 1995 (Vic) (see n 83 above). The congruence between the relevant English and Victorian law on this point is illustrated by the Victorian judgment having been almost entirely reliant on English authorities, including *Independent Broadcasting Authority v EMI Electronics Ltd and BICC Construction Ltd* [1978] EWCA Civ J1110-5, (1978) 11 Build LR 38. That said, English courts have more recently indicated a willingness to strictly apply fitness for purpose warranties, at least in the commercial context of design life warranties: see eg *MT Højgaard A/S v E.On Climate & Renewables UK Robin Rigg East Ltd* [2017] UKSC 59, [2018] 2 All ER 22.

[153] See, similarly, the way in which duties are extended to subsequent owners via s 37(2) of the Design and Building Practitioners Act 2020 (NSW).

dwelling,[154] whilst modelled on contractual duties, are binding even if the contracting parties agree otherwise.

As we noted in section III.A, this technique of restricting the parties' freedom to contract has been used, and with retrospective effect, by those parts of the BSA 2022 which, in certain circumstances, prevent landlords from enforcing terms that would allow them to recover the costs of interim security measures, or remediation, from leaseholders.[155] This occurs even if the current leaseholder and landlord are the original parties, and thus in privity of contract as well as privity of estate. As noted in section III.A, legislative control of the content of the rights and duties of landlords and leaseholders is far from unusual. As in relation to building contracts, it can be argued that long-term leasehold contracts have special features and important third-party aspects which justify external control.[156] This is consistent with a view of contract law which, rather than emphasising its conceptual unity as based on the agreement of the parties to the contract, instead notes the very different types of relationship to which such agreements can give rise, and argues that particular consequences can then be attached to particular types of relationship,[157] even in the absence of the consent of the parties and even, in some cases, in the face of the parties' contrary agreement.[158] Certainly, it is indisputable that the law-making power conferred by the law of contract is viewed rather differently when a gross inequality of bargaining power allows one party to legislate in their own interests, rather than in the parties' mutual interests, through the use of non-negotiable standard form contracts. It has been powerfully argued that there is a need for the state to control such one-sided law-making power.[159]

A third linked problem for those in multi-occupied residential dwellings relates to the discussion in section III.A and concerns fragmentation of ownership. The problem is acute in England, where there is no single entity, such as a condominium association, which can contract, or assert statutory rights, on behalf of all the occupiers. This can have unfortunate procedural consequences where, as under the DPA 1972, the duty imposed, modelled on a contractual duty, is owed to individual leaseholders. This has meant, for example, that it was not possible for a representative action to be brought on behalf of a group

[154] DPA 1972, s 2A, as inserted by BSA 2022, ss 134(1) and 170(3).

[155] BSA 2022, sch 8.

[156] See also S Blandy, S Bright and S Nield, 'The Dynamics of Enduring Property Relationships in Land' (2018) 81 *MLR* 85.

[157] See eg J English, 'Employment Contracts, Conditions, and the Relationship of Employment' (2024) 140 *LQR* 521, noting the distinct features of a 'relationship of employment' that arises where the parties enter a contract of employment. Note too the voluminous literature on relational contracts: see eg H Collins, 'Employment as a Relational Contract' (2021) 137 *LQR* 426.

[158] See eg *Street v Mountford* [1985] AC 809 (HL) and *Antoniades v Villiers* [1990] 1 AC 417 (HL).

[159] See eg WD Slawson, 'Standard Form Contracts and Democratic Control of Lawmaking Power' (1971) 84 *Harvard Law Review* 529.

of leaseholders, even when their claims stemmed from the same breach of duty, as each claim depended on showing that the specific apartment was unfit for habitation.[160] As Degeling and Gardner explain in their chapter,[161] such a narrow view of when a representative action can be brought can be questioned, even as a matter of current English law,[162] but it certainly demonstrates the difficulties faced where there is no single entity that can represent occupiers.

A fourth problem, which may also be seen as procedural in nature, comes from the rules as to limitation of actions. Many building safety defects may remain hidden for a long period after the completion of the relevant works: a breach of a contractual duty may thus be revealed only after the expiry of a statutory limitation period applying to contractual claims. The utility of the DPA 1972 to English claimants, for example, was thus impaired by its use of the standard contractual limitation period of six years from the date of breach.[163] As discussed by Bettini and Cappelletti in their chapter, the BSA 2022 makes radical, retrospective changes to the position, to capture breaches occurring in the 30-year period ending in June 2022. The Explanatory Notes to the Act state that a '30-year period has been chosen as evidence shows that this period captures all buildings affected by the relevant safety issues'. Whilst, as the legislation itself contemplates,[164] the retrospective nature of the change may lead to human rights challenges from affected defendants, a clear policy choice has been made to extend the means that may be used to promote the aim of remediating unsafe buildings. As we will see in the next section, this aim is also significant when considering the relationship between the building safety crisis and the law of torts.

C. Tort

As noted in a number of contributions to this book,[165] there is a lively and ongoing debate as to the nature and aims of the law of torts. As noted in section II.A, the building safety context has produced some decisions that have featured prominently in this debate. The contrasting rulings of the House of Lords in *Anns v*

[160] *Rendlesham Estates Ltd v Barr* [2014] EWHC 3968 (TCC), [2015] 1 WLR 3663.

[161] Degeling and Gardner (n 145).

[162] See the discussion in that chapter (primarily in its section III.E) of *Lloyd v Google* [2021] UKSC 50, [2022] AC 1217. Note too *Millharbour Management Ltd v Weston Homes Ltd* [2011] EWHC 661 (TCC), [2011] 3 All ER 1027: in a decision prior to *Rendlesham Estates*, two leaseholders were allowed to bring a representative DPA 1972 claim.

[163] As applied by the DPA 1972, this was six years from the date of completion of the work. It seems that the provisions of the Latent Damage Act 1986, allowing for the postponement of the point when the limitation period begins to run, do not apply to the DPA 1972.

[164] BSA 2022, s 135(3): 'Where an action is brought that, but for subsection (3), would have been barred by the Limitation Act 1980, a court hearing the action must dismiss it in relation to any defendant if satisfied that it is necessary to do so to avoid a breach of that defendant's Convention rights.'

[165] See eg the chapters of Bettini and Cappelletti (n 6), Chamberlain (n 43), Nolan (n 39) and Ti (n 59).

Merton LBC[166] and *Murphy v Brentwood LBC*,[167] for example, provide something of a litmus test, separating out those who commend the policy-focused reasoning in the former case[168] from those who see the latter decision as consistent with an approach that limits liability to breaches of a duty correlating to a specific right of the claimant.[169]

On the latter view, the key question in the building safety context, at least for a judge applying common law rules, is whether the carelessness of the defendant has simply caused pure economic loss, rather than damaging any property of the claimant. This will often be the case where, for example, no fire has damaged a claimant's apartment, but the claimant has had to contribute to the costs of expensive interim security measures and the value of their apartment has declined dramatically due to the looming remediation costs, to which the claimant may have to contribute. As Nolan has argued,[170] in an analysis recently echoed by Edelman J in the High Court of Australia,[171] it is essentially impossible to regard such a party as having a claim-right to the economic value of their apartment, and so, on a rights-focused view of the law of torts, no protection should be available. As Morgan notes in his chapter, such a view as to the scope of the tort of negligence may also have consequences for the interpretation of statutory provisions that allow a party to claim from a defendant who has breached a statutory duty, without expressly specifying whether such pure economic loss is recoverable.[172]

A characterisation of the loss resulting from building safety defects as 'purely economic', and hence beyond the scope of a negligence claim, whilst clearly defensible as a matter of private law logic, may seem problematic for two, related reasons.[173] First, from the perspective of an owner of all or part of an affected building, including, for example, a leaseholder in a multi-occupied residential block, the lack of a claim against a party whose carelessness has caused the defect may undermine the promise of private law as a means to protect their important interests. As noted in section III.A, absent some avenue of redress, the autonomy-conferring aspect of their property right will be severely reduced. It could be said in return that the law of torts is concerned only with the claim-rights associated with that property right, which correlate to the duties of third parties not to interfere, deliberately or carelessly, with the property itself, and so provides no protection from careless action which instead only impedes the exercise of liberties or powers associated with the property right and thus reduces its value.

[166] *Anns* [1978] AC 728 (HL).
[167] *Murphy* [1991] 1 AC 398 (HL).
[168] See eg J Conaghan and W Mansell, *The Wrongs of Tort* (London, Pluto Press, 1993) 34–35.
[169] See eg R Stevens, *Torts and Rights* (Oxford, Oxford University Press, 2007) 27–30.
[170] D Nolan, 'Rights, Damage and Loss' (2017) 37 *OJLS* 255.
[171] *Mallonland Pty Ltd v Advanta Seeds Pty Ltd* [2024] HCA 25 [71].
[172] See eg DPA 1972, s 1 and (if brought into force: see Morgan (n 35)) s 38 of the Building Act 1984.
[173] Note too the willingness of courts in Singapore to allow such claims for carelessly caused pure economic loss, as discussed in Ti's chapter (n 59) 122.

It may be, however, that in some contexts at least, as where the property right is in a dwelling occupied as a home, such a narrow view of the law of torts fails to take account of the private interests which lie behind, and justify the existence of, a property right. On this view, special rules in relation to dwellings may be justified by the special private interest in the exercise of powers and liberties that come from a property right in a home. In English law, this has already been recognised, to some extent, in the DPA 1972, and in its extension by the BSA 2022.

Second, it can be argued that the law of torts should be capable of giving effect to a broader public interest in building safety: this argument, unlike the first, extends to all buildings, including ones intended for commercial purposes. For example, as shown by Bettini and Cappelletti in their chapter, the Italian law of torts takes a quite different approach from that adopted by the House of Lords in *Murphy v Brentwood DC*.[174] As they show, Article 1669 of the Italian Civil Code imposes a liability, regarded by the courts as tortious, that is specific to building safety and which has been explained by the courts as motivated by a clear policy concern: the 'general interest of the public … in having long-lasting buildings which are robust and stable, so as to ensure the safety of citizens'.[175] This echoes the aim of the UK Building Regulations to secure 'reasonable standards of health and safety for persons in or about buildings (and others who may be affected by buildings, or matters connected with buildings)'.[176] Whilst thus intended to protect individuals, the duties imposed by those Regulations are standalone, or undirected, duties as they do not correlate to any claim-rights and so do not fit within a standard private law model. The government has the power, by bringing section 38 of the Building Act 1984 into force, to allow claims for those who have suffered 'damage' as a result of a breach of a duty imposed by building regulations. As Morgan notes in his chapter, there are some difficult questions as to how courts would give effect to such claims, and their classification as 'tort' claims or otherwise could have important practical effects.[177] As his chapter shows, however, the idea that certain public duties may have, as part of their rationale, protection of the exercise or enjoyment of private law rights and liberties – such as the liberty of an owner to make use of (their part of) a building – is far from foreign to private law, seen as it is in the law of public nuisance and of breach of statutory duty. This suggests that taking the interests that justify certain private law rights seriously may mean giving the holders of those rights protection not only when their rights are directly breached, but also where a breach of a public duty impedes the enjoyment of particular liberties (such as the freedom safely to use property) which are closely associated with the private law right.

Certainly, the BSA 2022 very clearly marks out building safety as an area in which parties are subject to liabilities going well beyond the general law of torts.

[174] *Murphy* [1991] 1 AC 398 (HL).
[175] Cass Civ (II) 17.7.2023 no 20450.
[176] Building Regulations 2010, reg 8.
[177] See section II of Morgan's chapter (n 35).

The provisions of sections 147–51, for example, create specific liabilities in relation to construction products, and (unusually) do make clear that economic loss can be recovered. In contrast to the DPA 1972, these provisions do not establish specific duties – they are rather phrased entirely in terms of liabilities. This necessarily makes an analysis in terms of individual rights inapplicable and so it might be argued, as is sometimes said in relation to liability in *Rylands v Fletcher*,[178] that the provisions do not, strictly, create torts.[179]

However, as one of us has argued elsewhere, it would be a mistake to regard liabilities, even if not arising from a breach of duty, as alien to private law: 'a full understanding of the nature of private law, and a solid platform for consideration of its justification, can only come from an integrated analysis of liability, rights, and duties'.[180] Vicarious liability is, after all, of vital importance to the operation of the law of torts and can arise where it is the defendant's employee, rather than the defendant itself, that has breached a duty. One possible justification for imposing such liability on a party which has not itself committed a wrong is that, where a breach of a private law duty has occurred, it may be necessary in the interests of 'social solidarity'[181] to ensure that the claimant has an effective remedy. The point, perhaps, is that the promise of private law in protecting important interests may be hollow if effective recourse is not available. As Sawtell makes clear in his chapter, the BSA 2022 goes far beyond the usual limits of private law in allowing courts to impose liability, for example by means of building liability orders and remediation contribution orders, on 'associated parties'.[182] The provisions, passed in haste, are complex but they are, at least in part, capable of being applied in a way that is consistent with some of the possible justifications for vicarious liability, such as deterrence and loss-spreading.[183] The way in which courts interpret their new powers to impose liabilities where it is 'just and equitable'[184] to do so will form potentially fascinating evidence as to the weight attached to such concepts that, as noted by Bettini and Cappelletti in their chapter, go well beyond the narrow set of considerations to which, in the view of some theorists, private law may pay heed.

[178] *Rylands v Fletcher* (1868) LR 3 HL 330.

[179] For the view that *Rylands v Fletcher* liability is not strictly part of the law of torts, see eg N McBride and R Bagshaw, *Tort Law*, 7th edn (London, Pearson, 2024) 12–14, 337–341.

[180] Robertson (n 12) 219. See too Morgan's point in section I of his chapter (n 35, 182) in relation to statutory torts: the exclusion of such instances from the category of torts may 'pose a problem for a narrow insistence on corrective justice, if it is unable to explain legal institutions with a strong resemblance to paradigm common law torts'.

[181] M Cappelletti, *Justifying Strict Liability* (Oxford, Oxford University Press, 2022) notes the prominent role 'social solidarity' has played in justifying impositions of strict liability in French and Italian law, stating that, in the view of influential analysts of French law, such as Saleilles and Josserand, '[t]he value of social solidarity required the community to support those of its members who suffered some sort of harm, even if caused without fault' (74–75).

[182] Sawtell (n 11) section IV.C; see BSA 2022, s 121.

[183] For discussion of possible justifications for vicarious liability, see M Cappelletti, 'A Pluralist View of Vicarious Liability in Tort' (2024) 140 *LQR* 61.

[184] See BSA 2022, ss 124 and 131.

IV. Conclusion: Private Law and Beyond

As shown by the Phase 2 report of the Grenfell Tower Inquiry, and as explored in McBride's chapter, building safety disasters can expose widespread failings in society.[185] In his statement on the publication of that report, Sir Martin Moore-Bick, the chair of the panel, stated that 'those who lived in the tower were badly failed over a number of years and in a number of different ways'.[186] UK Prime Minister Sir Keir Starmer in his own statement on the report accepted that the building's occupants were failed 'by just about every institution responsible for ensuring their safety',[187] including their government, their local authority (both as owner of the building and through its Building Control), their landlord and even their fire brigade.

In the light of these shocking failures, including 'systematic dishonesty on the part of those who made and sold the rainscreen cladding panels and insulation products',[188] it may seem that the role of private law is of marginal interest. Certainly, criminal prosecutions will play a prominent role in the response to the fire itself, and the prevention of future incidents will chiefly depend on reforms, including those recommended or endorsed by the Inquiry, of government oversight of construction, of regulatory systems, of fire safety practices and the fire service, as well as the introduction of licensing schemes for those working on the construction or refurbishment of higher-risk buildings. Nonetheless, in considering not only fire risks, but the wider building safety crisis, it is clear that private law does have a role to play, not least in setting the expectations of those affected by the crisis. It is certainly legitimate to ask whether private law is another of the institutions that has failed those who are affected by the building safety crisis.

Our argument in this chapter is that, in considering private law, as when considering an occupying owner of an apartment in a tower block, interdependence is a key idea. The position of the owner cannot be seen in isolation: their safety depends not just on the condition of their apartment, but on the state of other parts of the building, and it is often impossible, and always impractical, for them to act individually. Similarly, we have argued, core aspects of private law, such as property law, the law of contract and the law of torts, need to be understood together as interacting parts of a complex whole.

We saw in section II.A that the acute fragmentation of ownership in the English system of leasehold title has caused real difficulties in protecting individual apartment owners against the misconduct of third parties. It is similarly possible to

[185] McBride (n 4).

[186] Grenfell Tower Inquiry (n 89).

[187] Prime Minister's Statement in the House of Commons on Grenfell Tower Inquiry Final Report, 4 September 2024, https://www.gov.uk/government/speeches/prime-ministers-statement-on-grenfell-tower-inquiry-final-report-4-september-2024. The formal response to the report's recommendations came by way of the 'UK Government Response to the Grenfell Tower Inquiry Phase 2 Report' (CP 1248, February 2025).

[188] Grenfell Tower Inquiry, *Phase 2 Report* (n 1) [2.19].

take a fragmented view of private law and to argue, for example, that private law concerns duties which are bilateral not only in form, as they correlate to a claim-right of a specific other party, but also in the reasons which justify them, as those reasons must apply simultaneously to each party. However, such a view would, similarly, drastically curtail the usefulness of private law to the individuals whose conduct it governs and whose interests it seeks to protect.

We saw in sections II.B and II.C that changes introduced to English law by the BSA 2022, whilst radical in nature, and targeted at the specific issue of building safety, are not wholly alien to aspects of pre-existing private law. There are many cases in which, to advance a clear policy of addressing safety defects in high-risk buildings, the legislation has enlisted the standard form of private law action, whereby a specific claimant enforces a duty or liability of a specific defendant. It is clear, however, that the content of those duties and liabilities is affected by wider policy factors, and not determined solely by bilateral factors equally affecting both claimant and defendant. This means that, notwithstanding their form, many of the private law claims created are inconsistent with prominent theoretical models of private law, which focus solely on corrective justice as between claimant and defendant.[189] If such departures are necessary, however, to maintain the effectiveness of private law in protecting important interests, and to preserve its salience as a means of regulating behaviour, then one of the lessons of the building safety crisis may be that a narrow, rights-focused conception of private law may render it unfit to serve those whom it binds.[190]

The need for an integrated, coherent approach means that changes made to promote building safety should extend beyond the substance of private law to include the processes available to enforce private law claims. A model of private law centred around an individual's power to enforce a duty of a specific defendant may have unfortunate consequences when applied, for example, to a residential block containing many different leaseholders, all of whom suffer, in different ways, from construction defects. Just as a more collective approach, as seen for example in condominium arrangements, is needed to the allocation of ownership powers, it is also necessary when considering how owners of individual apartments may enforce both pre-existing claims, and new claims given under legislation such as the BSA 2022.

As argued by Degeling and Gardner in their chapter, the substantive changes made by the BSA 2022, for example in relation to building liability orders and remediation contribution orders, will be largely ineffective unless accompanied

[189] For examples of such views, see eg Weinrib, *The Idea of Private Law* (n 10); R Stevens, *Torts and Rights* (Oxford, Oxford University Press, 2007); A Beever, *A Theory of Tort Liability* (Oxford, Hart Publishing, 2016); A Ripstein, *Private Wrongs* (Cambridge, MA, Harvard University Press, 2016). For further difficulties with such views, and the implications they have for the range of reasons relevant to private law duties and liabilities, see N McBride, 'Must Private Law Be Private?' in J Gardner et al (eds), *Politics, Policy and Private Law*, vol 1 (Oxford, Hart Publishing, 2023).

[190] See McBride's chapter (n 4, 274) for discussion of different possible conceptions of the aims of private law.

by further procedural changes. Indeed, the analysis of Degeling and Gardner identifies a significant irony. Whereas those orders, and their availability against 'associated persons',[191] are premised on the idea that those who benefited from developing buildings shown to be defective should now bear the burden of the remediation of those buildings, there is no current mechanism for an individual who bears the litigation costs to ensure that such burden is shared with others who benefit from the remediation of the building. This provides a clear example, in a specific context, of a broader point recently made by Frederick Wilmot-Smith: it is not only idle, but also counterproductive, to argue for particular substantive rules of private law without also asking if a legal system offers, to those whom the rules are designed to protect, the procedures needed to enforce those rules.[192] The building safety crisis thus demonstrates the general dependence of private law on an adequate system of civil procedure,[193] and this in turn has implications for the state's role in funding that system.

The need for an integrated, coherent approach thus reveals an important link between private law and civil procedure. There is a similar interdependence between private law and the functioning of public bodies, and between private law and public law more generally. Building safety is just one of many areas, from consumer protection[194] to freedom of expression at universities,[195] in which private law interacts with, and responds to, public regulation. In this area of building safety, it is clear that the role of public bodies has had an important impact on the development of private law. The nature of this impact has varied over time, and in different jurisdictions. In England, for example, the fact that the defendant had 'broad shoulders' was one of the reasons given by Lord Denning for recognising a duty of care on a council in relation to its statutory task of 'seeing that houses were properly built';[196] similarly, in *Anns v Merton LBC*,[197] the defendant's duties under the Public Health Act 1936 to inspect buildings and pass byelaws maintaining building safety were crucial to the House of Lords' imposition

[191] As discussed in Sawtell's chapter (n 11).

[192] 'Norms and the Sword' paper presented at Obligations X conference, on file with authors.

[193] Part of that dependence, in a common law system, includes the need for litigation which can lead to judicial decisions declaring and developing the law. There is a concern that the salience of private law is dramatically reduced where disputes are settled confidentially, through arbitration or settlement: see eg H Genn, 'Why the Privatisation of Civil Justice is a Rule of Law Issue' (36th FA Mann Lecture, Lincoln's Inn, 2012) https://www.ucl.ac.uk/laws/sites/laws/files/36th-f-a-mann-lecture-19.11.12-professor-hazel-genn.pdf. L Mulcahy and W Teeder, 'Are Litigants, Trials and Precedents Vanishing After All?' (2022) 85 *MLR* 326 show that recent data from the UK suggest that 'the radical drop in the number of cases coming into the system has now abated', but they do note (at 351) that '[d]isputes such as those in the construction industry rarely find their way to the appellate courts at all because of the delay involved'.

[194] See eg the Australian Consumer Law (sch 2 to the Competition and Consumer Act 2010 (Cth)) which prohibits particular conduct in trade or commerce, and allows individuals to bring claims where such conduct causes loss.

[195] See the discussion in Morgan's chapter (n 35, 198) of the Higher Education (Freedom of Speech) Act 2023 (UK).

[196] *Dutton v Bognor Regis Building Co Ltd* [1972] 1 QB 373 (CA) 397–98.

[197] *Anns* [1978] AC 728 (HL) 758.

of a duty of care. As Nolan shows in his chapter, however, there are conceptual difficulties with constructing, from a standalone or undirected statutory duty, a duty of care owed to specific individuals in relation to economic loss. Further, the risk of widespread liability on public authorities was a major motivation for later English courts in retreating from the approach in *Anns*: in *Murphy*,[198] for example, Lord Bridge pointed out that the shoulders of a public authority are broad only 'because they are financed by the public at large'.

Conversely, it may be that private law holds some lessons for public law in how best to respond to a breach of a duty. Proponents of forms of a 'continuity thesis' have convincingly argued that private law is committed to ensuring, as far as possible, that even if a private law duty has been breached, if the reasons justifying that duty still exist, they should be given effect to, as far as possible, in the law's response to that breach of duty.[199] As formulated by John Gardner, the 'continuity thesis' means that, 'when a contract was breached or any other wrong was done to another person, various reasons went unconformed to, and those reasons are still awaiting conformity. The question is always, what is the best conformity with those reasons that is still available?'[200] It can be argued that such an analysis can apply even if the breach of the duty does not involve a wrong to another person, as there will still be reasons justifying that duty which, by definition, have not been met. If, for example, a developer can be shown to have breached its standalone or undirected duties under the Building Regulations, then there may be good reasons for allowing a local authority, on behalf of the persons affected by the breach, to bring a claim requiring the developer to pay for the remediation of that breach. Indeed, such an outcome could be reached through the remediation order provisions of the BSA 2022:[201] a public duty, enforced by a public body, but in a form inspired by private law.

It could be argued that, given the costs and inconvenience of litigation, as well as the general public importance of building safety, the enforcement of duties by public bodies should be the primary means of dealing with the building safety crisis. Certainly, adequately funded public bodies may play a vital role in enforcing standards that are based on, or significantly overlap with, private law duties. This can be demonstrated, for example, by the Australian Consumer Law (ACL),[202] which imposes standards on parties acting in trade or commerce,

[198] *Murphy* [1991] 1 AC 398, 482.

[199] See eg J Gardner, *Torts and Other Wrongs* (Oxford, Oxford University Press, 2019) ch 2; S Steel, 'Compensation and Continuity' (2020) 26 *Legal Theory* 250.

[200] J Gardner, *From Personal Life to Private Law* (Oxford, Oxford University Press, 2018) 102.

[201] BSA 2022, s 124. An 'interested person' can apply to the First Tier Tribunal for a remediation order, and such persons include, as well as parties with a legal or equitable interest in the relevant building, local authorities, fire and rescue authorities, the Building Safety Regulator, and the Secretary of State for Housing, Communities and Local Government.

[202] Competition and Consumer Act 2010 (Cth), sch 2.

including prohibitions on unconscionable conduct,[203] and misleading or deceptive conduct,[204] which can be enforced by the Australian Competition and Consumer Commission, and state and territory consumer protection agencies. The ACL, however, also allows for claims by individuals who suffer loss or damage as a result of a breach of its prohibitions[205] and, in developing rules to apply to such claims, the courts have clearly been influenced by existing private law principles.[206] In our view, private law would fail to perform one of its core functions if it formed no part of the efforts to address the building safety crisis.

So, in drawing attention to the possibility of a local authority seeking a remediation order, our aim is not to suggest that the building safety crisis should be addressed without any involvement of private law. Indeed, the language of the BSA 2022 as to who can seek such remediation orders recalls that of the Charities Act 2011 (UK), section 115, which allows 'any person interested' to bring a claim seeking to enforce the duties of charitable trustees.[207] The duties of a charitable trustee exist even if they do not correlate to a claim-right of a specific party with a power, for example, to waive the duty; the same is true of the duties of personal representatives administering an estate,[208] and of trustees of a discretionary trust who have a power to vary the class of objects.

It might be possible to take a very narrow view of private law, and to see all these cases as beyond its scope. That would, we think, be misguided. Even if, for example, a legatee of an unadministered estate does not yet have a specific claim-right, correlating to a duty of the personal representatives, that party does have a power to commence proceedings in order to hold those personal representatives to account, and that power exists to protect an important interest of the legatee. It is the provision of such an individual power of recourse, which its holder can choose to exercise or not, that forms a central – some might say defining[209] – characteristic of private law. It is the need to ensure that such powers are meaningful in practice which has such important implications for a system of civil procedure, and the costs it imposes on litigants.

Our conclusion, therefore, is that, just as private law forms one part of the causes of the building safety crisis, so it must be part of the response to that crisis.

[203] ACL, ss 20 and 21.

[204] ACL, s 18.

[205] See eg ACL, ss 236 and 237.

[206] See eg *Marks v GIO Australia Holdings Ltd* (1998) 196 CLR 494, although note the somewhat different approach taken in *Murphy v Overton Investments Pty Ltd* [2004] HCA 3, (2004) 216 CLR 388.

[207] See eg H Jing, 'Enforcing Charitable Trusts: A Study on the English Necessary Interest Rule (2021) *Legal Studies* 228.

[208] See eg *Commissioner of Stamp Duties (Queensland) v Livingston* [1965] AC 694 (PC), as discussed by C Mitchell, '*Commissioner of Stamp Duties (Queensland) v Livingston* (1964): Rights of Estate Beneficiaries and Trust Beneficiaries Compared' in B Sloan (ed), *Landmark Cases in Succession Law* (Oxford, Hart Publishing, 2019).

[209] See, for example, the 'civil recourse' theory developed by Goldberg and Zipursky, as set out in *Recognizing Wrongs* (n 21).

To be an effective part, two things must be true. First, we must draw on the full set of concepts and considerations that can already be seen within private law; these stretch beyond duties which correlate to claim-rights and reasons which apply simultaneously to both claimant and defendant. So, whilst the UK's Building Safety Act, for example, has been radical in imposing liabilities, the powers it confers on apartment owners to make particular claims (or defend claims against them)[210] do not depart from pre-existing private law forms, and are not based on reasons that are wholly alien to those already seen in parts of private law. Second, private law must be effectively supported by other institutions, such as civil procedure and public regulation. The building safety crisis may thus be seen as a 'private law moment', not only because it forces us to confront failings of private law, but also because it gives us an opportunity to show the promise of private law, by drawing on its full resources to give people the means by which they, themselves, can protect some of their most important interests. Like a complex building, private law can, in our view, endure and be fit for purpose, but only if it is regularly inspected and only if there is both the will, and the resources, to renovate it.

[210] See the discussion in section III.A above of sch 8 of the Act, which prevents enforcement by landlords of service charges in certain situations.

2

Tackling Building Safety Through Private Law: A Comparative Analysis

FABIANA BETTINI AND MARCO CAPPELLETTI

I. Introduction

In June 2017, highly flammable exterior cladding and other fire-safety defects resulted in a devastating fire that destroyed Grenfell Tower in London. Since then, a large-scale building safety crisis has unfolded in England and Wales, with thousands of residential buildings suffering from major fire-safety failures. Disasters similar to the Grenfell fire have occurred in multi-unit buildings across Europe, notable examples being the Tour Mermoz in France (May 2012),[1] the Torre dei Moro in Italy (August 2021)[2] and the Valencia apartment building fire in Spain (February 2024).[3]

These events clearly indicate that fire-safety failures are a common issue, but the range of potential defects affecting multi-unit residential buildings is not limited to those. Indeed, a wide variety of structural problems might affect these buildings after their initial construction or subsequent refurbishment: for example, weak foundations and compromised load-bearing walls can undermine the building's stability and cause its collapse; faulty plumbing, damaged roofing and poor ventilation can result in water leaks, mould growth and structural damage. Like fire-safety failures, structural building defects can have a serious impact on the lives of flat owners due to flats becoming unsafe, unmortgageable, unsellable, or reducing in value, and due to expensive remediation works and other interim measures being needed to remedy or at least mitigate these defects.

[1] F Lacas, 'ITA and Fire: "We Prohibit Certain products on Facades"' *Batiactu* (31 May 2018) www.batiactu.com/edito/suites-incendie-tour-mermoz-2012-53090.php.

[2] R Calabrese, 'Milan Torre dei Moro Destroyed by Fire' *edilportale* (30 August 2021) www.edilportale.com/news/2021/08/antincendio/milano-torre-dei-moro-distrutta-da-un-incendio_84372_2.html.

[3] C Martín-Gómez and MZ Bin Mohd Tohir, 'Valencia Apartment Block Fire: Can Safety Regulations Keep up with Innovation in Construction?' *The Conversation* (29 February 2024) theconversation.com/valencia-apartment-block-fire-can-safety-regulations-keep-up-with-innovation-in-construction-224321.

The recent disasters due to building failures have led governments to take action – for example, by implementing stricter regulations for preventative purposes,[4] or by supporting remediation works through the creation of dedicated funds.[5] Although public law responses to building safety issues are essential, it is also important to examine what role, if any, private law can play in tackling building safety issues. This question is most pressing for at least two reasons: private law rules may provide incentives for the proper construction and maintenance of buildings, and those affected by building failures may often seek redress through private law causes of action.[6]

The question of how private law responds to building-safety issues receives different answers depending on the specific private law rules featuring in a given legal system and on the way in which private law's functions are understood in that system. In this respect, a comparative analysis is particularly rewarding. First, it shows that the same problem, in this case building defects, can be addressed in different ways and with differing results across jurisdictions. Second, from a more theoretical standpoint a comparative analysis shows that different visions of private law exist, and hence that there is no universal truth regarding the role and aims of private law.

In this chapter, we offer a comparative analysis of how English and Italian private law – essentially property, contract and tort law – respond to defects in multi-unit residential buildings. We focus on the position of those who live there and their ability to recover pure economic losses resulting from those defects.

Each of the three main private law areas deserves close examination. Property law provides a framework for the allocation of ownership rights and responsibilities among the different parties within a building. In the context of building safety, looking at property arrangements is essential to understand who owns and controls the building, and is therefore in a position to take decisions that are critical for its maintenance and repair; but also who bears the loss caused by building defects and who might be able to seek redress and against whom. Besides property law, contract and tort law play a crucial role. Construction contracts and sale contracts are of primary relevance, because they enable – at least in

[4] See eg in France, Arrêté du 7 Août 2019 Relatif aux Travaux de Modification des Immeubles de Moyenne Hauteur et Précisant les Solutions Constructives Acceptables pour les Rénovations de Façade (Order of 7 August 2019 Relating to Modification Work on Medium-Rise Buildings and Specifying Acceptable Construction Solutions for Facade Renovations) www.legifrance.gouv.fr/jorf/id/JORFTEXT000038906954; in Italy, Decreto del Ministro Dell'interno 30 Marzo 2022 – Approvazione di Norme Tecniche di Prevenzione Incendi per le Chiusure d'Ambito Degli Edifici Civili (Approval of Fire Prevention Standards for the Area Closures of Civil Buildings) www.gazzettaufficiale.it/eli/id/2022/04/08/22A02207/sg.

[5] See eg in England and Wales, the Building Safety Fund (BSF): 'Building Safety Fund: Information for Leaseholders and Residents' UK Government (18 December 2023) www.gov.uk/guidance/leaseholder-and-resident-information-on-the-building-safety-fund#what-is-the-cladding-safety-scheme-css.

[6] See M Bell, S Bright, B McFarlane and A Robertson, 'Private Law and Building Safety: Problems and Promises', this volume, ch 1.

principle – contractual parties to set their expectations regarding the characteristics and quality of a building; if not fulfilled, these expectations can be enforced via an action for breach of contract. The law of torts too can provide routes for redress, whether for negligence or on the basis of strict liability causes of action, especially where parties are not in privity of contract.

Taken together, property, contract and tort law play a decisive role in defining and allocating the rights and responsibilities of all parties in cases of building defects. But, as the following discussion shows, different private law systems – in this chapter English law and Italian law – can take different approaches. To show this, the chapter is divided into two parts which focus on English law and Italian law, respectively. In section II, we first consider the ownership arrangement used in English blocks of flats, focusing on the freehold–leasehold structure and its implications in case of building defects, including what property remedies are available to leaseholders. We then analyse the avenues of redress available to them in contract and tort law, both at common law and via statute. As we engage in this analysis, we flag issues that are relevant to the discussion of Italian law, hence setting the scene for our comparative analysis. In section III, we turn to Italian law and first consider the ownership arrangements for multi-unit buildings, which there takes the form of condominium title, and we reflect on its implications for flat owners. We then proceed by looking at contract and tort law remedies. It is in this part of the chapter that we engage in most of our comparative analysis between English and Italian law. Finally, by way of conclusion in section IV, we provide some further and more general comparative reflections and we offer some thoughts on the different ways in which English and Italian legal actors tend to see the role and functions of private law.

II. English Law

A. Property Arrangements

English property law takes a distinctive approach to blocks of flats. Whereas multi-unit buildings are predominantly arranged as condominium title across the world,[7] including Italy, most English blocks rely on the freehold–leasehold scheme.[8] As will be imminently explained, this arrangement has an adverse impact on the position of leaseholders, as it deprives them of the power to take decisions

[7] Although they are called in different ways and their specificities vary: H Easthope, *The Politics and Practices of Apartment Living* (Cheltenham, Edward Elgar Publishing, 2019) 1–12. See also other chapters in this volume, including EC McKenzie, 'The Surfside Condominium Collapse: What Lessons Have Been Learned?' (ch 3).

[8] This is so despite the availability of a statutory alternative, the commonhold, which represents the English equivalent to condominium title. The commonhold was introduced by the Commonhold and Leasehold Reform Act 2002 and is regulated by the Commonhold Regulations 2004. For a critical

vis-à-vis building maintenance and repair and yet it forces them to sustain the costs of decisions made elsewhere, typically by freeholders. And although several legislative interventions have tried to redress the imbalance of power entrenched in the freehold–leasehold relationship, the result has been a set of piecemeal solutions that, while improving the position of some leaseholders, leaves many others unprotected.

Under a classic freehold–leasehold scheme, the freeholder owns title to the land and the building, which includes the building structure (including the roof, external walls and foundations) and the common parts (for example, stairwells and elevators). The leaseholders own title to the individual flats as long leases. A lease can vary in length, but it is usually very long (for example, 99 or even 999 years), and a leaseholder pays a considerable premium to acquire it. When the individual lease expires, the leasehold interest reverts back to the freeholder, who regains full ownership.[9] However, given the considerable length of the leases, the value of the freeholder's reversion is generally low compared to the value of the leasehold interests collectively considered.

This classic freehold–leasehold scheme can present greater levels of complexity, especially in high-rise blocks or large multi-block developments, giving rise to several possible variations in the ownership arrangement. To give just one example, the developer can retain the freehold while granting a lease of the building or parts of it to intermediate landlords, such as property investors or social housing associations,[10] which in turn can grant long leases of the individual flats to leaseholders. Such an arrangement creates a layered structure with numerous leases and 'multiple additional landlords who own the building or parts of it, separate from the freeholder of the land on which the building sits'.[11]

This diversity in ownership arrangements means that each block or development will have its own specificities, reflecting the different interests of the parties involved; in all cases though – from basic to more complex ones – the freehold–leasehold scheme gives rise to a significant fragmentation of property interests within the building as these interests will be held by (potentially many) different parties. As will be seen,[12] this contrasts with Italian law where, under the condominium regime, individual flat owners are also co-owners of the land, the building structure, and all its common parts and facilities.

assessment of commonhold, see C van der Merwe and P Smith, 'Commonhold – A Critical Appraisal' in E Cooke (ed), *Modern Studies in Property Law*, vol 3 (Oxford, Hart Publishing, 2005) 225.

[9] There are, however, exceptions to this where leaseholders have been given statutory rights to extend their lease or to enfranchise. On enfranchisement, see text to nn 19–20.

[10] In this case, the investors are head (or superior) leaseholders. For a discussion of the frameworks used in English blocks of flats, see S Blandy, 'Legal Frameworks for Multi-owned Housing in England and Wales: Owners' Experiences' in S Blandy, A Dupuis, and J Dixon (eds), *Multi-owned Housing: Law Power and Practice* (Surrey, Ashgate Publishing, 2016) 20, table 2.1.

[11] Explanatory Notes to the Building Safety Act 2022, para 913 ('Explanatory Notes').

[12] See section III.A below.

The ownership arrangements under the English freehold–leasehold scheme affect the allocation of rights and responsibilities among the freeholder and leaseholders in a significant way. As owner of the building, the freeholder has control over it and, among other things, may be responsible for carrying out maintenance and repair under the terms of the long leases.[13] Where there is an intermediate landlord, these obligations may be shared: for example, the freeholder may be responsible for the exterior and structure of the building, with intermediate landlords responsible for all the other 'inner' common parts of the building.[14] Also, it is often the case that the management of the building is entrusted by freeholders and landlords to professional managing agents, which assume such obligations for some or all of the common parts of the building. In any event, in the vast majority of blocks, the costs associated with maintenance and repair are passed on to the leaseholders via service charges, provision for which is contained in the terms of each individual lease. Service charges set out the costs that each leaseholder is liable to pay, usually in a set period of time, and they typically include costs relating to both small repairs and major remediation works. Importantly, though, the freeholders' and landlords' obligations to maintain and repair do not usually cover the remediation of inherent structural defects (such as defective foundations or unsafe cladding).[15]

The ownership arrangements and cost allocation arising under the traditional freehold–leasehold scheme have two important implications. On the one hand, freeholders and landlords stand in a privileged position: they control the building and, although they may have an obligation to carry out maintenance and repair under the terms of the lease,[16] there is much less incentive for them to do so promptly and properly given the relatively low value of their interest in the property and the fact that they are not personally impacted by the conditions of the building. On the other hand, leaseholders are left with little or no autonomy and control over the building,[17] despite the fact that they are ultimately responsible for bearing the costs of maintenance and repair. As we shall see when discussing Italian law, this marks a striking contrast with condominium title, where flat

[13] E Walsh, *A Guide to Landlord and Tenant Law* (Oxford, Routledge, 2018) 296.

[14] Explanatory Notes (n 11) para 640.

[15] Recent authorities have held that 'neither a covenant to repair nor a covenant to maintain is a covenant to remedy [inherent] structural defects, nor to make safe a building that was not safe when it was built': *Tower Hamlets LBC v Lessees of Brewster House and Malting House* [2024] UKUT 193 (LC). For a comment, see S Bright, 'Time to Revisit Whether Leaseholders Have to Pay?' *Housing After Grenfell* (26 July 2024) https://blogs.law.ox.ac.uk/housing-after-grenfell-blog/blog-post/2024/07/time-revisit-whether-leaseholders-have-pay. Cf S Garner and A Frith, *A Practical Approach to Landlord and Tenant*, 8th edn (Oxford, Oxford University Press, 2017) [7.37]–[7.40].

[16] Or under s 84 of the BSA 2022 in relation to higher-risk buildings (ie buildings that are at least 18 metres high or have at least seven storeys, and contain at least two residential units).

[17] This does not apply where the building is owned by leaseholders or where leaseholders have the right to manage: see text to nn 19–20.

owners take decisions as co-owners and are collectively responsible for the maintenance and repair of the building.[18]

With the purpose of improving the position of leaseholders, the law has intervened in various ways. First, leaseholders have been granted statutory rights to take over the management of the building via a right to manage company (RTM), or to acquire the freehold title to the building via enfranchisement.[19] In the latter case, leaseholders become members of a company that owns and manages the building (so the block becomes 'leaseholder-owned'), with effects similar to a condominium arrangement. Therefore, both RTM and collective enfranchisement can put leaseholders in a position of control and reduce or eliminate exploitation through service charges and poor management issues. However, the exercise of both statutory rights, and notably enfranchisement,[20] presents serious practical challenges, especially in larger blocks.

Secondly, the Landlord and Tenant Act 1985 offers leaseholders some protection in relation to service charges by enhancing transparency and accountability.[21] Most notably, the law prescribes that the amount of money recoverable via a service charge is limited to costs which are reasonable, and are incurred for works of reasonable standards, regardless of the express provisions of the lease.[22] Thirdly, leaseholders have the right to be consulted about major works and, if they are not, the recoverable costs will be limited to a prescribed amount.[23] The freeholder can, however, obtain dispensation from the First Tier Tribunal (FTT) from complying with the consultation requirement, and the Tribunal usually grants dispensation for works which are serious and urgent, such as remediation works for fire safety defects.[24] Overall, then, although these legislative interventions represent an improvement for leaseholders, at times they are not very effective in practice.

More radical and effective is the approach taken by the Building Safety Act 2022 (BSA 2022), which constitutes a response to the post-Grenfell building safety crisis. The BSA 2022 includes provisions protecting some leaseholders from the costs incurred or to be incurred to remedy building defects, whether arising in connection with the original construction of the building or with subsequent refurbishments or repairs.[25] The regime set out in sections 116–125 and Schedule 8 of the Act is a complex web of provisions that afford leaseholder protection in specific circumstances. For example, no service charge is payable to the landlord for building defects for which the landlord or someone associated with

[18] See section III.A below.
[19] See Commonhold and Leasehold Reform Act 2002.
[20] Garner and Frith (n 15) [23.04]–[23.05].
[21] LTA 1985, ss 18–30.
[22] LTA 1985, s 19.
[23] LTA 1985, s 20. The cap is set at £250.
[24] *Daejan Investments Ltd v Benson* [2013] UKSC 14, [2013] 1 WLR 854. See also S Bright, 'A Means to an End or an End in Themselves? Consultation and Dispensation for Fire Safety Works' (2024) 1 *Conveyancer* 40.
[25] BSA 2022, s 120.

the landlord is responsible because they either undertook or commissioned the works relating to the defect.[26] This protection is the widest of all because it applies to all leaseholders, and it is meant to make sure that those who created building defects will bear the costs of putting them right.[27]

All other protections set out in Schedule 8 cover only 'qualifying leaseholders', ie those for whom the flat is their principal home or those who own no more than three dwellings in the United Kingdom.[28] These leaseholders are shielded from the payment of service charges in two cases: if the landlord's net worth is above a specified threshold,[29] or if the value of the lease is less than £325,000 in greater London, or £175,000 in any other case.[30] In the first case, the idea is that a deep-pocketed landlord can easily absorb remediation costs, while in the latter case the aim is to offer complete protection to those leaseholders who are very unlikely to be able to contribute to remediation costs. Hence, both provisions are meant to allocate the costs of remediation and other mitigating measures in a way that avoids the negative implications resulting from concentrating such costs on leaseholders. Where none of the above applies, qualifying leaseholders may be required to contribute to remediation costs, but the amount recoverable by the landlord through service charges is capped at certain maximum limits.[31]

A further leaseholder protection is specifically envisaged in relation to defects requiring cladding remediation, as qualifying leaseholders do not have to pay any service charge in respect of the costs incurred for its removal or replacement.[32] Finally, the BSA 2022 empowers leaseholders (and other 'interested persons') to apply to the FTT for 'remediation orders' and for 'remediation contribution orders'. First, a remediation order can be issued requiring the landlord to remedy a relevant building defect (and hence to shoulder the relevant remediation costs).[33] Secondly, the FTT can, whenever it deems it to be 'just and equitable',[34] issue a remediation contribution order requiring the landlord, the developer and a person 'associated' with them to make a payment to a specified person (which includes leaseholders) to meet costs incurred in remedying a relevant defect arising from

[26] BSA 2022, sch 8 para 2.

[27] Explanatory Notes (n 11) para 1674.

[28] BSA 2022, s 119(2)(d).

[29] BSA 2022, sch 8 para 3 (the threshold is 'N × £2,000,000', where N is the number of relevant buildings that the landlord owns).

[30] BSA 2022, sch 8 para 4(1).

[31] BSA 2022, sch 8 para 5 sets the caps at £10,000 (£15,000 for flats in Greater London) for leases of up to £1 million in value; £50,000 for leases valued between £1 and 2 million; £100,000 for leases whose value is above £2 million.

[32] BSA 2022, sch 8 para 8.

[33] BSA 2022, s 123. On the meaning of 'relevant defect', see text to n 38.

[34] See BSA 2022, s 124(1). On the application of s 124, see eg *Triathlon Homes LLP v Stratford Village Development Partnership & Others* [2024] UKFTT 26 (PC), discussed further in the following chapters in this volume: J Morgan, 'Tort as a Tool of Government Policy: Section 38 of the Building Act 1984: Sleeping Beauty Awakes?' (ch 7) 181; D Sawtell, 'Rationalising Associate Liability under the Building Safety Act 2022' (ch 8) section VII; S Degeling and J Gardner, 'Procedural Challenges and Opportunities for Leaseholders' (ch 9) section II.B.

works done in the thirty-year period before the entry into force of the BSA 2022.[35] These provisions go some way towards affording leaseholders a degree of (indirect) participation in the governance of the block and shielding them from building defects and the costs of their remediation.

As can be appreciated from the foregoing analysis, the BSA 2022 protections represent a very significant improvement in the position of leaseholders. However, the level of protection offered varies according to several factors, such as the nature of the defect involved, the value of the lease granted and the wealth of landlords, creating a highly fragmented framework.[36] Moreover, all these leaseholder protections apply only to buildings that are at least 11 metres high or have at least five storeys, and are not owned by leaseholders collectively (leaseholder-owned blocks).[37] In addition, these protections apply only in relation to 'relevant defects', these being confined to defects causing a 'building safety risk', ie a risk 'arising from the spread of fire' or 'the collapse of the building or any part of it'.[38] In this way, the scope of application of these protections is significantly limited. On one side, it is not difficult to envisage defects which, while not relating to fire or collapse of a building, may still be very serious and impact substantially the safety and finances of leaseholders. On the other side, those living in low-rise blocks or leaseholder-owned blocks may well be unable to remove or mitigate the relevant building defects and thus remain trapped in unsafe and unsellable flats.[39]

In conclusion, the English freehold–leasehold scheme of flat ownership allocates rights and responsibilities so that freeholders and landlords have the power to make decisions in relation to the maintenance and repair of the building, but it is the leaseholders who sustain the (financial) costs of these decisions. Correcting this allocation has required ad hoc legislative interventions. Particularly significant is the BSA 2022, which shifts the burden of remediation costs from leaseholders to other parties such as freeholders, landlords, developers and other associated persons. However, the protections envisaged in the Act apply only to certain defects and buildings, and most of them cover only specified classes of leaseholders, hence resulting in a patchwork that gives complete protection to some leaseholders, partial protection to others, and no protection at all to others yet. The resulting overall framework remains highly fragmented.

[35] BSA 2022, ss 124(2)–(5) and 120(2)–(3).

[36] See eg S Bright, 'Resilient High-Rise Property? Grenfell Tower and Beyond' (2023) 8 *Journal of Law, Property, and Society* 9, 38.

[37] BSA 2022, s 117(2).

[38] BSA 2022, ss 120(2), 120(5).

[39] F Brown, 'Cladding Crisis: '"No End in Sight" for Flat Owners Still Trapped in Unsellable Homes Despite Major Repair Scheme' *Sky News* (28 July 2023) news.sky.com/story/cladding-crisis-no-end-in-sight-for-flat-owners-still-trapped-in-unsellable-homes-despite-major-repair-scheme-12928147.

B. Contract and Tort

As we observed in the previous section, the traditional property arrangement used in English blocks of flats has a significant impact on the ability of leaseholders to deal with building defects. This does not mean, however, that leaseholders, especially those who do not benefit from the new BSA 2022 protections, will necessarily be left unprotected. Other areas of private law, and notably contract and tort law, might provide avenues of redress. To these we now turn, showing their evolution and the interplay between common law and statutory remedies.

(i) Remedies at Common Law

English contract law is known to afford limited protection to purchasers of real property, including leaseholders buying flats in a block. Leaseholders are afforded some protection at common law if they buy a dwelling off-plan (directly from a developer who builds and sells it). In this case, a threefold implied warranty applies: the builder must do the work in a good and workmanlike manner, it must supply good and proper materials, and the building must be reasonably fit for human habitation.[40]

However, the scope of application of these warranties is limited in two ways: first, being contractual in nature, they only protect the initial purchaser against the builder/seller, and not subsequent purchasers of the leasehold interest; secondly, as they are confined to off-plan sales, they are not available to leaseholders who purchase a leasehold flat after completion of the building.[41] Wherever the three implied warranties are not available, purchasers can only obtain redress if they show a breach of contract by their immediate seller, but this is difficult for two reasons: first, it is unlikely that the sale contract includes an express warranty relating to the state and condition of the property; secondly, the caveat emptor rule applies, meaning that the seller will be answerable essentially only for hidden defects on grounds of misrepresentation. In any case, even if a purchaser of a leasehold flat had a right enforceable in contract, practical difficulties may arise. First, the leaseholder may well face problems in proving the defectiveness of the common parts of the building affecting their own flat.[42] Secondly, the leaseholder would need to bring the action within six years of the time of the breach,[43] which

[40] *Hancock v BW Brazier (Anerley) Ltd* [1966] 1 WLR 1317 (EWCA), 1332 (Lord Denning MR); *Greaves v Baynham Meikle* [1975] 1 WLR 1095 (EWCA), 1098.

[41] W Webb and T Coulson, *Chitty on Contracts*, 35th edn, vol 2 (London, Sweet & Maxwell, 2023) [40-081].

[42] S Bright and B McFarlane, 'Private Law Failings and Policy Development Following the Grenfell Tower Fire' in J Gardner et al (eds), *Politics, Policy and Private Law*, vol I: *Tort, Property and Equity* (Oxford, Hart Publishing, 2023) 127, 132.

[43] Limitation Act 1980, s 5.

is a relatively stringent limitation period especially for long latent defects, such as fire safety and hidden structural defects.

This paucity of contractual remedies has meant that greater pressure was put on the courts to provide remedies through tort law. However, English courts have refused to open that door, confirming on various occasions that the tort of negligence does not allow recovery for economic losses resulting from the acquisition of defective premises. In the leading case on this, *Murphy v Brentwood District Council*, the House of Lords first observed that to allow a duty of care in respect of economic losses would be to create a 'transmissible warranty of quality' as between parties not in privity – the builder and the subsequent buyers of the building.[44] As the established rule in relation to chattels is 'no duty' vis-à-vis economic loss, the same regime has to apply to real property, as there would be no principled or logical distinction between real property and chattels that could justify a differentiated treatment.[45] Secondly, the House of Lords put forward an 'institutional competence' argument. As Parliament had already legislated through the Defective Premises Act 1972 (DPA 1972), it would not have been 'a proper exercise of judicial power' to intervene in the same area and potentially disturb the allocation of losses and liabilities as determined by the Act.[46] As will be seen below, this second issue does not arise in Italy, where the courts routinely interpret code-based provisions and develop the law in very creative ways, especially in the sense of strengthening the protections afforded to the victims of building defects.

In conclusion, due to judicial self-restraint and (excessive?) caution, common law remedies in contract and tort do not provide valuable routes for redress to leaseholders suffering financial loss due to building defects.

(ii) Remedies in Legislation

More promising avenues of redress exist at statutory level. The DPA 1972 offers some protection to anyone who orders the construction of a dwelling (including freeholders and developers), and anyone who subsequently acquires a property interest in the dwelling (including leaseholders).[47] Under section 1(1), a duty is imposed on any party taking on work for or in connection with the provision of a dwelling to see that the work is done in a workmanlike or professional manner, with proper materials, so that the dwelling is fit for human habitation.[48] Following the

[44] *Murphy v Brentwood District Council* [1991] 1 AC 398 ('*Murphy*') (HL), 469 (Lord Keith). See also, in this volume, ESW Ti, 'The Role of Private Law in Promoting Building Safety: The Case of Singapore', ch 4 116; E Chamberlain, 'Building Safety in Canada: Has *Winnipeg Condominium* had an Impact?' (ch 5) 134–5; D Nolan, 'Defective Premises and Economic Loss: A Problem Best Left to Legislation?' (ch 6) section III.A.

[45] *Murphy* [1991] 1 AC 398, 469 (Lord Keith), 475 (Lord Bridge).

[46] ibid 457 (Lord Mackay).

[47] For other discussion in this volume of the DPA 1972, see the chapters by Nolan (n 44), and by Morgan, Sawtell, and Degeling and Gardner (all n 34).

[48] DPA 1972, s 1(1).

insertion of section 2A into the DPA 1972, the same regime has now been extended to work done to any part of *existing* dwellings, this typically covering refurbishment, repair or maintenance work.[49]

Originally, a significant obstacle to getting redress for building defects was the short limitation period to bring an action – six years from when the dwelling was completed. This was particularly unfavourable to leaseholders whose property suffered from defects that became discoverable only many years after the completion of the work, examples including defective foundations and flammable cladding. Following the BSA 2022, the position has significantly improved: for work done after the entry into force of the BSA 2022 (28 June 2022), the limitation period is 15 years from completion of the work, while in relation to past work it is possible to claim for work done in the 30 years preceding 28 June 2022.

Very importantly, redress is available under sections 1(1) and 2A of the DPA 1972 only if the defect makes the dwelling unfit for human habitation. The 'unfitness for human habitation' test is satisfied in, for example, cases of excessive dampness,[50] defective foundations,[51] lifts poorly installed in a tower block or lack of means of escape in case of fire.[52] More generally, it appears that any defect which renders the dwelling incapable of 'occupation for a reasonable time without risk to the health or safety of the occupants … or without undue inconvenience or discomfort to the occupants' would satisfy the test of unfitness for human habitation.[53] As currently understood and applied by the courts, then, the 'unfitness for human habitation' test under section 1(1) of the DPA 1972 looks reasonably broad and it seems to offer a good degree of protection to leaseholders. In this sense, the test is reminiscent of the 'seriousness of defect' test underpinning Article 1669 of the Italian Civil Code, one of the key provisions on building defects in the Italian context.[54]

However, the scope of application of the DPA 1972 has important limitations. In particular, the Act specifically targets works done for or in connection with a 'dwelling',[55] and courts have interpreted this notion as meaning that each flat constitutes a separate dwelling, while an entire building cannot be considered as such.[56] This limitation, within the freehold–leasehold scheme of building ownership, has two negative implications for leaseholders. First, as mentioned above,[57]

[49] See BSA 2022, s 134(1). This regime applies only to works completed after the coming into force of the BSA 2022 (28 June 2022).

[50] See eg *Andrews v Schooling* [1991] 1 WLR 783 (EWCA), 790; *Alderson v Beetham* [2003] EWCA Civ 408, [2003] 1 WLR 1686, [28].

[51] See eg *Harrison v Shepherd Homes Ltd* [2011] EWHC 1811 (TCC) esp [164].

[52] *Rendlesham Estates v Barr Ltd* [2014] EWHC 3968 (TCC), [2015] 1 WLR 3663, [82] (obiter of Edwards-Stuart J) ('*Rendlesham*'). Considerations that may be relevant to the test can be derived from the list of factors contained in s 10 of the Landlord and Tenant Act 1985.

[53] *Rendlesham* [2014] EWHC 3968 (TCC), [2015] 1 WLR 3663, [68] (Edwards-Stuart J).

[54] See text to nn 121–126.

[55] DPA 1972, s 1(1).

[56] *Rendlesham* [2014] EWHC 3968 (TCC), [2015] 1 WLR 3663, [33]–[46] (Edwards-Stuart J).

[57] See section II.A.

leaseholders have title to the individual flats, but not to the building, which is owned by the freeholder. It follows that, in case of defects which affect the whole building (eg external walls, common foundations), it is the freeholder who can sue the developer–builder whose works caused the defect. However, the freeholder may have few incentives to do so as the costs the freeholder incurs for remediation works can be passed on to the leaseholders via service charges.[58] Secondly, although leaseholders have a right to sue under the DPA 1972 provided that the construction works were done 'in connection with' their individual dwelling, each leaseholder who brings a claim against a defect in a common part of the building must show that their *individual* flat is unfit for human habitation as a result of that defect.[59] Hence, representative proceedings are barred, meaning that one leaseholder cannot act on behalf of all the others in relation to a defect in the common parts of the building,[60] with a potential increase in the litigation costs to be sustained by leaseholders in a block, both individually and in the aggregate. A separate question is whether an individual leaseholder, after proving that the defect made their own flat unfit for human habitation, can recover the cost of remediation for the entire building; a few decisions by the High Court answer this question in the affirmative,[61] and it will be interesting to see whether higher courts will confirm this approach.

As will be seen, these issues provide a useful opportunity for comparison with Italian law: there, the condominium administrator or even a single flat owner can sue on behalf of all flat owners regardless of whether the defect in the common parts affects any particular flat, and the recoverability of the cost of remediation for the entire building is undoubted.

All in all, the DPA 1972 does provide some valuable avenues of redress to those suffering financial loss because of building defects, particularly considering the extension of the duty under section 1 to work done to existing dwellings and the relaxation of the relevant limitation period. However, the scope of application of the DPA 1972 is limited in two significant ways: it depends on a test of unfitness for human habitation, and it is anchored to the notion of 'dwelling', which may pose various challenges to leaseholders as well as increase the relevant litigation costs.

(iii) New Protections under the BSA 2022

The BSA 2022 has introduced several new 'remedial weapons' to the benefit of leaseholders and other parties which may be affected by building defects.[62] These

[58] This is not always true following the enactment of the BSA 2022, as sch 8 prevents the landlord from passing the costs on to leaseholders in certain cases: see text to nn 25–39.

[59] *Rendlesham* [2014] EWHC 3968 (TCC), [2015] 1 WLR 3663, [33]–[46] (Edwards-Stuart J).

[60] ibid [88], but cf [89] (Edwards-Stuart J) (leaving the door open to representative proceedings where the defect in the common parts of a block affects all the flats in the same way).

[61] See eg ibid [226]–[242].

[62] Some of these protections, notably remediation orders, remediation contribution orders and protections relating to service charges contained in sch 8 have already been discussed in section II.A.

further measures will not be analysed in detail, but they are worth mentioning as they highlight the scale of the recent legislative intervention.

First, the BSA 2022 has intervened on the existing section 38 of the Building Act 1984 by extending its limitation period from 6 to 15 years.[63] Section 38, which has not yet come into force, provides that a 'breach of a duty imposed by building regulations, so far as it causes damage, is actionable'. If interpreted in a broad way, and particularly if the concept of 'damage' were construed as including economic loss, this provision would have great potential in terms of redressing the losses suffered due to building defects since it is not limited to specific categories of buildings or classes of claimants.

Secondly, section 130 of the BSA 2022 creates a new category of associate liability: it provides that a 'building liability order' may be made against entities associated with a party liable under the DPA 1972, under section 38 of the Building Act 1984, or as a result of a 'building safety risk'.[64] The idea behind this provision is that, where the party incurring primary liability for building defects is a thinly capitalised subsidiary company or a special purpose vehicle that dissolves on completion of the property development, the better capitalised wider group structure can be held liable for the remediation of the relevant defect.[65] Very significantly, an associated entity is exposed to a building liability order both prospectively and retrospectively (ie for work done in the 30 years preceding the entry into force of the BSA in 2022). This regime of associate liability is clearly driven by policy considerations. The test of control for determining association suggests that a key concern underlying the imposition of associate liability may well be deterrence, that is, providing incentives for those best placed to avoid or minimise the risk of defective buildings. This is certainly plausible in relation to prospective, forward-looking liability[66] because associated entities will have from now on an incentive to ensure the safety of their property developments. On the other hand, deterrence does not explain retrospective orders: the creation of a liability rule that targets behaviour or choices which, when made, were not legally recognised as giving rise to liability is unlikely to stimulate appropriate risk reduction. Rather, the retrospective imposition of associate liability appears to

[63] This Act is referred to in these footnotes as 'BA 1984'. On its s 38, see also the chapters by Nolan (n 44) and Morgan (n 34).

[64] For these purposes, a 'building safety risk' is defined as 'a risk to the safety of people in or about the building arising from the spread of fire or structural failure': s 130(6). Note that there is no minimum height requirement for the building.

[65] A similar scheme of associate liability is implemented by the BSA 2022, s 124 in relation to remediation contribution orders. As seen above (text to nn 34–35), orders of this type can be made not only against the landlord or the developer, but also against a party associated with that landlord or developer.

[66] For a similar suggestion, see Sawtell (n 34) 224. See also JH Arlen and WB MacLeod, 'Beyond Master–Servant: A Critique of Vicarious Liability' in MS Madden (ed), *Exploring Tort Law* (Cambridge, Cambridge University Press, 2005) 111 (arguably lending support to associate liability insofar as its prospective application is concerned with a view to promoting efficient risk reduction).

respond to other concerns, notably the compensation of victims and the spreading of losses.[67]

Thirdly, sections 148 and 149 of the BSA 2022 introduce entirely new causes of action which provide for the liability of manufacturers and sellers of specified construction products for personal injury, property damage, and economic loss, where the relevant construction products are in breach of regulations, inherently defective, or have been mis-sold, and where their use caused or contributed to a dwelling being unfit for human habitation. As a result, sections 148 and 149 provide another route for redress to leaseholders who are not in privity with the manufacturers or sellers of a defective construction product.[68]

Finally, section 144 of the BSA 2022 has introduced a 'new build home warranty' whereby the developer of a 'new build home' (which includes any dwelling) undertakes to remedy 'any specified defect' in the home connected with its development or the carrying out of other works, and to take out an insurance policy for the benefit of the purchaser against such defect for a period of at least 15 years starting from the date of purchase of the home.[69] Section 144 is not yet in force; the details of the warranty will be determined by the Secretary of State via regulations (eg as to the types of defect and risks covered, transmissibility of the warranty, and maximum or minimum amounts of cover). Depending on these details, then, the new build home warranty could have a very significant impact on the level of protection afforded to leaseholders (and other homeowners) against building defects.

C. Conclusion

Overall, until the enactment of the BSA 2022, all areas of English private law – property, contract and tort law – were quite unsupportive of leaseholders affected by building defects. Under the traditional freehold–leasehold scheme of flat ownership, leaseholders lacked power to take critical decisions for the remediation of the building, which could therefore be delayed or avoided by freeholders/landlords; at the same time, where action was taken, leaseholders were in most cases responsible for bearing the costs of remediation of such defects. In addition, and partly because of the property arrangement itself, the level of protection afforded in contract and tort was limited, both at common law and via statute.

The changes brought about by the BSA in 2022 have significantly improved the position of leaseholders. As explained, the BSA 2022 modifies some key mechanisms in property governance, essentially shifting the responsibilities for service

[67] A systematic analysis of the justifications behind associate liability is beyond the scope of the chapter.

[68] For more details and a critique see Bright and McFarlane (n 42) 146.

[69] Explanatory Notes (n 11) para 1183. Currently, most new homes are sold with NHBC structural warranties, which offer a range of moderately useful protections against building defects and physical damage resulting from such defects: see 'NHBC Warranty and Insurance Cover' (National House Building Council, 2024) https://www.nhbc.co.uk/builders/warranties-and-cover.

charges from some leaseholders to landlords and allowing leaseholders to seek remediation orders and remediation contribution orders. However, the BSA 2022 is highly selective in the choice of leaseholders, buildings and defects that can benefit from the new protective regime, and this results in a complex framework in which some leaseholders are only partially protected or are left totally unprotected from the negative effects of building defects. The BSA 2022 has also reformed existing liability rules such as the DPA 1972 and has created new ones such as associate liability and the liability of manufacturers/sellers of defective construction products. Importantly, the BSA 2022 has also made provision for the retrospective application of several of these liability rules.[70] This suggests that the allocation of the relevant losses (typically in the form of compensatory damages or remediation costs) is not based on fault or deterrence, but is instead grounded in justifications such as the protection of victims and the spreading of losses. In relation to the prospective application of liability rules, the BSA has extended the limitation period for several actions.[71] Besides giving claimants greater chances of success, especially in relation to long latent defects, a longer limitation period may also have a positive deterrent function: because it warns those responsible for building defects that their liability may be established many years after completion of the relevant works, it may encourage them to adopt measures and strategies that minimise the risk of such defects.

All these changes and innovations have reshaped the law and improved the position of leaseholders. On the one hand, it is certainly true that each avenue of redress has its own specific requirements and its own targets in terms of type/seriousness of defect and category of defendant, thereby creating a highly complex and fragmented system of protection.[72] This is arguably due to the ad hoc nature of the BSA 2022, which was conceived of more as a reaction to the building safety scandal than as a rational and comprehensive reform of the laws governing building defects and the losses stemming from them.

On the other hand, it seems undeniable that today most leaseholders would, at least in principle, be able to obtain some form of redress for losses resulting from serious building defects. Important caveats apply to this, though: because representative proceedings (or class actions) are not available for claims of this type, individual leaseholders must bring independent actions, with substantial and sometimes prohibitive aggravations of expenses and evidential difficulties;[73]

[70] This is true for both pre-existing rules, eg s 1 of the DPA 1972 and s 38 of the BA 1984, and new rules, eg s 124 (remediation contribution orders) and s 148 (defective construction products) of the BSA 2022.

[71] See eg DPA 1972, s 1; BA 1984, s 38; and BSA 2022, s 148.

[72] For example, leaseholders living in a low-rise building would not be able to enjoy the protections set out in ss 116–125 and sch 8 of the BSA 2022; if, in addition, those who built or contributed to the construction of the block were no longer in existence, it is difficult to see how the leaseholders would get any redress. This, of course, does not necessarily mean that it would be for the private law system to fill this protection gap.

[73] For some examples, see Bright (n 36) 29.

moreover, even if an individual leaseholder can recover the costs of remediation for an entire block of flats,[74] it remains to be seen if and how it can be ensured that the compensatory damages awarded to that leaseholder will be used for remediation works.[75] As we will explain below, none of these difficulties plagues Italian law due to its condominium system.

Some final observations on the nature and functions of private law are in order. Most interestingly for present purposes, there seems to be in the English context a perception that several statutory remedies for building defects constitute a significant (and perhaps unwelcome?) departure from classic private law principles. For example, Susan Bright and Ben McFarlane have argued that associate liability under section 130 of the BSA 2022 is a 'significant break with the conventional axiom of private law that only A, the party who owes a duty to B, is liable for breach of that duty',[76] and that the liability of developers under section 1 of the DPA 1972 departs from the principle that the 'justifications for A's duty to B should not be based on wider policy concerns but must apply specifically to each of A and B'.[77]

For now, we merely note that this critique assesses compliance of these statutory provisions with private law on the basis of some of the narrowest approaches to the selection of what rules, doctrines and justifications can legitimately form part of private law.[78] We will come back to this point in the concluding part of the chapter, where we compare the different understandings of private law in the English and Italian contexts and reflect on how this affects building safety issues.[79]

As will be seen immediately below, the situation in Italy is remarkably different from that found in England and Wales. This is due to the profoundly different property structures characterising the two legal systems, to a remedial apparatus that, particularly in tort law, is much more favourable to the victims of building defects in Italian law than in English law, and to the more flexible and creative approach adopted by Italian courts compared to English courts.

III. Italian Law

A. Property Arrangements

In contrast with English law, multi-unit buildings in Italy take the legal form of a condominium. This provides for ownership of individual flats within a building

[74] See *Rendlesham* [2014] EWHC 3968 (TCC), [2015] 1 WLR 3663; *Hunt v Optima* [2013] EWHC 681 (TCC), [97] (Akenhead J).

[75] This problem is identified by Bright (n 36) 30–31.

[76] Bright and McFarlane (n 42) 142. See also Sawtell (n 34) 224 (arguing that associate liability departs from conventional private law structures).

[77] Bright and McFarlane (n 42) 137. For an assessment of s 38 of the BA 1984 along similar lines, see ibid 143–44.

[78] Bright and McFarlane take as a yardstick for their assessment Weinrib's model of private law: ibid 136–38.

[79] See section IV below.

that is co-owned and governed collectively by the flat owners. A condominium is therefore a complex arrangement, according to which individual and collective ownership coexist in the building and, as we shall see, this complexity is reflected in a special body of rules contained in the Italian Civil Code (Cc).[80] Importantly, the condominium statutory regime applies automatically from the moment at which the individual flats are sold off by the builder or developer to future owners, and therefore the building becomes co-owned.[81] It is not possible to opt out of the condominium regime set out in the Code and choose a different property arrangement. Also, the vast majority of these statutory rules are mandatory, although some of them may be replaced by local rules tailored to the need of the specific building.

The availability of a statutory condominium regime in Italy presents some advantages compared to the English freehold–leasehold scheme. First, the condominium arrangement ensures legal uniformity across buildings at a basic level throughout the country. In contrast, the rules governing English blocks of flats are based on individual leases which the freeholder and the leaseholder negotiate, or which more often the freeholder imposes on all leaseholders in a block with little (if any) room for negotiation. Hence, compared to the Italian condominium regime, English leases vary from block to block, and while this might be thought to provide substantial flexibility and uphold freedom of contract, in reality it generates large-scale uncertainty in the allocation of rights and responsibilities and an almost systematic disadvantage for leaseholders.

Secondly, in Italian law the condominium regime predetermines the balance to be struck between the different interests in the building, individual and collective.

As we will see below, the law's approach leans towards the collective interest, to the point that it could be said that the ultimate goal of the condominium regime is to preserve the building itself and ensure that it stands the test of time and survives across different generations of owners. This contrasts with the position in English law, where it is the freeholder/landlord as owner of the building who is solely responsible for its preservation. However, as noted above,[82] freeholders and leaseholders have conflicting interests. For most freeholders the building is primarily a financial asset producing a reliable income stream, and they have little incentive to take care of it,[83] while for leaseholders a flat represents not just a financial investment but 'the locus for family life, the place of safety, privacy, continuity and permanence'.[84] The contrast which is embedded in the freeholder–leaseholder relationship is unknown to Italian law, as flat owners both own and manage the

[80] Arts 1117–1138 Cc. The condominium regime was contained in the original Code, which was enacted in 1942, but it has undergone an important reform in 2012 with the enactment of Legge 11.12.2012 n 220.

[81] The condominium regime also applies to a group of buildings which are in physical proximity, and which share common areas or services, such as gardens or parking lots: art 1117-bis Cc.

[82] See text to nn 10–18.

[83] See text to and following n 16.

[84] LF O'Mahony, 'The Meaning of Home: From Theory to Practice' (2013) 5(2) *International Journal of Law in the Built Environment* 156, 161.

building and the law aims to safeguard the collective interest of current and future co-owners.

The strong emphasis placed by the Italian regime on the collective interest of condominium owners is reflected in the governance of the building, which is entrusted to the assembly of co-owners and the administrator. Their functions and duties are mainly centred around the management of the building, which also includes both regular maintenance and the remediation of any defect that may affect the building. In respect of the latter, which is the focus of our analysis, the law does not contain rules which specifically address building defects; however, by allocating powers and duties within the building, the condominium regime greatly affects decision-making, allocation of costs, and standing in relation to building defects issues. Moreover, the statutory rules must be read in connection with other parts of the Civil Code, especially those concerning the possible routes for redress available to condominium owners in contract and tort law, and, in this sense, they form the basis of our discussion in section III.B below.

First, the assembly of co-owners has decision-making powers in relation to the condominium building on a wide range of issues.[85] Among other things, the assembly approves the condominium by-laws (*regolamento di condominio*), which contain all the specific rules governing the building, and an associated document (*tabelle millesimali*), which constitutes the basis for allocating both voting rights and costs among condominium owners in a fair and proportionate way.[86] Another important power of the assembly is to review and approve the quotation (prepared by the administrator) regarding the money contributions (*spese condominiali*) due by all co-owners for the management of the building in the subsequent year. However, these contributions only cover normal and foreseeable costs of maintenance and repair and do not include extraordinary building repairs, as in the case of building defects. For these, the law mandates the creation, possibly in advance, of a 'special fund' for an amount corresponding to the costs to be incurred.[87] In this respect, the assembly has the power to decide what works are required, to contract them out and to allocate the costs among co-owners. In practice, it is likely that in most cases of building defects, the co-owners will turn to the builder or developer to force them to carry out remediation works, or they will sue them to obtain compensation, as we will see in much more detail in section III.B.

So, compared to the English leasehold–freehold scheme, it seems that condominium governance is arranged very differently. In England and Wales, with the exception of leaseholder-owned or RTM blocks, leaseholders have no decision-making power regarding the block of flats, which sits with the freeholder, but they

[85] Art 1135 Cc.

[86] Art 1123 Cc. This document contains a calculation of the arithmetical value of each of the flats compared to the whole building. The criteria for this calculation include, but are not limited to, the size and floor height of the flat, the impact of weather conditions, brightness, proximity to greenery or services: G Terzago, *Il Condominio. Trattato Teorico-Pratico* (Milano, Giuffrè, 2022) 528–29.

[87] Art 1135(1) n 4, Cc.

are nevertheless those who bear the costs of any measures. Instead, co-owners in Italy are directly in charge of taking crucial decisions concerning the management, maintenance and repair of the building based on the majority principle, and at the same time, they are directly responsible for the costs incurred, which are allocated proportionately among them. Although this does not mean that condominium blocks are always managed in a peaceful and effective way, the fact that co-owners are those who own and manage the building is certainly advantageous compared to the freehold–leasehold scheme.

Along with the assembly, the governance of the condominium is entrusted to the administrator, who acts as agent of the co-owners and can either be one of the co-owners themselves or a professional third party (an individual or a company with certain characteristics). The assembly has the power to appoint the condominium administrator and it *must* appoint one in buildings with more than eight flats/co-owners.[88] The main role of the administrator is to manage and maintain the common parts of the building in furtherance of the collective interest of all co-owners, and while the letter of the Code confers on the administrator the power to take all the necessary measures to achieve that goal (*atti conservativi*), Italian courts have interpreted this power as a duty.[89] Moreover, where remediation works are unforeseeable, extensive or financially burdensome (*lavori di manutenzione straordinaria*), the administrator can take action without consulting with the assembly, which needs only to be informed.[90] To perform all these duties, the administrator has the power (again, judicially interpreted as a duty) to bring legal action against anyone whose actions affect the common parts of the building, whether a co-owner or a third party.[91] Therefore, in case of building defects that affect its structure (such as defective foundations or unsafe cladding) and require *manutenzione straordinaria*, the administrator could take legal action without being authorised by the assembly, although the practice suggests that it often seeks and obtains the assembly's approval beforehand.[92] It must, however, be mentioned that the administrator's power to sue does not preclude that possibility for co-owners: indeed, each co-owner can still bring claims to protect their interests in relation to both their individual units and the common parts of the building, as we will see below.[93]

Compared to English law, the role performed by the administrator in Italian condominium buildings stands out as unique and does not find any true correspondence there. In England and Wales, the responsibilities for maintenance and repairs are with freeholders and landlords, and although these may sometimes

[88] Art 1129 Cc and art 71-bis(3) disposizioni attuative Cc. Also, the assembly can always revoke the administrator's appointment and appoint a new one, regardless of whether the administrator breached any of its duties: art 1129(11) Cc.
[89] Art 1130(1) n 4, Cc (no authorisation from the assembly is needed).
[90] Art 1135(2) Cc.
[91] Art 1131(1) Cc.
[92] I Meo and M Jerovante, *Gravi Difetti Degli Edifici Condominiali* (Milano, Giuffrè, 2013) 73.
[93] Cass Civ Sez Un 18.4.2019 no 10934.

have a legal duty to take action, remediation works can nonetheless be delayed or avoided.[94] By contrast, the condominium administrator has a power-duty to act in the interest of co-owners and of the building itself, and if it fails to do so, it may incur personal liability vis-à-vis condominium owners and its appointment be revoked by the assembly.

In conclusion, the Italian statutory regime for condominium buildings entrusts co-owners and the administrator with substantial governance powers and duties. In the specific situation where a building is defective, either due to minor defects or more serious ones, the assembly of co-owners, each individual co-owner and/or the administrator can and sometimes *must* act to remedy the defect: it might be decided either that the condominium itself will remedy the defect and hence initially sustain the relevant remediation costs and then sue the party responsible for the defect, or that the condominium (typically through its administrator) will immediately sue anyone who, in law, can be made accountable for the defect and the losses resulting from it. In this latter respect, the law of contracts and the law of torts provide a number of potential routes for redress, to which we now turn.

B. Contract and Tort

In Italian law there is a handful of general provisions that can be relied upon by condominium owners in cases of defective buildings. These provisions are all set out in the Civil Code and are wide-ranging in nature, meaning that their scope of application goes well beyond multi-unit residential buildings, or even beyond buildings in general. Moreover, the provisions themselves are open-textured and therefore Italian courts have had to engage in relentless interpretive work which, as will be seen, is invariably geared towards a strengthening of the available protections. Finally, as the analysis below makes clear, while contractual remedies are of limited significance, Italian tort law provides the most valuable routes for redress.

(i) Contract Law

The main avenues of redress available to condominium owners in Italian contract law arise either from breach of construction contracts or for breach of sale contracts. Claims for building defects can be based on a breach of construction contract where condominium owners buy their flats off-plan from the developer or builder, whereas claims based on a breach of sale contract are available whenever the flats are sold, whether off-plan or subsequently. Construction contracts are also used for renovation works carried out on existing condominium buildings. The two contractual routes – construction contract and sale

[94] See text to and following n 16.

contract – have their own requirements and features, and therefore they are best analysed separately.

Where flats are bought off-plan, condominium owners can bring an individual action against the builder–developer for defects resulting from a breach of the construction contract. The Civil Code defines the construction contract as 'a contract by which one party takes on, with organisation of the necessary means and with management at its own risk, the performance of a work or a service in return for monetary consideration'.[95] The key provision about contractual liability is Article 1667 Cc, according to which the construction company must warrant that the work has been carried out in conformity with the contract and that it is free from defects. In this context, 'defect' refers to any deviation from the construction standards applicable to that type of work, and covers, for example, floor-plan variations, limited plaster detachments, inefficient insulation causing mould, inefficient rooftop impermeabilization causing water leaks, or inefficient central heating.[96] On this basis, there seems to be common ground between Italian law and English law because broadly the same types of defect can trigger liability in Italian law under Article 1667 Cc and in English law under the three implied warranties operating at common law for off-plan purchases.

The remedies available to condominium owners buying off-plan are set out in Article 1668 Cc. First, a condominium owner can demand that the building defect be remedied by the construction company at its own expense: certainly, when the defect damages the claimant's own flat, although it remains unclear whether remediation might be sought for a defect affecting the common parts only. As an alternative remedy, a condominium owner might demand that the price paid to purchase their flat be reduced.[97] In any event, the construction company remains liable in damages for any loss (personal injury, damage to other property and consequential economic losses) caused by the defect unless it proves that this was not due to its own fault.[98] Finally, if the defect is such that the building becomes *wholly* unsuitable for its intended purposes, the claimant can seek termination of the contract,[99] thereby obtaining restitution of the price paid. So, given the range of remedies available under Article 1668 Cc, and notably the possibility to seek the remediation of the defect, Italian law appears more favourable than English law, which typically allows for compensatory damages only.

[95] Art 1655 Cc.

[96] See eg M De Giorgi, *Vizi e Difformità Delle Opere* (Milano, Giuffrè, 2013) 7, 50–51.

[97] Art 1668(1) Cc.

[98] See eg Cass Civ (II) 14.5.2019 no 12803; Cass Civ (II) 17.1.2003 no 631; Cass Civ (II) 26.10.2000 no 14124. Cf De Giorgi (n 96) 28, 79–80 (noting that some courts and legal scholars qualify liability in damages as strict and thus independent of any fault in the construction company). See also Cass Civ (II) 11.4.2022 no 11606 (holding that if an individual flat owner claims damages under art 1668(1) Cc for defects affecting the common parts of the building, compensation for the entire loss caused to the condominium can be obtained only if the claimant sues on behalf of all flat owners, for otherwise they will be taken to sue in their exclusive interest and will be allowed only a sum proportional to their individual share of the common parts of the building).

[99] Art 1668(2) Cc; Cass Civ (II) 14.5.2019 no 12803.

Apart from off-plan sales, construction contracts are also used for renovation works, with either the assembly of co-owners or the condominium administrator commissioning a construction company to undertake the works.[100] In this situation, Articles 1667–1668 Cc can be invoked against any defect affecting the common parts of the building. The administrator can certainly act on behalf of co-owners, as its primary role is to protect the collective interest in the preservation of the whole building; but individual flat owners can also sue for defects affecting the building, and there is no need to prove that the defect affects their own flat. Compared to English law, condominium owners are in a better position than leaseholders. In England, renovation works are commissioned by the freeholder/landlord, and leaseholders do not have any means of controlling who carries out the work and how, and they have no avenues of redress against defects as they are not a party to the construction contract. In Italy, instead, condominium owners, individually or collectively, can directly sue for defects resulting from construction works and obtain their remediation (or any other remedy set out in Article 1668 Cc).

However, a general limitation on the usefulness of Articles 1667–68 Cc, both for off-plan buyers and renovation works, is represented by the existence of two strict time limits. First, the defect must be reported within 60 days of when the claimants acquired knowledge of the defect.[101] Secondly, the action is time-barred two years from the day on which the work was delivered (Article 1667(3) Cc). As a result, claims under Articles 1667–1668 Cc may certainly be useful in relation to building defects that become apparent quite soon, such as poor insulation causing water leaks or incorrect window/door fitting,[102] but this cause of action is of limited usefulness for hidden structural defects, such as flammable cladding or defective foundations. From the perspective of limitation periods, then, the actions under Articles 1667–1668 Cc are even less favourable than the English contractual action, which (as was noted above) is subject to an already stringent six-year limitation period.[103]

Besides bringing an action under Articles 1667–68 Cc, purchasers of condominium flats, whether off-plan or otherwise, may obtain redress against the seller by relying on the provisions governing the warranty for defects in the contract of sale of goods, which encompasses both movable and immovable property. When it comes to sale contracts, the level of protection ensured to purchasers in Italian law is markedly higher than that offered to leaseholders in English law.

[100] The administrator may or may not need to be authorised by the general assembly of condominium owners depending on whether the renovation works are extraordinary or routine.

[101] See eg Cass Civ (II) 18.5.1996 no 4619 (holding that, where the employer is a condominium, time starts running from when the administrator has knowledge of the defects, of their seriousness, and of their causal connection with incorrect construction works). However, if the defect was already acknowledged or concealed in bad faith by the construction company, the claimant has no duty to report them.

[102] De Giorgi (n 96) 7, 50–51.

[103] See main text to n 43.

Under Article 1490(1) Cc, 'the seller must warrant that the goods are free from defects that can render the goods unsuitable for their intended use or that can significantly decrease their value'. This legislatively mandated warranty offers broad protection: it applies to any contract of sale, regardless of whether the property is sold off-plan or only after it has been built, and it targets a wide range of defects – any defect rendering the property unfit for its use or significantly decreasing its value. So, for example, the buyer of a condominium flat can rely on Article 1490 Cc for a defect in a common part of the building which prevents the use of a garage bought with the flat and therefore reduces the value of the flat itself.[104] The approach of Italian law to warranties in sales contracts contrasts strikingly with English law where, as seen above, there are only three implied warranties for off-plan purchases and no implied warranty at all for other sales contracts.

Breach of warranty under Article 1490 Cc empowers the buyer of a condominium flat to bring an action against the seller claiming either termination of the contract or a price reduction.[105] The flat owner could also bring a claim to obtain remediation costs as well as damages for all further harm potentially caused by the defect, including loss of a chance to sell,[106] unless the seller proves to have ignored the defect without fault.[107]

While the law on sales contracts provides a prima facie favourable regime from a substantive point of view, the action is subject to strict time limits: the condominium owner must report any defect to the seller (and not to the condominium administrator) within eight days of the date the defect was discovered (unless the parties have agreed a different term) and, in any case, the claim is time-barred one year from the delivery of the good (Article 1495 Cc). Similar to what we observed in relation to Articles 1667–1668 Cc, the short limitation periods set out in Article 1495 Cc mean that a contractual action based on the seller's warranty for defects may be useful only for defects arising shortly after completion of the works. In this respect, the limitation periods applying in Italian law are less generous than those in English law as discussed above.

Overall, the avenues of contractual recourse available to Italian condominium owners and English leaseholders differ in many respects. Italian law imposes a wider range of contractual warranties that protect the purchasers of (real) property against the risk of defects, especially insofar as sales contracts are concerned. In addition, the rules on standing and the diverse range of remedies in claims based on construction contracts make it much easier for condominium owners than for leaseholders to obtain redress against building defects. In all these respects, Italian contract law looks more favourable than English law, although it must be

[104] Trib Busto Arsizio 14.6.2023 no 872.

[105] Art 1492(1) Cc. Termination means that the seller must repay the price as well as the reliance costs incurred by the buyer, while the buyer must return the property: see art 1493 Cc.

[106] Cass Civ (II) 7.3.2007 no 5202.

[107] Art 1494 Cc. An example would be where the defect was caused by the construction company and the seller could not identify it by using reasonable care.

borne in mind that contractual actions are subject to shorter limitation periods in Italy, and therefore they may be useless wherever knowledge of the relevant defect is acquired long after completion of the construction works or delivery of the property.

(ii) Tort Law

Besides actions in contract, various routes for potential redress for losses due to building defects are available in Italian tort law. There are three main causes of action that condominium owners may find helpful in seeking redress. As will be seen, the level of protection guaranteed is remarkably greater than that allowed in England and Wales.

a. Liability under Article 1669 Cc for Serious Defects

The most valuable avenue of redress for building defects in Italian law is contained in Article 1669 Cc. The provision relates to construction contracts and complements the contractual protection contemplated in Articles 1667–1668 Cc, but has a much broader scope of application and far-reaching effects that make it a crucial provision from the standpoint of the protection afforded to condominium owners. Moreover, as will be seen, Article 1669 Cc offers the opportunity for interesting comparisons with the DPA 1972, both in its original form and as amended by the BSA 2022.

Article 1669 Cc reads as follows:

> In the case of buildings or other immovables intended by their nature to last for a long period of time, if, within ten years of their completion, they totally or partially ruin due to a defect in the soil or a defect in the construction, or if they present an obvious danger of ruin or reveal a serious defect, the construction company is liable to the employer and their successors in title, provided that the defect is reported within one year of its discovery. The claim shall be time-barred one year from the date of the notice.

While the nature of this provision has long been controversial, with views oscillating between contractual, tortious and hybrid liability, Italy's highest appeal court (the Corte di Cassazione) has eventually embraced the view that Article 1669 Cc enshrines a tort liability rule.[108] In particular, it is now settled that Article 1669 is a special provision compared to the general tort rule contained in Article 2043 Cc, and it seeks to provide, to those ordering works, their successors in title and third parties more generally, a more effective redress against building defects.[109] Moreover, behind this head of liability lies the public policy concern to ensure that all buildings and other immovable property are safely and properly built so as to

[108] For a summary of this debate, see MC Cervale, *Struttura Dell'appalto e Responsabilità Dell'appaltatore* (Milano, Giuffrè, 2016) 145–55.

[109] Cass Civ Sez Un 3.2.2014 no 2284.

ensure they can withstand the test of time: in this respect, the Corte di Cassazione has recently emphasised that 'Article 1669 of the Civil Code is aimed … at protecting the general interest of the public … in having long-lasting buildings which are robust and stable, so as to ensure the safety of citizens'.[110]

Some comparative remarks with the DPA 1972 are in order here: first, while section 1 of the DPA 1972 is confined to dwellings, Article 1669 applies to all buildings, whether residential or of a different nature, hence possessing a far broader scope of application; secondly, the policy concern of protecting buildings as such seems to be absent from the DPA 1972, the original aim of which was to afford better protection to purchasers of new dwellings.[111]

The desire to provide a significant degree of protection to those affected by building defects is reflected in several aspects of Article 1669. First, defendants are subjected to a rigorous standard of conduct, as they will not be able to escape liability by proving the adoption of all reasonable care. Only proof of an act of a third party or an act of God will have an exonerating effect,[112] which confers on Article 1669 Cc a strict liability nature. Secondly, while the provision expressly mentions that a claim can be brought against the construction company, judges have interpreted it extensively to include as a potential defendant, first, any subcontractor to whom the construction company entrusted the work, and, secondly, the developer who avails itself of the work of contractors to construct the building, provided that the developer has the power to coordinate or supervise the contractors' work and therefore that the relevant defect can be traced to the seller's responsibility.[113] The reason for this extension lies in the desire to improve the position of purchasers and to circumvent the operation of the shorter and stricter limitation period associated with the general warranty for defects in the sale of goods, which, as seen above, is one year from delivery of the good.

Besides the construction company, courts have also clarified that a claim under Article 1669 Cc can be brought against all other parties who have been involved in various roles in the work and who, due to their professional negligence, have contributed to cause the defect, such as designers and construction managers.[114] Compared to English law, the broad range of potential defendants targeted by Article 1669 Cc is similar to that targeted by section 1 of the DPA 1972, showing how both regimes seek to cast their net wide and offer effective redress.

According to the letter of Article 1669 Cc, the action can be brought by those ordering works and by their successors in title, these including original condominium owners, whether they bought their flats off-plan or after completion, and any

[110] Cass Civ (II) 17.7.2023 no 20450.

[111] Law Commission, *Civil Liability of Vendors and Lessors for Defective Premises* (Law Com No 40, 1970) [7]–[8].

[112] Cass Civ (II) 27.2.1991 no 2123; Cass Civ (I) 6.12.2000 no 15488; Cass Civ (III) 17.1.2013 no 1026, [7.3].

[113] Corte d'Appello di Milano Sez IV 19.2.2021; Cass Civ (III) 13.1.2005 no 567; Cass Civ (II) 16.2.2012 no 2238; Cass Civ (II) 16.1.2020 no 777.

[114] Cass Civ (II) 23.7.2013 no 17874.

subsequent purchasers of the condominium flats.[115] Importantly, condominium owners can sue both for defects affecting their own flats and for defects affecting the common parts of the building.[116] The action can be also brought by the administrator on behalf of the condominium owners for defects affecting the common parts of the buildings,[117] such as external cladding or defective foundations. Moreover, the administrator can sue even if the defects affect only individual flats, and not the common parts of the building, but in this case it must have received a mandate from the condominium owners.[118]

A final important point on standing is that Italian courts have interpreted this aspect of Article 1669 Cc in a creative and expansive way and, given that the provision is now seen as a tort rule, they have extended the right to sue to any third party who is detrimentally affected by the serious defect.[119] Hence, neighbours, passers-by and anyone else who is harmed or suffers some loss due to serious defects in the building in question is entitled to seek redress under Article 1669. In light of this, Article 1669 is more generous on standing than section 1 of the DPA 1972, which grants the right to sue only to the person who ordered the works and to every person who acquires a property interest in the dwelling.

In terms of defects, Article 1669 targets 'serious defects' that affect the building or the land on which it is built.[120] Judges have interpreted expansively the meaning and scope of 'serious defect' as referring to 'alterations that, in an appreciable manner, reduce the enjoyment of the property as a whole, undermining its normal use, in relation to its economic and practical function and according to its intrinsic nature'.[121] Therefore, serious defects are not solely those that determine a risk of collapse, but also those that affect the overall structure and functions of the building, or part of it, and, as a result, undermine its normal enjoyment,[122] or significantly reduce its value.[123] Consistent with this approach, it has been specified that serious defects exist where unsuitable materials are used or the works are not done in a workmanlike manner, even if these defects affect secondary and ancillary elements of the building, such as cladding, window frames, flooring and installations, insofar as these defects undermine the long-term functioning of the building or its habitability, and remediation works can fix these defects.[124]

[115] Cass Civ (II) 29.3.2002 no 4622; Cass Civ (II) 16.11.2017 no 27250.

[116] Cass Civ (II) 10.4.2000 no 4485. See also A Pradelli, *Vizi e Difformità Nelle Costruzioni* (Milano, Giuffrè, 2011) 57; Meo and Jerovante (n 92) 75.

[117] Cass Civ (II) 6.2.2009 no 3040.

[118] Cass Civ (II) 8.11.2010 no 22656.

[119] Cass Sez Un 6.2.2014 no 2724.

[120] The article has been interpreted as applying to both the construction of new buildings and the maintenance and renovation of existing ones. See Cass Civ Sez Un 27.3.2017 no 7756.

[121] See Cass Civ (II) 18.6.2014 no 13882. Art 1669 is seen as a special regime carved out of art 1667, and hence a serious defect under art 1669 also constitutes a *vizio* under art 1667, while a *vizio* does not necessarily constitute a serious defect if it does not reach the required threshold of seriousness.

[122] Cass Civ (II) 17.11.2017 no 27315.

[123] On this point, see De Giorgi (n 96) 159.

[124] Cass Civ (II) 8.4.2004 no 8140.

Compared to section 1 of the DPA 1972, then, Article 1669 has a broader scope of application due to creative judicial law-making: any defect or alteration detrimentally affecting the functioning, enjoyment, use or even value of the building in an appreciable way is enough to trigger Article 1669, and this concept is broader than what amounts to a defect under the DPA 1972, even after the interpretation of 'unfitness for human habitation' provided in *Rendlesham*.[125]

With an action under Article 1669, a claimant could demand that the defendant remedies the building defects or pays a sum equivalent to the remediation costs.[126] Moreover, if it is shown that, notwithstanding the remediation works, the property is still not as valuable as it would have been without the building defects, it will be possible to obtain compensation for the residual financial loss.[127] As an alternative to these remedies, compensatory damages corresponding to the diminution in the market value of the building or of the individual flat might be awarded.

Overall, then, the administrator on behalf of all co-owners or each condominium owner may be able to obtain full redress for the losses suffered. Again, the type of protection afforded under Article 1669 is wider than the DPA 1972, which entitles claimants to compensatory damages only. To obtain an order requiring remediation works or a sum covering remediation costs, a leaseholder has to rely on sections 123 and 124 of the BSA 2022.

Very importantly, claims under Article 1669 Cc are subjected to three distinct time limits. First, the serious defect must exist before 10 years have passed from completion of the work. It is important to emphasise that this time limit refers to the coming into existence of the defect and not to the time period within which a claim must be brought. In other words, the condominium administrator or the individual condominium owner can rely on Article 1669 Cc even if they discover the serious defect after 10 years from completion of the work, so long as the defect itself came into existence within that time frame.[128] As can be appreciated, this constitutes a very favourable regime for the recovery of losses caused by building defects. What is more, this provision fits very well the needs of claimants affected by defects such as flammable cladding or defective foundations because this type of defect is invariably present since the completion of the works but may remain hidden for a long time after that. Secondly, the defect must be reported to the defendant within one year of its discovery, and this one-year time limit 'starts to run from the day on which the employer obtains an appreciable degree of objective knowledge of the seriousness of the defects and of their causal derivation from

[125] See text to nn 53–54. See also the chapters in this volume by Sawtell (n 34) 217–8 and Degeling and Gardner (n 34) 256–7.

[126] Cass Civ (II) 10.5.1995 no 5103, [2]. The compensatory damages awarded to claimants include 'all the costs necessary to remove the defects, including by carrying out works that are different and more onerous than those originally planned in the construction contract, provided that these works are useful to restore the normal functioning of the building': see Cass Civ (II) 4.3.2016 no 4319.

[127] See Meo and Jerovante (n 92) 32.

[128] See Cass Civ (I) 26.5.1993 no 5920; Cass Civ (II) 30.7.2004 no 14561, [1.1], [4.1]; Tribunale Bari (II) 24.2.2006 no 437. See also Pradelli (n 116) 75; Meo and Jerovante (n 92) 32.

the imperfect execution of the work' (eg, the date of the technical assessment).[129] Thirdly, the claim must be made within one year after reporting the defect to the defendant. These three time limits are cumulative, meaning that the action cannot be brought if any of them is not complied with.[130]

A comparison with the English regime on limitation periods is particularly interesting. Whereas claims under the DPA 1972 in its original form were subjected to a six-year limitation period and hence were of little value for leaseholders affected by long latent defects, the BSA 2022 has significantly improved the situation by extending that time limit prospectively to 15 years and by making possible retrospective claims.[131] As a result, both Article 1669 and section 1 of the DPA 1972 in its current form provide favourable limitation periods.

A final point concerns the so-called *polizza decennale postuma* ('decennial insurance policy'). This is an insurance policy that the builder–seller is obliged to take out for the benefit of purchasers and covers damage stemming from serious defects for which the builder–seller would be liable under Article 1669 Cc.[132] The insurance policy is operative for 10 years from completion of the works.[133] This compulsory insurance arrangement was first introduced in 2005 and received full implementation in 2022. This insurance scheme covers all physical and direct damage to buildings or their parts, but no insurance indemnity is owed in relation to 'loss of enjoyment of the building or any part of it, loss of profits and any other indirect damage such as, for instance, those stemming from the complete or partial interruption or suspension of economic activities, as well as loss in the value of the property'.[134]

Hence, the victims of serious building defects are provided with a reliable source of compensation wherever the builder–seller is not able to meet claims for damages only in relation to defects resulting in physical damage, but not otherwise. This decennial insurance policy is reminiscent of the compulsory insurance arrangements under the 'new build home warranty', introduced by section 144 of the BSA 2022. It remains to be seen, though, if, when and how the new insurance arrangements will be implemented in the English context, and it is therefore difficult at this stage to make any comparison between the two insurance regimes.[135]

Overall, the liability rule envisaged in Article 1669 Cc is generally a promising route of protection from serious building defects. Italian courts have interpreted all the elements of the provision in a way that is largely favourable to claimants,

[129] Cass Civ (II) 16.1.2020 no 777, [6.1] (also clarifying that manifestations of minor importance and mere suspicions are not sufficient).

[130] Cass Civ (II) 30.7.2004 no 14561, [4.1].

[131] See text following n 49.

[132] See Decreto Legislativo 20.6.2005 n 122, art 4; and Decreto 20.7.2022 n 154.

[133] Decreto 20.7.2022 n 154, art 4.

[134] Decreto 20.7.2022 n 154, art 18(a).

[135] As mentioned above (text following n 69) commencement of s 144 of the BSA 2022 is indefinitely delayed, and it will be for the Secretary of State to determine the content of the new build home warranty and of the relevant insurance policy.

from the meaning of 'serious defect' to the rules on standing and on limitation periods. Moreover, no distinction is made between different types of buildings, whichever their features and purposes, and liability can attach for defects originating either in initial works or in renovation/remediation works. As originally enacted, section 1 of the DPA 1972 did not come close to Article 1669 in terms of the level of protection granted: it was limited to initial works, it was (and still is) confined to dwellings, and its limitation period was very stringent. As amended by the BSA 2022, section 1 promises to achieve much more satisfactory results from the standpoint of leaseholders, as it covers any dwelling, it applies to renovation works as well, and the applicable limitation periods appear to be especially favourable to leaseholders, both prospectively and retrospectively. Moreover, the BSA 2022 allows for claims to be brought under the DPA 1972 against entities associated with the party primarily responsible for the defect,[136] an option that does not seem to be available under Article 1669 Cc as currently interpreted.

b. General Liability for Fault: Article 2043 Cc

Should Article 1669 Cc be unavailable for any reason, potential claimants could look elsewhere in Italian tort law for redress. In this respect, Articles 2043 and 2051 Cc could come into play.

Article 2043 Cc is the general provision governing fault-based liability in Italian tort law, stating that '[a]ny action which deliberately or negligently causes an unlawful harm to another obliges the party who committed that action to compensate the harm'.[137] For present purposes, there are three key points to consider: recoverability of pure economic loss, proof of fault and limitation period.

As in many other legal systems, the recoverability of pure economic loss in tort law is controversial.[138] Article 2043 Cc provides that only 'unlawful damage' (*danno ingiusto*) can be compensated. The concept of *danno ingiusto* performs the same function as the notional question of duty of care in the English tort of negligence:[139] they both reflect the selection of rights and interests deemed worthy of tort protection. Article 2043 Cc does not include any formal list of protected interests, but the courts have interpreted *danno ingiusto* so as to encompass property damage, personal injury and also some types of purely economic loss. In this latter respect, the Corte di Cassazione has developed the concept of 'right to the integrity of one's assets' (*diritto all'integrità patrimoniale*),[140] which can be found in many areas of Italian law and which, in tort law, has been used over the years to ensure that claimants could obtain compensation for financial loss due to,

[136] See text to nn 64–67.

[137] 'Qualunque fatto doloso o colposo, che cagiona ad altri un danno ingiusto, obbliga colui che ha commesso il fatto a risarcire il danno'.

[138] In this volume, see also E SW Ti, 'The Role of Private Law in Promoting Building Safety: The Case of Singapore' (ch 4) and the chapters by Chamberlain and Nolan (both n 44) and Morgan (n 34).

[139] See D Nolan, 'Deconstructing the Duty of Care' (2013) *LQR* 599.

[140] Cass Civ (III) 4.5.1982 no 2765, Il Foro Italiano 1982.I.2863.

for example, the wrongful death of a creditor caused by a third party,[141] loss of a chance of monetary gains (eg relating to a missed job opportunity)[142] or interference with contractual relations.[143]

On this basis, it would be in principle open to Italian courts to allow a claim for financial losses resulting from building defects. This could be supported by the broader approach taken in Italian law, which confers a special status on buildings and affords substantial protection to owners of real property, as evidenced by Article 1669 Cc. This contrasts with the position in English law, where buildings are not considered as especially worthy of protection in general and when it comes to the recoverability of pure economic losses, as the House of Lords also reaffirmed in *Murphy*.[144] In addition, Italian courts have routinely engaged in creative interpretation and law-making, without feeling particularly constrained by the letter of the law; this marks a contrast with the approach adopted in *Murphy*, where the House of Lords refrained from intervening in the same area where the Parliament had legislated through the DPA 1972.[145]

If Italian courts decided to allow claims for financial losses due to building defects under Article 2043 Cc, the same remedies as those available under Article 1669 Cc could be sought:[146] an order to the defendant to undertake remediation works or to pay a sum equivalent to the remediation costs[147] or, alternatively, damages reflecting the diminution in the market value of the property.

Compared to Article 1669 Cc, Article 2043 presents an advantage and a disadvantage. The disadvantage is that, while Article 1669 is a rule of strict liability, liability under Article 2043 rests on fault. Hence, a condominium owner or the administrator will have to identify the party whose conduct caused the building defect (eg the construction company, construction manager or designer), and then prove their fault. This may be no easy task, not least because a defendant who complied with best (or even standard) practices at the time of the construction works may, on that very basis, argue that their conduct was entirely reasonable and therefore that the fault requirement could not be satisfied.

However, compared to Article 1669, Article 2043 is advantageous when it comes to time limits. As seen above, Article 1669 Cc covers only defects that came into existence within 10 years of completion of the work. Now, according to the letter of Article 2947 Cc, a claimant bringing an action in tort under Article 2043 Cc faces a limitation period of five years, commencing to run from the time of the tortious act or fact. This may suggest that the limitation period applying to Article 2043 Cc is markedly less favourable to claimants than that applying to

[141] Cass Civ Sez Un 26.1.1971 no 174.

[142] Cass Civ sez lavoro 19.11.1983 no 6906, Il Foro Italiano 1984.I.1830; Cass Civ sez lavoro 19.12.1985 no 6506, Il Foro Italiano 1986.I.383.

[143] Cass Civ (I) 6.5.1980 no 2996, Il Foro Italiano 1980.I.1886.

[144] *Murphy* [1991] 1 AC 398 (HL).

[145] See text to n 46.

[146] See text to and following nn 127–128ff.

[147] Cass Civ (III) 4.3.1998 no 2402.

Article 1669 Cc, but the judicial interpretation of Article 2947 produces a very different result. Indeed, Italian courts invariably hold that the five-year time limit for actions grounded in the general law of torts starts to run from when the harm has manifested itself and thus from the moment the harm is 'objectively perceptible and recognisable'.[148] This happens, the courts have explained, when a reasonable person in the claimant's position would have had sufficient knowledge to become aware of the existence of the harm and of its causal connection with the defendant's conduct.[149] This approach appears to be particularly useful for building defects, especially those that materialise a long time after completion of the works, given that the five-year limit would start running from the moment at which a reasonable flat owner or administrator would have become aware of the building defect.[150] Overall, while Article 2043 Cc is less favourable to claimants than Article 1669 Cc from the standpoint of the relevant standard of conduct, it would provide an alternative route for redress if Article 1669 Cc were not available.

c. Liability under Article 2051 Cc

A further avenue of recourse in tort which may be available to condominium owners, and which finds no equivalent in English tort law, is Article 2051 Cc. According to this, '[e]veryone is liable for the damage caused by things in [their] keeping, unless [they prove] that the damage was the result of a fortuitous event'. The interpretation of this article by courts has been fairly broad: the 'keeper' of a thing is anyone who is in a position to 'control the thing, remove situations of danger that may have materialised, and exclude others from coming into contact with the thing';[151] 'thing' is any physical thing, movable or immovable, in solid, liquid or gaseous state.[152] Moreover, liability for the harm caused by things in one's keeping is strict: the defendant can escape liability only by proving the occurrence of a fortuitous event that was the exclusive cause of the harm.[153]

For our purposes, what is key is that the condominium, understood as the flat owners taken collectively, is regarded in law as the keeper of the common parts of the building. As a result, co-owners have a duty to ensure that crucial maintenance or repairs are carried out; if they do not do so and the defective common part causes damage to an individual flat (or even a third party), the condominium

[148] Cass Civ (III) 9.5.2000 no 5913; Cass Civ (III) 7.10.2011 no 20609, [5.2]–[5.5].

[149] Cass Civ (III) 25.5.2010 no 12699; Cass Civ Sez Un 18.11.2008 no 27337; Cass Civ Sez Un 11.1.2008 nos 576 and 580.

[150] It is worth noting that, if there is a change in the ownership of the building/flat, the new owner is not entitled to sue for the damage caused to the property before the transfer of ownership, unless the transfer expressly includes also the transfer of the right to sue: see Cass Civ Sez Un 16.2.2016 no 2951, [67]–[73] (settling a judicial conflict of views on this issue).

[151] See eg Cass Civ (III) 8.2.2012 no 1769.

[152] M Cappelletti, *Justifying Strict Liability: A Comparative Analysis in Legal Reasoning* (Oxford, Oxford University Press, 2022) 53.

[153] Cass Civ (III) 18.9.2015 no 18317, [1.2].

will be liable vis-à-vis the individual flat owner for that damage.[154] This means that all condominium owners are jointly and severally liable, in the sense that a claimant flat owner will be able to seek full compensation from any one of them, and the payer will then have a recourse action against all the others.[155]

Importantly, this liability extends to cover damage caused by building defects which are attributable to the construction company's original works.[156] Hence, wherever this is the case, an individual flat owner might decide to bring an action under Article 2051 Cc against the condominium for any loss due to the building defect, including purely economic ones. As seen above,[157] Italian courts allow in principle compensation of this type of loss under Article 2043 Cc, and there is nothing which would prevent them from stating that the same would be possible under a strict liability rule such as Article 2051 Cc.[158] As a result, individual flat owners may recover a sum corresponding to the diminution in value of the property, or a sum equivalent to the remediation costs. Finally, it must be noted that the limitation period applying to Article 2051 is the same as that applying to Article 2043 Cc: five years from when the harm was objectively perceptible and recognisable.

Overall, Article 2051 is a useful resource for individual owners in condominiums because they can sue the condominium itself for its failure to keep the common parts in good repair or to remedy defects in the building promptly and effectively. This regime has no equivalent in English law, where leaseholders cannot sue other leaseholders, as responsibility for repairing the building lies with the freeholder/landlord.

C. Conclusion

Since the enactment of the Civil Code in the 1940s, Italian private law has taken building safety very seriously. This is true in general and in relation to residential

[154] Cass Civ (II) 15.4.1999 no 3753. The Corte di Cassazione has instead excluded that the administrator can qualify as keeper of the common parts for the purposes of art 2051 Cc. However, the administrator is liable to condominium owners for its failure to manage and maintain the common parts, including remedying defects, on the basis of the power-duty conferred on it by art 1130 Cc. Moreover, even if the condominium as such is liable under art 2051, art 2043, or even art 2049 (vicarious liability) Cc to any individual condominium owner or third party for the loss caused by a defective common part, the condominium has recourse against the administrator if the loss can be traced back to the administrator's failure to discharge its duties. Finally, it may well be that liability can only attach to the administrator personally, as where the administrator omits to implement a deliberation of the condominium assembly. On all these aspects, see Terzago (n 86) 454–66.

[155] GD Nuzzo, *Il Nuovo Condominio: Spese, Ripartizione e Gestione* (Trani, Edizioni Ad Maiora, 2016) 555.

[156] Cass Civ (III) 20.8.2003 no 12211, [3.2].

[157] See text to nn 141–144.

[158] Indeed, it is clear that there are cases in which compensation for pure economic loss would be allowed in the context of strict liability torts: for some examples, see M Bussani and VV Palmer, *Pure Economic Loss in Europe* (Cambridge, Cambridge University Press, 2003) 174–76, 193–94.

buildings in particular. The combination of a condominium regime with the contract and tort routes for redress set out in the Code creates a legal regime very favourable to condominium owners.

Compared to the English approach, there are marked differences as regards property arrangements. First, unlike English leaseholders, condominium owners have full control and decision-making autonomy in relation to the building; there is no other party who has an interest in the building (eg freeholder/landlord) and who takes decisions on their behalf. In this sense, co-owners are in a better position than English leaseholders. On the other hand, condominium owners have full and direct responsibility for the building, including for the remediation of defects, and have to bear the relevant costs. There is no freeholder or landlord who can shield them from such responsibilities.

In this respect, it may be thought that condominium owners are in a worse position than English leaseholders because the freeholder or landlord is primarily responsible for looking after the building. In reality, we have observed that English leaseholders, despite lacking autonomy, are ultimately made responsible for the costs incurred by their landlord. As explained above, the BSA 2022 has modified key mechanisms in property governance, most notably by reshaping the law on service charges relating to the remediation or mitigation of building defects. These changes have certainly improved the position of many leaseholders, but the several distinctions set out in the Act have created a landscape of piecemeal solutions which are clearly in need of further rationalisation. The Italian law on condominium looks, in this sense, more rational and certainly more comprehensive, as it does not discriminate among different categories of condominium owners, types of building, or defects.

Besides the advantages of a condominium regime, condominium owners can rely on private law causes of action to obtain redress for losses suffered as a result of building defects. In this respect, too, the difference with English law is marked. Under Italian law, the parties ordering construction works benefit from a general contractual warranty against construction companies, and this warranty is clearly broader than the implied warranties in English law because it is not confined to off-plan purchases but extends to renovation works. Moreover, the condominium regime positively affects the rules on standing as both the administrator and any condominium owner has the right to sue the builder for defective work, unlike in England and Wales where leaseholders do not order works on defective common parts and therefore have no right to bring a contractual action in that respect. Finally, the range of remedies available in Italy for breach of a construction contract is significantly broader than in English law.[159]

In relation to sale contracts, Italian law provides to the buyers of real property the same (generous) warranties for defects as those offered to the buyers of chattels, marking a striking contrast with English law. Moreover, within the realm

[159] See text to nn 97–99.

of real property sales, Italian law does not draw any distinction between off-plan purchases and purchases taking place at a later stage, hence giving condominium owners the same degree of protection in the two scenarios. Thus, it seems fair to say that, from a substantive point of view, condominium owners receive a more favourable treatment in Italian contract law compared with leaseholders in English contract law. Having said that, the difference is attenuated by the fact that contractual actions in Italian law are subjected to stricter time limits than in English law and that, therefore, contractual remedies in Italian law may be not very useful, at least in relation to long latent defects.

Where we find the strongest response of Italian private law to building defects is in the context of tort law. There, the key provision is Article 1669 of the Civil Code. All the ingredients of this provision – its strict nature, the rules on standing for both claimants and defendants, the types of buildings covered, the meaning of 'serious defect', and the ten-year time limit for the coming into existence of the defect – show the commitment of Italian law to encouraging the proper construction of buildings as well as to ensuring as much protection as possible to those adversely affected by building defects.

Buildings are meant to last for many decades, if not centuries, and it is therefore essential that they are built properly and that, if not, those harmed as a result can obtain redress. In this sense, the threat of tort liability under Article 1669 places an incentive on builders and other parties taking on work for the construction or renovation of buildings to ensure that these are safe and sound. At the same time, it provides a promising avenue of redress for all losses, including purely economic ones, suffered because of a building defect.

Notably, while the application of Article 1669 to all buildings was already set out in the letter of Article 1669 since its enactment in 1942, all its other ingredients – who can sue/can be sued, the meaning of serious defect, the ten-year time limit – have been developed by the courts in subsequent decades so as to promote the provision's main goals, namely compensation and deterrence. This picture contrasts sharply with English tort law. Focusing on a comparison between Article 1669 Cc and the DPA 1972, what emerges is that Article 1669 offers more extensive protection than the DPA 1972 in the light of the rules on standing, of the 'serious defect' test compared with that of 'fitness for human habitation', and of the types of buildings protected – all buildings as opposed to dwellings only. The only respect in which the DPA 1972 is more favourable than Article 1669 Cc concerns time limits: as explained above, the BSA 2022 has extended the limitation period applying to the DPA 1972 to 15 years from completion of the works, and it has also established its retrospective application, hence setting out a regime on time limits that finds no equivalent in Italian tort law.

For situations in which Article 1669 Cc cannot be invoked, routes for redress might be available in the Italian general law of torts, namely liability based on fault (Article 2043 Cc) and liability for the deeds of things (Article 2051 Cc). As seen above, these liability rules might give condominium owners the opportunity to recover economic losses resulting from building defects. Again, this marks a contrast with English law: there, as seen above, judges have barred the recoverability of economic losses of this type under the tort of negligence, and no liability rule comparable to Article 2051 Cc exists. However, there are some liability rules which have been introduced in English law via the BSA 2022 – for example, the liability of manufacturers/sellers of construction products under sections 148 and 149 of the BSA 2022 as well as the new category of associate liability under section 130 of the same Act – which improve the position of leaseholders and offer a degree of protection that may not be available in Italian law.[160]

Overall, the Italian condominium arrangement and the robust regime of contract and tort protections benefiting flat owners in Italy reflects an awareness *within private law* of the special importance of buildings that has been difficult to find in the English context; at least until the enactment of the BSA 2022. Italian private law has long been equipped to deal effectively with defects affecting multi-unit residential buildings (or, for that matter, buildings in general). The combination of a condominium regime with private law causes of action shows that Italian private law acknowledges the complexity of buildings and accords them a special status. Aware that the governance of common parts is critically important for the life of a building, Italian law has developed a complex web of detailed rules under the condominium regime. These rules are key not merely in the day-to-day management of the building, but also in situations where serious defects might threaten the health, safety and finances of flat owners. In this respect, condominium owners will be well placed to take action, whether by themselves or through the administrator, and seek redress. At the same time, Italian private law sets out liability rules in contract and tort which, on the one hand, provide incentives for the construction of safe and sound buildings and, on the other hand, afford to those harmed by building defects valuable avenues of redress, most notably through Article 1669 Cc.

Ultimately, if we look at building safety through the lens of private law, what emerges is that Italian law appreciates the special role of buildings, including multi-unit residential buildings, and that it seeks to ensure both the stability and duration of such buildings as well as the compensation of the victims of building defects. Conversely, if one looks at private law through the lens of building safety, what emerges is that private law is seen as a system of rules geared towards the achievement of societal considerations such as stable property governance, the minimisation of the risk of harm and the compensation of losses. This provides a contrast with English law, where legal actors often embrace a less policy-oriented understanding of private law.[161]

[160] Italian law does of course include a regime of products liability that implements the well-known EU Directive 374/85. Moreover, art 1669 Cc imposes liability on construction companies *and* their subcontractors, this presenting some similarities with the English category of associate liability, but a comparison between these regimes of liability is beyond the scope of the chapter.

[161] See text to nn 76–79.

IV. Private Law Aims and Building Safety

The comparative analysis undertaken in this chapter reveals that private law plays a role in addressing building safety issues. We have seen that property, contract, and tort rules and doctrines affect the allocation of rights and duties of the parties responsible for, and affected by, building defects. This allocation might differ across jurisdictions, and it does differ dramatically as between English law and Italian law. This has been analysed at length above, and we hope that our comparative analysis has shed some light on the interaction between private law and building safety in both England and Italy. By way of concluding remarks, a few general points emerge which are worth emphasising.

First, a private law system might accord special status to buildings and thus subject them to special rules. It is not difficult to see the special character of buildings, especially if one focuses on those of residential nature: dwellings not only represent the most significant financial investment in the lifetime of most buyers, but they provide them with a sense of safety and stability, playing a key role in shaping their lives and those of their families. If defective, buildings can threaten one's health and safety or more generally their ability to live a life of their own choosing, including financially, with potentially devastating effects. Given all this, it is not difficult to make a prima facie case for why buyers of real property should benefit from more, not less, contract law safeguards than buyers of goods, or why it might be desirable to enhance the level of tort protection by allowing for the recoverability of economic losses resulting from defective buildings.

As seen above, Italian private law recognises significantly reinforced protections from building defects, mainly through the tort provision set out in Article 1669 Cc, which has no equivalent in the private law regime governing chattels. English private law has traditionally adopted another vision of buildings. The legislature has certainly provided some protection to those with a property interest in dwellings through the DPA 1972, but this piece of legislation achieved little and it has not been meaningfully complemented (until 2022) by further measures. For their part, the courts have consistently refused to reserve any special treatment to buildings in tort law, holding that there is no basis for distinguishing between chattels and immovables in relation to the recoverability of economic losses stemming from defects.[162] Perhaps even more striking is the position in English contract law: many implied warranties are recognised in relation to contracts for the sale of goods,[163] but very few in relation to contracts for the sale of real property, this resulting in a more favourable regime for buyers of goods than for buyers of realty! Coupled with the mechanisms triggered by the freehold–leasehold scheme in the context of multi-unit residential buildings, the approach of English contract and

[162] See text to nn 44–45.

[163] See eg Sale of Goods Act 1979, ss 12–15A.

tort law has probably contributed decisively to the poor position in which leaseholders find themselves today.

A further key and related point relates to issues of institutional competence. Is it for the courts or the legislature to devise private law rules governing the recoverability of losses resulting from building defects? In a chapter in this volume, Donal Nolan argues that the legislature is much better placed to do so.[164] We agree: measures tackling building safety issues are likely to have several socioeconomic implications, and Parliament is better equipped than judges to assess them and to strike a balance between all the conflicting factors and considerations at stake. On the other hand, one might wonder what the courts should do if faced with legislative inaction. Until 2022, Parliament's only meaningful intervention for England and Wales was the DPA 1972 which, as discussed, offered only limited protection against building defects. What is more, the DPA 1972 was intended to start providing some protection without in any way 'foreclose[ing] or imped[ing] future development of the common law in this and other construction contexts'.[165] In light of this, English courts could (and perhaps should) have done more.

An oft-mentioned problem with judicial law-making is that, if the courts are not careful, liability developments might send shock waves through the economy,[166] with potentially serious socioeconomic consequences. While this might be true, the reasons for concern should not be exaggerated and, in this sense, the experience of other legal systems can be helpful. As shown in this chapter, Italian courts have embarked on creative judicial law-making in private law, a prominent example being their development of liabilities under Article 1669 Cc. This provision merely sets out the skeleton of a liability rule for building defects, and it has been the courts who have interpreted it as a tort rule and have developed all its elements in a very expansive way, from the rules on standing and the time limits to the meaning of 'serious defect'. In this latter respect, while it is true that, as Nolan argues,[167] a legislative definition of defect might be better than a judicial one, it can be readily appreciated from the letter of Article 1669 Cc that the Italian legislature did not give any meaningful indication as to the content of 'serious defect', and that it was entirely in the hands of judges to develop the concept. Italian courts have successfully done this on a case-by-case basis, without any troublesome side effect or unwarranted consequence. In a meaningful sense, then, it could be said that the liability regime based on Article 1669 Cc (and this is true of countless other code-based provisions) is very much the product of the Italian courts, not Parliament.

To be sure, there is no doctrine of binding precedent in Italian law, and hence judges can experiment as they see fit because later courts can always ignore previous decisions if these are ill-advised. English courts, by contrast, are under a system of stare decisis, and therefore they need to be more careful in creating

[164] Nolan (n 44).
[165] J Stapleton, 'Duty of Care and Economic Loss: A Wider Agenda' (1991) 107 *LQR* 249, 269.
[166] ibid 277.
[167] Nolan (n 44), cf Morgan (n 34).

new remedies or innovating too much, for steps of this type will, however unwarranted, be binding on later courts. This suggests that English judges are right in approaching legal change somewhat more cautiously than their Italian colleagues. But even so, English courts have often been creative in the past in all sorts of different contexts, literally creating new causes of action or remedies and/or developing existing ones, and hence it is somewhat surprising that they chose such a low-profile approach in the context of building defects.[168] The traditional caution of English courts in this area seems to be a missed opportunity, especially in light of the building safety crisis which has emerged recently and which proper private law rules might have avoided or at least mitigated if adopted 35 years ago when the opportunity arose.[169] Going forward, after the enactment of the BSA 2022, English judges will be called to interpret statutory provisions and develop them in the way they think more appropriate. Besides straightforward matters of textual interpretation, their work will often require value judgements and, in this respect, very much will turn on the goals that the courts decide to ascribe to the relevant provisions. Will these be about vindicating some norm of individual responsibility, deterring harmful conduct, compensating/spreading losses or some other goal?

This brings us to a final and broader point concerning the role and functions of private law. This is not the place to engage in an all-encompassing analysis of the English and Italian understandings of private law, but a few remarks can nevertheless be made.

Many approaches to the functions and goals of private law are possible but one key aspect with which every private law scholar should grapple is whether, and to what extent, private law pursues the doing of individual justice and/or the promotion of broader societal aims. Are these two sets of goals mutually exclusive, or complementary? In Italy, the general tendency is to point out the multifunctional dimension of private law. For example, tort law is thought to pursue a plurality of goals, including justice between the parties, the compensation/spreading of losses, and the prevention of accidents. The idea that private law could be just about individual justice between the particular claimant and the particular defendant has virtually no currency. This marks a contrast with England and Wales, where private law is often presented as an ethical system of individual responsibility and where ideas such as compensation, spreading or deterrence are frowned upon as valid reasons for the existence of private law rights and responsibilities.

The approach one takes to issues of this type affects in a profound way what private law can accomplish. To illustrate this, consider one of the leading corrective justice theorists, Ernest Weinrib,[170] and the impact his approach would have on building safety. Weinrib's model of private law is particularly narrow, as it

[168] For a critical assessment of this judicial approach, see Stapleton (n 166) esp 267–77.

[169] *D&F Estates v Church Commissioners* [1989] AC 177 (HL); *Murphy* [1991] 1 AC 398 (HL). We are happy to acknowledge that ours is only a guess and that it is easier to assess someone else's choice – in this case that of English courts – in hindsight rather than at the time that choice was made.

[170] See EJ Weinrib, *The Idea of Private Law* (Oxford, Oxford University Press, 2013).

categorically excludes from the list of acceptable justifications for private law rights and responsibilities all reasons that do not pertain to the correlative relationship between claimant and defendant. In other words, no policy reason is admitted in private law because it is morally indefensible to allocate rights and responsibilities based on considerations external to the interaction between claimant and defendant. Unsurprisingly, many of the provisions included in the BSA 2022 as well as section 1 of the DPA 1972 do not comply with Weinrib's model and therefore 'significantly disrupt some core principles of private law'.[171] Measured against that standard, it is certainly true that these provisions are a failure, but it is unclear why private law should seek to comply with that model in the first place. A quick look at private law's main areas – property, contract and tort – shows that both English law and Italian law have never sought to conform to models such as Weinrib's and that they do take into account policy considerations all the time.

So, while the new category of associate liability under section 130 of the BSA 2022 may not be reconcilable with Weinrib's model, it is certainly in line with English law and the law of many other jurisdictions as these are all familiar with vicarious liability and with justifications such as deterrence and the compensation/spreading of losses. Similarly, the liability of developers under section 1 of the DPA 1972 may well be non-excludable and extended to future owners,[172] but there is nothing extravagant about this, for both features characterise (for example) Article 1669 Cc[173] and can be easily explained both in terms of deterrence and compensation.

In sum, the view one takes regarding the aims of private law and what can or cannot constitute a valid reason for the existence of private law rights and obligations obviously affects what private law could and should do. In this sense, adopting a narrow approach such as Weinrib's would dramatically curb the reach of private law, for example leading to the abolition of essential doctrines such as vicarious liability or, in the building safety context, preventing the creation of valuable routes for redress such as those introduced with the BSA 2022.

By contrast, adopting a vision of private law which is open to a plurality of goals and considerations – and this is overwhelmingly the majority position in many legal systems across the world – gives (or should give) lawmakers, including judges, the opportunity to develop the law in a way that can contribute to the resolution of legal issues. While public law actions may well be necessary to deal effectively with emergencies such as the building safety crisis in the United Kingdom and beyond, the potential of private law for contributing positively to the resolution of difficult issues should not be downplayed, both currently and for its long-term effects. In this sense, the Italian experience looks instructive, and the private law adjustments and innovations included in the BSA 2022 seem to go in the same direction.

[171] Bright and McFarlane (n 42) 147; see text to nn 76–78.
[172] ibid 137.
[173] See Cass Civ (III) 6.11.2008 no 26609 on non-excludability.

3

The Surfside Condominium Collapse: What Lessons have been Learned?

EVAN C McKENZIE

I. Introduction

On 24 June 2021, Champlain Towers South (CTS), a condominium building in Surfside, Florida, collapsed suddenly during the night, killing 98 people. An investigation is underway to determine the precise structural mechanism of the building collapse, but this may not be completed for years. However, it is clear that private and public institutions could and should have acted sooner to prevent this catastrophe.

In the aftermath of the disaster, a number of private and public entities investigated the events that preceded the building collapse. They produced reports and recommendations intended to inform industry practices and public policies in order to prevent or reduce the likelihood of such disasters in the future, not only in the State of Florida, but in relation to the United States' 140,000 condominiums.

This chapter analyses and critically assesses these reports in the context of a policy process in Florida that led to passage of a new statute regulating condominium association practices. The reports were generated by:

1. a Miami-Dade County Grand Jury that investigated the building collapse;
2. the Federal National Mortgage Association;
3. a select committee of condominium lawyers chosen by the Florida state bar association;
4. the Community Associations Institute: a trade association that is active in the condominium law and policy arena;
5. the Florida state legislature, in the course of passing a law requiring condominium associations to conduct inspections, maintain adequate reserve funds and perform certain repairs; and
6. the final court settlement of multiple wrongful death and property loss claims against multiple defendants, including the condo association.

The goal of the chapter is to identify assumptions and evaluate findings concerning the ways in which building safety is protected or jeopardised by the structure and practice of condominium association private government, and by the regulatory framework within which such associations operate.

Although there is a clear consensus that a variety of private and public actors were responsible for the collapse of CTS, the dominant approach that emerged from the policy process was an intense focus on condominium boards and unit owners. The recommendations that became law in Florida, and to some extent nationally, involve taking away from boards and owners the discretion they have always had about when and how to maintain their buildings, and imposing new financial obligations on them that may prove difficult to bear. This reflects an abandonment of the most basic assumption about condominium ownership: that the owners and their elected representatives could be counted upon to maintain the buildings in perpetuity.

Condominium housing came to the United States in 1961, which means that the oldest condominiums there are now over 60 years old. Condominium buildings are multi-unit structures that look like apartment buildings but are actually a type of home ownership. When someone buys a condominium unit, they acquire an individual interest and a common interest. The individual interest consists of the airspace of the buyer's unit and the inner finished surfaces of the walls, ceiling and floor. The rest of the building, including everything behind the paint, panelling and carpets, is in common ownership, with all the unit owners being tenants in common. Each owner acquires a percentage of the entire building, minus the individually owned units. That percentage is assigned by the developer before units are sold, and that ownership percentage is also the unit owner's voting percentage in association affairs as well as the percentage of total assessments for maintenance and repair that the unit owner has to pay. The condominium association is a not-for-profit corporation that manages, but does not own, the building through a board of directors elected by the unit owners.

A number of scholars and professionals have for many years been pointing out two related and troubling facts. First, many condo buildings are ageing and in need of major and very expensive repairs, including structural components that are critical to safety. Second, paying for these repairs is entirely the responsibility, and at the discretion, of owner-run condominium associations, many of which have been deferring maintenance and underfunding a sinking fund or reserve accounts simply because they have the power and the incentive to do so. Consequently, when the time comes, the associations do not have sufficient funds to pay for necessary repairs from their reserves, which requires them to impose large lump sum 'special assessments', often in the tens of thousands of dollars, that many owners are financially unable to pay. The inability of many associations to fund these repairs contributes to situations in which the associations end up simply going out of existence, with unit owners deciding to sell to investors who buy their buildings, terminate the condo association and operate the former condo as an apartment building.[1]

However, despite calls for some sort of fix involving private practices or public policy, state and federal policy-makers had little to no interest in addressing these facts as problems that required a solution. Condominium finances were left in the hands of condo boards and their professional advisers. That laissez-faire approach was called into question with the collapse of CTS while the building was in condominium ownership and being managed by a functioning condominium association. In the State of Florida and elsewhere, condominium finances suddenly came to be viewed as a problem with potentially life-and-death implications that required the attention of private and public institutions.

Scholars generally view the public policy process, or policy cycle, as being composed of stages. There are many models, but typically they include *agenda setting* when problems rise to public attention; *policy formulation*, where various solutions are considered; *decision making*, where a solution is adopted; *implementation*, where policies are put into practice; and *policy evaluation*, where policy-makers get information concerning how well the policy is working. Evaluation of policies that have been adopted often leads back into agenda setting and the policy cycle continues for another round.[2]

The collapse of CTS was a 'focusing event' that put condo finances on the public policy agenda, and on the agendas of private organisations with an interest in shaping those policies.[3] This chapter examines the positions that private and public organisations took as the State of Florida moved toward a significant policy change.[4]

The positions are reflected in reports that were made available to the public. There have been several reports and analyses of the CTS disaster. The final word on the physical causes of the building collapse will come from the National Institute of Standards and Technology (NIST), and that is anticipated to take years as they sort through the warehoused rubble, hold hearings and conduct tests.[5] I have chosen

[1] E McKenzie, 'Private Covenants, Public Laws, and the Financial Future of Residential Private Governments' (2019) 52 *UIC John Marshall Law Review* 715; E McKenzie, 'Chicago's "Deconversion" Waves and the Fragility of Condominium Associations' in R Lippert and S Treffers (eds), *Condominium Governance and Law: Global Urban Perspectives* (London, Routledge, 2020); E McKenzie, 'Climate Change Could Cost Condo Boards Billions. They Aren't Ready For It' *Washington Post* (2 July 2021) https://www.washingtonpost.com/outlook/surfside-condo-climate-change-cost/2021/07/01/b6699a98-da76-11eb-9bbb-37c30dcf9363_story.html.

[2] HD Lasswell, *The Decision Process: Seven Categories of Functional Analysis* (College Park, MD, University of Maryland Press, 1956); J Kingdon, *Agendas, Alternatives and Public Policies* (New York, Harper Collins, 1984).

[3] TA Birkland, 'Focusing Events, Mobilization, and Agenda Setting' (1998) 18 *Journal of Public Policy* 53.

[4] Florida is not the only state that began to consider policy changes following the CTS disaster, but, as the state where the collapse occurred and because it has so many condo associations, it became the state that went through the policy cycle first.

[5] NIST posted to its website in February 2025 that it had made a report to Congress which noted that the investigation team had, amongst other things, 'completed all experimental work on the physical evidence from the building's structural elements'; see www.nist.gov/disaster-failure-studies/champlain-towers-south-collapse.

to examine here what I believe to be the six most comprehensive and consequential public and private responses to the disaster that were in some way part of the movement towards policy change.

They are, in rough chronological order:

1. The 15 December 2021 *Final Report of the Miami-Dade County Grand Jury* that investigated the roles of public and private actors in the collapse of the building.[6] I will discuss this first because it contains a detailed account of events that is helpful in understanding the other reports.
2. The 13 October 2021 *Lender Letter LL-2021-14* from the powerful Federal National Mortgage Association (Fannie Mae), the private/public entity that purchases and securitises home mortgage loans and sets conditions for the loans that it will buy.[7] This policy announcement is important for its national scope and sweeping impact on condominium finances.
3. The 12 October 2021 *Report of the Florida Bar RPPTL Condominium Law and Policy Life Safety*
4. The *Advisory Task Force*, a select committee of condominium lawyers chosen by the Florida Bar Association.[8] This report is notable for its detailed explanations of Florida condominium law and practice, and for its apparent influence on the changes in the law.
5. The October 2021 *Condominium Safety Public Policy Report* from the Community Associations Institute (CAI), a national trade association that represents professionals who supply services to condominium associations.[9] CAI trains lawyers, property managers and other vendors, and is arguably the most influential lobbying group active on condominium-related public policy issues. This report also appears to have been influential on the changes in the law.
6. The May 2022 *Florida Senate Bill SB4-D* and related *Bill Analysis and Impact Statements* from the Florida state legislature. This law requires condominium associations to conduct certain inspections, maintain adequate reserve funds, and perform particular types of repairs. It appears to enact some of the recommendations of the Florida Bar Task Force and the CAI.[10] In June 2023, the legislature passed, and the governor of Florida signed, a so-called 'glitch

[6] Miami-Dade County Grand Jury, 'The Surfside Condo Collapse Tragedy: Recommendations to Make Buildings Safer' (Spring Term Final Report, Miami-Dade County, 15 December 2021).

[7] Letter from Federal National Mortgage Association to All Fannie Mae Single-Family Sellers (13 October 2021) ('Lender Letter LL-2021-14').

[8] Condominium Law and Policy Life Safety Advisory Task Force, 'Report of the Florida Bar Real Property, Probate & Trust Law Condominium Law and Policy Life Safety Advisory Task Force' (Florida Bar, 12 October 2021).

[9] Community Associations Institute, 'Condominium Safety Public Policy Report: Reserve Studies and Funding, Maintenance, and Structural Integrity' (Community Associations Institute, October 2021), https://dualauth.caionline.org/HomeownerLeaders/DisasterResources/Documents/CAI%20Condo%20Safety%20Public%20Policy%20Report%2010%2029%2021old.pdf.

[10] SB 4D, 2022D (Fla 2022) ('Building Safety Bill').

bill' that addressed a number of the details of SB 4-D that had come under criticism and made some changes to the law while leaving the basic elements of 4-D in place.[11]

7. I also summarise the 30 August 2022 *Final Order and Judgment* filed by Florida state judge Michael Hanzman in the case titled *In Re Champlain Towers South Collapse Litigation*.[12] This is the main consolidated lawsuit that involves a court-administered settlement process aimed at compensating victims as fast as possible through an allocation of responsibility to all possible defendants. Understanding how the case was resolved is helpful in understanding issues that arise in the reports.

II. Reports on the CTS Collapse

A. Miami-Dade County Grand Jury

The first post-collapse document that merits consideration is a report of the Miami-Dade County Grand Jury that was filed at the end of 2021. The report is based on an investigation that was conducted to improve building safety and not to attribute criminal liability to anyone or issue any criminal indictments. The report begins by noting that the precise cause of the collapse will not be known until the NIST and other engineers and consultants complete their work. The focus of the Grand Jury report was instead to examine the policies and practices of government officials, professionals and residents regarding building safety, maintenance and oversight. The report found that, '[u]nfortunately, as to Champlain Towers South there were failings at every level and for all of the participants'.[13]

At CTS, the disaster began at 1:14 am with the collapse of the massive concrete structural slab that served as the pool deck and the roof of the parking garage. Eight minutes later, the central and eastern wings of the building collapsed in just 12 seconds. It does not seem necessary to wait for the final NIST report to make the obvious point that, if the structural slab had not collapsed, the residential wings would not have collapsed a few minutes later. It cannot have been a coincidence that one event quickly followed the other.

The Grand Jury report finds that the CTS condo board had known for years that the pool deck slab had serious structural problems and needed very expensive repairs. The slab was made of steel-reinforced concrete that was protected by a

[11] SB 154, 2023 (Fla 2023) ('Glitch Bill').

[12] Final Order and Judgment, *In Re Champlain Towers South Collapse Litigation* (2021) (No 2021-015089-CA 01); MI Goldberg, 'In Re Champlain Towers South Collapse Litigation' (CTS Receivership, 2021) https://ctsreceivership.com/; Plaintiffs' Motion for Preliminary Approval of Class Action Settlement and for Certification of Settlement Class, *In Re Champlain Towers South Collapse Litigation* (2021) (No 2021-015089-CA 01) ('Plaintiffs' Motion').

[13] Miami-Dade County Grand Jury (n 6) 1.

waterproofing layer. The association was first told in 1996 that the waterproofing in the concrete slab had failed, the concrete was cracking and repairs were needed to protect the steel reinforcing bars from water.[14]

When water penetrates steel-reinforced concrete, the steel reinforcing bars ('rebar') rust, lose their strength and swell to up to four times their normal diameter. The bond between the steel and the concrete weakens, which in turn weakens the concrete itself. The swelling rebar exerts enormous pressure on the concrete from the inside, causing it to crack, and eventually, chunks of the concrete begin to fall off, a process known as 'spalling'. At this point the rebar becomes exposed to the air and additional moisture.

This process had been going on for years at CTS, and the condo board was well aware of it. The CTS condo board received a structural engineering report from Morabito Consultants in 2018 that warned them again of the failure of the waterproofing layer, which had caused serious concrete damage to the slab, the walls of the garage, and the columns and beams that supported the buildings. All of this required extensive repairs. The report contains photos of cracking and spalling of parking garage columns and other building components. The report stated:

> [T]he waterproofing below the Pool Deck & Entrance Drive as well as all of the planter waterproofing is beyond it [*sic*] useful life and therefore must all be completely removed and replaced. *The failed waterproofing is causing major structural damage to the concrete structural slab below these areas. Failure to replace the waterproofing in the near future will cause the extent of the concrete deterioration to expand exponentially. … It is also important to note that the replacement of the existing deck waterproofing will be extremely expensive* as removal of the concrete topping slab to gain access to the waterproofing membrane will take time, be disruptive and create a major disturbance to the occupants of this condominium building … [Morabito Consultants'] review of the Parking Garage signs of distress/fatigue [including]. … *Abundant cracking and spalling of varying degrees was observed in the concrete columns, beams, and walls* … most of the concrete deterioration needs to be repaired in a timely fashion.[15]

This dire situation could, and should, have been repaired years before the building collapsed, but the Grand Jury found that 'regular and routine maintenance and repairs were not being conducted' at CTS:

> It appears that the enormous costs of making those repairs had led owners and officers to 'Kick the can down the road'. … [T]his unfortunate scenario has replicated itself in condominiums all over South Florida; a failure of condo boards to implement much needed repairs and maintenance has led to unsafe building structures throughout South Florida.[16]

[14] SR Kim and L Romero, 'Pool Deck, Garage Ceilings of Collapsed Surfside Building were Problematic as Early as 1996, Documents Show' *ABC News* (14 July 2021) https://abcnews.go.com/US/pool-deck-garage-ceilings-collapsed-surfside-buildingproblematic/story?id=78832334.

[15] F Morabito, 'Champlain Towers South Condominium Structural Field Survey Report' (Morabito Consultants, 8 October 2018) https://www.wfla.com/wp-content/uploads/sites/71/2021/06/8777-collins-ave-structural-field-survey-report.pdf, 7 (emphasis added).

[16] Miami-Dade County Grand Jury (n 6) 9–10.

Perhaps as disturbing as the condo board's failure to authorise necessary repairs was the inadequacy of public building inspection processes. The Grand Jury reported that the town of Surfside reviewed the Morabito report that clearly explained serious problems with the building, and nonetheless said that the building was 'in very good shape'.[17] Going further, the Grand Jury noted the desperately inadequate state of affairs in the neighbouring city of Miami with respect to mandatory building inspections. These 40-year inspections were required by the South Florida Building Code and were the responsibility of the Unsafe Structures Division of the Miami Building Department, but the department had only one inspector, and it suffered from a five-year backlog with 6,400 pending cases in the city of Miami alone. This included 2,212 buildings for which 40-year recertification reports had not been not submitted; 1,606 buildings with reports submitted but not approved; and 2,582 buildings that were tagged as unsafe.[18]

A building safety inspection regime this inadequate is better categorised as a form of de facto privatisation in which local governments have simply abdicated their responsibilities and rely on condo boards and apartment building owners to do their job for them. The responsibility of the Building Department in this case is to make sure that buildings are safe for people to live in, which would seem to be a high priority of state and local governments.

The Grand Jury's recommendations, which are advisory, were focused on building certification, maintenance and repair, and aim at reforming both government and condo board behaviours. Some of their recommendations focus on public actors, such as shortening the 40-year building recertification process;[19] mandating certain qualifications for building inspectors;[20] providing two years of advance notice to condo boards of an impending inspection requirement, so that they can begin the process sooner;[21] creating a criminal penalty for making false statements on a building recertification report;[22] and expanding the Unsafe Structures Division of the Miami Building Department.[23]

Other recommendations emphasised increased regulation of condo boards in carrying out their maintenance responsibilities, including imposing specific duties and more detailed obligations on condo associations to maintain buildings; to conduct inspections at least every 10 years;[24] and to report to government.[25] The Grand Jury recommended being increasingly specific regarding what components must be inspected, and what qualifications inspectors must have.

[17] ibid 17.
[18] ibid 14.
[19] ibid 2.
[20] ibid 16.
[21] ibid 11–12.
[22] ibid 15.
[23] ibid 14.
[24] ibid 10–11.
[25] ibid 21.

It is noteworthy that, while the report sought to increase the responsibilities of condo boards, and would clearly require that condo unit owners pay higher charges than many of them can afford, it did not clearly address the question of where the resources are to come from to maintain buildings to higher standards. This is a recurring theme in the other reports as well.

B. Federal National Mortgage Association

On 13 October 2021, just four months after the CTS collapse, a policy change was announced by the powerful Federal National Mortgage Association, known as Fannie Mae. This is a federal government-sponsored corporation that buys home mortgages from banks, packages them as mortgage-backed securities and sells them on the bond market. Fannie Mae is one of the largest US corporations with assets of over US$4 trillion, and it sets conditions under which it will purchase mortgages that banks must comply with in order to sell to them and preserve their own liquidity. In Lender Letter LL-2021-14, Fannie Mae notified lenders across the nation that they were setting more stringent requirements for purchase of loans secured by condominium units.[26] The new rules were occasioned by the CTS collapse:

> Our condo and co-op project standards policies are designed to support the ongoing viability of condo and co-op projects. In the wake of the tragic collapse of the Champlain South Tower in Surfside, Florida, residential buildings with ageing infrastructure and significant deferred maintenance are a growing concern across the nation. This concern is expected to increase over the next decade as the majority of residential condo and co-op buildings were built more than twenty years ago. Lenders and other industry stakeholders have asked for clear guidance on how to manage emerging risk related to residential projects. In response to the concerns about projects with significant deferred maintenance, we are issuing temporary requirements that impact the eligibility of condo and co-op projects containing attached units. These requirements apply to all loans secured by units in projects with five or more attached units, regardless of the type of project review or review waiver.[27]

Under the new rules,

> [l]oans secured by units in condo and co-op projects with significant deferred maintenance or in projects that have received a directive from a regulatory authority or inspection agency to make repairs due to unsafe conditions are not eligible for purchase.[28]

[26] The policy in LL-2021-14 was intended to be temporary. In November 2023, these requirements were incorporated into Fannie Mae's Selling Guide: Federal National Mortgage Association, 'Selling Guide FAQs: B4-2.1-03 Ineligible Projects' (Fannie Mae, 7 May 2023) https://selling-guide.fanniemae.com/sel/b4-2.1-03/ineligible-projects.

[27] Federal National Mortgage Association (n 7) 1.

[28] ibid.

The burden is on the lender to get this information from the condo association, or the loan is ineligible for purchase, because:

> The lender is expected to obtain the financial documents necessary to confirm the association has the ability to fund any repairs. If the special assessment is related to safety, soundness, structural integrity, or habitability, all related repairs must be fully completed or the project is not eligible.[29]

In addition, Fannie Mae required that all condo associations must contribute to their reserve funds annually an amount equal to at least 10 per cent of their operating budget.[30]

The net effect is that Fannie Mae is protecting itself from loss occasioned by condo associations that engage in deferred maintenance or inadequate funding of reserves, or that find themselves confronted with an unexpected need to perform major repairs. It would be hard to overstate the impact of these policy changes on the market for condominium units, and therefore on condo associations. Fannie Mae is the main force in the secondary mortgage market, buying two-thirds of all mortgages. If they will not buy a mortgage from a bank, no bank that is in the business of making these 'conforming loans' will make the loan at all. This means that the prospective purchaser can choose between buying the unit with cash; paying a higher interest rate to get an 'non-conforming' loan from some other bank that makes higher-risk and higher-interest rate loans; or simply buying a condo in a different building that does not have these maintenance and repair problems.

Nothing in the Fannie Mae letter addresses the common situation where, as at CTS, the reason the condo association has not done repairs, or has not maintained an adequate reserve fund, is that many if not most of the owners do not have sufficient disposable income to do those things. As with the Florida Bar Task Force report, Fannie Mae is focusing on the actions of condo boards. It is using its enormous financial leverage over banks to force boards to do whatever is necessary to conform with higher, but not clearly specified, reserve fund and maintenance standards.

The lender letter was greeted with opposition from the CAI (see section II.D below), which recommended that the policy be delayed and not implemented for at least one year. While stating its support for Fannie Mae's objective of enhancing condo safety, the CAI argued that reporting on the financial condition of condos would be based on subjective and unreliable information, would leave condo boards uncertain about how to comply, and would lead to the denial of mortgage applications from creditworthy borrowers who sought to buy in buildings that were actually safe.[31]

[29] ibid 2.
[30] ibid.
[31] Letter from JM Towles and TM Skiba to The Honourable Sandra Thompson (17 February 2022) https://www.caionline.org/getmedia/5acff66d-5239-4c5f-8cc3-fdb038c31c23/GSE-FHFA-Coalition-Letter-6-21-2023.pdf.

C. Florida State Bar Association Select Task Force

Within two days after the collapse of CTS, some of Florida's most prominent condominium and planned community lawyers began conversations about how they could influence the inevitable public policy debate regarding the role that condominium governance played in the disaster. The Real Property, Probate, and Trust Law Section of the Florida Bar convened a special ten-person task force (including top Florida condo lawyers) that began meeting on 9 July 2021, only 16 days after the building collapsed. The Condominium Law and Policy Life Safety Advisory Task Force held 19 meetings at which it heard from and questioned experts in condominium reserve studies, accounting, insurance, development practices, governance and property management, as well as local government.

On 12 October 2021 the Task Force issued a report that reflected not just a deep understanding of Florida condominium law, but more importantly, how that law is implemented in actual practice. The report concludes that the main problems are the fact that condo boards have ultimate responsibility for building repair and maintenance, but that there is an 'inherent conflict' between the

> need for investment for deferred and long-term maintenance and structural repair, and the desires of the unit owners in the election of and direction to boards of directors of condominium associations to manage and operate their condominiums in a cost effective manner, be market-sensitive, avoid special assessments, and avoid excessive or unaffordable charges to unit owners.[32]

The Task Force found that the 'lack of uniform maintenance standards or protocols, and the broad discretion given to boards to determine when, how, and if life safety inspections and necessary repairs should be performed, requires legislative intervention.'[33]

The Task Force report made specific recommendations in 12 areas of law and practice that relate to this problem. The most important recommendations increase the number of specific responsibilities placed on the shoulders of condo boards in all buildings with three or more storeys, and add to their powers to carry them out. The Task Force recommended changing the law to:

- require boards to perform 'timely maintenance, repair and replacement of structural and life safety systems';[34]
- empower boards to impose 'special assessments' and take out loans for necessary maintenance without voting or approval by the unit owners;[35]

[32] Condominium Law and Policy Life Safety Advisory Task Force (n 8) 8.
[33] ibid.
[34] ibid 10.
[35] ibid 12.

- require boards to arrange for periodic structural and life safety inspections of their buildings,[36] and disclose the reports to all unit owners, as well as to local government if required by local law;[37]
- make it possible for any unit owner to sue the association if the inspections or necessary repairs are not conducted;[38]
- obtain casualty insurance for the full replacement cost of the building.[39]

They also recommended that developers be held accountable for defects in original construction; that condominiums should be subject to termination if the building has become 'economically obsolete';[40] that federal, state and local government should create means-tested programmes to make low-interest, long-term loans available to condo boards for necessary repairs;[41] that property managers should be better trained regarding building maintenance and life safety issues, and that they should be subject to legal liability for giving bad advice on these matters;[42] and that local governments should lose sovereign immunity, and thus have legal liability for negligent inspections and building approvals.[43]

Clearly, the most specific and consequential reforms the Task Force recommended all involve placing increased responsibilities on condo boards to get their buildings inspected regularly, raise the money for necessary repairs, and have them performed. Associations would be subject to lawsuits for failing to do all of that. The key question then becomes: how is it to be paid for? And here the Task Force recommends that unit owners lose their ability to block special assessments or borrowing, so that boards could take such actions without member approval.

The net effect of these recommendations is that condo owners and boards would lose ultimate control over the maintenance and repair of the buildings they own. Owners would have to pay the full costs of building maintenance and repair, according to the recommendations of professionals required to be hired by the board, whether or not the owners want, or can afford, to bear those costs. Those among them who choose to serve on the board will be placing the association in legal jeopardy if they fail to make the members pay.

The most basic assumption of condominium ownership in the United States has always been that unit owners and their boards can be trusted to maintain their buildings. Condominiums are created and operated primarily on principles of property and contract law, within the limits set by state condominium property

[36] ibid 15.
[37] ibid 15–16.
[38] ibid 17.
[39] ibid 34.
[40] ibid 25.
[41] ibid 29.
[42] ibid 32.
[43] ibid 33.

Acts. These private law arrangements have structured the relationships between unit owners and their elected boards and officers, including the process of paying for and conducting building maintenance and repair. The Task Force recommendations amount to a tacit admission that this assumption is false, and that where building safety is concerned, condo boards and owners should have a substantial part of their discretion taken away from them, and that public law should play a stronger and more prescriptive role than it has to date.

D. The Community Associations Institute

The CAI was founded in 1973, and is the United States' leading national, state and local trade association representing the lawyers, property managers, and other contractors and vendors who are retained by condominium and homeowners' boards of directors to help them run the associations for which they are responsible. It is the nation's primary organisation for the training and certification of these professionals, and it offers training courses for board members as well. The CAI is also the most influential interest group on condominium and homeowners' association issues in Washington DC and in state capitols.

Like many interest groups, the CAI produces a steady flow of research reports that are intended to inform and influence public policy on issues of concern to its members. Soon after the collapse of CTS, in October 2021, the CAI issued a report titled, *Condominium Safety Public Policy Report: Reserve Studies and Funding, Maintenance, and Structural Integrity.*[44] The report was prepared by a task force selected on a national basis by the CAI, and states that it involved the participation of 600 people over three months. The findings and recommendations of the report are similar to those of the Florida Task Force in a number of significant respects, particularly in the emphasis on enacting laws that put increased and more specific responsibilities on condo boards. These recommendations include:

- Mandating structural safety inspections for new buildings no later than five years after occupancy of a building.[45]
- For existing buildings, requiring inspections within two years after passage of the recommended new statutory requirements, and then at least every 10 years for the first 20 years of the building life, and every five years thereafter.[46]
- Giving boards the power to impose special assessments and borrow for immediate repairs without a vote of the unit owners.[47]

[44] Community Associations Institute (n 9).
[45] ibid 26.
[46] ibid 4.
[47] ibid 12.

- Mandating periodic reserve studies.[48]
- Mandating disclosure of these studies to the owners and potential buyers.[49]
- As a best practice, 'anticipating procedures for disposition of the project when the buildings and systems are economically obsolete'.[50]

The similarities in some of the CAI recommendations to those of the Florida Bar is interesting in that there was a connection between the CAI and the Task Force. One of the 10 members of the Florida Bar Task Force was attorney Joseph E. Adams, whose biography in the report identifies him as the former Chair of the Community Associations Institute's Florida Legislative Alliance, the lobbying arm of the CAI in Florida. He is also the managing shareholder of the Naples and Fort Myers offices of the firm of Becker and Poliakoff, a firm that was characterised in the press as 'the nemesis of condo safety reformers'. The Becker firm was instrumental in 2010 in persuading the Florida legislature to repeal a law passed in 2008 that required condominium associations to conduct periodic reserve studies.[51] It was also the firm that represented the CTS condo association in the period leading up to the building collapse, and its insurers paid US$31 million on the firm's behalf in the lawsuit settlement.[52]

It may be the case that the collapse of CTS was a 'focusing event' that changed prevailing views within the industry, and sparked a sudden support for governmental oversight over reserves and building maintenance that had been remarkably absent.[53] However, as will be seen below, the eventual legislative response relies almost exclusively on regulatory policy that increases responsibility of condo boards and imposes significantly increased costs on condo owners, while not placing similarly increased responsibilities and costs on local or state government or the professionals who advise them.

[48] ibid 11.

[49] ibid.

[50] ibid 28.

[51] B Wallman, L Huriash, M Ariza and S Norris, 'Becker & Poliakoff Law Firm the "Nemesis" of Condo Safety Reformers' *South Florida Sun-Sentinel* (3 October 2021) 1); P Prazan, 'Florida Used to Encourage More Condo Inspections and Repair Plans' *NBC Miami* (9 July 2021) https://www.nbcmiami.com/news/local/surfside-condo-collapse/florida-usedto-encourage-more-condo-inspections-and-repair-plans/2492014/. There were other situations where the Becker firm lobbied against state-imposed condo safety regulations. Becker also lobbied successfully to allow older Florida high-rise condos to opt out of a requirement to install fire sprinklers. Becker shareholder Donna DiMaggio Berger said of this victory, 'We hope this is a harbinger of future campaigns where community associations drive the bus, as it were, on determining the issues affecting their communities. It's vital that these decisions are made on the association level rather than the state level': DD Berger and ES Bogdanoff 'Florida Legislature Approves Landmark Bill Allowing High Rises to Opt-Out of Installing Fire Sprinkler and Engineered Life Safety Systems' *BeckerLawyers.com* (16 May 2017) https://beckerlawyers.com/florida-legislature-approves-landmark-bill-allowing-high-rises-to-opt-out-of-installing-fire-sprinkler-and-engineered-life-safety-systems/.

[52] Plaintiff's Motion (n 12) 24–26. See Class Action Settlement Agreement, *In Re Champlain Towers South Collapse Litigation* (2021) (No 2021-0150890-CA-01) 15.

[53] Birkland (n 3) 53.

E. Florida Senate Bill 4-D

The law that was passed by the Florida legislature in response to the tragedy at CTS adopts in large part the basic approaches seen in the Florida Bar Task Force and CAI reports. The state government's attempted solution to the problems at CTS is premised largely on placing more responsibilities on condo boards and more costs on unit owners.

The changes required by Senate Bill 4-D became effective on 26 May 2022, and applied to condo and cooperative buildings over three storeys in height. The similarities to the Bar and CAI reports were obvious. The essence of the Bill was to place specific obligations on the shoulders of condo boards to pay for and coordinate a detailed regimen of structural building inspections and repairs. The association must first do a 'milestone' inspection of the building, and thereafter do another inspection every 10 years. The deadline for these initial 'milestone' inspections to be completed for older condos was set for 31 December 2024. For newer condos, the initial inspections were to be done by the end of the year when the condominium building reaches either 25 years or 30 years old, depending upon how close the building is to the Florida coastline, with coastal condos being subject to the earlier deadline. The inspections had to be done by a licensed architect or engineer.

Every 10 years after the milestone inspection, associations had to do a special type of reserve study called a 'structural integrity reserve study', or SIRS for short, regarding the need for, and cost of, repair of most major building components, including roofs, load-bearing walls, floors, foundations, fire protection systems, electrical systems, waterproofing and painting, windows, plumbing and anything else that might affect the foregoing.[54] And associations were prohibited from waiving contributions to reserves for these repairs, or using those reserve funds for anything else.[55] The law also established that it is a breach of a board member or officer's fiduciary duty if the association fails to complete the required structural integrity reserve study.[56] This provision subjects the board member or officer to the potential for being sued by any unit owner for breach of fiduciary duty.

After the law was passed, criticisms began to surface concerning some of the Bill's provisions on the grounds that they would be hard, if not impossible, for associations to comply with, at least by the deadlines set in the original Bill. A consensus quickly emerged that changes had to be made. Another Bill, SB 154, was introduced on 10 February 2023, and referred to in the industry as the

[54] Building Safety Bill (n 10) 41.
[55] ibid 4.
[56] ibid 38.

'Glitch Bill';[57] it passed quickly with unanimous votes of both houses of the state legislature and was signed by the governor on 9 June 2023.[58]

The Glitch Bill left the major provisions of SB 4-D in place but made numerous changes to some of the language in the original bill to make compliance easier. It clarified that the requirements of SB 4-D applied only to buildings that included residential condominiums or housing cooperatives,[59] which would exempt commercial condominiums consisting entirely of businesses. It also addressed a major concern with SB 4-D, which was that the 31 December 2024 deadline for milestone inspections was unrealistic. It appeared that there were not enough licensed architects and engineers in the state of Florida to perform the inspections on thousands of condo buildings by the end of 2024. SB 154 loosened that requirement so that the inspections could be performed by 'a team of professionals' working under the supervision of an architect or engineer.[60] Building components with greater than a 25 year remaining life were exempted from the reserve requirement. Additionally, buildings that were about to turn 30 years old and had little time to get the inspections done were given an additional year to comply.

The Bill also changed the definition of the SIRS to facilitate compliance. The original Bill required visual inspections of a list of building components, and concerns emerged that some of these components were not readily subject to visual inspection short of taking the building apart. Others, such as windows, were in many cases the responsibility of unit owners, not condo boards, to maintain and repair. The Glitch Bill addressed these concerns as well, specifying that the association was only responsible for reserving money to repair building components that it was responsible for maintaining, and exempting floors and foundations from these requirements.[61] The legislature also modified the mandatory reserve requirement so that it only applied to budgets adopted after the end of 2024. Local government building code enforcement agencies were given increased discretion in implementing the law, so that they could extend the milestone inspection deadline for good cause.[62] Otherwise, the new law reflects little concern with the dramatic failures of government oversight that were documented in the Grand Jury report.

The striking thing about this new law, even taken with the revisions in SB 154, is that, except for requiring developers to do benchmark inspections, and empowering government agencies to enforce these provisions against association leaders, it focuses almost entirely on condo boards and officers. It is essentially a list of

[57] KM Koushel, '2023 Legislature Responds with Condominium "Glitch Bill"' *Bilzin Sumberg* (12 June 2023) https://www.bilzin.com/insights/publications/2023/06/legislature-responds-with-condominium-glitch-bill.

[58] 'CS/CS/SB 154: Condominium and Cooperative Associations' (The Florida Senate, 13 June 2023) https://www.flsenate.gov/Session/Bill/2023/154.

[59] Glitch Bill (n 11) 5–6.

[60] ibid 5, 25.

[61] ibid 6.

[62] ibid 7.

mandates that are imposed on condo boards. There is even a process by which a state agency can punish a board member or officer for failing to turn over association records to owners on demand, to the tune of a fine of up to US$5,000. This raises questions concerning how many people will volunteer to serve as condo board members and officers under this regime.

Commentators noted that SB 4-D effectively raised the cost of living in a condominium in the State of Florida.[63] The law says nothing about where condo owners are supposed to acquire the funds to pay for detailed inspections and reserve studies, much less do the building repair and maintenance that is required of them. Yet, we know that many owners at CTS lacked funds to pay their share of the costs for necessary repairs, and that this was one of the underlying problems at CTS, because it led the condo board to put off the repair work for too long. The fact that the cost issue was not on the list of matters addressed in SB 154 indicates that it was not an oversight.

III. The Court Settlement Process

The most dramatic private law response to the CTS collapse to date has been the massive litigation settlement involving the victims of the building collapse. This had the potential to be a legal nightmare lasting years, if not decades, as often happens with mass disaster litigation. However, all the wrongful death and property loss cases were consolidated before a single judge, Michael A Hanzman, Circuit Court Judge for the Complex Division of the 11th Judicial Circuit in Miami-Dade County, a Florida state court judge who put pressure on all defendants to create a pool of money to resolve the victims' claims within one year, leaving the defendants to sort out later any complex disagreements about percentages of joint and several liability, indemnification, and contribution.

Judge Hanzman appointed attorney Michael I Goldberg as receiver for the Champlain Towers South Condominium Association. Goldberg's role involved handling the financial and legal affairs of the association for the benefit of those affected by the tragedy, and he created a website to publicise all relevant legal documents on the progress of the consolidated cases.[64] The judge also appointed a mediator, Bruce W Greer, a prominent Miami attorney with extensive mediation experience, whose main function was to broker a settlement with any and all defendants for the benefit of the victims.

[63] D Lyons, 'Condo Owners Brace for Steep Costs With Post-Surfside Reforms on the Way' *SunSentinel* (25 July 2022) https://www.sun-sentinel.com/2022/07/25/condo-owners-brace-for-steep-costs-with-post-surfside-reforms-on-the-way/; A Machado, 'Cost of Condo Living on the Rise after Partial Collapse of Champlain Towers South in Surfside' *NBC Miami* (22 July 2023) https://www.nbcmiami.com/news/local/cost-of-condo-living-on-the-rise-after-the-partial-collapse-of-champlain-towers-south-in-surfside/3058705/.

[64] Goldberg (n 12).

The task of settling with the victims was complicated by the fact that there were, and still are, competing theories of responsibility regarding what caused the tower to collapse. There is no doubt that the condo association had been informed of serious concrete spalling that jeopardised the structure of the building, and failed to repair it. There were also claims that excavation and construction at a neighbouring site contributed to destabilising the building. Additionally, the CTS board was being advised by lawyers, engineers and other professionals who arguably could bear some potential liability if it were shown that they had failed to advise the association fully of the risks. Before the collapse, CTS was being advised by a law firm that did in fact pay to settle claims against them arising from their work for the association. The security system had a building alarm that might have alerted people to leave their units, but that alarm allegedly did not sound. All possible responsible parties were sued by those who had lost loved ones and/or their homes, and these defendants in turn cross-claimed against each other, creating a Gordian knot of high-stakes litigation.

All plaintiffs, including unit owners, relatives of those who died and anyone else who claimed to have suffered any loss, were consolidated into a class, and all their cases were included within a single class action. Defendants included the condominium association; professionals who had been retained by the association; the association's security company; design, engineering, waterproofing and construction firms who had worked on CTS; the Town of Surfside; and firms connected with construction work on the neighbouring condominium building (which arguably had destabilised CTS).

Through a complex process of negotiation, most of the potentially responsible parties paid into a settlement fund, typically through their insurance carriers, in order to discharge any potential claims of liability. For example, the association's security company paid over US$517 million; the association's law firm, Becker and Poliakoff, paid US$31 million; and the Town of Surfside paid US$2 million.[65]

On 9 August 2022, Judge Hanzman approved a final settlement fund of approximately US$1,074,000,000,[66] and a Claims Administration Procedure was set in motion for plaintiffs to make claims on that fund,[67] with the claims being reviewed

[65] Order Granting Class Plaintiffs' Motion for Preliminary Approval of Class Action Settlement and Certification of the Settlement Class at 24–25, *In Re: Champlain Towers South Collapse Litigation* (2022) (No 2021-015089-CA-01).

[66] ibid 2.

[67] Plaintiffs' Motion (n 12) 4. The claims process was established in the settlement agreement. All settling parties seeking to be released from potential liability deposited the agreed-upon amount in a settlement fund. The overall Settlement Administrator was attorney Michael I Goldberg, a distinguished bankruptcy lawyer who the judge handling the case, Circuit Judge Michael Hanzman, had earlier appointed as receiver for the condo association. Class Action Settlement Agreement at 19, 30. The process for making a claim on the settlement fund involves submitting a claim form for review by the two Claims Administrators, attorney Robert L Parks and retired Judge John W Thornton, who would determine whether the claimant qualified for any payment. The amounts of payments would ultimately be determined by the Claims Administrators and Judge Hanzman: Class Action Settlement Agreement (n 52) 8.

by a panel of experienced attorneys. Judge Hanzman's determination to see the victims compensated quickly came to fruition, although it remained for those who contributed to the settlement fund to sort out their respective claims against each other. It is important to note that this legal process ended in a settlement that sacrificed any exhaustive and authoritative fact-finding process, such as a trial, in the interest of compensating the victims. It did not resolve the question of how and why the building collapsed, or why nothing was done to prevent that from happening. It simply resolved the claims of those who had lost their loved ones and/or homes.

IV. Conclusions

The collapse of Champlain Towers South was a focusing event that put the relationship between the finances of condo associations and building safety on the policy agenda of public and private organisations in Florida and elsewhere in the United States. The documents reviewed here were written by knowledgeable people with professional expertise, and they reflect a consistent view of the nature of the problem that needs to be solved, as well as how to solve it.

The reports do not definitively address the physical cause of the collapse, which will eventually be determined by the NIST. The lawsuit settlement is the most authoritative statement on that so far, and the settlement makes it clear that there were numerous responsible parties, and the causation picture is complex. For example, it may eventually be learned that there were defects in the original construction, and that construction activities at nearby properties may have contributed to structural instability in the CTS building foundation.

But even with the physical causation issue unresolved, the documents reviewed in this chapter reflect an overriding consensus that the building collapse is largely attributable to the failure of the condominium association to properly maintain and repair the building. The condo owners, through their association, chose to maintain inadequate reserves, deferred necessary maintenance and failed to act on the recommendations of experts who advised major and expensive repairs. Remarkably, the association had been paralysed by internal conflict over necessary repairs from the time they learned of the cost of repairs until the building collapsed and took so many lives with it. The repairs were estimated to cost more than US$15 million and there were 136 units in the building, which means that the average cost would have been over US$110,000 per unit.[68]

[68] Five members of the board of directors resigned in 2019 in frustration at the internal conflict over the high cost of repairs, with one of them, the board president at the time, saying: 'This pattern has repeated itself over and over, ego battles, undermining the roles of fellow board members, circulation of gossip and mistruths' (Beth Reinhard, Tik Root, Brady Dennis and Jon Swaine, 'Majority of Florida Condo Board Quit in 2019 as Squabbling Residents Dragged Out Plans for Repairs' *Washington Post* (30 June 2021) https://www.washingtonpost.com/investigations/majority-of-florida-condo-board-

The consensus that this condo association should have done more to prevent disaster led directly to agreement that what happened at CTS is not just a one-off tragedy. The experts who studied this situation, and the policy-makers who eventually took action, became convinced that many other associations were in a similar state of ignorance about the state of their buildings and were engaged in the same risky practice of deferring necessary maintenance. From the emergence of condominium housing in the early 1960s on, condo finances were viewed as a private matter best left to condo boards and owners. But if a large number of associations in Florida were overlooking potentially dangerous structural problems, then condo finances had to be seen as a matter of public concern. The tragedy at CTS became a focusing event that turned the legislature's view of condo finances from seeing it as a condition that was best left to market forces, to viewing it as a policy problem that needed to be addressed.

The policy problem, as it is framed in these reports, is that under the current state of affairs, condo boards cannot be relied upon to inform themselves sufficiently regarding the condition of their buildings, and condo owners cannot be trusted to fund necessary repairs. At CTS and elsewhere, the reports say, the members and boards they elect do not pay for necessary inspections of their buildings, and then often underfund reserve accounts, not realising the potential consequences. When problems become evident and the money is not there to conduct repairs, owners then resist paying the huge special assessments that become necessary.

Clearly the main assumption animating the state legislature in passing SB 4-D was that action was needed to prevent dangerously deferred maintenance at other Florida condos. The Grand Jury reported noted that 'a failure of condo boards to implement much-needed repairs and maintenance has led to unsafe building structures throughout South Florida'.[69] The solutions proposed in these reports reflect an emphasis on removing a great deal of the discretion that condo unit owners and their elected boards have always had to manage and maintain their buildings as they see fit.

This is in fact a revolutionary change, although that fact is not acknowledged in the reports, because the institution of condominium housing has always been based on several assumptions about building maintenance. Stated simply, they are:

- economic self-interest in enhancing property values would ensure that condo unit owners would be willing to pay what was necessary to keep their buildings in proper repair;
- that condominium association private governments, in the form of not-for-profit corporations run by elected boards of directors, were a proper and adequate vehicle for overcoming collective action problems and making good decisions about these properties; and

quit-in-2019-as-squabbling-residents-dragged-out-plans-for-repairs/2021/06/30/43592282-d98e-11eb-ae62-2d07d7df83bd_story.html).

[69] Miami-Dade Grand Jury (n 6) 10.

- the resources of the owners and their elected boards would be adequate to keep buildings repaired and functioning properly indefinitely.

Senate Bill 4-D reflects a new, implicit, legislative consensus that the first two of these assumptions are wrong, and that state public policy must be premised on a different set of assumptions about boards, members and resources. None of the reports explicitly raises fundamental questions about the basic model of condominium governance that they implicitly undermine, but the evidence of a paradigm shift is in the proposals and the laws that followed them. These new laws and policies abandon reliance on market forces and self-interest, and instead require condo boards to hire experts, inform themselves, maintain reserves, raise money for repairs, and carry them out in a timely manner. Boards are required to obtain and follow professional recommendations on matters that have always been within the discretion of condo boards and unit owners. And the legislation also removes owner discretion to ignore major problems, underfund reserves and block board efforts to raise necessary funds through special assessments. Where structural issues are concerned, the old laissez-faire approach has been abandoned.

The third assumption regarding the adequacy of owner resources appears to remain in place in the new legal regime, because the changes in law and policy do not provide increased institutional support and funding to achieve higher levels of building maintenance and repair. But this is strange, in that owner resistance to undertaking expensive repairs was a critical factor in the unfortunate decisions and non-decisions made there that led to the fatal building collapse.

In my view, the best way to explain the legislature leaving the third assumption in place when events at CTS suggest that it is as flawed as the other two assumptions is simply to consider the enormous costs involved in condo building maintenance in the State of Florida.[70] Those costs still lie in private hands, and there is presently no willingness to bail out struggling condo owners and shift their repair costs to the general public. The political problems that would go with doing that are obvious.[71]

Yet, a more comprehensive examination of the reasons for the CTS collapse might frame the problem differently. Putting the matter in a broader context would require acknowledging the overreliance on the resources of condominium owners and boards that has characterised this policy area since condominiums became available in the United States in 1961. Empowering boards to levy special

[70] A recent estimate by the Community Associations Institute, based on census data, put the total number of condo units in the state at over 1.5 million. They also reported that in large buildings (over 50 units) 59% of those units were in buildings built before 1990. With an enormous stock of large, old condo buildings, all of which must inevitably require major repair, it is hard to imagine a state legislature voting to hand that cost to the public: Community Associations Institute, 'Florida Condominium Data and Statistics' (Community Associations Institute, 2 September 2021) https://dualauth.caionline.org/Advocacy/Priorities/condolegislation/Documents/Building%20Data%20and%20Statistics/Florida%20Condominium%20Datarevised.pdf.

[71] This is a theme underpinning many of the chapters in this volume; notably, NJ McBride, 'Private Law in the Ruins' (ch 10).

assessments and borrow money without owner approval merely increases the burden on owners. Placing boards in the position of having to raise the money for mandated repairs means that they must resort to liens and foreclosure to make owners pay the special assessments and contribute to the loan payments. A more meaningful response to this disaster could address this problem and find ways to make funds available to owners and boards, beyond their own resources, to meet their new maintenance and repair responsibilities.

Moreover, there are other costs to consider. It is becoming clear that any attempt to determine the real cost of a condominium unit must include the inevitable costs of complying with stricter environmental laws. In the near future, the costs facing condo owners and their boards will include not just paying for regular and deferred maintenance, but for updating their buildings in many ways to comply with the coming wave of laws requiring higher levels of energy efficiency, so that cities and states can meet net-zero carbon emission goals.[72]

It can be argued that financial programmes to aid condo owners are not necessary, because once again there is a market solution in the form of investor buyouts. Facilitating termination of 'economically obsolete' condos can be viewed as a necessary last resort, which involves state laws that enable investment groups to acquire a super-majority of units and force the remaining owners to sell at fair market value. Such drastic measures underscore the financial fragility of many condo associations, a situation that is for the most part ignored by these reports.[73] On the other hand, these buyouts reduce the supply of 'affordable' owner-occupied housing for people of modest or limited means, and the lack of affordable owner-occupied housing in many markets is increasingly perceived as a significant problem or even a crisis. When these investment groups buy up all the units in a condo building, terminate the condo association and convert the property into rental apartments, it reduces the supply of the most affordable single-family units available to entry-level buyers, people on fixed incomes and those of modest means who wish to experience the benefits of home ownership.[74]

The rise of residential private government, including condo associations, is ultimately a widespread privatisation of responsibilities that were historically carried out by local government. Many of the things that condo owners pay for would otherwise be covered by tax dollars and delivered by municipalities, government contractors or special districts. Yet, condo owners pay their property

[72] E McKenzie, 'Net Zero and Condominiums: Emerging US Policies and Practices' (Housing After Grenfell, 13 March 2023) https://blogs.law.ox.ac.uk/housing-after-grenfell-blog/blog-post/2023/03/net-zero-and-condominiums-emerging-us-policies-and.

[73] The financial fragility of many condominium associations, particularly older ones occupied by people of modest or fixed incomes, has been well-documented. See the analyses by Attorney T Berding and by McKenzie (n 1).

[74] See D Madden and P Marcuse, *In Defense of Housing: The Politics of Crisis* (London, Verso Books, 2016).

taxes like other homeowners, as well as their private assessments.[75] Perhaps policies that intentionally increase the costs they must bear, in order to meet public policy objectives such as safer buildings and reduced carbon emissions, could come with increased access to resources. For example, there could be low-interest loans guaranteed by the federal government, offsetting property tax reductions, or grants-in-aid. Low-interest loan programmes are among the recommendations emerging from these reports, and those proposals would offer owners some relief. Owners would, of course, have to repay loans, so there would be no unjust enrichment at public expense.

In any case, it seems clear that increasing the financial burden on condo owners without doing anything to enable them to meet those burdens is a partial solution, at best, to the situation highlighted by the collapse of CTS. And going forward, public policies and private practices need to take into account the full cost of condominium housing and make that cost known to buyers in advance.

Finally, it should be noted that while particular individuals associated with CTS, and responsible for it, made errors of judgement, it is also true that policy decisions made decades earlier by officials at higher levels of responsibility are part of the picture. There is a public dimension to this private catastrophe. The lessons that are learned from CTS, and the changes in policy and practice that result, should encompass all levels of responsibility. They should provoke us to think deeply about how the policy changes of the last four decades have undermined and disarmed government agencies that were established to protect us. The result is that, as homeowners, consumers and citizens, people are exposed to risks of physical harm and economic loss that they understand dimly if at all.

[75] The State of New Jersey, in recognition of the quasi-governmental nature of many functions that condos and homeowners' associations perform, enacted the Municipal Services Act. This law requires municipalities to reimburse private communities for their costs if their members have to pay through their association for snow and leaf removal, street lighting, recycling, and removal of solid waste. The logic of this law is that, as local taxpayers, the private community residents pay full property taxes that cover these services, but they may also be paying a second time for private provision of these same services to their own private community. NJ Rev Stat § 40:67-23.3 (2023).

4

The Role of Private Law in Promoting Building Safety: The Case of Singapore

EDWARD SW TI

I. Introduction

Singapore is a tiny granite rock situated just north of the equator. Lacking land, and indeed any kind of natural resource, means that the trend for urban development in the city-state will always be densification; 96 per cent of residents in Singapore already live in multi-owned housing, ie high-rise apartments.[1] Singapore is also a rapidly greying nation.[2] It has been observed that persons over 70 years old are four times more vulnerable in the event of a fire,[3] and fire safety is a critical aspect of building safety. Safety features and measures in the erection and maintenance of dwellings and structures are thus vital, due to the horrendous outcomes that would result if building safety were not assiduously maintained due to Singapore's urban and demographic reality.

While the statutory regime is at the heart of building safety in Singapore, this chapter focuses less on the statutory rules per se but more on how courts have applied, sometimes creatively, the relevant legislation, and what effect this has on building safety. More importantly, this chapter also considers tort law in Singapore, and, in respect of negligently caused building defects, compares Singapore with England, Australia and Canada. It is contended that Singapore's liberal approach in identifying a duty of care for pure economic loss more robustly promotes building safety compared to these jurisdictions.

Following this introduction, section II presents an overview of the statutory framework governing building safety works in Singapore, with a focus on the Building Control Act 1989, the Planning Act 1998 and the Building Maintenance

[1] ESW Ti, 'Big Houses on a Small Island: Legislating Singapore's "Good Class" Bungalows' (2022) 23 *International Journal of Housing Policy* 612.

[2] According to UN standards, Singapore will be a 'super aged' country by 2026, with one in four citizens aged 65 and above by 2030: 'What Is Age Well SG?' (Age Well SG, 17 May 2024) https://www.agewellsg.gov.sg/about/.

[3] *Singapore Parliamentary Debates, Official Report* (5 August 2019) vol 94 (Anthea Ong).

and Strata Management Act 2004. Section III considers fire risks to buildings and how Singapore's legislation has sought to respond to this. The heart of the paper lies in section IV, which comparatively considers how tort interacts with building safety. Section V concludes. As the first comprehensive review of building safety law in Singapore, it is hoped that this case study provides expanded considerations of what building safety entails, and may be of relevance to improving safety standards everywhere.

II. The Statutory Framework

The primary statute governing building safety works in Singapore is the Building Control Act 1989 (BCA). The BCA covers the control of building works; the duties of developers; qualified persons; site supervisors and builders; when a building may be occupied; the establishment of accredited checkers; dangerous buildings and occurrences; inspection of buildings; and the licensing of builders. Given that the BCA was enacted in response to two building tragedies, it is apposite to briefly consider the Act's legislative history.

A. Historical Overview of the BCA

The first iteration of the Building Control Act (1973) was precipitated by a building fire tragedy. On the morning of 21 November 1972, a fire destroyed the Robinson's department store at Raffles Place resulting in the death of nine people and the destruction of property worth approximately S$21 million. A three-person Commission headed by FA Chua J found that the fire was caused by a short circuit as a result of the overloading of an electrical branch circuit on the ground floor.[4] The fire had been 'allowed to be nursed in the loft stores without being detected',[5] and the Commission found that criticisms levelled at the fire brigade in respect of poor firefighting performance were unjustified. Indeed, the Commission found that the brigade had done well in containing the fire.[6]

Among other things, the Commission recommended that the Public Utilities Board grade the licensing of electrical contractors to ensure that only contractors with the requisite professional expertise and experience be allowed to undertake electrical installations.[7] This led to the enactment of the Electrical Workers and Contractors Licensing Act 1974, the predecessor Act to the current Electricity Act 2001. The Commission also recommended the introduction of legislation to

[4] Parliamentary Deb 30 November 1973, vol 32 col 1314 (Encik Othman Bin Wok, Minister for Social Affairs).
[5] ibid.
[6] ibid.
[7] ibid cols 1315–16.

enable the authorities to implement 'a system of periodic inspections of places of public resort to check on unauthorised additions and alterations to buildings which might endanger the safety of the public'.[8] This recommendation, among other things, resulted in the enactment of the Building Contract Act 1973. The 1973 Act consolidated the then existing law by repealing part III of the Local Government Integration Act (Cap 210) which dealt with building activities, as well as significantly enhancing the financial penalties for carrying out building works without the written permission of the Building Authority.

The second major iteration of the Building Control Act (1989) came about following Singapore's first major building failure. This occurred in 1986 when Hotel New World, a six-storey hotel with a basement carpark, collapsed, resulting in the deaths of 33 people. An independent commission attributed the collapse of the building to its 'grossly inadequate structural design', 'unsatisfactory construction', the 'imposition of large loads not allowed for in the design during the building's lifespan' (of a mere 15 years), and the absence of proper maintenance.[9]

The Hotel New World tragedy resulted in the establishment of the Building Construction Authority and the enactment of the 1989 Act to better regulate building works safety in Singapore.[10] Among other things, the amendments implemented the system of independent accredited checkers, requiring construction supervision by qualified persons and site supervisors, as well as mandatory inspection of buildings at regular intervals by structural engineers.[11] Then Minister for National Development S Dhanabalan observed that one of the main purposes of the legislative changes was to prevent a situation where the design of the structure was 'carried out by an unqualified person, such as a draughtsman under the supervision of an irresponsible engineer, as happened in the case of the Hotel New World'.[12] Subsequent amendments to the BCA have been relatively minor, and the current BCA largely conforms to the tenor of the 1989 Act.

B. The BCA and Building Safety Works

Building safety works is the paramount focus of the BCA. In *Management Corporation Strata Title Plan No 3322 v Tiong Aik Construction Pte Ltd*,[13] the Singapore Court of Appeal traced the legislative history of the BCA, and identified that it was evident from *Hansard* records that building safety, rather than

[8] ibid col 1315.

[9] Commission of Inquiry into the Collapse of Hotel New World, *Report of the Inquiry into the Collapse of Hotel New World* (16 February 1987).

[10] Parliamentary Deb 16 February 1989, vol 52, cols 668–85.

[11] ibid col 668 (S Dhanabalan, Minister for National Development).

[12] ibid col 670.

[13] *Management Corporation Strata Title Plan No 3322 v Tiong Aik Construction Pte Ltd* [2016] SGCA 40, [2016] 4 SLR 521 ('*Tiong Aik*').

issues such as the quality of workmanship, was the raison d'être of the statute.[14] Following the collapse of Hotel New World, the Act was enacted in 1989 to 'ensure that … buildings [were] designed, checked, constructed, and maintained to safe standards'.[15] Parliament also maintained its focus on structural safety and the soundness of buildings in the 2007 debates on amendments to the BCA. Then Minister of State for National Development Grace Fu stated that 'building safety cannot be left to chance, and complacency has no place in any construction project'.[16] More recently, the purpose of the Act has again been judicially recognised by the Court of Appeal to be the improvement of safety standards in all areas of the construction industry.[17]

One way the Act seeks to enhance building safety is by holding Qualified Persons (QPs) and Accredited Checkers (ACs) criminally accountable for breaches so as to deter professional practice that may put public safety at risk.[18] During the parliamentary debates in 2007, amendments were made to the Act to increase the range of sanctions that may be meted out where building professionals are negligent or incompetent, with Minister Fu asserting to the House that, post amendments, custodial sentences would be 'common' for serious offences that could cause death or injury.[19] The government explained that it had considered that custodial sentences were also imposed on professionals under the respective building control laws in jurisdictions such as Hong Kong SAR, California and New York City.[20]

The reliance on QPs and ACs in the case of major building works essentially places the burden of responsibility on the building professionals, and even the fact that the statutory body administering the BCA, the Building and Construction Authority ('the Authority') may have approved certain drawings does not mean that the professionals cannot be held liable.

In *Ser Kim Koi v GTMS Construction Pte Ltd*,[21] the appellate division of the Singapore High Court dealt with a case where an owner engaged an architect to construct three bungalows. An issue the Court had to deal with was whether a glass barrier parapet at the outdoor deck of one of the bungalows was sufficiently tall so as to protect persons from injury caused by falling.[22] While the trial judge found that the glass barrier was 1 metre in height and thus in compliance with the

[14] ibid [36]–[38].

[15] Parliamentary Deb 30 March 1988, vol 50, col 1739 (S Dhanabalan, Minister for National Development).

[16] Parliamentary Deb 20 September 2007, vol 83, col 2062 (Grace Fu Hai Yien, Minister for National Development).

[17] *Nam Hong Construction & Engineering Pte Ltd v Kori Construction (S) Pte Ltd* [2016] SGCA 42, [2016] 4 SLR 604 [23].

[18] *Leong Sow Hon v Public Prosecutor* [2020] SGHC 228, [2021] 3 SLR 1199 [41].

[19] Parliamentary Deb 20 September 2007, vol 83, cols 2078–79 (Grace Fu Hai Yien, Minister for National Development).

[20] ibid.

[21] *Ser Kim Koi v GTMS Construction Pte Ltd* [2022] SGHC(A) 34, [2023] 1 SLR 1097.

[22] ibid [149], [151].

regulation, the appeal court held that, from where the measurements should be taken, the glass parapet was only 0.55 metres.[23] The trial judge had also held that, since the Authority approved the submitted drawings (which included the originally constructed glass parapet), the architect should not be faulted for the design. This point was also overruled by the appellate division.[24]

The appellate court stated that the Act provides for a scheme where the responsibility for accuracy, design, compliance and adequacy of engineering or architectural matters falls squarely upon the shoulders of QPs such as architects, engineers and ACs, with these professionals charged with the responsibility to ensure that the building works comply with the regulatory requirements. Loh JAD noted that the Commissioner of Building Control may, based on the required certificates signed by these professionals, approve the submitted plans *without* checking the designs and calculations of any building works, although the Act also empowers the Commissioner to carry out random checks on the detailed structural plans, design calculations or geotechnical aspects of any building works before granting the approval. Although this appears particularly onerous to the professionals involved, the ruling may be said to enhance building safety because the fact that the designs were approved by the regulators does not remove the responsibility of the qualified person to ensure that the building works truly conform to the regulations.

One issue linking the statutory control of building works with private law is the interaction of statutory duties and common law claims. In *Animal Concerns Research & Education Society v Tan Boon Kwee*,[25] the Singapore Court of Appeal noted that breaches of the BCA did not 'obviously create'[26] a private cause of action because the statutory breach would only attract purely criminal sanctions under the statute. Neither, however, did the Court hold that a reading of the relevant section – in that case, section 10 – indicate that Parliament intended to preclude common law civil remedies in respect of pure economic loss. In *Animal Concerns*, the apex court reversed the lower court's decision and held a clerk of works liable for negligently failing to supervise the levelling of a site meant to construct an animal shelter for the appellant, a registered charity. Damages on the basis of pure economic loss for the cost of remedial work were awarded to the charity.[27] Although the trial judge dismissed this action in negligence on the basis that there was no statutory duty to supervise 'backfilling',[28] thus implicitly holding that the statute exhaustively set out the clerk's duty of care, the Court of Appeal rightly held that the clerk of works also owed duties at common law.[29]

[23] ibid [151].
[24] ibid [152].
[25] *Animal Concerns Research & Education Society v Tan Boon Kwee* [2011] SGCA 2, [2011] 2 SLR 146 ('*Animal Concerns*').
[26] ibid [81].
[27] ibid [32], [103].
[28] A process of bringing in earth from elsewhere to raise the lower regions: ibid [9].
[29] ibid [82].

Gary Chan observes that the case demonstrates two important points: first, that the Court recognised a common law duty of care despite the fact that Parliament did not intend to confer a private right of action to the victim who suffered pure economic loss; and second, because the statute did not exclude a cause of action in negligence, it permitted a common law duty of care to be established where there was a voluntary assumption of responsibility.[30] It remains open therefore to a homeowner to argue that breaches of the BCA provide the evidentiary basis giving rise to private causes of action.

C. Building Maintenance and Strata Management Act 2004

A significant proportion of Singaporean resident households – some 77 per cent of private property owners – reside in strata dwellings.[31] Special mention is thus made to the Building Maintenance and Strata Management Act 2004 (BMSA). Issues of multi-ownership mean that the organisation of unit owners, especially in relation to expending funds for building safety, is challenging.[32] The imposition of regular 'sinking funds' that unit owners must pay under section 39 of the BMSA, as well as strata regulations governing by-laws[33] and general maintenance,[34] are thus statutory innovations to overcome these practical problems. The solemness of the obligation on the part of strata owners to collectively maintain the building is shown by the fact that the failure by a strata unit owner to pay their contribution dues for the maintenance of the development results not just in the imposition of interest,[35] but may even lead to a criminal conviction.[36]

Remarkably, the Management Corporation (MC) of the development may also seek the sale of the strata lot to recover the unpaid arrears if the lot owner has failed to pay their dues 30 days after a written demand for the contribution.[37] This extraordinary power has no parallel in other jurisdictions and underscores the legal responsibility imposed on lot owners collectively to maintain the development. In relation to the proper financial management of the MC's accounts, an annual audit must be conducted by a public accountant.[38] While the MC is

[30] G Chan, 'Finding Common Law Duty of Care from Statutory Duties: All Within the *Anns* Framework' (2016) 24 *Tort Law Review* 14, 28.

[31] 'Households' (Department of Statistics Singapore, 28 May 2022) https://www.singstat.gov.sg/find-data/search-by-theme/households/households/latest-data.

[32] cf EC McKenzie, 'The Surfside Condominium Collapse: What Lessons Have Been Learned?', this volume, ch 3.

[33] Building Maintenance (Strata Management) Regulations 2005.

[34] Building Maintenance and Strata Management (Lift, Escalator and Building Maintenance) Regulations 2016.

[35] BMSA, s 40(6).

[36] BMSA, s 40(10).

[37] BMSA, s 43.

[38] BMSA, s 45.

statutorily empowered to borrow moneys[39] for the benefit of the development, this is virtually unheard of in Singapore in practice, with most management corporation strata titles (MCSTs) having healthy cash balances.

Building safety is also enhanced via the BMSA as the legislation specifically allows for strata owners to install safety equipment in their units even if this contradicts any by-law of the strata development.[40] Safety equipment refers to features such as window grilles, screens, balustrades, railings or fences that prevent people from falling over the edge of an outdoor-facing balcony, terrace, window or door; any screen or device to prevent entry of animals or insects on the lot; an intruder alarm or monitoring system; and any lock or security mechanism designed to protect against intruders.[41] A recent paper by Tang Hang Wu observed that children falling from windows and balconies of buildings is a 'silent epidemic' happening all over the world, including Singapore.[42] Installation of safety equipment is thus a right and is not subject to consent from other strata owners.

A related but distinct concern with living in a high-rise apartment is how ground-floor apartment units can protect themselves against 'killer litter', ie objects thrown or dropped from the upper floors. Tang notes that 'some of the causes for killer litter can range from people suffering from mental health issues, unsupervised children, anti-social behaviour and objects placed on balconies such as flowerpots and laundry poles falling down due to a gust of wind'.[43] The Strata Titles Board has held that an owner of a lot (typically the ground floor apartment owner) may install awnings as protective coverings without the consent of other lot owners.[44] This is justified on the basis of prescribed by-law 5(3)(c),[45] which provides that a lot owner may alter the common property to 'install any structure or device to prevent harm to children'. Notably however, in *Foo Siang Yean v MCST Plan 2245*,[46] the Strata Titles Board held that a by-law which 'allows for the installation of structures or devices to prevent harm to children' *at a limit of 2 metres* was not inconsistent with the prescribed by-law 5(3)(c). Any awning meant to protect against killer litter may thus be legitimately limited to a cover not exceeding 2 metres.

[39] BMSA, s 38(9).
[40] BMSA, s 37A(1).
[41] BMSA, s 37A(3).
[42] HW Tang, 'Conceptualizing Condominium Law and Children: Comparing the State of Strata Titles Law in New South Wales and Singapore' (2023) 16 *Journal of Property, Planning and Environmental Law* 36, 42.
[43] ibid 45.
[44] ibid 46.
[45] Building Maintenance (Strata Management) Regulations 2005, sch 2.
[46] *Foo Siang Yean v Management Corporation Strata Title Plan No 2245*, STB Case Reference STB 109 of 2022 [31].

III. Fire Risks and Building Safety

While control of building works and inspection of buildings via the BCA was promulgated in 1973 following the Robinson's department store fire, the BCA itself does not regulate fire risks to buildings. Instead, the Fire Safety Act 1993 (FSA) seeks to prevent fires from occurring in buildings.[47] The BCA and FSA are, however, interconnected because the Building Authority will not permit a newly constructed building to be used (by withholding the certificate of statutory completion) if approval under the FSA relating to fire safety has not been obtained.[48]

On 4 May 2017, a fire broke out at an industrial building at 30 Toh Guan Road resulting in the death of a 54-year-old woman.[49] Investigations revealed that the composite panels used as cladding on the building's external walls were not of Class 0 standard as required under the Fire Code.[50] The composite panels on the building were supplied by an overseas manufacturer through a local sole distributor, and following an investigation it was revealed that the distributor mixed two models of composite panels from the same 'Alubond' brand – one of which meets the Fire Code requirement for use as cladding, while the other was certified as Class 0 on full assembly for use on roofs and internal walls, but not for use as cladding.[51] Notably, the Fire Code's requirements for Class 0 cladding predated the tragedy.

Following a parliamentary question filed by a member of the House regarding what lessons Singapore could learn from the Grenfell Tower tragedy, the minister replied stating that Singapore's Civil Defence Force (SCDF) would study the investigation report of the London Fire Brigade when it was released to see whether changes to Singapore's fire regulations were needed.[52] In addition, the minister highlighted the existing regulatory regime for construction projects, including the fact that the QP was responsible for ensuring that building materials conformed to the prevailing Fire Code. Subsequent to this, the SCDF also issued notices to owners of more than 40 buildings that their claddings were non-compliant with the Fire Code. The member who filed the parliamentary question expressed surprise at this revelation as she had understood that all buildings in Singapore, including the 40 identified, having been issued with Fire Safety Certificates, were already compliant with fire safety requirements.[53] Sadly, the cladding death that

[47] Fire Safety Act 1993, s 2(1) states that the terms 'building' and 'building works' have the meaning given by the Building Control Act 1989.

[48] Building Control Regulations 2003, reg 42(2)(fa).

[49] The Court heard that the flames 'raced up the eight-storey façade of the building and took the life of a 54-year-old woman': S Alkhatib, 'Man Allegedly Duped 3 Building Contractors into Believing the Cladding he Sold was Fire-Safety Certified' *Straits Times* (2 March 2020) https://www.straitstimes.com/singapore/courts-crime/man-allegedly-duped-3-building-contractors-into-believing-the-cladding-he.

[50] Singapore Civil Defence Force, 'SCDF Takes Immediate Actions to Ensure Fire Safety of Buildings' (News Release, 24 August 2017) https://www.scdf.gov.sg/docs/default-source/scdf-library/news-releases/press-release---cladding-(final-24-aug---updated-on-7-dec).pdf, 2–3.

[51] ibid.

[52] Parliamentary Deb 5 August 2019, vol 94 (Sylvia Lim).

[53] ibid.

occurred in Singapore uncannily portended the Grenfell Tower tragedy which occurred about a month later on 14 June 2017.

In 2017, 2018 and 2019, the Grenfell Tower tragedy (and, in 2019, the Notre Dame cathedral fire in Paris) was discussed in Singapore's parliament. According to the Minister of Law, one explanation given to explain why the tragedy in Singapore differed from Grenfell Tower was that local requirements for fire escape routes are very stringent, and have to be fire protected as well.[54] Another parliamentarian observed that, while the external cladding in both cases accelerated the spread of the fire, the 'Grenfell Tower also had similar deficiencies [as the Kyoto Animation building][55] in lacking a fire sprinkler system and having only one stairway, which the survivors later reported were blocked and full of smoke, an indication that the fire doors had failed'.[56] Assuming these observations are true, it is evident that a building's internal footways and having basic firefighting implements, independent of the combustibility of the cladding, also contribute to building safety.

Regulatory responses in Singapore following the Toh Guan Road and Grenfell Tower tragedies included empowering the Commissioner to order building owners to install fire safety measures, including buildings which predate 1974 (the year when Class 0 cladding became mandated). The Commissioner is also empowered to stop the use of non-compliant fire safety products by tightening control over the entire supply chain. Prior to the 2017 tragedies, the FSA only allowed for limited enforcement action to be taken against some persons in the supply chain. Following legislative amendments in 2017, however, it is now a crime to supply non-compliant fire safety products,[57] for any test laboratory to issue a false test report,[58] for any person who is not an accredited certification body to certify such products,[59] and when non-compliant products find their way into the market or into buildings, the Commissioner may issue directions to any party with possession, charge or control of the product to recall, cease supply, remove or dispose of the product, as well as to rectify any contravention.[60] These amendments thus allow the authorities to go 'upstream' to punish suppliers who provide non-compliant products and building materials.

A pure economic loss would accrue if it were discovered, prior to any accident, that non-compliant cladding had been installed in a building, and the building's owners can seek damages to make good on such cladding defects. Such losses may

[54] *Singapore Parliamentary Debates, Official Report* (10 January 2018) vol 94 (K Shanmugam, Minister for Home Affairs and Minister for Law).

[55] In 2019, an arsonist killed 36 people by using petrol to set fire to a three-storey animation building in Kyoto, Japan. Some architects opined that the spiral staircase structure and lack of sprinklers may have contributed to the extent of the harm caused by the fire: 'Spiral Stairs, No Sprinklers May Have Contributed to Deadly Japan Animation Studio Fire' *Straits Times* (19 July 2019) https://www.straitstimes.com/asia/east-asia/spiral-stairs-no-sprinklers-may-have-contributed-to-deadly-japan-animation-studio.

[56] *Singapore Parliamentary Debates, Official Report* (5 August 2019) vol 94 (Chia Shi-Lu).

[57] FSA, s 70.

[58] FSA, s 67.

[59] FSA, s 69.

[60] FSA, s 73(2).

be either vindicated by articulating an actionable statutory duty for breach of the FSA or, as the following discussion shows, via Singapore common law.

IV. Private Law

On one view the various regulatory controls imposed by planning, building control and fire safety law may be seen as incursions to the Blackstonian view of private law, which sees property as the concentration of absolute rights of use, exclusion, transfer and immunity from expropriation.[61] If, however, the prevention of harm as stated by Honoré as one of his 11 incidents of ownership[62] is accepted as a necessary aspect of being a property owner, then perhaps the statutory regime discussed above can even be said to be complimentary to the private law concept of *property*.

A. Negligence Liability of Builders Vis-a-Vis Purchasers without Privity

Although it is clear that a contractual duty of care will normally be owed to a person who engaged the builder, or between a direct purchaser of a new home with the developer, it is less intuitive whether, and to what extent, a duty of care exists between the builder and/or their subcontractors with the successors of the landowner or even tenants of the property. In cases of pure economic loss, English case law has denied the existence of a duty of care to downstream purchasers and tenants even where it is clear that remediation is necessary to make the building safe.[63] The position in England is that pure economic loss for defective buildings is not actionable in negligence. In chapter 6 of this volume, Donal Nolan argues that legislation rather than case law should provide remedies for pure economic loss stemming from defective buildings; however, he sets out cogent arguments as to why there is pressure for a tort remedy in defective premises cases.[64] Although, as Nolan notes, the problem of economic loss caused by defective premises has 'bedevilled the Commonwealth courts for over half a century',[65] in Singapore a line of cases recognise a duty of care for such losses, while providing for defences to

[61] ESW Ti, 'Of Landlords and Tenants: Property in the Midst of a Pandemic' (2022) 43 *Statute Law Review* 284, 293.

[62] AM Honoré, 'Ownership' in AG Guest (ed), *Oxford Essays in Jurisprudence* (Oxford, Oxford University Press, 1961).

[63] *D&F Estates Ltd v Church Commissioners for England* [1989] AC 177 (HL) ('*D&F Estates*'); *Murphy v Brentwood District Council* [1991] 1 AC 398 (HL) ('*Murphy*').

[64] D Nolan, 'Defective Premises and Economic Loss: A Problem Best Left to Legislation?', this volume, ch 6.

[65] ibid 151.

builders and architects depending on the nature of these defects. This is in contrast with the view put forward by Nolan that legislation rather than case law should provide remedies for pure economic loss stemming from defective buildings.[66] In the following segment, I endeavour to distil three key principles governing this area of law, with a discussion of the main cases which support them, as well as a comparative discussion with the laws of England, Australia and Canada.

(i) A Service Provider Involved in the Construction or Design of a Defective Building can be Held Liable in Tort in Respect of Pure Economic Loss

In *RSP Architects Planners & Engineers v Management Corporation Strata Title Plan No 1075*,[67] bricks and brick tiles fell from a gable end wall on the fifth storey of a condominium development, Eastern Lagoon, and damaged the roof of a third-storey unit in a neighbouring block located within the same development. This failure of the wall cladding occurred in November 1992, just six years after the building was constructed.[68] In response, the Public Works Department issued an order dated 29 May 1993 requiring the MCST to appoint a professional engineer to inspect the condition of the affected walls and execute the required rectification works.[69] The matter involved the MCST because the outer walls and roofs of constituent buildings within the development constitute common property.

The case is interesting because a claim in pure economic loss by the strata management corporation against the architect was allowed by the Singapore court even though there was, and there remains, clear authority at English common law against such claims.[70] Although the falling bricks and brick tiles caused physical damage to the roof and contents of the level-three unit, in this action MCST sought to recover the cost of rectification of the wall claddings which had not fallen, which was done to avoid future injury to persons and/or damage to property.[71] Such rectification works, being losses not sustained in consequence of injury to person or damage to property, were classified by the court as pure economic loss.[72]

Singapore's position in this regard is comparatively liberal compared to those of England and Australia.[73] In *D&F Estates*,[74] the House of Lords dealt with a case

[66] ibid.
[67] *RSP Architects Planners & Engineers v Management Corporation Strata Title Plan No 1075* [1999] SGCA 30; [1999] 2 SLR(R) 134 ('*RSP*').
[68] ibid [4].
[69] ibid [5].
[70] *D&F Estates* [1989] AC 177; *Murphy* [1991] 1 AC 398.
[71] *RSP* [1999] SGCA 30; [1999] 2 SLR(R) 134 [12].
[72] ibid.
[73] See, further, Nolan (n 64) section III; J Morgan, 'Tort as a Tool of Government Policy: Section 38 of the Building Act 1984: Sleeping Beauty Awakes?', this volume, ch 7, section IV.
[74] *D&F Estates* [1989] AC 177.

in which a tenant sued the contractors engaged by its landlord for the cost of remedial works, carpet cleaning and loss of rent (the tenant had subtenants) because of defective plastering which had fallen off. In rejecting the claim for pure economic loss, Lord Oliver held:

> A cause of action in negligence at common law which arises only when the sole damage is the mere existence of the defect giving rise to the possibility of damage in the future, which crystallizes only when that damage is imminent, and the damages for which are measured, not by the full amount of the loss attributable to the defect but by the cost of remedying it only to the extent necessary to avert a risk of physical injury, is a novel concept.[75]

In the same vein, the Lords in *Murphy*[76] rejected a house-owner's claim for economic loss arising from the purchase of a pair of semidetached houses constructed on a foundation approved by the local council's consulting engineer. Despite the approval, the foundation proved faulty and serious cracks appeared on the properties. As he could not afford to make the requisite repairs, the owner sold the property with the defects unremedied at £35,000 below what its market value otherwise would have been, and claimed against the council for this loss, alleging that his family had been subjected to an imminent risk to health and safety because gas and oil pipes had broken, and there was a risk of further breaks.

Lord Keith held that the right to recover for pure economic loss did not extend beyond the situation where the loss had been sustained through reliance on negligent misstatements, as in *Hedley Byrne*.[77] On his part, Lord Oliver held that there was insufficient proximity between the council's actions and the ultimate loss sustained by the homeowner to justify extending the scope of the duty of care in such a circumstance.[78] As actual loss to property and/or human life would have been actionable in both the English cases – not being pure economic loss – it appears somewhat perverse that there is an economic incentive on the part of the plaintiff to sustain the loss rather than nip the problem in the bud and proactively ensure the building is safe. As the Supreme Court of Canada observed in *Winnipeg Condominium*,[79] a case discussed below, maintaining a bar against recoverability for the cost of repairing dangerous defects in relation to contractors and subsequent property purchasers 'provides no incentive for plaintiffs to mitigate potential losses and tends to encourage economically inefficient behaviour'.[80] Apart from the potential injury to life, rectification works may well be less costly than reconstruction following building failure.

[75] ibid 213–14.

[76] *Murphy* [1991] 1 AC 398.

[77] ibid 468, citing *Hedley Byrne & Co Ltd v Heller & Partners Ltd* [1964] AC 465.

[78] ibid 485–86.

[79] *Winnipeg Condominium Corporation No 36 v Bird Construction Co* [1995] 1 SCR 85 ('*Winnipeg Condominium*'). See, further, E Chamberlain, 'Building Safety in Canada: Has *Winnipeg Condominium* Had an Impact?', this volume, ch 5.

[80] ibid [37].

D&F Estates and *Murphy* were both rejected by the Singapore Court of Appeal in *RSP*.[81] Instead, the Court held that, in building defect cases involving pure economic loss, it should first be determined whether there was a sufficient degree of proximity in the relationship between the party who had sustained the loss and the party who was said to have caused the loss which would give rise to a duty of care to avoid the kind of loss sustained. And, if such a degree of proximity were found, the court should next consider whether there was any material factor or policy which precluded such a duty from arising.[82]

The articulation of this two-stage test was made by an earlier Singapore case, coincidentally involving the same architects.[83] This was not a novel legal standard but an adaptation of the test laid out by the Australian High Court in *Bryan v Maloney*.[84] In describing the decision as 'undoubtedly'[85] a landmark Australian decision, the Court of Appeal in *Ocean Front* also noted that the High Court of Australia had declined to follow the English authorities of *D&F Estates* and *Murphy*.[86]

The Singapore Court was referring to the 1995 case of *Bryan v Maloney*, in which a majority of the Australian High Court held that there was a relationship of proximity between the parties to avoid the kind of damage suffered even by subsequent owners such as Mrs Maloney, given that the house 'is a permanent structure to be used indefinitely … and is likely to represent … the most significant investment which the subsequent owner will make during his or her lifetime'.[87] The Court also held that it was 'obviously foreseeable … that the negligent construction of the house with inadequate footings is likely to cause economic loss, of the kind sustained by Mrs Maloney, to the owner of the house at the time when the inadequacy of the footings first becomes manifest'.[88]

Although the test in *Bryan* is endorsed in Singapore, the High Court of Australia in *Brookfield Multiplex Ltd v Owners Corporation Strata Plan No 61288*[89] limited pure economic loss claims by downstream purchasers to vulnerable home-owners of the class identified in *Bryan*.[90] Matthew Bell and Wayne Jocic thus note that *Multiplex* brings Australia's common law in line with the 'limited province of tort' expressed by the English House of Lords in *Murphy*.[91] Although the current

[81] *RSP* [1999] SGCA 30, [1999] 2 SLR(R) 134 [32].
[82] ibid [31].
[83] *RSP Architects Planners & Engineers v Ocean Front Pte Ltd* [1995] SGCA 79, [1995] 3 SLR(R) 653 ('*Ocean Front*').
[84] *Bryan v Maloney* (1995) 182 CLR 609 ('*Bryan*').
[85] *Ocean Front* [1995] SGCA 79, [1995] 3 SLR(R) 653 [49].
[86] ibid [55].
[87] *Bryan* (1995) 182 CLR 609, 625.
[88] ibid.
[89] *Brookfield Multiplex Ltd v Owners Corporation Strata Plan No 61288* [2014] HCA 36, (2014) 254 CLR 185 (HCA) ('*Brookfield Multiplex*'). See, further, Nolan (n 64) 160–1.
[90] M Bell and W Jocic, 'Negligence Claims by Subsequent Building Owners: Did the Life of *Bryan* End Too Soon? (2017) 41 *Melbourne University Law Review* 1, 12.
[91] ibid 3.

Australian position provides that non-vulnerable plaintiffs must protect themselves via contract,[92] there is no such distinction under Singapore law.

The High Court of Australia in *Mallonland*[93] most recently dealt with the issue of pure economic loss claims, albeit not in the context of building defects. The appellants in *Mallonland* had purchased grain contaminated with the seed of another plant, which resulted in the appellants suffering pure economic loss in the form of reduced income and increased expenditure. The sole issue before the appellate court was whether the grain producers owed a duty to take reasonable care in its production process to avoid the risk that the appellants would sustain purely economic losses by reason of a hidden defect in the bags of grain because of the presence of the contaminating seeds.[94]

In affirming the lower court's decision that no duty of care existed, six of the seven members[95] of the High Court held that reasonable foreseeability, while a necessary element of the tort, is by itself not sufficient to ground pure economic loss.[96] Further, the Court held that, while a duty of care may be established where a defendant has assumed a responsibility towards a plaintiff to take reasonable care to avoid economic loss to the plaintiff,[97] this may be negated or limited by words or conduct.[98] In referencing *Brookfield Multiplex*, the High Court in *Mallonland* articulated that the lack of vulnerability was determinative in finding that there was no duty of care owed by the builder to the owners corporation to avoid pure economic loss resulting from latent defects in the common property.[99]

It is submitted that *Mallonland* does not detract from the principles articulated in *Brookfield Multiplex*[100] regarding the affirming relationship between the assumption of responsibility and vulnerability. Both cases are, however, a retreat from the more plaintiff-friendly two-stage test articulated in *Bryan* which does not mention the concept of vulnerability in the decision. In following *Bryan* rather than more recent Australian decisions, the approach in Singapore thus more easily allows for pure economic loss claims in tort to be found against builders and contractors.

In declining to follow English authorities, the *RSP* court observed that *Murphy*, in holding that there was no proximate duty of care between the council and the homeowner, found there were no special factors distinguishing negligence in the construction of a building from negligence in the manufacture of consumer

[92] ibid 4.
[93] *Mallonland Pty Ltd v Advanta Seeds Pty Ltd* [2024] HCA 25 ('*Mallonland*').
[94] ibid [1]–[2] (Gageler CJ, Gordon, Steward, Gleeson, Jagot and Beech-Jones JJ).
[95] Edelman J concurred with the decision of the majority but wrote a separate opinion. In the main, he disagreed with adopting vulnerability as the central salient feature to found a duty of care: ibid [102]–[103].
[96] ibid [32].
[97] ibid [33].
[98] ibid [34].
[99] ibid [41].
[100] ibid [22].

goods.[101] In this regard Lord Keith expressed caution as introducing an implied warranty of quality may open the floodgates for such claims:

> [I]f such a duty is incumbent upon the local authority, a similar duty must necessarily be incumbent also upon the builder of the house. If the builder of the house is to be so subject, there can be no grounds in logic or in principle for not extending liability upon like grounds to the manufacturer of a chattel. That would open on an exceedingly wide field of claims, involving the introduction of something in the nature of a transmissible warranty of quality.[102]

The Court in *RSP*, however, agreed with the reasons expressed in *Bryan* justifying treating chattels and buildings differently – first, that the investment in real property is likely to represent a very significant investment in an individual's lifetime; and second, that the permanence of realty gives rise to a much greater expectation than a chattel.[103] Thean JA held that both these arguments apply a fortiori in Singapore, where land is not only scarce but expensive, and to treat houses and consumer goods alike 'ignores simple realities'[104] which are instrumental in dictating the degree of reliance placed upon the persons building or designing the built structure.[105] Singapore's pragmatic adoption of *Bryan* (sans any requirement of vulnerability), rather than following the House of Lords and subsequent developments in Australian law, is to be welcomed. As Bright and McFarlane note, 'the inability to recover in tort for carelessly caused pure economic loss has particularly harsh consequences for purchasers of domestic property'.[106]

In *RSP*, the MCST of the development incurred costs in carrying out rectification to the damaged unit, as well as reinforcement works to the wall claddings to avoid future injury to persons and/or damage to property. Although the architects argued that they owed no duty of care to the MCST for its pure economic loss, the Court disagreed, holding that there was a sufficient degree of proximity in the relationship between the architects and the MCST justifying the existence of a duty to exercise reasonable care to avoid the loss sustained by the MCST. Writing for the Court, Thean JA held that the architects were engaged by the developers to design and supervise the construction of the condominium and in this regard, the developers had relied on the architects' exercise of reasonable care and skill.[107] Linking the duty owed to the developer to that owed to the MCST, Thean JA held that the management corporation 'was merely a statutory creation and was a successor to the developers with respect to the common property'.[108]

[101] *RSP* [1999] SGCA 30, [1999] 2 SLR(R) 134 [43].
[102] *Murphy* [1991] 1 AC 398 (HL) 469.
[103] *RSP* [1999] SGCA 30, [1999] 2 SLR(R) 134 [43].
[104] ibid [43].
[105] ibid.
[106] S Bright and B McFarlane, 'Private Law Failings and Policy Development Following the Grenfell Tower Fire' in J Gardner et al (eds), *Politics and Policy of the Private Law: Volume 1: Tort, Property and Equity* (Oxford, Hart Publishing, 2023).
[107] *RSP* [1999] SGCA 30, [1999] 2 SLR(R) 134 [38].
[108] ibid.

The appellate court thus found an adequate relationship of proximity because the defendant architects knew that the MCST would depend on their care and skill in the design of the construction of the common property.[109] Regarding the design breaches committed by the architects, the appellate court in *RSP* endorsed the trial court's findings that RSP (1) failed to provide movement joints in the gable ends walls, (2) failed to provide adequate wall ties between the inner and outer leaves of the cavity brickwork, and (3) failed to provide an adequate method of adhesion in the claddings.[110] One argument made by the architects asserted that the damage suffered was due to the bad workmanship on the part of the main contractors, and as they had supervised the works adequately they should not be held responsible for bad workmanship. This was rejected by the Court flowing from the finding of fact that the design of the wall was flawed – 'even if the walls had been built to the utmost quality, they would have still collapsed because of the poor design'.[111]

A related issue is whether the MCST would have had a direct cause of action against the developer. Although there is good authority in Singapore that a developer can be held liable for pure economic loss caused by bad workmanship,[112] the Court held on the facts that, while the MCST depended on the developer to 'unite resources and to co-ordinate the execution of the project',[113] it depended on the architect to 'get the design of the building right'.[114] Thus, it appears that the design failure on the part of the architect meant that neither the developer nor the subcontractor engaged to actually lay the bricks and tiles on the wall would have been found liable as the architect's breaches in design was the material cause of the loss. What is clear, however, is that the case is authority for holding that in general, service providers either further upstream or downstream can be held tortiously liable for pure economic loss. Notwithstanding, it should be noted that where a homeowner does not have privity with the developer and where the developer itself is not negligent, such a developer is generally entitled to rely on the 'independent contractor' defence in tort.

(ii) In the Absence of Privity, a Non-negligent Builder is Generally Entitled to Rely on the 'Independent Contractor' Defence if Sued in Tort

In *Seasons Park*,[115] one issue before the Court of Appeal involved the 'independent contractor' defence which was raised by a developer who was sued for

[109] ibid.
[110] ibid [47].
[111] ibid [57].
[112] *Ocean Front* [1995] SGCA 79, [1995] 3 SLR(R) 653.
[113] *RSP* [1999] SGCA 30, [1999] 2 SLR(R) 134 [39].
[114] ibid.
[115] *Management Corporation Strata Title Plan No 2297 v Seasons Park Ltd* [2005] SGCA 16, [2005] 2 SLR(R) 613 ('*Seasons Park*').

defects appearing in the common property of a condominium development. There, the Court endorsed the general rule that the developer's tortious duty is simply to exercise proper care in appointing an independent contractor,[116] and, where this was done, it would not generally be vicariously liable for the negligence of its independent contractor, workers or agents in the execution of the building works.[117] It is noted that the Court of Appeal articulated the 'independent contractor' defence as one where the developer or builder is not vicariously liable for the tortfeasor's negligence because the negligent party was not an employee or akin to an employee, being an independent contractor. As Goudkamp notes, however, this may be somewhat of a misnomer because this 'defence' is better understood as a denial of one of the requisite elements for establishing the tort.[118]

Seasons Park noted that, from a contract perspective, where the developer has agreed to deliver a unit or building in accordance with certain specifications but has failed to do so, it would be found liable, regardless of any fault on the developer's part. In respect of such a contractual claim, the developer cannot plead in defence that it has engaged competent professionals to design the project and supervise its construction, and an experienced contractor to build it.[119] In respect of subpurchasers, ie owners who did not purchase the property from the developer, the Court clarified that such persons could only sue in contract if the original purchaser is willing to lend their name to being a co-plaintiff (subject to the subpurchaser indemnifying the original purchaser as to costs and other possible liabilities) to the action in contract.[120]

Although Chao JA is technically right in stating that such arrangements could be set out in the agreement for the subsale from the original purchaser to the subpurchaser, this suggestion may be commercially unwieldy because there is little incentive for the original purchaser to agree. Further, depending on how much time has passed since the original sale, the first purchaser may no longer exist (passed away or wound up), or simply be uncontactable. Another problem is one of timing. If the defect only arose after the original purchaser conveyed the property to its subpurchaser, then the bundle of assigned rights may not include any actionable claim against the builder.[121] Owners who do not purchase their property from the developer should therefore be aware that in the absence of fault on the part of the developer, their recourse would lie in tort, against the contractor or architect which breached its proximate duty of care in the execution or design of the building works.

[116] ibid [37].
[117] ibid. The Court noted that at common law, ultra-hazardous activity and works done in or on a highway would be non-delegable ([38]). These exceptions do not apply in the construction of a building.
[118] See J Goudkamp, *Tort Law Defences* (Oxford, Hart Publishing, 2016) 46.
[119] ibid [42].
[120] ibid [43].
[121] *Dawson v Great Northern and City Railway Company* [1905] 1 KB 260, 268–9.

(iii) The BCA Imposes Statutory Non-delegable Duties on Builders and Architects Only in Respect of Building and Structural Safety

In *Tiong Aik*,[122] the MCST of a condominium development sued the builder and architect for building defects in the development's common property that were caused by their subcontractor's negligence. These defects did not compromise the building's structural safety. The MCST's arguments that the architect and builder owed it non-delegable duties to ensure that the common property was designed and built with reasonable care was rejected by the appellate court. The *Tiong Aik* court noted, 'in the context of the tort of negligence, a person is generally only held liable for his [*sic*] own carelessness, and not for the carelessness of others'.[123]

There are two key exceptions to this principle: vicarious liability and non-delegable duties.[124] In respect of vicarious liability, a non-negligent employer may be liable for torts committed by its employees, but would not be liable for the negligence of its independent contractors.[125] In respect of the doctrine of non-delegable duties, the law (either common law or statute) provides that delegation does not enable the duty-bearer to escape tortious liability because the legal responsibility for the performance of the duty resides in the duty-bearer.[126]

One difference between the two exceptions is that, while vicarious liability is secondary, the tortious liability imposed pursuant to a breach of non-delegable duty is primary.[127] In the case of vicarious liability, the employer's liability is said to be secondary because liability does not arise because of its own negligence, but because of its employee's negligence.[128] In the case of a breach of a non-delegable duty, however, this is said to attract primary liability because the employer itself has breached a certain non-delegable duty.[129] In the case of breaches of non-delegable duty attracting primary liability, this means that the developer would be directly responsible for the tort, whereas in the case of vicarious liability, the obligation on the part of the developer arises only if the builder or workmen who is the directly responsible party fails to fulfil it.

Regarding vicarious liability, *Tiong Aik* affirms the position articulated in *Seasons Park*: where an independent contractor is concerned, only the party that itself is negligent would be held liable in tort, and it is reasonable for a builder or developer to rely on a subcontractor to discharge its duty with the requisite care and skill.

[122] *Tiong Aik* [2016] SGCA 40; [2016] 4 SLR 521.
[123] ibid [19].
[124] ibid [25].
[125] ibid [19].
[126] ibid [21].
[127] G Chan, *The Law of Torts in Singapore*, 2nd edn (Singapore, Singapore Academy of Law, 2016) [19.001].
[128] *Tiong Aik* [2016] SGCA 40; [2016] 4 SLR 521 [20].
[129] ibid [25].

Tiong Aik also considered the ambit of non-delegable duties at length, and, importantly, held that the language of the BCA only gives rise to limited non-delegable duties on the part of builders and architects, in the main concerning building safety, construction in accordance with approved plans, and compliance with building regulations.[130] In so holding, the appellate court rejected the MCST's arguments that there was a non-delegable statutory duty placing legal responsibility on the builder and architect to ensure that *all* aspects of the building and design of the condominium were completed with reasonable care.[131] The Court emphasised that the BCA only sought to impose legal responsibility and protect building occupiers and owners in respect of building and structural safety, and not in relation to other aspects of the construction such as workmanship or aesthetic flaws.[132]

This appears to contrast with the earlier mentioned English case of *Murphy*. As pointed out in Nolan's analysis of that case, their Lordships had reasoned that recovery for defects in quality was a matter for contract. No distinction could be drawn between dangerous and non-dangerous defects: once the danger was discovered, the gist of the complaint was not the danger itself, but the inability to use the dangerous thing without incurring repair costs.[133]

While English tort law excludes claims for pure economic loss, Singapore tort law permits a tort claim for both dangerous and non-dangerous defects, where the builder or architect (as the case may be) is at fault. However, in relation to dangerous defects in Singapore, the courts have held that there exists a non-delegable duty on the part of the builder or architect even when these parties have not been personally negligent.

Compared to Singapore and England, Canada appears to take a middle-road approach. Chamberlain[134] notes that in *Winnipeg Condominium*[135] the Supreme Court of Canada found that a subsequent purchaser could sue a contractor for the costs of repairing building defects, provided that those defects posed a 'real and substantial danger to the occupants of the building'.[136] La Forest J left open whether damages should also be recoverable in the case of non-dangerous defects.[137] The English cases of *D&F Estates* and *Murphy* were not followed by the Canadian court. Under English law, the costs of repairing building defects of any kind – as opposed to the losses caused by physical damage – are considered pure economic losses and hence unrecoverable in tort. Based on her empirical research, Chamberlain postulates that *Winnipeg Condominium* contributes to building safety in Canada by providing an incentive for dangerous defects to be repaired before they cause

[130] ibid [33].
[131] ibid.
[132] ibid [35].
[133] Nolan (n 64) 157.
[134] Chamberlain (n 79) esp section II.
[135] *Winnipeg Condominium* [1995] 1 SCR 85.
[136] ibid [21].
[137] ibid [41].

physical injury.[138] Because Singapore permits claims for pure economic loss for all types of building defects (on a negligence standard), as well as imposing a non-delegable duty in relation to dangerous defects, it seems that tort law in Singapore can also be said to enhance building safety.

Although it was invited to do so by the MCST, the appellate court in *Tiong Aik* declined to hold that there was at common law a *general* non-delegable duty imposed on the builder and the architect to build and design buildings with reasonable care (regardless whether the defect related to structural safety).[139] Again referring to the purpose of the BCA to deal with the structural safety and soundness of a building, the Court reasoned that imposing a broad non-delegable duty of care on construction professionals would be 'inconsistent with the spirit'[140] of the Act, and possibly inconsistent with parliamentary intention.[141] A policy consideration that did appear to give the appellate court some pause, however, was that, without a non-delegable duty imposed on builders and architects, 'management corporations might have to take up additional applications to ascertain the correct defendant, and might even end up suing a defendant who could not meet the full judgment sum'.[142] Nonetheless, in maintaining its position that no broader non-delegable duty should exist, the Court held that this was 'part and parcel of any litigation and was an ordinary risk endemic in any investment, including the purchase of a property'.[143]

Considering the case law in Singapore, what can be concluded is this: where building and structural safety is concerned, builders and architects are saddled, via the BCA, with a non-delegable duty and cannot rely on downstream subcontractors to defray such risk. However, where the defects do not relate to safety, builders may rely on the 'independent contractor' defence to avoid vicarious liability for the negligence of the persons they engage to do the work. Further, where safety is a concern, both direct costs caused by the defect as well as the funds needed to rectify defective works, ie pure economic loss, are compensable even in the absence of privity because the courts recognise that there is a duty of care owed to the occupant by the person legally responsible for the work.

Compared to England, Canada and Australia, this aspect of tort law is considerably more liberal, and has the effect of enhancing building safety. By giving a direct cause of action in tort to a victim, builders and architects alike are incentivised to place building safety at the heart of their work, an outcome that comports with the purpose of the statutory regime.

[138] Chamberlain (n 79) 149.
[139] *Tiong Aik* [2016] SGCA 40, [2016] 4 SLR 521 [64].
[140] ibid [72].
[141] ibid [72].
[142] ibid [89].
[143] ibid [89].

B. Occupier's Liability

The Singapore courts have taken a pragmatic and balanced approach to occupier's liability, even in the face of the immediacy of a tragedy. In *ICB*,[144] a case stemming from the Hotel New World collapse, the Court of Appeal dismissed a claim by an invitee seeking compensation under occupier's liability. The Court reasoned that, even though there were signs of unusual danger to the building, it was difficult for the occupier to ascertain the *extent* of the unusual danger at that point in time – and the Court should not be swayed by retrospective harm to hold the occupier liable.

Although Singapore used to adopt the traditional invitee–licensee–trespasser trichotomy to determine the duty of care owed to someone who came on land, the Court of Appeal in *See Toh Siew Kee v Ho Ah Lam Ferrocement (Pte) Ltd*[145] held that the trichotomy created a 'complex, confusing and unpredictable legal landscape'.[146] The appellate court also held that the arbitrary distinction between the static condition of property and dynamic activities done on property is not founded on logic or principle but 'is rooted in convoluted English legal history'.[147] The *See Toh Siew Kee* Court thus held that the law on occupier's liability is a mere subset of the general law of negligence.[148] Accordingly, VK Rajah JA stated that the appropriate test to establish a duty of care owed by the occupier would be dependent on proximity and policy considerations as set out in *Spandeck Engineering (S) Pte Ltd v Defence Science & Technology Agency*.[149]

In coming to its decision, the Court explained that the high population density of Singapore results in more significant 'neighbourly' considerations, and the urban realities of Singapore are a far cry from the origins of the common law's feudalist landlord. VK Rajah JA thus held that the proximity test advocated would incentivise rational cost-avoiding measures because the occupier who controls the premises would be in the best position to prevent injury to entrants. It remains an open question whether this reasoning if applied in *ICB* would have led to a successful claim for occupier's liability.

Subsequently, in *Singapore Rifle Association v The Singapore Shooting Association*,[150] the Court of Appeal reviewed *See Toh Siew Kim*. The Court explained that, in respect of occupier's liability law in Singapore, this was essentially a fact-sensitive analysis of whether there is a prima-facie duty of care on the part of an occupier under the first stage of the *Spandeck* approach. Further, while in the great majority of cases occupiers would de jure owe lawful entrants a prima-facie

[144] *Industrial Commercial Bank v Tan Swa Eng* [1995] SGCA 54, [1995] 2 SLR(R) 385 ('*ICB*').

[145] *See Toh Siew Kee v Ho Ah Lam Ferrocement (Pte) Ltd* [2013] SGCA 29, [2013] 3 SLR 284.

[146] ibid [26].

[147] ibid [21].

[148] ibid [122].

[149] *Spandeck Engineering (S) Pte Ltd v Defence Science & Technology Agency* [2007] SGCA 37, [2007] 4 SLR(R) 100.

[150] *Singapore Rifle Association v The Singapore Shooting Association* [2018] SGCA 42.

duty of care because there would be sufficient legal proximity, the mere fact that a person is an occupier with control over the property and/or the activities carried out there is not necessarily determinative in this regard.[151] Applying this formulation to potentially dangerous buildings means that occupiers would in most cases come under a reasonable duty to inform entrants to the land of these risks. The scope of this duty may even extend to prevent entry on the land altogether, should the potential harm to an entrant be particularly high, eg someone with known sensitivities.

C. Nuisance and the Duty to Provide Lateral Support

In *Xpress Print v Monocrafts Pte Ltd*,[152] the Singapore Court of Appeal departed from the old common law rule in *Dalton v Angus*[153] to hold that all landowners owe strict duties of care in relation to their adjacent plots, regardless of whether the land is in its natural state or the land has a building on it. *Dalton* provides that there is only a duty to provide lateral support to neighbouring land for whatever occurs naturally on the land. As buildings are not natural, a landowner would not ordinarily owe a duty to provide lateral support to a building constructed on the land. However, *Dalton* preserves the common law rule that the provision of lateral support can be gained by prescription, ie if one landowner had been providing lateral support to a building on his neighbour's land for 20 years, the landowner cannot thereafter cease to provide such support. Yong CJ described the old common law as a 'curious proposition':

> If my neighbour's land is in its natural state, I may not remove the soil on my land without providing alternative support for his [*sic*] land; but if my neighbour expends money and effort in building a bungalow on his land, then I may excavate with impunity, even though his bungalow may crumble to the ground. Yet, my liberty to ignore the support required by his house is not perpetual, but lasts only for 20 years, at which time any indolence in pursuing my right to remove my soil is transformed into a positive right of support in respect of his dwelling.[154]

Yong CJ departed from the natural state/prescription test in *Dalton* and held that Singapore's high land-use pattern justified the right of support because landowners must use their own property in such a manner as not to injure that of another. In holding that the law must adapt itself to modern conditions and local policies, the Court of Appeal thus held:

> We are of the view that the proposition that a landowner may excavate his [*sic*] land with impunity, sending his neighbour's building and everything in it crashing to the ground,

[151] ibid [24].
[152] *Xpress Print v Monocrafts Pte Ltd* [2000] SGCA 37, [2000] 2 SLR(R) 614 ('*Xpress Print*').
[153] *Dalton v Angus* [1881] 6 App Cas 740.
[154] *Xpress Print* [2000] SGCA 37, [2002] 2 SLR(R) 614 [34].

> is a proposition inimical to a society which respects each citizen's property rights, and we cannot assent to it … the current state of affairs cannot be allowed to persist.[155]

Accordingly, Yong CJ held that a landowner has a right of support in respect of their buildings from neighbouring lands from the time such buildings are erected, and that the right is infringed as soon as, but not until, damage is sustained in consequence of the withdrawal of that support.[156] The measure of damages to be awarded is the general tort measure, ie all foreseeable losses suffered by the injured party as a result of the wrongful act.[157]

Xpress Print is a prime example of how private law can buttress building safety. There are, however, some unanswered puzzles regarding the case and its aftermath. What is the scope of a neighbouring landowner's duty with respect to lateral support if the adjacent landowner claiming support had not obtained planning permission, or had constructed an illegal structure? Although this was not addressed, it is postulated that, if the construction was beyond the load contemplated by the site, then no duty should exist because the illegality should not enjoy tortious protection. Another point of consideration is dealing with provisions to the State Lands Act 1920 which came about some 15 years after *Xpress Print*. In May 2015, the new section 10 of the State Lands Act 1920 provided that there is an implied easement of mutual subjacent support for all landowners which allows entry into the subservient tenement to install or maintain support. The Explanatory Statement to the State Lands Bill 2015 reads:

> The new section 3C [now section 10] clarifies the common law on natural rights of subjacent support. For every parcel of land, the new section 3C implies in favour of the grantee or lessee of the parcel of land, and as appurtenant thereto, an easement for the subjacent support of that parcel of land by the subterranean space capable of affording support. This is in line with the Court of Appeal decision in *Xpress Print Pte Ltd v Monocraft Pte Ltd*.[158]

What remains unsettled is whether section 10 of the State Lands Act 1920 has fully codified *Xpress Print* or whether both case law and statute are discrete sources of rules which are similar albeit different. Section 10's expansion of landowner obligations in relation to the nature of the obligations owed to adjacent lots suggests that *Xpress* may have been only partially codified. In *Xpress*, the Court held that there was a duty on the adjoining landowner not to excavate his land without first securing adequate support for his neighbour's building.[159] In *Afro-Asia Shipping Company v Da Zhong Investment* (a case predating the implied easements under

[155] ibid [37].
[156] ibid [51].
[157] ibid [52].
[158] Explanatory Notes to the State Lands (Amendment) Bill 2015, 9.
[159] P Pillai, 'The Primacy of the Principle of Reciprocity in the Singapore Land Regime' (2001) 13 *Singapore Academy of Law Journal* 198, 210.

the State Lands Act 1920), this was observed as prohibiting an active interference with existing support.[160]

The adjacent neighbour is thus not obligated to undertake positive duties unless any original support was removed and *Xpress Print* is consistent with *Dalton* which categorises the right of support to buildings (acquired by prescription) as a negative easement.[161] This is in line with the notion that a right of support in this context does not obligate a neighbour to take any active steps to maintain lateral support, with the servient tenement's compliance being passive in nature.[162] In contrast, however, section 10(2)(a) of the State Lands Act 1920 implies a positive obligation on subjacent landowners to allow the installation and erection of structural supports in their parcel of land.[163] Such positive duties appear to depart from the original exhortation of 'not to injure'.[164]

Significantly, *Xpress Print* stated that the action for the breach of the appellant's right of support was 'akin to an action in nuisance'.[165] Although the *Xpress Print* court analogised an action for the breach of the right of support to an action in nuisance, commentators have appeared to categorise a breach of the right of support as a type of nuisance instead.[166] Thus, in *Eng Yuen Yee v Grandfort Builders Pte Ltd*, the Court held that an action for the breach of the right of support articulated in *Xpress Print* is either akin to an action in nuisance or is itself a type of actionable nuisance.[167] If this is true, then apart from the statutory easement granted under the State Lands Act 1920, building owners suffering building subsidence due to excavation works done on their neighbour's land may rely on *Xpress Print* to found a cause of action in nuisance.

D. Contracts for the Sale of Land, Planning Permission and Latent Defects in Title

How does the caveat emptor maxim when buying land interact with any duty of disclosure on the part of a vendor? Patent defects, whether in quality or title, need not be actively disclosed. In respect of latent defects, there is a duty on the part of a

[160] *Afro-Asia Shipping Company (Pte) Ltd v Da Zhong Investment Pte Ltd* [2003] SGHC 286, [2004] 2 SLR(R) 117 [59].

[161] *Halsbury's Laws of Singapore*, 2nd edn (1999) vol 14(2), para 170.0392.

[162] K Gray and SF Gray, *Elements of Land Law*, 5th edn (Oxford, Oxford University Press, 2009) 20.

[163] State Lands Act 1920, s 10(2)(a).

[164] E Chew, 'Digging Deep into the Ownership of Underground Space: Recent Changes in Respect of Subterranean Land Use' (2017) *Singapore Journal of Legal Studies* 1, 11.

[165] *Xpress Print* [2000] SGCA 37, [2002] 2 SLR(R) 614 [52].

[166] HW Tang and K Low, *Tan Sook Yee's Principles of Singapore Land Law*, 4th edn (Singapore, LexisNexis, 2019) [20.14]; MA Jones, AM Dugdale, M Simpson (eds), *Clerk & Lindsell on Torts*, 21st edn (London, Sweet & Maxwell, 2014) [20]–[139] to [20]–[146]; HW Tang, 'The Right of Lateral Support of Buildings from the Adjoining Land' (2002) *Conveyancer and Property Lawyer* 237, 257; and Pillai (n 159) 201.

[167] *Eng Yuen Yee v Grandfort Builders Pte Ltd* [2018] SGHCR 1 [23].

vendor to disclose latent defects of title but there is no duty on the part of a vendor to disclose latent defects of quality.[168] In *Huang Ching Hwee*, the purchaser sought to rescind a contract for the sale of land on the basis that there was a latent defect of title because the vendor had carried out significant alterations and demolitions to parts of the two-storey bungalow without planning permission. These alterations included, among other things, constructing a roof over the patio, demolishing the garage and installing new roofing to parts of the dining and kitchen area.[169] Under the BCA, these alterations constituted 'building works' and thus are considered to be 'development' of the land requiring planning permission under the Planning Act 1998.

Notwithstanding, the appellate court held that the failure to obtain planning permission was a latent defect of quality which the vendor was not obliged to disclose because there was no inevitability that the planning authorities would take action against the property owner for failing to obtain planning permission.[170] Khoo J, who delivered the judgment of the Court, reasoned that there was no evidence that the alterations made to the property actually contravened the building regulations but merely that the approval for the works had not been obtained.[171] This suggests that the Court considered that the alterations were not illegal per se, but the vendor had simply failed to seek the requisite planning permission. Presumably because the purchaser did not argue that the alterations affected the property's safety, Khoo J observed that, 'where no questions [*sic*] of safety is involved, there is no reason to believe that approval to retain the works must necessarily be ruled out'.[172] This dictum suggests that, if a question of safety arises from the unauthorised works, this could lead to enforcement action against the property owner, and so this would amount to a latent defect in title. With respect, it is difficult for a purchaser to prove that the alterations may cause the property to be structurally unsafe – because no submissions for the alterations were made to the authorities at the time, there is simply no evidence either way.

If it is accepted that an important aspect of obtaining planning permission for building works is to ensure minimum standards of safety – because a qualified architect or engineer is needed to sign off the plans – then the appellate court's judgment may arguably be too liberal. For instance, under part 4 of the BCA, the Commissioner may order building works to stop if they deem it dangerous, and appoint a qualified person to carry out the requisite investigations and tests.[173] It would seem at odds with the spirit of the BCA if a failure to obtain the requisite planning permission for building works is deemed safe unless evidence were presented to prove otherwise. It may be more prudent for the court to hold that

[168] *Huang Ching Hwee v Heng Kay Poh* [1992] SGCA 79, [1992] 3 SLR(R) 452.
[169] ibid [3].
[170] ibid [53]–[56].
[171] ibid [53].
[172] ibid.
[173] BCA, s 23.

the failure to obtain permission for 'building works' amounts to a latent defect in title unless there is expert evidence to show that the alterations did not make the building unsafe, and hence, following the Court of Appeal's logic, that the regulatory authorities would not take enforcement action against the property owner.

Finally, it should be noted that the principle of caveat emptor in the contract for the sale of land between a non-developer vendor and the purchaser operates on a different plane from the rule that allows for claims made by a purchaser against a negligent builder or architect for pure economic loss. The former prevents the purchaser from suing the vendor in the subsale, but does not bar the subpurchaser from suing a negligent builder or architect.

V. Conclusion

This chapter has given an overview of the statutory regime governing building safety in Singapore, and discussed its close and sometimes overlapping interplay with private law. In tort, it is clear that Singapore law gives subpurchasers tortious recourse against builders and architects where these professionals have been negligent, even for pure economic loss cases, and regardless of whether the building defects pertained to safety per se. This is considerably more generous than the position in England and Australia, which, in the main, bars pure economic losses of this kind, and Canada, which allows such claims only where they relate to building safety concerns.

Additionally, the courts in Singapore have imposed a non-delegable duty on builders and architects for building defects relating to safety – this means that the professionals would not be able to rely on the independent contractor defence to avoid liability. Builders and architects in Singapore can only escape liability if (1) they have not been negligent in appointing or supervising the subcontractor and (2) the defect does not relate to building safety. The Singapore position is characteristically pragmatic. Given the urban realities of Singapore, limiting liability in the tort of negligence to actual physical loss would be unnecessarily pedantic, even if more consistent with English tort law. In respect of private law, this chapter has also considered the law of nuisance, the duty to provide lateral support and latent defects of title in contracts for the sale of land.

In the two English cases highlighted,[174] tensions between private law principles and building safety have not been resolved in ways that promote the latter. Whether private law should explicitly consider building safety in the development of its jurisprudence is thus an interesting question this chapter poses. What can be said is that while there can be no perfect system to govern building safety, several features in Singapore's legal system that advance building safety may certainly be of interest, especially to other densely populated cities.

[174] *D&F Estates* [1989] AC 177; *Murphy* [1991] 1 AC 398.

5

Building Safety in Canada: Has *Winnipeg Condominium* Had an Impact?

ERIKA CHAMBERLAIN*

I. Introduction

In this chapter, I provide a Canadian perspective on the role of private law in promoting building safety. The natural focus of such a study is the 1995 Supreme Court of Canada decision in *Winnipeg Condominium Corporation No 36 v Bird Construction Co Ltd*,[1] which established that subsequent purchasers of buildings could sue builders for the costs of repairing dangerous defects. Although *Winnipeg Condominium* is well known as representing a category of recoverable pure economic loss, its practical impact has not, to my knowledge, been carefully studied. As explained below, *Winnipeg Condominium* is based on the policy rationale that it is preferable to repair dangerous defects before they cause injury. Thus, in theory at least, it should contribute to building safety in Canada. The centre of this chapter is an empirical review of the cases that have applied the principles of *Winnipeg Condominium*. I aimed to gain insight into the types of defects that have been considered sufficiently dangerous to merit recovery in tort for preventive repair, as well as any additional principles that have been considered by the Canadian courts (such as the latency of the defect and the imminence of the danger). My review also uncovered an interesting case study from Atlantic Canada, where several dozen buildings had to be remediated as a result of faulty roof joists produced by one manufacturer. This was the clearest instance of *Winnipeg Condominium* being used as part of an effective building safety campaign. In particular, the engineering experts who were retained pursuant to some early tort

* I would like to thank Shan Malhi, Western University JD Candidate 2025, for his extensive background work on the empirical analysis in this paper.

[1] *Winnipeg Condominium Corporation No 36 v Bird Construction Co Ltd* [1995] 1 SCR 85 ('*Winnipeg Condominium*').

claims helped to uncover widespread problems with welding quality, leading to province-wide campaigns of inspection and remediation. These cases thus illustrate how tort law and tort litigation can play a role in the complex systems of quality control, professional regulation and government oversight in the construction industry.

My review also helped to identify some future research questions and new legal issues related to dangerous defects that are currently before the courts. Finally, I assess the continuing influence of *Winnipeg Condominium* in light of recent Supreme Court of Canada jurisprudence on the duty of care as it relates to pure economic loss. In spite of the Supreme Court's increasing emphasis on the parties' contractual arrangements, the lower courts remain persuaded by the policy rationale of repairing dangerous defects before they cause harm. On the whole, it seems that *Winnipeg Condominium* has had a positive, albeit modest, effect on building safety in Canada. It has helped both commercial and residential building owners to recover the costs of preventive repairs, particularly in buildings with structural defects, before catastrophe occurs. That said, the tort claims are primarily about cost-shifting rather than about whether repairs will be undertaken, and so the primary beneficiaries may well be property insurance companies. But, to the extent that *Winnipeg Condominium* has shifted the costs of repair to the parties responsible for the defects, it should also provide an incentive for builders to construct buildings without dangerous defects in the first place. This is an important contrast to jurisdictions in which negligent builders are able to avoid liability to subsequent purchasers – a situation that provides weak incentives for building safety and sits uneasily with a sense of justice for the average homeowner.

II. The Decision in *Winnipeg Condominium*

Winnipeg Condominium was the Canadian entry in a series of building defect cases decided by the apex courts in Commonwealth jurisdictions between the 1970s and 1990s.[2] These cases debated whether building defects were a form of property damage or pure economic loss, and whether that distinction was even plausible.[3] They also reflected broader trends in each jurisdiction whether and on what bases to expand or retract the scope of negligence liability, and the appropriate approach to recognising novel duties of care. This included arguments on the role of policy considerations in the duty analysis and on the potential for concurrent liability in tort and contract. *Winnipeg Condominium* can be understood in light of these contexts.

The defect in question involved the masonry of a 15-storey apartment building. Specifically, a large piece of stone cladding (about a storey high) had fallen from

[2] For a helpful summary, see S Todd, 'Policy Issues in Defective Property Cases' in JW Neyers, E Chamberlain and S Pitel (eds), *Emerging Issues in Tort Law* (Oxford, Hart Publishing, 2007) 199, 200–11; and D Nolan, 'Defective Premises and Economic Loss: A Problem Best Left to Legislation?', this volume ch 6, section III.

[3] See Sir R Cooke, 'An Impossible Distinction' (1991) 107 *LQR* 46.

the ninth floor of the building down to the street below. Thankfully, no one was injured. Following that incident, the Condominium Corporation commissioned inspections of the cladding, and ultimately had all the cladding replaced, at a cost exceeding C$1.5 million. It sued the general contractor, masonry subcontractor and architectural firm in negligence. The claim was struck out by the Manitoba Court of Appeal,[4] which applied the House of Lords decision in *D&F Estates Ltd v Church Commissioners for England*[5] in concluding that the plaintiff's expenses were a form of economic loss. As Lord Bridge explained,

> liability can only arise if the defect remains hidden until the defective structure causes personal injury or damage to property. … If the defect is discovered before any damage is done, the loss sustained by the owner of the structure, who has to repair or demolish it to avoid a potential source of danger to third parties, would seem to be purely economic.[6]

The House of Lords and Manitoba Court of Appeal found that such economic loss is non-recoverable unless it is governed by contract or a relationship of reliance between the parties.[7]

The Supreme Court of Canada agreed that the loss in question was pure economic loss. However, unlike the English courts, the Supreme Court found that this loss should be recoverable in negligence, even if the plaintiff was a subsequent purchaser of the building who had no contractual relationship with the builder.[8] Although a subsequent purchaser would not be able to enforce contractual provisions relating to, for example, higher-quality materials or 'special ornamental features', the requirement that the building be constructed in accordance with reasonable standards was an independent duty in tort.[9] A duty of care could be established through an analysis of reasonable foreseeability and proximity (a concept that was still loosely defined in 1995), and was amply supported by reasons of policy.

Indeed, having reviewed the English jurisprudence, LaForest J, writing for the Court, found that the rule of non-recovery created exactly the wrong kind of incentives. He explained:

> Apart from the logical force of holding contractors liable for the cost of repair of dangerous defects, there is also a strong underlying policy justification for imposing liability in these cases. Under the law as developed in *D&F Estates* and *Murphy*, the plaintiff who moves quickly and responsibly to fix a defect before it causes injury to persons or

[4] *Winnipeg Condominium Corporation No 36 v Bird Construction Co* (1993) 85 Man R (2d) 81 (CA).

[5] *D&F Estates Ltd v Church Commissioners for England* [1989] AC 177 (HL) ('*D&F Estates*').

[6] *D&F Estates* [1989] AC 177, 206 (HL). For criticism of the English approach, see JG Fleming, 'Anticipatory Repairs of Dangerous Defects' in NJ Mullany (ed), *Torts in the Nineties* (Sydney, LBC Information Services, 1997) 59–60, complaining that the House of Lords 'paid no regard to tort law's overriding aim and function of preventing accident losses. … While motivated to slay the dragon of tortious economic loss, their Lordships sacrificed its traditional protégé, the victim of physical risk.'

[7] *Winnipeg Condominium* [1995] 1 SCR 85 [16].

[8] The Supreme Court stressed that, unlike in England, concurrent liability in contract and tort was an accepted part of Canadian law: see ibid [23]–[26].

[9] ibid [25].

> damage to property must do so at his or her own expense. By contrast, the plaintiff who, either intentionally or through neglect, allows a defect to develop into an accident may benefit at law from the costly and potentially tragic consequences. In my view, this legal doctrine is difficult to justify because it serves to encourage, rather than discourage, reckless and hazardous behaviour. Maintaining a bar against recoverability for the cost of repair of dangerous defects provides no incentive for plaintiffs to mitigate potential losses and tends to encourage economically inefficient behaviour.[10]

This reasoning is important for the subject of this book because it stresses the preventive function of allowing recovery for the costs of repairing dangerous defects; building owners should be encouraged to repair defects before they lead to tragedy. In theory, then, the rule in *Winnipeg Condominium* should improve building safety in Canada.

Significantly, recovery pursuant to *Winnipeg Condominium* is limited to defects that pose a 'real and substantial danger'.[11] This was relevant to several issues. First, keeping in mind that the duty of care at the time was based largely on the issue of reasonable foreseeability, the foreseeability of 'real and substantial danger' to inhabitants brought the purported duty of care in line with other, uncontroversial cases where the defendant's negligence posed a foreseeable risk of physical injury.[12] Second, it helped to distinguish the tortious duty from the contractual one, which would include matters such as the quality of materials or workmanship, but was limited to the original purchaser.[13] Third, it was relevant to the main policy issue in the case, namely, that the law should provide an incentive for building owners to repair dangerous defects before they cause injury.[14] Finally, the requirement of 'real and substantial danger' helped to counter arguments about potentially indeterminate or disproportionate liability. According to the Court, damages would be limited to the costs of bringing the building to a non-dangerous state, and liability would only extend for the 'useful life of the building'. LaForest J explained that this would 'practically' be a shorter period in most cases, since '[w]ith the passage of time, it will become increasingly difficult for owners of a building to prove at trial that any deterioration in the building is attributable to the initial negligence of the contractor and not simply to the inevitable wear and tear suffered by every building'.[15]

Notably, LaForest J rejected Lord Keith's argument in *Murphy v Brentwood District Council* that a purchaser's 'decision to repair a dangerous defect is analogous to a decision to discard a defective article. In either case … the cost of repair

[10] ibid [37].

[11] ibid [21]. The Court (ibid [41]) discussed but declined to formally decide whether the duty of care should be extended to cover non-dangerous defects or defects affecting habitability. Subsequent lower-court decisions have largely rejected this extension of liability. See PT Burns & J Blom, *Economic Interests in Canadian Tort Law* (Markham, Ontario, LexisNexis, 2009) 382–83.

[12] *Winnipeg Condominium* [1995] 1 SCR 85 [36].

[13] ibid [33], [42].

[14] ibid [37].

[15] ibid [49]–[50].

cannot be characterised as recoverable loss because the owner of the defective article may simply discard it and thereby remove the danger.'[16] LaForest J found this argument to be perhaps appealing as a matter of 'abstract logic', but 'unrealistic' when it came to the choices faced by homeowners.[17] Given that a home represents, for most people, their largest and longest-term investment, they are unlikely to simply 'discard' or sell the home just because they identify a dangerous defect. Instead, it is reasonably foreseeable (to the builder and others) that they will incur the expenses of repairing the defect.[18]

All that said, the Court did not provide much guidance in terms of what kinds of defects would be considered 'real and substantial danger[s]', or how trial judges might draw the line between dangerous and non-dangerous defects.[19] LaForest J's formulation suggests that it is the *danger* that must be substantial, not the injury (although the potential injuries in *Winnipeg Condominium* were unquestionably serious). It is tempting to assume that the Court intended for the potential injuries themselves to be serious, which would counter arguments that repair costs could be disproportionate to the potential injuries averted. Thus, one aspect of this empirical study is to reveal what kinds of defects have been considered dangerous by the lower courts applying *Winnipeg Condominium*.

III. Empirical Analysis of Decided Cases

A. Methodology

In conducting the empirical portion of this study, I reviewed all cases that directly applied *Winnipeg Condominium* in the context of building defects for the period

[16] ibid [39], citing *Murphy v Brentwood District Council* [1991] AC 398 (HL).

[17] ibid [40].

[18] The Canadian courts have not, for the most part, extended this reasoning to dangerously defective *goods*, which can more readily be discarded. See recently *1688782 Ontario Inc v Maple Leaf Foods Inc* [2020] SCC 35, [2020] 3 SCR 504 ('*Maple Leaf Foods*'), involving contaminated ready-to-eat meats (which, as the majority noted, cannot feasibly be 'repaired' either, [58]). However, this issue is to be decided on a case-by-case basis because some goods cannot practically be discarded. The majority in *Maple Leaf Foods* cited *Plas-Tex Canada Ltd v Dow Chemical of Canada Ltd* [2004] ABCA 309, 245 DLR (4th) 650 in this regard at [52] (defective polyethylene resin used to construct 3,000 miles of natural gas pipeline). See also *Hughes v Sunbeam Corporation* (2001) 61 OR (3d) 433 (CA), where the Ontario Court of Appeal certified a class action against a manufacturer of defective smoke alarms on the basis that, although defective smoke alarms themselves are not dangerous, reliance on them could be. The Court acknowledged that a defective smoke alarm could be discarded, but concluded that this was an issue to be determined on the basis of a full factual record and did not prevent certification of the proceeding.

[19] One early commentator suggested that this would cause significant difficulties in applying *Winnipeg Condominium*. See N Rafferty, 'Case Comment: *Winnipeg Condominium v Bird Construction* – Recovery of Purely Economic Loss in the Tort of Negligence: Liability of Builders to Subsequent Purchasers for Construction Defects' (1996) 34 *Alberta Law Review* 472, 484. See also Nolan (n 2) 164–5.

from 1995 to July 2023.[20] Cases in which the damage had already occurred were excluded because they did not involve the possibility for preventive action or the promotion of safety. With one exception (explained below), I also excluded cases involving dangerous chattels, as well as cases that cited or discussed *Winnipeg Condominium* but did not apply it to the factual circumstances.

For the included cases, I identified: the relevant defects, the type of defendant(s) (eg contractor, architect, engineer, developer, inspector), and whether the defect was considered by the court to pose a 'real and substantial danger'. I also noted any additional considerations that the court took into account, such as whether the defect was latent or patent, and whether the danger was considered to be 'imminent'.

B. Results

Overall, 28 cases met the study criteria, of which 17 were resolved in favour of the plaintiff.[21] All but three of the cases involved residential buildings, including the common property of condominium corporations.

Of the 11 cases in which the defendant was successful,[22] seven were cases where the defects were considered non-dangerous (eg poor-quality roofing material,[23] hardwood floors poorly installed,[24] deficient HVAC system leading to poor air quality[25]), and five involved defects that were patent when the plaintiff purchased the building (eg leaks and mould,[26] ineffective sump pump[27]). Recovery was denied in these cases on the basis that the plaintiff had the opportunity to negotiate a purchase price that reflected the need to repair these defects. Two cases

[20] The search was conducted using the KeyCite feature of the Westlaw database. This captured all cases with written decisions citing *Winnipeg Condominium* at any stage of the proceedings, in the provincial superior and appellate courts, and the Supreme Court of Canada. The search was then sorted for relevance in terms of 'building + defect', with cases individually reviewed by a research assistant to identify those meeting the study criteria.

[21] If there was an appeal decision in a case, only the last reported decision in the litigation was counted.

[22] Some cases involved more than one basis for deciding in favour of the defendant.

[23] *Heinicke v Cooper Rankin Ltd* [2006] MBQB 273, [2007] 2 WWR 112 ('*Heinicke*') (use of untreated pine shakes as roofing material).

[24] *Hanoski v Cornerstone Homes Ltd* [2011] SKPC 75, (2011) 373 Sask R 260. The plaintiff was nevertheless successful in contract.

[25] *Clark Builders and Stantec Consulting Ltd v GO Community Centre* [2019] ABQB 706, (2019) 57 Atla LR (7th) 475 [156] ('"hot and stuffy" is not equivalent to dangerous', even in a recreational facility).

[26] See eg *Cardwell v Perthen* [2007] BCCA 313, (2007) 68 BCLR (4th) 117 [48], where the Court explained that purchasers could not sue for defects that could be discovered by a reasonable inspection and/or reasonable inquiries. Here, the effects of the leaky roof were readily observable (eg damp patches on the ceilings, swelling of walls, mould in nooks).

[27] *Thériault v Lanthier* [2010] ONSC 655, [2010] OJ No 1545 (QL). When he purchased the home, the plaintiff had disregarded the home inspector's report, which raised concerns of water infiltration.

were dismissed on account of expired limitation periods,[28] and another because the defendant's work had met the standard of care.[29]

In three cases, the defendant had argued that the defect must be not only dangerous but *imminently* dangerous. The appeal courts of Alberta,[30] Saskatchewan[31] and Ontario[32] all rejected this argument, explaining that it was neither required nor consistent with the reasoning in *Winnipeg Condominium*.[33] This issue is discussed in further detail in section V.B below.

Of the cases involving dangerous defects, the largest number (eight) concerned structural weaknesses, including poorly welded joists that could lead to roof collapse, poorly constructed retaining walls,[34] cracks in load-bearing walls[35] and the use of non-draining backfill.[36] The cases typically referred to the potential for collapse under heavy snow and ice build-up, which is of particular concern in parts of Canada. Other defects included water seepage into electrical fixtures,[37] dampness in the basement[38] and sewage/septic problems.[39] Although the cases in this latter group involve defects that could, over time, cause negative effects to the health and safety of occupants (eg respiratory or gastrointestinal conditions), one could argue that those effects are of a different character than what was at issue in *Winnipeg Condominium*. In particular, while the courts have rejected a requirement that the danger be 'imminent', the dangers involved in the leading appellate cases, such as *Winnipeg Condominium* or, in the case of chattels, *Rivtow*

[28] *Armstrong v West Vancouver (District)* [2003] BCCA 73, (2003) 233 DLR (4th) 102; *Toronto Standard Condominium Corp No 2073 v Printing Factory Lofts Inc* [2016] ONSC 6600, (2016) 72 CLR (4th) 306 ('*Printing Factory*').

[29] *Coglan v Ergas* [2009] BCSC 1170, (2009) 86 RPR (4th) 71.

[30] *Vargo v Hughes* [2013] ABCA 96, (2013) 360 DLR (4th) 653 (substantial structural defects, which could lead to collapse of roof or floors).

[31] *Roy v Thiessen* [2005] SKCA 45, (2005) 252 DLR (4th) 475 (condensation leading to rotting and decomposition of structural beams).

[32] *Mariani v Lemstra* (2004) 246 DLR (4th) 489 (Ont CA) ('*Mariani*') (cracking in load-bearing wall could lead to collapse under heavy snow load if not repaired).

[33] In a case decided subsequent to the study period, the British Columbia Court of Appeal also rejected the suggestion that the danger must be 'imminent in the sense of bound to happen immediately'. Rather, it must be a 'presently existing risk': *Centurion Apartment Properties Limited Partnership v Sorenson Trilogy Engineering Ltd* [2024] BCCA 25, [2024] 3 WWR 532 [79] ('*Sorenson Trilogy*') (structural weaknesses sufficiently serious to lead the municipality to order the evacuation of building residents). Leave to appeal *Sorenson Trilogy* to the Supreme Court of Canada was refused on 19 September 2024 (SCC docket 41192).

[34] *Globalnet Management Solutions v Cornerstone CBS Building* [2018] BCCA 303, [2018] 12 WWR 577. The Court accepted that the dangerousness of the retaining walls did not require expert evidence.

[35] *Mariani* (2004) 246 DLR (4th) 489.

[36] *Wesley v Geneau* [2020] ONSC 868, (2020) 98 CLR (4th) 189 ('*Wesley*'). The defendants, the vendors of the residential property, appeared to have deliberately concealed the defects.

[37] *Roy v Thiessen* [2005] SKCA 45, (2005) 252 DLR (4th) 475.

[38] *Mariani* (2004) 246 DLR (4th) 489.

[39] *Remmington v JDC Contracting* [2011] ABPC 18, (2011) 2 CLR (4th) 130. Exposed sewage can cause contamination of food and water.

Marine Ltd v Washington Iron Works,[40] tend to involve at least the risk of sudden or catastrophic injury, rather than the gradual onset of chronic injury. This issue was not expressly discussed in the decided cases, but could well be the subject of future argument.

The vast majority of cases involved defendants who were contractors or subcontractors. A smaller number involved engineers,[41] previous owners,[42] architects[43] and municipal inspectors or regulators.[44] As described in section V.C, one case was brought against a developer who had no involvement in physical construction.[45]

C. Limitations

This study is subject to the obvious – and perhaps substantial – limitation that it is restricted to decided cases. It therefore excludes cases that were not the subject of any decision (ie that were abandoned or settled without any judicial involvement). Notably, those cases may have been settled, in part, *because of* the decision in *Winnipeg Condominium*, in that they were not worth defending. This makes it difficult to know the extent to which *Winnipeg Condominium* has contributed to overall building safety in Canada. Its influence may well be more widespread than what this study reveals.

IV. Case Study: Defective Roof Joists in Atlantic Canada

My empirical analysis uncovered a noteworthy series of events and litigation that demonstrated *Winnipeg Condominium*'s potentially broader impact on building safety. In the 1980s and 1990s, two buildings (a warehouse and a Sears store) in Atlantic Canada suffered catastrophic roof collapses after heavy snowfalls.[46] The

[40] *Rivtow Marine Ltd v Washington Iron Works* [1974] SCR 1189 (Laskin J, dissenting). The case involved a defective crane. There had already been a collapse of a similar crane, which killed the operator. Laskin J's dissenting opinion was ultimately adopted by the Court in *Winnipeg Condominium* [1995] 1 SCR 85 [36].

[41] *Friskie v Parkview Homes Ltd* [2005] CanLII 49748 (Sask QB); *Printing Factory* [2016] ONSC 6600, (2016) 72 CLR (4th) 306.

[42] *Wesley* [2020] ONSC 868, (2020) 98 CLR (4th) 189.

[43] *Heinicke* [2006] MBQB 273, [2007] 2 WWR 112.

[44] ibid; *Timmerman v Selkirk & District Planning Area Board* [2007] MBQB 194, (2007) 218 Man R (2d) 125, affd [2008] MBCA 52, (2008) 228 Man R (2d) 77. Note that claims against municipal inspectors are permitted in Canada pursuant to *Ingles v Tutkaluk Construction Ltd* [2000] SCC 12, [2000] 1 SCR 298.

[45] *Condominium Corporation No 0522151 (Somerset Condominium) v JV Somerset Development Inc* [2022] ABCA 193, [2023] 4 WWR 589.

[46] There was also a roof collapse at a mall in Southwestern Ontario in 2000, killing one employee. Although the collapse was blamed on heavy snow build-up on the mall's flat roof, there was no suggestion that Robb Engineering joists were involved. Casualties could well have been higher – the collapse occurred during the height of the Christmas shopping season, but the mall had not yet opened for the

collapses were blamed on defective roof joists that had been manufactured by a company called Robb Engineering (later acquired by Dominion Bridge Company). Following the collapses, there were investigations by professional engineers and government information campaigns in the Atlantic provinces, in which owners of private residential and commercial buildings were advised to inspect any joists produced by Robb Engineering. Many government buildings were also affected. In total, some 70 buildings had to be remediated in Newfoundland and Labrador, including 15 schools.[47] The scope of the danger caused by the defects was, thus, relatively broad.

The incidents and the inspection campaign prompted litigation that led to three reported decisions directly applying *Winnipeg Condominium*. The first was a Nova Scotia Court of Appeal decision, *North Sydney Associates v United Dominion Industries*.[48] The plaintiff was the owner of a shopping mall the roof joists of which had been manufactured by Robb Engineering. Following the reports of other roof collapses, the plaintiff hired three different sets of engineers to inspect the joists at the mall, each of whom found missing, poor-quality and cracked welds. The plaintiff was awarded over C$550,000 at trial to repair the welding and restore the building to a non-dangerous condition. The defendant's primary argument on appeal was that the plaintiff had repaired more joists than were necessary to restore the building to a non-dangerous condition. The defendant argued for a precise burden of proof: that the plaintiff should have to prove an exact number of missing welds, cracked welds, porous welds, etc, rather than simply that there were '3,300 deficient welds of various types'.[49] The Court of Appeal rejected this argument because the trial judge had relied on the evidence of three different experts who had inspected every visible weld on every joist; he had not blindly accepted the testimony of a mall owner who was afraid that the roof would collapse.[50] Moreover, the plaintiff had established that the costs of inspecting every single joist (which would have required approximately 1,000 hours of work at a rate of C$100/hour) far exceeded the costs of simply remediating all the welds.[51] The Court of Appeal thus agreed that the remediation methods employed by the plaintiff were reasonable in the circumstances.[52]

The next case, *Loblaws v United Dominion Industries Ltd*,[53] was brought by the owner of a warehouse that had suffered a collapse; in other words, there had already been substantial property damage. The owner of the building sued United

day: see 'Snow-Covered Roof Collapses at Ontario Mall' *CBC News Online* (17 December 2000) https://www.cbc.ca/news/canada/snow-covered-roof-collapses-at-ontario-mall-1.218652.

[47] See *Loblaws v United Dominion Industries Ltd* (2007) 265 Nfld & PEIR 204 (NLTD) [14] ('*Loblaws*').

[48] [2006] NSCA 58, 268 DLR (4th) 491, affg [2005] NSSC 206, (2005) 235 NSR (2d) 263 ('*North Sydney*').

[49] ibid [22].

[50] ibid [23].

[51] ibid [29].

[52] ibid [31].

[53] *Loblaws* (2007) 265 Nfld & PEIR 204.

Dominion Industries for the costs of remedial work on the portion of the building that had not yet collapsed. The post-collapse inspections had found poor-quality welding in many of the joists.[54] Some joists evidenced a welding technique ('puddle welding') that was not approved by the Canadian Standards Association. The expert report concluded that the welding was 'consistently inferior', with evidence of poor workmanship and 'a near total lack of quality control'.[55] The expert opined that there was a 'real and substantial danger of collapse' which could occur 'with little or no warning'.[56] Another expert testified as to long-standing problems with Robb Engineering's welding standards, saying, 'At no time in my professional career have I witnessed such a blatant disregard for the obligations imposed upon a steel fabricator … as displayed by Robb Engineering when producing open web steel joists.'[57] He pointed to a lack of proper training for the welders and a lack of inspection of joist welds, concluding that 'the Robb joist line was allowed to exist, as if it was in a Regulatory vacuum'.[58]

The judge in the case quoted extensively from *Winnipeg Condominium* and had little difficulty concluding that a duty of care existed in the circumstances.[59] Based on the consistent evidence of the engineers who testified, he also concluded that the welding defects were dangerous and not merely shoddy workmanship.[60] This was no surprise, given that part of the roof had already collapsed. The judge was also generous when it came to awarding damages to the plaintiff, which had conducted a comprehensive remediation programme. While, in hindsight, a less extensive programme might have been sufficient to render the building non-dangerous, 'the plaintiff did not have the benefit of hindsight … at the time it was making a determination as to how the building ought to be remediated'.[61] Thus, as in the *North Sydney* case, the judge rejected the defendant's suggestion that each weld be individually inspected to determine whether it needed to be replaced, rather than simply replacing them all. Given the latency of the defects, it was not clear to the judge that the defendant's approach would have mitigated costs in any event. The judge also noted that, in *Winnipeg Condominium*, the Court had indicated that defendants could be liable for the 'reasonable cost of repairing the defects', meaning that the plaintiff is not limited to the bare minimum needed to render the building non-dangerous.[62] On the facts, the plaintiff's repairs were reasonable.

[54] ibid [6]. An engineer hired to advise on the remediation work reported that 69% of the joists inspected had one or more broken welds [45].

[55] ibid [13].

[56] ibid.

[57] ibid [22].

[58] ibid. In contrast, the defendant's expert suggested that the roof collapse was primarily due to overloading of the joists by snow, ice, and various equipment and services on the roof [25].

[59] ibid [101]–[102].

[60] ibid [129]–[130].

[61] ibid [133]. Keep in mind that part of the building had already collapsed; the plaintiff could not inordinately delay the repairs.

[62] ibid [135].

The third tort case arising from the roof collapses in Atlantic Canada was *Burnac Corp v United Dominion Industries Corp.*[63] It also involved a shopping mall and followed a similar pattern to the *Loblaws* and *North Sydney* decisions (ie there were many defective roof joists, there was a real and substantial danger of collapse and the remediation efforts were found to be reasonable, not excessive). In addition, *Burnac* featured expert evidence indicating that Robb Engineering was aware of its welding problems but did not adequately address them,[64] and that it falsely advertised that its joists met national welding standards. When a welding supervisor raised this misstatement, he was told by management 'that they could not make joists in compliance with [the standard] and stay competitive'.[65] The plaintiffs were ultimately awarded nearly C$1.5 million in 'hard' construction costs and over C$850,000 in 'soft' construction and inspection costs.

These three cases are useful illustrations of the role of *Winnipeg Condominium* in enhancing building safety in Canada by encouraging (or at least supporting) building owners to repair dangerous defects before they cause harm. At the same time, it seems reasonable to conclude that the respective building owners would have carried out the repairs regardless of the applicable tort principles to avoid the risk of roof collapse (which could cause significant property damage and possible injury or loss of life, in addition to making the building unavailable for commercial use for many months).

The cases are also interesting, however, as illustrations of the role of private law within a broader campaign of building safety in a jurisdiction. Following the first collapse in Newfoundland (which resulted in the *Burnac* litigation), the Association of Professional Engineers and Geoscientists of Newfoundland (APEGN)[66] sought information from various parties (the mall owners and the City of St John's, among others) about the cause of the collapse, with no success.[67] However, through the investigations and inspections conducted in furtherance of litigation, the professional engineers who had been engaged by the building owners developed the opinion that the collapse was due to faulty welding of roof joists manufactured by Robb Engineering. Then, after the *Loblaws* collapse, APEGN wrote to the Province of Newfoundland and Labrador to express its suspicions about the Robb joists, and subsequently provided a list of potentially at-risk buildings to the government.[68]

[63] *Burnac Corp v United Dominion Industries Corp* [2007] NSSC 40, (2007) 62 CLR (3d) 211 ('*Burnac*').

[64] After United Dominion acquired Robb Engineering, their experts also made recommendations to Robb Engineering's management about improving welding quality: *Burnac* [2007] NSSC 40, (2007) 62 CLR (3d) 211 [20]–[24].

[65] ibid [26].

[66] Now the Professional Engineers and Geoscientists of Newfoundland and Labrador.

[67] See G Follet, *Report on the Open Web Steel Joist Remediation Program for the Province of Newfoundland and Labrador*, vol 1 (The Open Web Steel Joist Task Review Board, 2005) 1.

[68] ibid. The buildings were those constructed between 1970–83, containing Robb joists. This was later extended to all buildings constructed after 1963: Open Web Steel Joist Task Review Board, 'Robb Engineering OWSJ Updated Information' (Report, November 2006) 2.

In response, the province created a Technical Evaluation Board to promote investigation of buildings, and to provide advice on risk management, public interest matters and operational guidelines, among other tasks.

The government of Newfoundland and Labrador undertook an assessment of all public buildings in the province that used open web steel joists (some 1,000 buildings). It also issued a public advisory regarding the need to conduct structural assessments of all private buildings built prior to 1985 that used open web steel joists.[69] It was hoped that, between the government and APEGN, all public and private buildings using joists manufactured by Robb Engineering would be identified, inspected and, if necessary, remediated. In the meantime, it was also recommended that building owners clear snow and ice from their roofs to prevent collapse. Following alerts from the government of Newfoundland and Labrador, inspection campaigns were also carried in Nova Scotia[70] and Prince Edward Island.[71] In Nova Scotia, information packages were distributed to the owners of hundreds of private buildings, including a list of potential defects associated with Robb Engineering joists. The Nova Scotia government also had to repair 85 public buildings (out of 2,200 that were inspected), at a reported cost of C$8 million.[72]

Thus, in addition to the reported cases in which *Winnipeg Condominium* was applied to cover the costs of preventive repairs, the relevant tort litigation (and the engineers who were retained by the plaintiffs) helped to spawn a massive inspection and remediation campaign of public and private buildings in the Atlantic region. It is impossible to know how many additional, potentially catastrophic roof collapses were thus averted; however, it seems safe to conclude that the litigation indirectly helped to render a large number of buildings non-dangerous.

V. The Future of *Winnipeg Condominium*

In this section, I assess the ongoing relevance of *Winnipeg Condominium* in the light of recent Supreme Court of Canada jurisprudence on the duty of care as it relates to pure economic loss. Although it appears that *Winnipeg Condominium* may have narrower application going forward, it is still being applied and even extended in the Canadian courts.

[69] Minister of Works, Services and Transportation, 'Government Recommends Inspections of Open Web Steel Joists' (Government of Newfoundland and Labrador, 19 February 1997).

[70] Department of Housing and Municipal Affairs, 'Open Web Steel Joist Info Campaign' (Government of Nova Scotia, 8 June 1998).

[71] No defects were identified in public buildings in PEI: 'PEI Public Buildings Pass Joist Inspection' *CBC News* (12 January 2001) https://www.cbc.ca/amp/1.264512.

[72] ibid.

A. *Winnipeg Condominium* after *Maple Leaf Foods*

The Supreme Court of Canada's 2020 decision in *1688782 Ontario Inc v Maple Leaf Foods*[73] has brought the continuing relevance of *Winnipeg Condominium* into question.[74] This is for three main reasons. First, the majority in *Maple Leaf Foods* approached *Winnipeg Condominium* through corrective justice or a 'rights-based' theory,[75] and thus focused on the correlative right and duty on which the case was purportedly founded.[76] The majority indicated that the defendant's duty in *Winnipeg Condominium* corresponded to '*the plaintiff's rights in person or property*'.[77] Brown and Martin JJ explained, 'the law views the plaintiff as having sustained actual injury to its right in person or property because of the necessity of taking measures to put itself or its other property "outside the ambit of perceived danger"'.[78] The majority reasoned that the scope of the defendant's duty was thus limited by 'this normative basis for the duty's recognition – that it protects a right to be free from injury to one's person or property'.[79]

This became critical for a variety of reasons given the facts in *Maple Leaf Foods*. The case was a class proceeding brought by Mr Sub franchisees to recover the economic loss and reputational injury they suffered following a recall of lunchmeats supplied by Maple Leaf Foods for potential contamination with listeria. The individuals who were foreseeably at risk of physical injury in *Maple Leaf Foods* were the potential *consumers* of tainted lunchmeat, not the Mr Sub franchisees (who suffered economic loss).[80] Thus, the plaintiff franchisees did not have a relevant right that correlated to the defendant's duty to provide lunchmeat that was safe for human consumption. If this reasoning is extended to dangerous

[73] *Maple Leaf Foods* [2020] SCC 35, [2020] 3 SCR 504.

[74] See B Feldthusen, '*16888782 Ontario v Maple Leaf Foods Inc*: The Secret Death of *Winnipeg Condominium*' (2021) https://dx.doi.org/10.2139/ssrn.3729537.

[75] The Court in *Maple Leaf Foods* [2020] SCC 35, [2020] 3 SCR 504 [18]–[19] cited, for example, EJ Weinrib, 'The Disintegration of Duty' (2006) 31 *The Advocates' Quarterly* 212 and R Stevens, *Torts and Rights* (Oxford, Oxford University Press, 2007).

[76] *Maple Leaf Foods* [2020] SCC 35, [2020] 3 SCR 504 [41]. I say 'purportedly' because this did not figure in LaForest's judgment and is arguably an effort to impose a theory some 25 years after the fact. Brown and Martin JJ (ibid [45]) suggested that he was explaining the principle from *Winnipeg Condominium*, 'properly understood'.

[77] *Maple Leaf Foods* [2020] SCC 35, [2020] 3 SCR 504 [45] (original emphasis). The majority quoted from P Benson, 'The Basis for Excluding Liability for Economic Loss in Tort Law' in DG Owen (ed), *Philosophical Foundations of Tort Law* (Oxford, Oxford University Press, 1995) 427, 429: the plaintiff's economic loss 'is analogized to physical injury to the plaintiff's person or property'. It is worth noting Brown J's prior career as a torts professor sympathetic to corrective justice theory.

[78] *Maple Leaf Foods* [2020] SCC 35, [2020] 3 SCR 504 [45], quoting Benson (n 77) 440.

[79] ibid [46]. The 'property' referred to here is presumably personal property, not the building itself. Hence the majority's reference to the plaintiff's 'other' property.

[80] ibid [57]. The majority similarly noted (ibid [81]) that the duty of care in *Donoghue v Stevenson* [1932] AC 562 was owed by the manufacturer to the ultimate consumer, not to an intermediary who might suffer economic loss from that same act of negligence.

building defects, it could result in a narrower applicability of *Winnipeg Condominium*. For instance, owners of commercial buildings are not typically concerned about their own bodily integrity or personal property interests, but rather, those of their tenants and patrons. According to the majority in *Maple Leaf Foods*, it would be inappropriate to 'bootstrap' the duty owed by a defendant to the commercial owner (ie a duty not to cause economic loss through the costs of repairs) to the duty owed to patrons who might suffer physical injury or damage to their personal property.[81] This interpretation could have the effect of limiting the applicability of *Winnipeg Condominium* to residential building owners, whose own physical safety and personal property interests are at risk if their homes have dangerous defects.[82]

Second, the majority in *Maple Leaf Foods* found that, even if the general principles underlying *Winnipeg Condominium* are still valid and applicable, plaintiffs must now also account for the element of proximity, which was expressly recognised by *Cooper v Hobart* in 2001.[83] This involves an assessment of the relationship between the parties.[84] As Bruce Feldthusen aptly pointed out in a case comment on *Maple Leaf Foods*, the combined effect of the majority's rights-based approach and its emphasis on proximity means that *even* a plaintiff who is *personally* at risk of physical injury would still be required to prove proximity with a builder who negligently created the relevant dangerous building defect.[85]

Finally, when conducting its proximity analysis, the majority in *Maple Leaf Foods* placed considerable emphasis on the contractual matrix among the parties. The plaintiffs were franchisees of Mr Sub. The franchise agreements required them to purchase their ready-to-eat meats from Mr Sub, which in turn purchased them from Maple Leaf Foods. Accordingly, through their multipartite agreement, the franchisees were restricted to purchasing meats from Maple Leaf Foods. They argued that this made them vulnerable in the case of a recall of potentially contaminated meats. The majority accepted this vulnerability, but reasoned that it was voluntarily undertaken by the plaintiffs, who had decided to operate their restaurants as franchises (rather than as independent operations). The plaintiffs had to accept the disadvantages of being a franchisee along with its advantages (eg the goodwill of the franchisor's trademark, cooperative marketing and the franchisor's

[81] ibid [81]. The majority thus criticised the trial decision in *376599 Alberta Inc v Tanshaw Products Inc* [2005] ABQB 300, (2005) 379 AR 1, where the manufacturer of a 'foam' used for a nightclub dance party was found to owe a duty of care to the nightclub and its patrons. According to Brown and Martin JJ, the duty of care in that case was owed only to the patrons (who were at risk of physical injury (skin and eye irritation)), not to the nightclub (which was only at risk of economic loss through occupier's liability to its patrons).

[82] Claims by condominium corporations, too, could face new hurdles under this approach. See B Feldthusen's critique (n 74).

[83] *Maple Leaf Foods* [2020] SCC 35, [2020] 3 SCR 504 [60], referring to *Cooper v Hobart* [2001] SCC 77, [2001] 3 SCR 537.

[84] Notably, recent Supreme Court jurisprudence suggests that parties may have proximity in some aspects of their relationship but not other aspects. See *Maple Leaf Foods* [2020] SCC 35, [2020] 3 SCR 504 [65], discussing *Deloitte & Touche v Livent Inc (Receiver of)* [2017] SCC 63, [2017] 2 SCR 855 [27]–[28].

[85] Feldthusen (n 74) 4.

buying power).[86] The majority found it inappropriate to circumvent this contractual arrangement by imposing a duty of care in tort.[87]

While it is important not to overstate the impact of this reasoning, it seems to signal a shift away from the more flexible approach to concurrent liability that was applied in *Winnipeg Condominium*. Feldthusen expressed the suspicion that, after *Maple Leaf Foods*, it would not be possible for commercial building owners to sue for the costs of repairing dangerous defects because (a) the defects pose no risk to the owners' physical safety, and (b) the risks of economic loss could have been allocated by contract. The parties in *Winnipeg Condominium*, an expensive building project, were not in a power imbalance, and would undoubtedly have been advised by competent lawyers and engineers. As Feldthusen concluded, '[t]his is precisely the situation that cries out for deference to contract so forcefully embraced by the majority in *Maple Leaf*.'[88] Although *Maple Leaf Foods* was a 5:4 decision (and the dissent did not even mention *Winnipeg Condominium*), it could potentially lead to a substantial narrowing of liability for dangerous defects.

B. Must the Danger be 'Imminent'?

The Supreme Court's decision in *Maple Leaf Foods* also – perhaps unintentionally – reopened questions about whether the dangerous defect must be 'imminently' dangerous. In stressing that the duty of care in *Winnipeg Condominium* corresponds to the plaintiff's rights in person or property, the majority concluded:

> In our view, this normative basis for the duty's recognition – that it protects a right to be free from injury to one's person or property – also delimits its scope. This is because this basis vanishes where the defect presents no imminent threat.[89]

The notion of imminence was not part of the decision in *Winnipeg Condominium*; as noted above,[90] this requirement has also been rejected by the appellate courts in Alberta, Saskatchewan, Ontario and, subsequent to *Maple Leaf Foods*, British Columbia. Accordingly, its addition would pose a significant change in the law.

[86] *Maple Leaf Foods* [2020] SCC 35, [2020] 3 SCR 504 [88]–[89]. The four dissenting judges (ibid [148]–[150]) stressed the unequal bargaining power between the franchisees and the franchisor, which meant that their ability to negotiate for more favourable terms was practically limited.

[87] ibid [90]. The franchise agreement included a provision allowing franchisees to seek permission to purchase supplies from other vendors, but the plaintiffs did not avail themselves of these provisions. This failure to adequately protect themselves from loss was also persuasive to the majority: ibid [94].

[88] Feldthusen (n 74) 5. See Feldthusen's earlier critiques of the decision in *Winnipeg Condominium* for altering the allocation of risk under contract: '*Winnipeg Condominium Corporation No 36 v Bird Construction Co*: Who Needs Contract Anymore?' (1995) 25 *Canadian Business Law Journal* 143. See also C Chisick, '*Winnipeg Condominium Co No 36 v Bird Construction Co*: The Death of the Contractual Warranty?' (1997) 25 *Manitoba Law Journal* 393, which compares the scope of recovery in *Winnipeg Condominium* to industry practice and statutory new home warranty provisions.

[89] *Maple Leaf Foods* [2020] SCC 35, [2020] 3 SCR 504 [46].

[90] Text to nn 30–33.

Several of the cases included in this study involved defects that were dangerous but not necessarily imminently so. For instance, defects to foundations, beams or load-bearing walls pose a risk of roof collapse, particularly under heavy snow or ice build-up, but it is not always the case that the roof is in danger of imminent collapse. Adding a requirement of imminence would seem contrary to the reasoning and spirit of *Winnipeg Condominium*: surely the homeowner would want to make the repairs before a heavy snowfall (a not uncommon occurrence), after which the repairs would be too late.[91] Further, heavy snowfall is reasonably foreseeable to builders in Canada, and is factored into building standards.[92]

This suggests that the use of 'imminence' by the majority in *Maple Leaf Foods* may have been inadvertent.[93] The majority did not signal any intention to modify the principles of *Winnipeg Condominium* in this regard, and so did not provide any justification for this potential new requirement. The facts in *Maple Leaf Foods* involved contaminated lunchmeats, which could be easily discarded and so did not present a risk – imminent or otherwise – to the plaintiff franchisees. Moreover, the case cited by the majority with respect to imminent harm, *Blacklaws v 470433 Alberta Ltd*,[94] involved a time share with inadequate sewage systems, and the Court had found that the buildings in question 'were not really defective'.[95] Indeed, the Alberta Court of Appeal had expressly distinguished its own decision in *Blacklaws* when it rejected the requirement of imminence.[96]

C. Subsequent Treatment

Despite some scholarly predictions of its demise, *Winnipeg Condominium* has been applied and even expanded since the decision in *Maple Leaf Foods*. While *Maple Leaf Foods* seemed to suggest that the proximity analysis would be governed by the contractual matrix among the parties, a recent British Columbia Court of Appeal decision concluded that the contractual allocation of risks would not necessarily

[91] On this point see also D Nolan, 'Preventive Damages' (2016) 132 *LQR* 68, 86–87. Nolan helpfully points out that waiting for a danger to become imminent would likely make the repairs more expensive. Nolan suggests that the focus should be on the likelihood and gravity of the damage.

[92] See DE Allen, 'Snow Load on Buildings' (National Research Council Publications Archive, 1959); Canadian Standards Association, 'Managing Changing Snow Load Risks for Buildings in Canada's North' (Standards Council of Canada, 2014) https://www.scc.ca/en/managing-changing-snow-load-risks-for-buildings-canadas-north.

[93] On this point, the majority may well be guilty of what Nick McBride describes as 'degraded language', which 'gives the judiciary a great deal of latitude in deciding a case': see his 'Private Law in the Ruins', this volume, ch 10, section I.D. Of course, the same might be said of the concept of a 'dangerous' defect.

[94] *Blacklaws v 470433 Alberta Ltd* [2000] ABCA 175, [2000] 11 WWR 476.

[95] ibid [62].

[96] *Vargo v Hughes* [2013] ABCA 96, (2013) 252 DLR (4th) 475 [23]. They noted that there was not even a threat of physical harm to the plaintiffs in *Blacklaws*. The British Columbia Court of Appeal also reasoned that the word 'imminent' was meant to distinguish dangerous from non-dangerous defects: *Sorenson Trilogy* [2024] BCCA 25, [2024] 3 WWR 532 [79].

be determinative. *Centurion Apartment Properties Limited Partnership v Sorenson Trilogy Engineering Ltd*[97] involved an apartment building that was so structurally unsound that the municipality ordered its immediate evacuation. The plaintiff, which was not the original purchaser of the building,[98] had no contract with the defendant engineering firm (which admitted negligence), but each party had a contract with the design-build firm. Notably, the contract between the design-build firm and the engineers limited the engineers' liability in contract and tort to the amount of the fees it received from the design-build firm. All three parties were presumably sophisticated commercial entities and could have negotiated different contractual arrangements. Nevertheless, the Court of Appeal concluded that a duty of care in tort could arise between the engineering firm and the plaintiff owners, and that the engineers could possibly be liable for the costs of remediating the building's defects to make it fit for occupancy.

In particular, the Court of Appeal found the alleged duty to be analogous to the duty in *Winnipeg Condominium*, in that both cases involved negligence leading to dangerous defects, and both plaintiffs had to take remedial action to prevent injury to inhabitants during the useful life of the building.[99] Further, the Court reasoned that the duty to create a building safe for human occupancy arises outside any contractual standards of quality.[100] The Court expressly accepted the underlying policy justification to repair dangerous defects before they cause injury, and concluded that the defendant should not be protected by contractual defences, especially in the absence of a contract with the plaintiff.[101]

Finally, in its efforts to reconcile *Winnipeg Condominium* and *Maple Leaf Foods*, the Court stressed that *Maple Leaf Foods* did not involve a real and substantial danger that had to be averted, but a temporary loss of a product supply and related business goodwill.[102] This is the type of loss that is appropriately allocated by contract. In contrast, both *Winnipeg Condominium* and *Sorenson Trilogy* involved dangerous defects, and the alleged 'contractual tower' put forward by the defendant engineers did not override the plaintiff's reasonable expectations that the engineers would design a building that was fit for occupancy, or the broader policy rationales that promote building safety.[103] In other words, the British Columbia Court of Appeal found that *Winnipeg Condominium* was still relevant as a matter of law and policy, in spite of its apparent narrowing in *Maple Leaf Foods*.

[97] *Sorenson Trilogy* [2024] BCCA 25, [2024] 3 WWR 532.

[98] The transaction by which Centurion acquired title was somewhat convoluted, involving various trusts and share purchases. In effect, Centurion was not far removed from the original purchase of the property, and to describe it as a 'subsequent' purchaser would be misleading: ibid [16]–[21].

[99] ibid [88].

[100] ibid.

[101] ibid.

[102] ibid [94].

[103] ibid [102].

Next, in *Condominium Corporation No 0522151 (Somerset Condominium) v JV Somerset Development Inc*,[104] the Alberta Court of Appeal was even open to the expansion of *Winnipeg Condominium* to new categories of defendants. The Court dismissed a motion for summary judgment by a developer who was sued for the costs of replacing the defective balconies in a 215-unit condominium building. The balconies had become structurally unstable due to water penetration and rot, and thus fell below the minimum load-bearing capacity under the Alberta Building Code. The condominium corporation decided to replace all the balconies.[105] The Court was willing to accept that structurally unstable balconies posed a real and substantial danger; the main issue was whether the scope of *Winnipeg Condominium* could be extended to developers who sold the units but did not have any involvement in their physical construction. Overturning the decision of the chambers judge,[106] the Court decided that it was arguable that a developer could be in a proximate relationship with subsequent purchasers, such that the principles of *Winnipeg Condominium* would apply. They were not willing to make that determination on the summary judgment motion, and allowed the action to proceed.[107]

An unanswered question in *Somerset* was the applicable standard of care; that is, if the developer were found to owe a duty of care, how would it fulfil that duty?[108] Would it be sufficient if the developer hired competent architects and contractors, or would they also be required to supervise and monitor the work of the contractors? Depending how this is answered, there is a potential that developers could be left on the hook for the negligence of all other parties who contribute to dangerous defects.

While we should be cautious in drawing conclusions from these cases, it seems that the predictions of *Winnipeg Condominium*'s demise in the wake of *Maple Leaf Foods* were premature. Even in cases involving commercial parties, which were not vulnerable and could have negotiated different allocations of risk, the policy of promoting the timely repair of dangerous building defects continues to be persuasive among Canadian judges. This suggests that, for the time being, tort law will continue to be relevant to building safety in Canada.

[104] *Somerset* [2022] ABCA 193, [2023] 4 WWR 589.

[105] The Court did not determine whether replacement was warranted or whether the balconies could have been made non-dangerous through less expensive means: *Somerset* [2022] ABCA 193, [2023] 4 WWR 589 [32].

[106] The chambers judge had reasoned that a developer, 'without more', owed no duty of care to detect or present construction defects, nor was it vicariously liable for the negligence of contractors. See the summary in *Somerset* [2022] ABCA 193, [2023] 4 WWR 589 [12].

[107] Notably, any common law duty of care would now be superseded by the statutory duties in the Alberta New Home Buyer Protection Act 2012 (Alb), which came into force in 2014. Section 4 of that Act provides, among other things, a deemed agreement between the builder and the prospective owner and subsequent purchasers that the home is free from certain defects for a designated amount of time, including defects in the building envelope (five years) and structural defects (10 years).

[108] *Somerset* [2022] ABCA 193, [2023] 4 WWR 589 [31].

VI. Conclusion

The decision in *Winnipeg Condominium* seems to have contributed in some way to building safety in Canada, even if judging only by the roof collapse cases in Atlantic Canada. That said, the owner of a commercial building has other incentives (such as its own liability, its insurance contracts, business disruption and bad publicity) to undertake remedial repairs. The defects in most of the other successful claims were not especially alarming, although they were undoubtedly worrisome for the homeowners. It probably seems fairer to say that, in most cases, *Winnipeg Condominium* primarily served to shift the costs of repairs that the owner (or owner's insurer) would have undertaken in any event, unless the owner decided it was preferable to sell the building at a loss. If the owner chose to sell, the next purchaser presumably would lose any opportunity to sue for the cost of repairs, because at that point the defects would be considered 'patent', and would be factored into the costs of purchase.

To that extent, *Winnipeg Condominium* has probably helped to shift the costs of repairs to the party responsible for the defects, whether that it is the builder, architect or otherwise. This can indirectly improve building safety, in that it provides an incentive for these defendants to design and construct buildings without dangerous defects (in the same way that manufacturers' liability provides an incentive to improve product safety). Thus, whether it encourages preventive repairs by building owners or shifts the costs of repairs to the negligent party, *Winnipeg Condominium* must be taken to have contributed to building safety in some respects. Further, the Atlantic Canada roof collapse cases illustrate how tort law and tort litigation can play an important role in broader building safety campaigns, led by professional engineers, inspectors and government. While tort law may not be the primary driver of building safety in Canada, it is part of a complex system of regulation and standards enforcement that promotes harm prevention and responsibility for safe construction.

6

Defective Premises and Economic Loss: A Problem Best Left to Legislation?

DONAL NOLAN

> There are two questions that should be answered before making any decision. First, who should make the decision? Second, what is the best decision? We should not jump over the first question in our haste to answer the second.[1]

I. Introduction

The problem of economic loss caused by defective premises has bedevilled the courts in Commonwealth jurisdictions for over half a century.[2] In this chapter I argue that the courts should never have got involved with the problem in the first place but should instead have left it to legislatures to resolve. After a troublesome two decades of litigation in the United Kingdom, the House of Lords recognised the wisdom of this course in *Murphy v Brentwood District Council*.[3] *Murphy* stands in stark contrast to the more liberal decisions which predated it in New Zealand and the UK, and postdated it in Australia and Canada, although the most recent decisions of the High Court of Australia and the Supreme Court of Canada have significantly closed the gap with the *Murphy* approach. (New Zealand has chosen to follow a different course.) In the meantime, legislatures throughout the common law world have been roused to intervene, albeit often only when prompted to do so by political pressures arising out of events (such as the 'leaky buildings' scandal in New Zealand and the building safety crisis in the UK) for which the executive and legislative branches of government bear much of the responsibility in the first place.

[1] *Cosmopolitan Homes Inc v Weller* 663 P 2d 1041 (Colo 1983) 1051 (Rovira J) ('*Cosmopolitan Homes*').

[2] The problems began with *Dutton v Bognor Regis Urban District Council* [1972] 1 QB 373 (EWCA) ('*Dutton*').

[3] *Murphy v Brentwood District Council* [1991] 1 AC 398 (HL) ('*Murphy*').

The concern of this chapter is with tort claims for pure economic loss arising out of a defect in premises that the claimant owner blames on the negligence of a builder or construction professional involved in their construction, conversion or renovation. Actions in respect of personal injury or property damage lie beyond the scope of the chapter, as does the boundary between property damage and pure economic loss in so-called 'complex structure' cases.[4] Nor does the chapter deal with claims against a surveyor or valuer instructed to advise on the condition or value of the premises at the time of their acquisition by the claimant. The additional complications arising from defective premises claims against local authorities accused of failing properly to discharge their supervisory functions are also excluded from the analysis, although with the caveat that many of the leading authorities on the issues that are considered were in fact concerned with claims of this kind.

It is important to recall at the outset why it is that there is such pressure for a tort remedy in defective premises cases. First, the default rule in sales of real property is caveat emptor, with the result that a buyer's contractual remedies against the vendor are generally limited to instances of positive misrepresentation.[5] This can be contrasted with sales of chattels, where the implied terms in the contract for the sale of goods confer generous protection on buyers, the exclusion of which is generally impermissible where the buyer is a consumer.[6] Second, even where there is contractual protection, as will usually be the case with sales of new builds, this will only avail the initial purchaser, while the long latency period of many defects means that the limitation period (in the UK, six years from the breach of contract) has often expired before the problem becomes apparent. Third, purchases of residential property otherwise than for investment are usually by far the most significant financial commitments that the buyers make in their lives, so that if things go wrong the consequences are often devastating. Fourth, insurance protection in respect of pre-existing defects may not be available, or may be prohibitively expensive.[7] Fifth, defects in premises are often easy to conceal, and may lie dormant for many years, so that there is a greater temptation for builders to cut corners than there is for, say, producers of manufactured goods, where problems are more likely to manifest themselves quickly, thereby damaging the

[4] On which, see D Nolan, 'Damage to "Other Property": Exploring the Boundary Between Property Damage and Pure Economic Loss' in E Peel and R Probert (eds), *Shaping the Law of Obligations: Essays in Honour of Professor Ewan McKendrick KC* (Oxford, Oxford University Press, 2023).

[5] Of course, in principle a buyer can negotiate for greater protection, but a consumer purchaser is unlikely to do this, and even commercial purchasers will struggle to get it: see M Bell and W Jocic, 'Negligence Claims by Subsequent Building Owners: Did the Life of *Bryan* End Too Soon?' (2017) 41 *Melbourne University Law Review* 1, 22.

[6] See eg Sale of Goods Act 1979, ss 12–15.

[7] A noteworthy form of insurance in the UK context is the National House-Building Council's 'Buildmark', whereby owners of new-build homes are given a warranty against defective workmanship and materials for two years from completion and insured against some structural defects for a further period. See further, P Britton and M Bell, *Residential Construction Law* 2nd edn (Oxford, Hart Publishing, 2025) paras 7.2.1ff (though note that the cover provided has recently changed).

producer's commercial reputation. Sixth, although statutory inspection regimes may afford some protection to purchasers, much depends on the rigour of the scheme and its enforcement, and even rigorous inspection regimes can be circumvented. And finally, although buyers can obtain additional protection from surveys and valuations carried out at the time of acquisition, the cost of a full structural survey is prohibitive for most residential purchasers, and no survey can be guaranteed to identify a latent defect.[8]

For all these reasons, financial loss caused by defective premises is a significant social problem, and a strong case can be made for a tort remedy in respect of it. However, my concern in this chapter is not with whether such a remedy should be available, but with whether it should be fashioned by courts or legislatures. My argument that it should be left to legislatures is far from original. On the contrary, it is a consistent theme of the more restrictive judicial decisions in this area and was heavily relied upon by the House of Lords in *Murphy*. According to Lord Keith, for example, there was much to be said for the view that 'in what is essentially a consumer protection field … the precise extent and limits of the liabilities which in the public interest should be imposed upon builders … are best left to the legislature'.[9] Similarly, Lord Oliver did not think it right for the courts 'to create at large new principles in order to fulfil a social need' that had already been perceived by the legislature.[10]

By contrast, another argument that was made in *Murphy*, which we might term the 'legislative pre-emption' argument, seems to me to be weak. Several of their Lordships argued that, since the UK Parliament had already provided some protection to residential purchasers of defective premises in the Defective Premises Act 1972, it was not appropriate for the courts to expand those protections through common law development.[11] The difficulty with this argument is that it seems to rest on a presumed legislative intention, when in fact it is simply impossible to know what the legislature's intention actually was (whether in 1972 or later, when *Murphy* was decided), if indeed it makes any sense to speak of the legislature's

[8] Furthermore, in the case of apartments, it is unlikely that a survey will encompass the apartment building itself.

[9] *Murphy* [1991] 1 AC 398, 472.

[10] ibid 492. See also 457 (Lord Mackay LC), 482 (Lord Bridge), 498 (Lord Jauncey); *Junior Books Ltd v Veitchi Co Ltd* [1983] AC 520 (HL) 537 (Lord Brandon) ('*Junior Books*'); *D&F Estates Ltd v Church Commissioners for England* [1989] AC 177 (HL) 208, 210 (Lord Bridge) ('*D&F Estates*'); *Bryan v Maloney* (1995) 182 CLR 609 (HCA) 644 (Brennan J) ('*Bryan*'); *Woolcock Street Investments Pty Ltd v CDG Pty Ltd* [2004] HCA 16, (2004) 216 CLR 515 [233] (Callinan J) ('*Woolcock Street Investments*'); *Brookfield Multiplex Ltd v Owners-Strata Plan No 61288* [2014] HCA 36, (2014) 254 CLR 185 [134] (Crennan, Bell and Keane JJ), [186] (Gageler J) ('*Brookfield Multiplex*').

[11] See *Murphy* [1991] 1 AC 398, 472 (Lord Keith), 480–81 (Lord Bridge), 491 (Lord Oliver), 498 (Lord Jauncey). See also *D&F Estates* [1989] AC 177, 207–208 (Lord Bridge). In fairness to their Lordships, their references to the 1972 Act were bundled up with more persuasive points about the competency of the courts, and/or the unprincipled nature of the common law liability sought to be imposed, with the result that it is unclear if they really attached much, if any, weight to a presumed legislative intention to limit recovery to the circumstances set out in the 1972 Act.

'intention' in this respect at all.[12] If common law principle requires that a remedy be given, then it is no answer to say that legislation covers the field unless the legislation itself excludes such a remedy, which the 1972 Act did not. Conversely, the fact that the legislature is thought to favour a remedy is not a good reason for the courts to create one if this flies in the face of common law principles.[13]

II. Judge-Made Law and Legislation

My preference for legislative solutions to the defective premises problem rests on the existence of fundamental differences between judge-made law and legislation. To understand what these are, it is helpful to begin with Albert Venn Dicey's seminal discussion of what he called 'judicial legislation' (by which he meant judge-made law).[14] According to Dicey:

> Judicial legislation aims to a far greater extent than do enactments passed by Parliament, at the maintenance of the logic or symmetry of the law. The main employment of a Court is the application of well-known legal principles to the solution of given cases, and the deduction from those principles of their fair logical result.[15]

As a result, Dicey observes, judges acquire a 'logical conscience', and 'come to care greatly … for consistency'.[16] And he also argues that judicial legislation 'aims rather at securing the certainty than at amending the deficiencies of the law', so that a well-trained judge tends to feel that a fixed and certain rule (even if not 'the best rule conceivable') promotes justice more than 'good laws which are liable to change and modification'.[17] Similarly, Benjamin Cardozo wrote that the judge 'is not to innovate at pleasure. … He is to draw his inspiration from consecrated principles.'[18]

For reasons that Dicey and others have identified, there are vitally important distinctions between the law-making roles of judges and legislatures. One is that while legislation is generally only prospective in effect, judge-made law is not, so that if the courts were 'to apply to the decision of substantially the same case one principle to-day, and another principle to-morrow, men would lose rights which they already possessed'.[19] Another is that, although legislatures passing new

[12] For a contrary view to that of their Lordships in this regard, see J Stapleton, 'Duty of Care and Economic Loss: A Wider Agenda' (1991) 107 *LQR* 249, 268–69.

[13] cf *Invercargill City Council v Hamlin* [1996] AC 624 (PC) 643 ('*Invercargill*').

[14] AV Dicey, *Lectures on the Relation between Law & Public Opinion in England During the Nineteenth Century* (London, Macmillan, 1905) Lecture XI.

[15] ibid 362.

[16] ibid.

[17] ibid 364.

[18] BN Cardozo, *The Nature of the Judicial Process* (New Haven, CT, Yale University Press, 1921) 141.

[19] Dicey (n 14) 365. See also *Philipp v Barclays Bank UK plc* [2023] UKSC 25, [2024] AC 346 [22]. But legislation can of course also have retrospective effect: see eg Building Safety Act 2022, s 14 (liability for defective cladding).

statutes usually seek to reconcile them with existing laws (by appropriate amendments or repeals), in principle each piece of legislation is written on a clean slate.[20] By contrast, new judge-made law becomes part of a complex web of rules that must as a matter of principle be coherent and consistent,[21] with the result that '[r]espect for precedent is the necessary foundation of judge-made law'.[22] Third, while a court makes a ruling on particular facts, legislatures 'establish abstract rules of general applicability'.[23] Fourth, legislation is 'always formally drafted and univocal',[24] which means that it is better suited to the task of drawing sharp lines than court decisions, the judgments in which are inevitably more nuanced[25] and more casually written, and which may be complicated by the presence of multiple judgments, including dissenting opinions. And finally, whereas legislators derive their legitimacy from the people they represent, judges derive theirs from membership of a professional class trained to exercise judgment and to engage in a specialised form of reasoning based primarily on precedent and the use of analogy. This is why it is that common law judges refer to earlier decisions as 'authorities', since it is from these that they identify the rules and principles they are bound to apply. And it is also why in modern legal parlance the phrase 'judicial legislation' is a term of opprobrium, amounting as it does to the claim that the courts have overreached themselves, and strayed into the sphere of the legislature.[26]

It follows from all this that, '[e]ven when a reform seems most plainly desirable, the conditions under which the judge works often make it preferable that the change should come from the legislature'.[27] And it also follows that there are significant limits, not only on *what* the courts should do, but also on *how* they can do it. For example, even if it would be beneficial for a judge to lay down an arbitrary line for reasons of legal certainty, the form that judgments take makes it hard for a judge to do this. Such a line is also difficult to reconcile with the application of principle and precedent, and it will be hard to hold to it in later cases, where those same forces will tend towards the expansion of the rule beyond the limits first

[20] A D'Amato, 'Judicial Legislation' (1979) 1 *Cardozo Law Review* 63, 64. The contrary view that legislation should also be principled (see eg R Dworkin, *Law's Empire* (London, Fontana Press, 1986) ch 6) is so completely at odds with established practice that it is hard to take seriously, at least as a prescription for legislative action. More realistic is Dicey's observation that 'Parliament in most instances pays little regard to any general principle whatever': Dicey (n 14) 368 n 1.

[21] See *Fairchild v Glenhaven Funeral Services Ltd* [2002] UKHL 22, [2003] 1 AC 32 [36] (Lord Nicholls): 'To be acceptable the [common] law must be coherent. It must be principled.'

[22] Dicey (n 14) 365. By contrast, statute law 'is not precedent-driven': N Duxbury, *Elements of Legislation* (Cambridge, Cambridge University Press, 2013) 15.

[23] Duxbury (n 22) 13.

[24] ibid 15.

[25] Not least because a judgment must be read as a whole and is not structured like a statute. Hence there will frequently be several passages in one judgment which deal with the same issue, and from which the ratio on that point must be gleaned.

[26] See eg *Murphy* [1991] 1 AC 398, 471 (Lord Keith) (referring to the decision in *Anns v Merton London Borough Council* [1978] AC 728 (HL) ('*Anns*')), 473 (Lord Bridge) (referring to the decision in *Dutton* [1972] 1 QB 373).

[27] ER Thayer, 'Judicial Legislation: Its Legitimate Function in the Development of the Common Law' (1891) 5 *Harvard Law Review* 172, 201.

set down.[28] No such constraint applies to legislation, which frequently lays down arbitrary rules that are dutifully applied by the courts,[29] but which have no 'wider "gravitational" effect'.[30] Furthermore, the form that legislation takes means that it can 'trim, compromise and split the difference in a way in which the common law simply cannot'.[31]

III. The Defective Premises Case Law

It is impossible to evaluate the judicial response to the problem of economic loss caused by defective premises without an account of the case law in this area. However, for reasons of space the account will be kept as brief as possible. It will be helpful to divide the discussion up by country, beginning with the United Kingdom.

A. United Kingdom

The first case in which a Commonwealth court awarded damages in negligence for economic loss caused by defective building work is *Dutton v Bognor Regis Urban District Council*,[32] where the English Court of Appeal held that the owner of a house with defective foundations could recover compensation from a local authority that had failed to undertake a sufficiently thorough inspection of the foundations when the house was being built. The claim was mistakenly treated as one for physical damage, rather than pure economic loss. The same error was made in *Anns v Merton London Borough Council*,[33] where the House of Lords held that the owner of premises with a defect which posed an imminent danger to the health or safety of the occupiers could recover the cost of making the property safe from those – in the case itself, another local authority – whose negligence was to blame for the existence of the defect. According to Lord Wilberforce, the claim was one in respect of 'material, physical damage'.[34]

[28] See J Morgan, 'Causation, Politics and Law: The English – and Scottish – Asbestos Saga' in R Goldberg (ed), *Perspectives on Causation* (Oxford, Hart Publishing, 2011) 63.

[29] See eg the Compensation Act 2006, s 3 (a provision regarding tort liability which is limited to a single disease, namely mesothelioma, even though the disease has no unique characteristics that would justify this special treatment).

[30] Morgan (n 28) 91.

[31] ibid 87.

[32] *Dutton* [1972] 1 QB 373, described by WVH Rogers in a case note as 'an unfortunate decision' ('Defective Premises – The Council Will Pay' [1972A] *CLJ* 211, 214), and – a few years later – by IND Wallace as 'perhaps the most remarkable and far-ranging decision extending liability in the law of tort for many years' ((1977) 93 *LQR* 16, 18).

[33] *Anns* [1978] AC 728.

[34] ibid 759.

In *D&F Estates Ltd v Church Commissioners for England*,[35] where the House of Lords refused to apply *Anns* to a non-dangerous defect, doubts began to be cast on the correctness of *Anns* itself.[36] Matters came to a head in *Murphy* – another defective foundations case – where the House of Lords overruled *Anns*, and held that in general pure economic loss caused by the acquisition of defective premises was not recoverable in tort, even if the defect was a dangerous one.[37] In essence, their Lordships' reasoning was that recovery for defects in quality was a matter for contract, and that no distinction could be drawn in this regard between dangerous and non-dangerous defects, since once the danger was discovered, the gist of the complaint was not the danger itself, but the inability to use the dangerous thing without incurring repair costs.[38] Their Lordships were also adamant that no principled distinction could be drawn between defective premises and defective chattels.[39] It followed that the logical end point of the *Anns* doctrine was recovery for all defects of quality in both premises and chattels, which would 'open up an exceedingly wide field of claims, involving the introduction of something in the nature of a transmissible warranty of quality'.[40] Lord Keith said:

> In my opinion, it is clear that *Anns* did not proceed upon any basis of established principle, but introduced a new species of liability governed by a principle indeterminate in character but having the potentiality of covering a wide range of situations, involving chattels as well as real property, in which it had never hitherto been thought that the law of negligence had any proper place.[41]

Unsurprisingly, in the three decades since *Murphy* was decided, there has been little in the way of negligence litigation on these issues in the United Kingdom. What case law there has been has concerned either the dividing line between property damage and pure economic loss,[42] or Lord Bridge's suggestion in *Murphy*[43] that recovery might be permitted for the cost of demolition or repair required to prevent a dangerous defect causing damage to persons or property beyond the boundaries of the premises themselves.[44]

[35] *D&F Estates* [1989] AC 177.
[36] See ibid 213 (Lord Oliver), 206 (Lord Bridge).
[37] Although, like *Anns*, *Murphy* concerned a claim against a local authority for negligent inspection of a building under construction, another decision of the House of Lords handed down on the same day extended the no-recovery rule to claims against builders: *Department of the Environment v Thomas Bates & Son* [1991] 1 AC 499 (HL) ('*Thomas Bates*').
[38] See *Murphy* [1991] 1 AC 398, 465, 470 (Lord Keith), 475 (Lord Bridge), 488–89 (Lord Oliver).
[39] ibid 469 (Lord Keith), 475 (Lord Bridge), 498 (Lord Jauncey).
[40] ibid 469 (Lord Keith).
[41] ibid 471.
[42] See Nolan (n 4) 235–39.
[43] *Murphy* [1991] 1 AC 398, 475.
[44] Such a claim was allowed in *Morse v Barratt (Leeds) Ltd* (1993) 9 *Construction Law Journal* 158 (Ch D), but rejected in *Thomas v Taylor Wimpey Developments Ltd* [2019] EWHC 1134 (TCC), [2019] PNLR 26. In these circumstances, the cost of obviating the threat to third parties is arguably justified on grounds similar to those underlying actions for 'preventive damages', as discussed in D Nolan, 'Preventive Damages' (2016) 132 *LQR* 68.

B. Canada

Although the Canadian courts have taken a more liberal approach to economic loss caused by defective premises than the House of Lords in *Murphy*, they have limited recovery (as in *Anns*) to cases where the defect is a dangerous one. The key decision is *Winnipeg Condominium Corp No 36 v Bird Construction Co Ltd*,[45] which concerned an apartment building from which a large piece of concrete cladding had fallen from the ninth storey to the street below. The Supreme Court of Canada held that the owners of the building could recover the cost of replacing the building's cladding from the contractor who had installed it because it posed 'a real and substantial danger' to the occupants.[46] La Forest J concurred with the reasoning of Laskin J in *Rivtow Marine Ltd v Washington Iron Works Ltd*,[47] where he held (in a partially dissenting opinion) that the manufacturer of a defectively dangerous crane should be liable in tort to the crane's owner for the cost of making it safe to use because prevention of threatened harm resulting in economic loss should not be treated differently from the curing of damage actually done. La Forest J also argued that allowing recovery of the cost of making dangerously defective buildings safe would incentivise their owners to mitigate potential losses and encourage economically efficient and socially responsible behaviour. Whether damages were recoverable in respect of non-dangerous construction defects was left open.[48]

However, in its recent decision in *1688782 Ontario Inc v Maple Leaf Foods Inc*,[49] a majority of the Supreme Court of Canada signalled a more restrictive approach to negligence claims for economic loss than had previously been taken by that court. According to their Honours, to recover for such loss a plaintiff must establish both that it was the result of an interference with a legally recognised right (there being no general tort right 'protecting against the negligent … infliction of pure economic loss'[50]) and that there was sufficient proximity between the parties. They reconciled this analysis with *Winnipeg Condominium* by holding that economic loss recovery in the case of a dangerous defect 'was founded upon the idea that, in the eyes of the law, the defendant negligently interfered with rights in person or property'.[51] It followed that that decision should not be extended to the cost of repairing non-dangerous defects in buildings and products, which did not 'implicate a right protected under tort law', and were 'better channelled through the law of contract'.[52]

[45] *Winnipeg Condominium Corp No 36 v Bird Construction Co Ltd* [1995] 1 SCR 85 ('*Winnipeg Condominium*') and, more generally, E Chamberlain, 'Building Safety in Canada: Has *Winnipeg Condominium* Had an Impact?', this volume, ch 5. See also *City of Kamloops v Nielsen* [1984] 2 SCR 2.

[46] *Winnipeg Condominium* [1995] 1 SCR 85, 116.

[47] *Rivtow Marine Ltd v Washington Iron Works Ltd* [1974] SCR 1189.

[48] *Winnipeg Condominium* [1995] 1 SCR 85, 119–20.

[49] *1688782 Ontario Inc v Maple Leaf Foods Inc* [2020] SCC 35, [2020] 3 SCR 504 ('*Maple Leaf*').

[50] ibid [19].

[51] ibid [46].

[52] ibid [47].

C. Aotearoa – New Zealand

The New Zealand courts have taken the most liberal approach to the question under consideration of any major Commonwealth jurisdiction. This approach dates back to *Bowen v Paramount Builders (Hamilton) Ltd*,[53] a decision of the New Zealand Court of Appeal handed down shortly before *Anns*. In *Bowen* a subsequent purchaser of a building comprising two flats that had subsided recovered the cost of putting things right from the builders responsible for defects in the building's foundations. Even though the first-instance judge had pointed out that the claim was one for 'the diminished quality of the article',[54] the Court of Appeal insisted that it was not a claim for pure economic loss but for property damage, so that it fell within the scope of the *Donoghue v Stevenson*[55] principle.

Later decisions of the New Zealand courts have followed the generous course set in *Bowen*. In *Invercargill City Council v Hamlin*,[56] for example, the Court of Appeal refused to follow *Murphy*, holding that a local authority charged by statute with inspecting construction work to ensure compliance with building by-laws owed a duty of care to downstream purchasers of the building, on the basis that potential home buyers relied on local authorities to carry out this function with due care.[57] Unlike in Canada, in New Zealand liability is not limited to dangerous defects, but extends to all departures from minimum construction standards as set out in the relevant building codes. Furthermore, in *Body Corporate No 207624 v North Shore City Council*,[58] a majority of the Supreme Court of New Zealand refused to restrict the duty recognised in *Hamlin* to residential premises, although, in a dissenting opinion broadly supportive of the *Murphy* approach, William Young J disagreed. According to his Honour, limiting the duty to residential property was 'the least bad option in what is currently an extremely unsatisfactory situation'.[59]

D. Australia

The Australian case law on this issue is complex and difficult to set out with precision, for reasons including Australia's federal system and that many defective building cases are decided (at least, at first instance) by tribunals that have a degree of latitude in dispensing 'practical justice'. The overall pattern is, however, clear: an

[53] *Bowen v Paramount Builders (Hamilton) Ltd* [1977] 1 NZLR 394 (NZCA) ('*Bowen*').
[54] *Bowen v Paramount Builders (Hamilton) Ltd* [1975] 2 NZLR 546 (NZSC) 555–56 (Speight J).
[55] *Donoghue v Stevenson* [1932] AC 562 (HL).
[56] *Invercargill City Council v Hamlin* [1994] 3 NZLR 513 (NZCA) ('*Hamlin*').
[57] The *Hamlin* decision was affirmed by the Privy Council ([1996] AC 624 (PC)) on the basis that it was up to the New Zealand courts to determine, in the light of local conditions, whether such a duty of care ought to be recognised.
[58] *Body Corporate No 207624 v North Shore City Council* [2012] NZSC 83, [2013] 2 NZLR 297 ('*Spencer on Byron*').
[59] ibid [290].

initially liberal approach that has gradually become more restrictive. The key early decision is *Bryan v Maloney*,[60] where a majority of the High Court of Australia rejected the *Murphy* analysis and held that a housebuilder who had installed inadequate footings owed a duty of care to a downstream purchaser of the property who suffered economic loss as a result. The recognition of the duty of care – which was not restricted to dangerous defects – was based on the existence of a relationship of close proximity between the parties, coupled with policy considerations said to support its recognition. However, Brennan J dissented, essentially endorsing the *Murphy* approach, and the decision was met with a distinct lack of enthusiasm in some quarters, in part because of the uncertainty it generated.[61] One source of uncertainty was whether the liability recognised in *Bryan* extended to commercial or investment property. That question eventually came before the High Court in *Woolcock Street Investments Pty Ltd v CDG Pty Ltd*,[62] where it was held (Kirby J dissenting) that an engineering company which designed the foundations of a warehouse and office complex owed no duty of care to a subsequent purchaser in respect of economic loss caused by structural problems because the buyer could have protected itself against such loss by the terms of its contract with the vendor who sold it the property.

As Stephen Todd has observed, the reasoning of the joint majority judgment in *Woolcock Street Investments* was hardly 'a ringing affirmation' of *Bryan*,[63] and the High Court rowed back further from its initially expansive approach to liability in *Brookfield Multiplex Ltd v Owners–Strata Plan No 61288*.[64] The defendant in *Brookfield Multiplex* was a building company which had constructed a mixed-use building for a developer, which had then sold the lots in a part of the building that was to be used for serviced apartments. The common property was vested in an owners' corporation, which brought a negligence action against the defendant when defects in the common property became apparent some years after the building's completion. The High Court held that the defendant had not owed the plaintiff a relevant duty of care, essentially on the basis that subsequent purchasers had not been vulnerable to lack of care on its part, because the contracts of sale had contained detailed provisions regarding the quality of the building work. In their joint judgment in *Brookfield Multiplex*, Crennan, Bell and Keane JJ essentially endorsed the *Murphy* analysis, which they described as the approach 'that better accords with the coherent development of the common law'.[65] Although *Brookfield Multiplex* does not close the door on tort claims for economic loss in this context, it is viewed as a highly restrictive decision, which bars such claims

[60] *Bryan* (1995) 182 CLR 609.
[61] See eg *Zumpano v Montagnese* [1997] 2 VR 525 (VCA) 528, where Brooking JA lists more than 30 questions that he says arise as to the scope of the *Bryan* decision.
[62] *Woolcock Street Investments* [2004] HCA 16, (2004) 216 CLR 515.
[63] S Todd, 'Policy Issues in Defective Property Cases' in JW Neyers, E Chamberlain and SGA Pitel (eds), *Emerging Issues in Tort Law* (Oxford, Hart Publishing, 2007) 205.
[64] *Brookfield Multiplex* [2014] HCA 36, (2014) 254 CLR 185.
[65] ibid [164].

except in 'special cases of vulnerability', where the plaintiff was unable to protect themselves from such loss.[66]

E. Other Common Law Jurisdictions

Finally, reference should be made to the position in Singapore and the United States.[67] In *RSP Architects Planners & Engineers v Ocean Front Pte Ltd* ('*Ocean Front*'),[68] the Singapore Court of Appeal refused to follow *Murphy*, holding that the developer of a condominium complex owed a duty of care in respect of economic losses caused by defects in its construction to the management corporation of the development. This approach was later upheld in *RSP Architects Planners & Engineers v Management Corporation Strata Title Plan No 1075*,[69] where the Court of Appeal observed that 'to treat houses and consumer goods alike would be to ignore simple realities'.[70] It was also pointed out that no equivalent of the statutory tort liability created by the UK's Defective Premises Act 1972 exists in Singapore. However, in a more recent case concerned with economic loss caused by a defective ship's engine, the Court of Appeal said that the relationship between the parties in *Ocean Front* had been 'as close to a contract as could reasonably be', and that it should be treated as 'a special case' arising from the statutory provisions regarding strata title or at least 'confined to defects in buildings'.[71]

The multitude of state jurisdictions in the United States makes it difficult to summarise the law on this issue in that country, but the predominant view seems to be in line with the *Murphy* analysis, refusing recovery in defective premises cases by applying the general rule barring negligence recovery of pure

[66] See *Roberts v Goodwin Street Developments Pte Ltd* [2023] NSWCA 5, (2023) 110 NSWLR 557 [196] (Kirk JA and Griffiths AJA). See also Bell and Jocic (n 5). The extensive statutory protections now available to homebuyers in many Australian states may themselves be considered to reduce their 'vulnerability': see *Owners–Strata Plan No 74602 v Brookfield Australia Investments Ltd* [2015] NSWSC 1916 [131]. *Raymond v Lewis* [2024] QCA 43 provides an illustrative example of the current position: the Queensland Court of Appeal overturned a finding at trial that the plaintiff homeowners were vulnerable in the relevant sense so as to give rise to a duty of care, largely on the basis that the Court regarded the plaintiff as capable of having had an independent building inspection done, so that they fell outside the narrow residual confines of *Bryan* (1995) 182 CLR 609: see [2024] QCA 43 [53] (Mullins P; Morrison JA and North J agreeing). In *Mallonland Pty Ltd v Advanta Seeds Pty Ltd* [2024] HCA 25, the High Court of Australia confirmed the narrowness of the gateway to imposition of a duty of care in negligence to protect against pure economic loss. See, further, section V.C below.

[67] See also in this volume, respectively, ESW Ti, 'The Role of Private Law in Promoting Building Safety: The Case of Singapore' (ch 4) and EC McKenzie, 'The Surfside Condominium Collapse: What Lessons Have Been Learned?' (ch 3).

[68] *RSP Architects Planners & Engineers v Ocean Front Pte Ltd* [1995] 3 SLR(R) 653.

[69] *RSP Architects Planners & Engineers v Management Corporation Strata Title Plan No 1075* [1999] SGCA 30, [1999] 2 SLR(R) 134. See, further, Ti (n 67).

[70] ibid [43].

[71] *Man B&W Diesel SE Asia Pte Ltd v Pt Bumi International Tankers* [2004] SGCA 8, [2005] 2 LRC 1 [44] (Chao Hick Tin JA).

economic loss.[72] In *Calloway v City of Reno*,[73] for example, the Supreme Court of Nevada held that the economic loss rule applied in construction defect cases, and barred a claim by the owners of townhouses against subcontractors they blamed for alleged defects in the framing of the buildings. Expectancy interests created by agreement were a matter for contract, said the Court, and not tort.[74] Some American jurisdictions do, however, recognise an exception to the economic loss rule in defective premises cases, at least where residential property is involved.[75]

F. Two Observations

Before we leave the Commonwealth case law, two general observations should be made about it. The first is that the standard of the reasoning in the more liberal decisions is generally quite poor. The early decisions in *Dutton*, *Bowen* and *Anns* rested on a mistake as to the nature of the loss, which was simply asserted rather than analysed. Lord Denning's treatment of the problem in *Dutton* was crude and outcome-oriented, and there is little evidence that he considered the broader implications of the decision.[76] Lord Wilberforce's judgment in *Anns* was remarkably thin and unimpressive (at least on this issue[77]) and it is not surprising that that decision gave rise to so many problems of interpretation and application in the decade or so before it was overruled. Turning to the leading expansionary cases of the 1990s, the majority judgment in *Bryan* also seems rather undercooked, resting as it does on the twin pillars of a rather vacuous 'proximity' analysis (an approach soon after disavowed by the High Court of Australia[78]) and a series of assertions about the policy implications of allowing recovery. The contrast with the standard of the reasoning and the depth of the analysis in the two later High Court cases is marked. Similar criticisms can be levelled at the

[72] See *Brookfield Multiplex* [2014] HCA 36, (2014) 254 CLR 185, 239.

[73] *Calloway v City of Reno* 993 P 2d 1259 (Nev 2000).

[74] See also *Aas v Superior Court of San Diego County* (2000) 12 P 3d 1125 (Cal 2000).

[75] See generally, DF Partlett, 'Defective Structures and Economic Loss in the United States' in Neyers, Chamberlain and Pitel (n 63) 242, who observes that so 'various and inconsistent' is the US case law 'that the approaches taken in England, Australia, Canada and New Zealand can all be found somewhere in the kaleidoscope'.

[76] For example, his assumption that local authorities would rarely have to pay damages because claims would be covered by builders' insurance policies was false, as such policies do not generally cover latent defects causing economic loss. Hence the burden of compensating building owners largely fell on local authorities. See J Smillie, 'Compensation for Latent Building Defects' [1990] *New Zealand Law Journal* 310, 312.

[77] Most of Lord Wilberforce's speech is devoted to the statutory powers and limitation points. The analysis of what we would now recognise as the economic loss question was confined to a mere two pages (*Anns* [1978] AC 728, 758–60). For criticism of the 'relative insouciance' of the speech, see IND Wallace, 'Negligence and Defective Buildings: Confusion Confounded?' (1989) 105 *LQR* 46, 56.

[78] *Sullivan v Moody* [2001] HCA 59, (2001) 207 CLR 562.

reasoning of the New Zealand Court of Appeal in *Hamlin*, which is also grounded on notions of proximity,[79] and some aspects of which (such as the emphasis placed on local conditions) have been criticised in the more recent New Zealand case law.[80] *Winnipeg Condominium* is a more carefully reasoned decision, in which La Forest J strives to provide clarity as to the scope and rationale of recovery, although the policy analysis is again rather conclusory and has been the subject of sharp criticism by Canadian commentators.[81]

The second general observation is that the judgments which adopt a more liberal approach to the defective premises issue are dominated by discussion of policy, whereas the judgments that take a more restrictive line are typically focused on points of principle. Hence policy reasoning is to the fore in the decisions in *Dutton*,[82] *Bryan*,[83] *Winnipeg Condominium*,[84] *Hamlin*[85] and *Spencer on Byron*.[86] By contrast, the reasoning in *Murphy* is almost exclusively principled in nature, with discussion of policy relegated to a single short paragraph in the speech of Lord Keith.[87] More liberal judicial voices have questioned the emphasis which their Lordships placed in *Murphy* on the distinction between property damage and pure economic loss,[88] while the reliance on principle and the absence of policy analysis has been heavily criticised by commentators,[89] some of whom have resorted to rather extreme language to make their point.[90] Clearly the gap between Dicey and many contemporary legal scholars is a yawning one.

[79] See eg *Hamlin* [1994] 3 NZLR 513, 533–34.

[80] Indicative of the standard of the policy analysis in *Hamlin* is the reliance placed by Richardson J on the fact that New Zealand experienced a housing boom in the 1950s and 1960s: *Hamlin* [1994] 3 NZLR 513, 524. Quite why this was relevant was not explained.

[81] See eg JP Palmer, 'Bird: A Confusion Between Property Rules and Liability Rules' (1995) 3 *Tort Law Review* 240; B Feldthusen, '*Winnipeg Condominium Corporation No 36 v Bird Construction Co*: Who Needs Contract Anymore?' (1995) 25 *Canadian Business Law Journal* 143.

[82] See eg *Dutton* [1972] 1 QB 373, 390, 397.

[83] See eg *Bryan* (1995) 182 CLR 609, 623, 627–28.

[84] See eg *Winnipeg Condominium* [1995] 1 SCR 85 (SCC) 97, 100, 103, 117, 120.

[85] See eg *Hamlin* [1994] 3 NZLR 513, 546.

[86] See eg *Spencer on Byron* [2012] NZSC 83, [2013] 2 NZLR 297 [26]. See also *Invercargill* [1996] AC 624, 642.

[87] See *Murphy* [1991] 1 AC 398 (HL) 472. According to Lord Jauncey (at 498) the policy issues raised by such cases were a matter for Parliament. The assertion that *Murphy* was a policy decision (see eg J Conaghan and W Mansell, *The Wrongs of Tort* (London, Pluto Press, 1993) 35; *Hamlin* [1994] 3 NZLR 513, 546) is hard to fathom.

[88] Hence the distinction is described as 'metaphysical' in *Hamlin* [1994] 3 NZLR 513, 521 (Cooke P), and 'essentially technical' in *Bryan* (1995) 182 CLR 609, 623 (Mason CJ, Deane and Gaudron JJ); cf *Brookfield Multiplex* [2014] HCA 36, (2014) 254 CLR 185 [67] (Crennan, Bell and Keane JJ) (of 'critical importance' that the loss is purely economic).

[89] See eg R O'Dair, '*Murphy v Brentwood District Council*: A House With Firm Foundations?' (1991) 54 *MLR* 561, 564 (one of the 'most disappointing aspects' of the decision). See also *Canadian National Railway Co v Norsk Pacific Steamship Co Ltd* [1992] SCR 1021 (SCC) 1146 (McLachlin J) (criticising the 'doctrinal tidiness which is the motivating spirit of *Murphy*').

[90] See eg Conaghan and Mansell (n 87) 34, describing the reasoning of the House of Lords as 'bizarre' and commenting that it is 'startling that they see anything rational and coherent in what they are doing'.

IV. Principle and Policy

I now turn to the core of my argument that the courts should not seek to provide common law solutions to the problem of economic loss caused by the acquisition of defective premises, but should instead leave the issue to be resolved by legislatures. There are three key planks to my argument. The first is that the various solutions that have been tried are all contrary to principle. The second is that they rest on determinations of policy which are best left to legislatures to make. And the third is that they give rise to a range of problems, many of which are intractable. I will elaborate on the first two points in this part of the chapter, before moving on in the next part of the chapter to discuss the third.

A. Principle

My discussion of the objections of principle to common law tort claims for economic loss in this context will be brief because I have previously set out the relevant arguments in depth elsewhere. My starting point is that a right not to suffer pure economic loss is a conceptual impossibility,[91] so the claim that awards of damages for economic loss caused by defective premises are correcting a wrong[92] is mistaken. What the courts have in fact been doing, I believe, is fashioning various liability rules[93] of differing levels of complexity. And while it is true that the courts have been known to create bespoke liability rules in the tort context, such as the rule in *Rylands v Fletcher*,[94] doing so within a negligence framework is certain to cause incoherence because the tort of negligence is a wrong. This incoherence, and the knock-on effects it generates, can be minimised if the rule has both a clear and precise rationale, and bright-line boundaries.[95] As we shall see, however, neither of these conditions has been met in the context under discussion.

The Canadian solution of limiting liability to dangerous defects looks on its face to be more principled than the more liberal approach in New Zealand. However, although it is possible to analyse the award of 'preventive damages' in cases such as *Anns* and *Winnipeg Condominium* as a response to an infringement of rights

[91] See D Nolan, 'Rights, Damage and Loss' (2017) 37 *OJLS* 255, 261–71.

[92] See eg Todd (n 63) 228. It is rare for courts to formulate the objection to economic loss recovery in the terms set out in the text, but see *Aas* 12 P 3d 1125 (Cal 2000) 1137–38 (unless a construction defect has led to personal injury or damage to other property the plaintiff has not suffered harm that grounds a claim in tort).

[93] On the distinction between wrongs and liability rules, see D Nolan and A Robertson, 'Rights and Private Law' in D Nolan and A Robertson (eds), *Rights and Private Law* (Oxford, Hart Publishing, 2011) 15–18.

[94] *Rylands v Fletcher* (1868) LR 3 HL 330 (HL). Perhaps not an auspicious precedent.

[95] See eg *White v Jones* [1995] 2 AC 207 (HL), though even there Lord Mustill (dissenting) argued that it was a mistake for the courts to fashion a bespoke remedy which could not be reconciled with wider principles.

to bodily integrity and property, or alternatively as a principled exception to the general bar on pure economic loss recovery grounded in those rights, in my view this analysis is ultimately unpersuasive. For reasons that I have set out elsewhere,[96] the objections of principle to the Canadian doctrine set out in *Murphy* seem to me to be convincing.

Finally, even though the argument that claims for disappointed contractual expectancies are properly a matter for contract may look conclusory, it is noteworthy how much support the argument seems to have,[97] and it does seem to me to have some force when it comes to the overall coherence of private law. As the House of Lords pointed out in *Murphy*, it is hard to see how as a matter of principle (as opposed to policy) the courts can distinguish between claims for economic loss caused by the acquisition of defective real property and defective personal property. And even if it is borne in mind that allowing such claims in tort does not strictly speaking create a transmissible warranty of quality, since negligence must still be established on the part of the builder or producer, the tension that this creates between the law of tort and the law of contract seems real enough. This can be seen most clearly when one considers the reductio ad absurdum of tort recovery for mere quality defects, which is surely the tort claim brought by a subsequent purchaser of a house against a painter employed by the previous owner in the New South Wales case of *Goulding v Kirby*, and framed as a claim for 'diminution in the value of the house by reason of the condition of the painting work'.[98] The view that such a claim does not belong in tort 'is not just arid doctrine'.[99] There is after all a close relationship between price and quality,[100] and giving the claimant in such a case a tort claim prima facie threatens to undermine allocations of contractual risk, even if ultimately this can be avoided by a complex set of second-order principles qualifying the tort liability rule.

B. Policy

My claim regarding the policy implications of allowing claims for economic loss in this context is not that they point either in favour of or against such actions, but that it is impossible to know. In those circumstances, the policy determination should be made by elected legislators, rather than unelected judges. That the policy issues in this area are complex and contestable seems obvious, and has sometimes been

[96] Nolan (n 44) 78–81.

[97] For judicial endorsements of the argument, see not only *D&F Estates* and *Murphy*, but also *Maple Leaf* [2020] SCC 35, [2020] 3 SCR 504 [47], and much of the US case law, including *Calloway* 993 P 2d 1259 (Nev 2000) [9], [10]. The argument has also been accepted by scholars who are hardly died-in-the-wool doctrinalists, including S Waddams, *Dimensions of Private Law: Categories and Concepts in Anglo-American Legal Reasoning* (Cambridge, Cambridge University Press, 2003) 158.

[98] *Goulding v Kirby* [2002] NSWCA 393 [4].

[99] *Spencer on Byron* [2012] NZSC 83, [2013] 2 NZLR 297 [244] (William Young J).

[100] Indeed, there is a market for shoddy goods, such as flawed porcelain and stoneware.

conceded by the judges who use policy to justify imposing liability.[101] Consider, for example, the claim that imposing liability will encourage builders to take more care when undertaking construction work. Although this seems perfectly plausible, it can be argued against it that, by the time many defects become apparent, the building contractor responsible has often gone out of business, whether through insolvency or otherwise. It is also telling in this regard that the New Zealand 'leaky buildings' scandal, which affected many thousands of homes built from the mid-1990s onwards, occurred in a jurisdiction with a long-standing and very generous (to claimants) tortious liability regime in the defective premises context, dating back to the late 1970s. It would appear that the deterrent effect of tort law was lost on the builders involved. Similarly, the policy argument that was put forward in *Winnipeg Condominium* for recovery in respect of dangerous defects, that this would encourage owners to put things right before any damage was done, is highly speculative, not least because a person living in a dangerous building clearly has powerful incentives to make it safe regardless of the tort liability rules, or else to sell it at a loss and live elsewhere.[102]

Furthermore, where there is deterrence, there is also the possibility of overdeterrence. Note, for example, Lord Oliver's extrajudicial claim that in the aftermath of *Anns* local authorities concerned about liability required builders to dig 'extravagantly deep foundations', thereby significantly increasing construction costs.[103] There is also evidence from the United States that liability rules in this area have a significant knock-on effect on the price of new homes.[104] And while of course higher prices may be considered an acceptable trade-off for greater consumer protection, decisions with such marked redistributive effects would seem to be better suited to legislatures than to courts.

Another reason that policy is an insecure foundation on which to rest common law rules is that the social conditions that inform the policy analysis may change. In the 1990s, for example, it was argued that particular characteristics of the New Zealand building scene pointed towards tort liability in this context.[105] By the 2010s, it seems that those conditions were no longer present,[106] so that the policy base of the generous liability rules had partially collapsed, and other arguments had to be deployed to shore it up. In the same way, justifying liability by reference to the vulnerability of the buyer assumes that buyers in general (or alternatively some categories of buyer) are unable to protect themselves against the negligence of builders in other ways, such as through first-party insurance.

[101] See eg *Spencer on Byron* [2012] NZSC 83, [2013] 2 NZLR 297 [214].
[102] *Murphy* [1991] 1 AC 398, 472.
[103] Lord Oliver of Aylmerton, 'Judicial Legislation' (1989) 2 *Leiden Journal of International Law* 3, 18. For evidence of defensive practices by local authority building inspectors in New Zealand in the 1980s, see Smillie (n 76) 312.
[104] See Partlett (n 75) 243–44.
[105] See *Hamlin* [1994] 3 NZLR 513, 525–26, 546.
[106] See *Spencer on Byron* [2012] NZSC 83, [2013] 2 NZLR 297 [126].

However, the availability of such protection is a highly contested question,[107] which may again vary over time, and according to local conditions.

The problems with basing common law liability in this type of case on policy considerations are highlighted by William Young J in his dissent in *Spencer on Byron*. As his Honour points out, judges are rarely faced with a tabula rasa on which they can create a liability rule that they consider to be ideal in policy terms because even the most policy-oriented judge is still constrained by the previous authorities. Furthermore, because judges lack the empirical evidence that would be necessary for a properly informed policy judgment, in making duty of care decisions on policy grounds they inevitably rely 'on what can be no more than hunches'.[108] His Honour's conclusion was that the extension of liability to non-residential buildings gave rise to 'policy issues of a kind which the courts are not well-placed to assess and quite likely to get wrong'.[109]

To reiterate, my point is not that the policy arguments for liability are necessarily weak. It is rather that these are complex questions, which do not admit of easy answers. In those circumstances whether a special tort liability rule for defective premises is justified on policy grounds is an issue best left to legislatures to resolve, because they have both the democratic legitimacy to make such a decision, and the resources to ensure that it is properly informed.[110]

V. Problems

Common law claims for economic loss caused by the acquisition of defective premises give rise to a range of anomalies and practical problems. The precise form that these take varies according to the liability rule adopted, although certain issues consistently recur, including problems of line-drawing, limitation difficulties and the need for second-order rules to avoid undermining contractual allocations of risk.

A. Benchmarking

We can usefully start with the more generous approach to liability that permits a property owner to recover in respect of quality defects even if they pose no danger.

[107] Compare Todd (n 63) 227 (such protection not generally available to residential purchasers) with Feldthusen (n 81) (arguing that such protection is available, and that the courts should leave buyers to obtain it through contract and not impose tort liability). And witness also the somewhat involved – and not always persuasive – discussion of the possibility of contractual protection in *Brookfield Multiplex* [2014] HCA 36, (2014) 254 CLR 185.

[108] *Spencer on Byron* [2012] NZSC 83, [2013] 2 NZLR 297 [237].

[109] ibid [315]. See also NJ McBride, 'Private Law in the Ruins', this volume, ch 10, section II.

[110] See *Junior Books* [1983] AC 520, 537; *Bryan* (1995) 182 CLR 609, 644; *Aas* (2000) 12 P 3d 1125 (Cal 2000) 1142. See also Stapleton (n 12) 276–77.

An obvious problem with this approach is the relationship between quality and contractual expectations. As has often been pointed out, where there is a contract between the parties for provision of a chattel or premises, the question of acceptable quality can only be assessed by reference to the circumstances in which the contract was made, including the purpose for which the chattel or premises are intended to be used, and the other terms of the contract, including price.[111] Where the claim is one in tort between parties who are not in a contractual relationship, this is not possible, with the result that the question of acceptable quality is at large.[112]

It follows that a court which allows tort claims for mere defects in quality must choose some external benchmark as an objective, extracontractual standard of quality.[113] And yet it is difficult to know on what basis such a benchmark is to be selected, particularly when it will potentially apply across a wide range of premises, including things like specialist commercial plant, built to complex contractual specifications.[114] Furthermore, regardless of which external benchmark is chosen, it may mean that a defendant is held liable in negligence for failing to meet a higher quality standard than she bargained to provide in the contract pursuant to which she did the work.[115] This creates a paradox, whereby the person who paid for the work is entitled to a lesser quality standard than a third party who did not.[116] Finally, the benchmark needs to be kept in mind when damages are assessed because the claimant is entitled only to be put back in the position that they would have been in had the defendant exercised reasonable care to achieve compliance with the benchmark in question, and this may lead to other complications.[117]

In the more recent New Zealand premises cases, the benchmark has been compliance with the Building Code,[118] but this gives rise to other problems. First, the liability rule that results is a strange hybrid of negligence and breach of statutory duty, whereby the defendant owes a duty to take reasonable care to avoid causing economic loss by failing to comply with the Building Code (or some variant of this formula). The action for breach of statutory duty proper rests on a

[111] *Minchillo v Ford Motor Co of Australia Ltd* [1995] 2 VR 594 (VCA) 598–99.

[112] *Junior Books* [1983] AC 520, 551–52; *Woolcock Street Investments* [2004] HCA 16, (2004) 216 CLR 515 [100].

[113] S Todd et al, *Todd on Torts*, 9th edn (Wellington, Thomson Reuters New Zealand, 2023) 347.

[114] See *Rolls-Royce New Zealand Ltd v Carter Holt Harvey Ltd* [2005] 1 NZLR 324 (NZCA) [69].

[115] *Cosmopolitan Homes* 663 P 2d 1041 (Colo 1983) 1049–50; *Spencer on Byron* [2012] NZSC 83, [2013] 2 NZLR 297 [303]. See also the facts of *Woolcock Street Investments* [2004] HCA 16, (2004) 216 CLR 515, and of *Woollahra Municipal Council v Sved* (1996) 40 NSWLR 101 (NSWCA), where one of the defects was the absence of a waterproof membrane which the people for whom the house was built had ordered the builders not to install.

[116] See *Bryan* (1995) 182 CLR 609, 644.

[117] For example, whether such an award should be made where the cost of repair far exceeds any possible benefit or increase in value (as in the contract case of *Ruxley Electronics and Construction Ltd v Forsyth* [1996] AC 344 (HL)).

[118] *Spencer on Byron* [2012] NZSC 83, [2013] 2 NZLR 297 [47]. There are parallels here with *Anns*, where the duty was 'to take reasonable care … to secure that the builder does not cover in foundations which do not comply with byelaw requirements': *Anns* [1978] AC 728, 758 (Lord Wilberforce).

presumed legislative intention, but here the courts have (in effect) made the Code privately actionable without any reference to Parliament's intentions. Indeed, in theory, the negligence rule could be framed in this way even if the Code made clear that it was not intended to give rise to private rights. Second, the complexity of a negligence rule relating to the exercise of reasonable care to comply with a set of regulations generates an obvious risk of confusion between the scope of the duty (compliance with the Code) and the standard of care (which is that of a reasonable builder, architect, etc). And, finally, changes in the Code will of course also have a knock-on effect on the content of the builder's tort obligation.[119]

B. Dangerousness

In *Junior Books Ltd v Veitchi Co Ltd*, Lord Brandon argued that the problem of the external quality benchmark is obviated by the limitation of the liability rule to dangerous defects.[120] However, this is not necessarily true, as Stephen Waddams points out:

> It may be thought obvious that a building is defective if slabs of stone fall off, but this will not be so in all cases. If a building required a new roof after ten years, it would not be assumed that the original roof was defective in the absence of proof that roofs were expected to have a longer life than ten years. The fact that the roof, if left unrepaired, might become dangerous does not affect this point.[121]

Similarly, a building may be dangerous if used in one way but safe if used in another.[122] In the absence of contractual markers relating to expected use, it may be difficult in such a case to determine whether the owner has cause for complaint or not.

In any case, the limitation of liability to dangerous defects leads to a raft of other problems, as the UK courts discovered in the years following *Anns*.[123] One is that the logic of the rule allowing recovery for dangerous defects in premises is that the owner is in practical terms forced to repair because the premises cannot simply be discarded, as, say, a dangerously defective toaster could be.[124] However, it is impossible to draw a bright line between premises and chattels in this respect: there may

[119] The additional complications which would result from attempts to provide an external benchmark for mere quality defects in goods have thus far been avoided, since (as far as I know) no jurisdiction has been foolish enough to permit such claims.

[120] *Junior Books* [1983] AC 520, 552.

[121] Waddams (n 97) 159.

[122] See eg *Thomas Bates* [1991] 1 AC 499, where structural defects made a building dangerous if it was loaded up to its design capacity, but not if it was not.

[123] Critics of *Murphy* seem to put on rose-tinted spectacles when it comes to the post-*Anns* era. The contemporary case law and literature make it perfectly obvious that *Anns* ushered in a period of chaos and confusion. See eg Wallace (n 77) 47 ('it is notorious that the courts have found themselves entangled in a jungle of difficulties caused by [*Anns*]').

[124] See *Winnipeg Condominium* [1995] 1 SCR 85, 119.

be premises of little value that can straightforwardly be demolished by a wealthy owner, and many chattels (such as cars) where disposal may not be a practical solution to an owner of limited means. Ultimately this seems to me to undermine the argument for limiting economic loss recovery to dangerous premises.[125] But even if that is not accepted, it makes it hard to hold the line at premises, and it is no coincidence that Canada is the only jurisdiction surveyed in which recovery for economic loss caused by the acquisition of chattels has been permitted.[126] This raises further problems, however, such as how the courts decide which kinds of chattels are covered by the liability rule and which are not, and what external standard to apply to determine whether a chattel is unreasonably dangerous.[127] By contrast, systems that do not distinguish between dangerous and non-dangerous premises simply leave chattels out of the picture altogether.[128]

Another problem with limiting liability to dangerous defects is that it gives rise to serious line-drawing difficulties.[129] Several different tests have been used to determine whether a defect is 'dangerous', such as whether it is a 'real and substantial danger'[130] or poses a 'present or imminent danger to the health or safety' of the occupiers,[131] but whatever formula is used its boundaries are inevitably going to be too fuzzy for it to provide a clear test for use by the courts. What about a long-term health risk from damp or mould, for example, or defective weatherboards that might in an extreme case let water into the house?[132] If recovery is to be limited to dangerous defects, then a statutory definition is likely to work much better.[133]

Further difficulties may also arise if recovery is limited to dangerous defects. Suppose that a defect is not currently dangerous, for example, but will become so if not dealt with. And suppose that the cost of repair will be much greater by the time the danger arises. If the owner repairs now, are they barred from recovering the cost on the ground that there was no danger, and so no cause of action? What if they wait until there is danger and then sue for the larger sum? Was putting off the repair contributory negligence, or even a novus actus interveniens?[134] And what if the owner sells for a discount and then wants the diminution in value, and not

[125] See Nolan (n 44) 78–81.

[126] See eg *Hughes v Sunbeam Corp (Canada) Ltd* (2003) 219 DLR (4th) 467 (Ont CA). The logic of this position is accepted by the majority in *Maple Leaf* 2020 SCC 35, [2020] 3 SCR 504, according to whom (at [51]) it is 'the feasibility of discarding the thing as the means of averting the danger' which determines whether recovery is permitted. Note how, like the vulnerability test used in Australia, this test is highly fact-specific, and hence likely to generate uncertainty.

[127] This may depend, for example, on what the chattel is used for, how long it is supposed to last, etc.

[128] See Todd (n 63) 206 (Australia), 211 (New Zealand).

[129] See Palmer (n 81) 247.

[130] *Winnipeg Condominium* [1995] 1 SCR 85, 116 (La Forest J).

[131] *Anns* [1978] AC 728, 760 (Lord Wilberforce).

[132] See *Porirua City Council v Stieller* [1986] 1 NZLR 84 (NZCA).

[133] See eg Building Safety Act 2022, s 62 (defining a 'building safety risk' as 'a risk to the safety of people in or about a building' arising from 'the spread of fire' or 'structural failure' as regards the building).

[134] *Murphy* [1991] 1 AC 398, 480.

the cost of repair?[135] More generally, where the touchstone of liability is danger, are only those endangered owed a duty of care, or does this extend to an owner out of occupation?[136] And what precisely should the measure of the damages be in dangerous defect cases? Doubtless at least some of these issues can be satisfactorily resolved, but just posing these questions demonstrates the complexity involved in limiting liability to dangerous defects.

C. Vulnerability

Mention should also be made of the importance that has been attached by the Australian courts to the plaintiff's vulnerability.[137] There is, of course, a clear link between this approach and many of the key policy concerns in this area, as outlined at the start of the chapter. In particular, the financial consequences of defective building work are likely to be more devastating for a residential purchaser than for a commercial party or investor,[138] and they are likely to have less bargaining power in the sale negotiations. There is therefore an obvious rationale for limiting the tort liability rule to such cases, as indeed legislative interventions have mostly done. Nevertheless, trying to achieve this result by common law means generates seemingly insoluble line-drawing difficulties. In theory, the courts could simply lay down an arbitrary line (as legislation usually does) and then stick to it. However, what Dicey called the 'logical conscience' of the common law judge baulks at laying down arbitrary rules, and at holding the line in later cases when faced with such a rule. And in this context any bright-line rule will inevitably be arbitrary: there are plenty of private purchasers who are wealthy and sophisticated enough to negotiate a good deal, or to pay for alternative protection, and plenty of commercial purchasers who may lack the resources and bargaining power to do either.[139] It is not therefore surprising that the Australian courts have taken a more nuanced approach, whereby they assess the vulnerability of the plaintiff on the facts. However, this adds greatly to the complexity of litigation, and threatens to reduce the law to a wilderness of single instances.[140] Furthermore, it is doubtful

[135] As in *Murphy*, where the claimant had sold the house, and diminution in value was the measure of damages used by the Court of Appeal: [1990] 2 All ER 269. This decision is an excellent example of the difficulties with assessing damages on the *Anns* approach.

[136] There was much discussion of this issue in the aftermath of *Anns*: see eg JH Holyoak and DK Allen, *Civil Liability for Defective Premises* (London, Butterworths, 1982) para 5.41.

[137] See generally, Todd (n 63) 225–29. And for the intellectual antecedents of this approach, see Stapleton (n 12) 270–71.

[138] See Partlett (n 75) 248–49.

[139] A point made by Chambers J in *Spencer on Byron* [2012] NZSC 83, [2013] 2 NZLR 297 [197]–[198]. More generally, it may be harder for commercial purchasers to negotiate alternative protection than is sometimes assumed: see Todd (n 63) 222–23 ('at most only limited alternative rights of action' available to commercial owners).

[140] Indeed, if 'carried to its logical extreme' the vulnerability approach 'would make it hard to predict the outcome of any particular case': *Spencer on Byron* [2012] NZSC 83, [2013] 2 NZLR 297 [298] (William Young J). The *Raymond v Lewis* case referred to in n 66 provides an example of this

whether the courts are in a position to make such an assessment accurately in the first place.[141]

Line-drawing problems are also inevitable if the focus is switched from the nature of the purchaser to the nature of the premises. A hard-and-fast distinction between residential and non-residential premises is impossible to achieve because many premises are mixed use. Residences are used for work, workplaces for living in, and so on. These difficulties are well documented[142] and are again best resolved by a statutory definition,[143] preferably one as precisely phrased as possible. Moreover, for the courts to determine whether a duty of care is owed solely by reference to this distinction seems unprincipled. As Todd says, if the courts are going to allow claims for economic loss caused by defective premises, 'there is no good stopping point' in terms of distinguishing different types of purchaser or building: 'Seemingly it is all or nothing.'[144] However, this then means allowing recovery in many situations where the policy case for it seems weak, such as where a bank repossesses a defective house.

D. Limitation

A recurrent theme of the law in this area has been difficulties with limitation of actions. The *Anns* doctrine was notoriously problematic in this respect. To some extent, this was attributable to the characterisation of the harm in *Anns* as physical damage to property, as opposed to pure economic loss,[145] but the suggestion that, once the harm is properly classified as economic loss, the limitation problems fall away[146] is naive. On the contrary, negligence claims for pure economic loss tend to generate intractable limitation problems, for the simple reason that there is no single moment in time at which a claimant can definitively be said to have suffered 'loss', which is in principle when the cause of action is complete, and hence when the limitation period starts to run.[147] It follows that in cases of economic loss caused by defective premises a departure from the default negligence rules regarding limitation of actions is needed. However, limitation is now generally governed

conundrum, since the homeowner was found at trial to be vulnerable in the relevant sense but this was reversed on appeal.

[141] Witness the disagreement on this issue between the majority and Kirby J in *Woolcock Street Investments* [2004] HCA 16, (2004) 216 CLR 515.

[142] See eg ibid [17] (Gleeson CJ, Gummow, Hayne and Heydon JJ); *Spencer on Byron* [2012] NZSC 83, [2013] 2 NZLR 297 [206]–[214].

[143] See *Brookfield Multiplex* [2014] HCA 36, (2014) 254 CLR 185 [135] (distinction between domestic and commercial purposes unstable, 'at least in the absence of a statutory definition').

[144] Todd (n 63) 228.

[145] Eventually Parliament stepped in and passed the Latent Damage Act 1986 to try to resolve the issues.

[146] See eg *Invercargill* [1996] AC 624, 648.

[147] See Nolan (n 91) 261–71.

by statute, and (unlike legislatures) courts are clearly not in a position to create bespoke rules for particular types of case.[148]

The problems that have resulted are again well documented. Is the loss suffered, for example, when the claimant pays too much for the defective property, or only when the defect is discovered, or reasonably discoverable?[149] And what if one owner discovers the defect and then sells the premises to a buyer who pays full price, oblivious of the defect?[150] Applying a discoverability test, it seems that the original owner must have had a cause of action (despite in fact suffering no loss), in which case does the limitation period for the buyer's claim run from the same time as the seller's, or from the time of the sale, or from the time at which the buyer discovered (or could reasonably have discovered) the defect?[151] Finally, where liability is dependent on the dangerousness of the defect, when does the cause of action arise?[152] Once again, these difficulties demonstrate the challenges of fashioning a workable common law solution to the defective premises problem.

E. Other Problems

Three other difficulties to which this kind of litigation gives rise should also be flagged. The first is the 'double jeopardy' problem.[153] Suppose that the owner settles with the builder and pockets the compensation, but then sells the property for its full value, because the problem is not obvious. Can the new owner sue as well (and if not, why not)? The second difficulty is the 'transferred loss' problem. Suppose that a vendor of premises warrants their soundness and freedom from defects, and that it later becomes apparent that they are defective because of the negligence of, say, an architect who advised on the foundations. And suppose that there is no contractual link between the vendor and the architect. If the buyer recovers compensation from the vendor on the warranty, should the vendor be entitled to an indemnity from the architect in tort?[154] The third difficulty relates to the work in fact taken on by the defendant. Suppose this time that the architect

[148] On limitation periods in the defective premises context generally, see Britton and Bell (n 7) ch 10.

[149] As tends now to be assumed: see eg *Hamlin* [1994] 3 NZLR 513, 534; Partlett (n 75) 249.

[150] Note that in this scenario it is not necessarily the case that the buyer has been careless. It is conceivable that the seller in fact discovered the defect before it became reasonably discoverable. Indeed, it is even possible to imagine circumstances in which a defect becomes reasonably discoverable at one point in time, and then ceases to be reasonably discoverable at a later date!

[151] See S Todd, 'Difficulties with Leaky Building Litigation' (2012) 20 *Tort Law Review* 19, 30–31, discussing *North Shore City Council v Body Corporate 188529* [2010] NZSC 158, [2011] 2 NZLR 289.

[152] This moment is particularly difficult to pinpoint if (as under the *Anns* principle) it is a condition of recovery that the danger is 'imminent', a notably elusive concept.

[153] As to which, see G Robertson, 'Defective Premises and Subsequent Purchasers' (1983) 99 *LQR* 559; Todd (n 151) 32–33.

[154] See *Riddell v Porteous* [1999] 1 NZLR 1 (NZCA), discussed in S Todd, 'Defective Buildings – Relational Loss and Negligent Owners' (1999) 7 *Tort Law Review* 81.

designing the foundations is not paid to undertake an investigation of the soil which a reasonable architect would undertake before doing the task. It seems rather harsh on the architect to make them liable for not undertaking a task which they were not paid to undertake in the first place. And while the obvious solution is to say that the terms of the contract under which the architect was engaged limit the scope of their duty to the third-party purchaser,[155] as a matter of principle it is not obvious why the purchaser should be prejudiced by the terms of a contract to which they were not a party.[156] Problems such as these are likely to be easier to solve through legislative provision than by judicial development, constrained as the latter is by general negligence principles. For example, regarding the last point, the legislation can simply limit the defendant's duty to the work in fact taken on.[157]

VI. Legislative Solutions

Many of the problems thrown up by allowing common law claims for economic loss caused by the acquisition of defective premises can be avoided by providing statutory remedies instead. The contrast between the two approaches to the issue was highlighted by Lord Bridge in *D&F Estates*:

> The statutory development enacted by the Defective Premises Act 1972 effected clear and precise changes in the law imposing certain specific statutory duties subject to carefully defined limitations and exceptions. … The common law developments have effected changes in the law which inevitably lack the kind of precision attainable by statute though limits have had to be and still are being worked out by decisions of the courts in a spate of ensuing litigation.[158]

Various different techniques have been employed in the legislation that has been passed in this area. The most prominent of these are the use of a contractual privity exception in favour of subsequent owners to allow them to recover under warranties deemed to be included in their residential building contracts;[159] the statutory generation of a negligence duty of care;[160] and the use of a more bespoke approach which is not parasitic on an existing conceptual structure such as contract or negligence. My sense is that this last option is the superior one, and that in particular the use of a negligence framework, as in recent New South Wales legislation, is likely to lead to similar problems to those thrown up by the common law

[155] *Woolcock Street Investments* [2004] HCA 16, (2004) 216 CLR 515 [28].
[156] See the objections put forward by Todd (n 63) 220–21.
[157] See eg Defective Premises Act 1972, s 1(1) ('DPA 1972').
[158] *D&F Estates* [1989] AC 177, 193.
[159] See eg Domestic Building Contracts Act 1995 (Vic) ss 8–9; Building Act 2004 (NZ) ss 362I–J. Typically provisions of this kind imply various warranties into domestic building contracts, which can be relied on by subsequent owners.
[160] See eg Design and Building Practitioners Act 2020 (NSW) pt 4.

developments.[161] It is at any rate an advantage of a legislative solution that it is not necessarily tied to concepts, such as negligence, which may not be conducive to the achievement of an optimal solution.

A good example of a bespoke statutory remedy which avoids many of the problems thrown up by common law development is that provided by section 1 of the UK's Defective Premises Act 1972. Certain aspects of the 1972 Act illustrate the advantages of a statutory remedy. First, the protections the Act affords are offered to 'a clearly-defined category of persons beyond [contractual] privity',[162] namely owners and tenants of dwellings. Second, the Act uses objective quality benchmarks derived from the terms implied into contracts for the construction of dwellings.[163] These benchmarks are well established in contract,[164] which suggests that they are workable standards to employ, and means that there is a body of case law on which to draw when applying the 1972 Act. And the reliance of the benchmarks on a threshold of 'habitability' excludes minor quality defects without opening up the can of worms that is 'dangerousness'.[165] Third, the Act is limited to work undertaken 'for or in connection with the provision of a *dwelling*'.[166] This has the effect of furthering the policy goal of protecting more vulnerable property purchasers while avoiding the kinds of problems that common law attempts to distinguish between different kinds of premises have thrown up.[167] Fourth, the Act does not impose a duty of care, but a stricter duty to bring about a particular result, which may be better suited to the achievement of that policy goal. Fifth, the Act straightforwardly rules out exclusion of the liability it creates,[168] although it provides protection to defendants sued for following binding instructions given

[161] ibid. According to the central provision (s 37), '[a] person who carries out construction work has a duty to exercise reasonable care to avoid economic loss caused by defects in or related to a building for which the work is done, and arising from the work, which is owed to owners and successive owners of the relevant land'. Remarkably, though many of the terms in this provision are defined, 'defect' is not, with the result that the legislation fails to provide an objective benchmark against which the quality of the work can be assessed See, further, J Morgan, 'Tort as a Tool of Government Policy: Section 38 of the Building Act 1984: Sleeping Beauty Awakes?', this volume, ch 7, 187.

[162] S Whittaker, 'Privity of Contract and the Tort of Negligence: Future Directions' (1996) 16 *OJLS* 199, 202.

[163] The duty is to 'see that the work [taken on] is done in a workmanlike or, as the case may be, professional manner, with proper materials and so that as regards that work the dwelling will be fit for habitation when completed' (DPA 1972, s 1(1)).

[164] The threefold implied warranty on which the DPA 1972 relies dates back at least as far as *Miller v Cannon Hill Estates Ltd* [1931] 2 KB 113 (KBD).

[165] Crucially, there is no scope for the defendant to argue that 'habitability' is a higher quality standard than they bargained to provide, since fitness for habitation is a purpose which 'must be achieved whatever [the dwelling's] price or position in the market': Whittaker (n 162) 202.

[166] DPA 1972, s 1(1) (emphasis added). This wording does not encompass most refurbishment work (*Jenson v Faux* [2011] EWCA Civ 423, [2011] 1 WLR 3038), but s 2A of the Act now extends the s 1 duty to such work, if done in the course of a business. The specificity of the DPA 1972 in this respect can be contrasted with common law duties of care, where it is often unclear what kind of work is covered.

[167] See similarly the limitation of the transmissible warranties imposed by the Building Act 2004 (NZ) to a 'household unit', a term very precisely defined in s 7 of the Act.

[168] DPA 1972, s 6(3).

to them by the person for whom the work in question was being done.[169] And finally, the fact that time runs from the completion of the work, and not from the occurrence of the loss, neatly side-steps the limitation problems that have arisen in common law claims.[170] And while it is not obvious that the Act avoids some of the other difficulties to which the common law developments have given rise, such as the 'double jeopardy' problem,[171] these could no doubt readily have been resolved by suitable drafting.[172] Overall, the Act is 'an attractive model for … imposition of liability for defects in quality beyond privity'.[173]

VII. Conclusion

Some years after the House of Lords handed down its decision in the causation case of *Fairchild v Glenhaven Funeral Services Ltd*,[174] Lord Hoffmann, who had given one of the judgments allowing the claimants' appeals, suggested that it might have been better had their Lordships dismissed the claims for want of proof of causation, and let Parliament overturn that decision by legislation.[175] Unlike Parliament, he said, the House 'could not simply erect a rule with arbitrary limitations'.[176] Judges were 'supposed to declare the principles of the common law', and if allowing the claims in *Fairchild* could not be reconciled with those principles, then it would have been better to have dismissed the appeals. After touching on the multifarious problems to which the *Fairchild* decision gave rise, he concluded:

> In retrospect, I think the most satisfactory outcome would have been for their Lordships in their judicial capacity to have adhered to established principle, wrung their hands about the unfairness of the outcome in the particular case, and recommended to the Government that it pass appropriate legislation. Then judiciary and legislature would each have been functioning within its proper sphere: the judges not creating confusion in the common law by trying to legislate for special cases and Parliament amending the common law where fairness and the public interest appeared to demand it.[177]

[169] ibid s 1(2).

[170] ibid s 1(5). This is presumably why the Latent Damage Act 1986 was limited to negligence and did not encompass claims under the 1972 Act. Legislation in other jurisdictions also uses readily ascertainable dates for the start of the limitation period, such as the date of the grant of occupancy certification or date of first occupation (Building Act 1993 (NT), s 160) or the date of the act or omission on which the claim is based (Building Act 2004 (NZ), s 393(2)).

[171] The duty that s 1 creates is owed to (inter alia) 'every person who acquires an interest (whether legal or equitable) in the dwelling', which would seem to allow for the possibility of claims by successive owners in respect of the same defect.

[172] See eg Domestic Building Contracts Act 1995 (Vic), s 9 (right to sue on implied warranties extended to 'the owner *for the time being*' of the relevant building (emphasis added)).

[173] Whittaker (n 162) 202.

[174] *Fairchild v Glenhaven Funeral Services Ltd* [2002] UKHL 22, [2003] 1 AC 32.

[175] Lord Hoffmann, '*Fairchild* and After' in A Burrows, D Johnston and R Zimmermann (eds), *Judge and Jurist: Essays in Memory of Lord Rodger of Earlsferry* (Oxford, Oxford University Press, 2013).

[176] ibid 65.

[177] ibid 68.

Similar sentiments had previously been expressed by Jonathan Morgan in an insightful paper on the *Fairchild* saga. According to Morgan, *Fairchild* was 'an essentially legislative attempt to carve out an exceptional category, doomed to failure by the common law's ineluctable method of reasoning by analogy'.[178] Far better, he writes, to have left the creation of such a category to Parliament.

The history of common law and legislative responses to the social problem of economic loss caused by the acquisition of defective premises bears witness to the wisdom of these words. In this chapter, I have argued that the House of Lords was right in *Murphy* to stick to principle, reject claims for such loss, and leave it to Parliament to provide a properly tailored and workable solution. In the words of an American judge, dissenting in a case where the majority imposed tort liability for economic loss caused by defective building work:

> There is no principled way for this court – or any court – to limit the reasoning to the case of homebuilders; it can do so only by judicial fiat. While such line-drawing is appropriate for a legislative body – indeed that is its primary function – it is singularly inappropriate for a judicial body.[179]

As Lord Hoffmann points out, the 'development of the law is not solely the province of one branch of government but ought to be a partnership between all three'.[180] And if in the case of defective premises Parliament was slow to act, then the responsibility for that lies squarely with the politicians. The judges were simply doing their job.

[178] Morgan (n 28) 64–65.
[179] *Cosmopolitan Homes* 663 P 2d 1041 (Colo 1983) 1050 (Rovira J).
[180] Hoffmann (n 175) 69.

7

Tort as a Tool of Government Policy: Section 38 of the Building Act 1984: Sleeping Beauty Awakes?

JONATHAN MORGAN

I. Introduction: Developing Statutory Liability for Defective Buildings

How can tort law advance government policy? To pose this question immediately takes a position in tort's Theory Wars[1] by considering tort law's regulatory potential. Today's intellectually dominant theorists reject the very suggestion.[2] However, *statutory* torts are difficult to accommodate in a pure account of corrective justice, correlative rights and duties, unsullied by public policy. Tort lawyers are paying more attention to the role of statute within this stronghold of common law reasoning.[3] This chapter examines the nature of 'statutory torts', concentrating specifically on actionability of the Building Regulations in English law.

Liability for defective buildings has vexed courts around the common law world for the past half-century.[4] Prior to the disastrous Grenfell Tower fire in London in 2017, it was not such a high priority for the British government and legislature. The tragedy has revived political interest in building safety. Some notable changes in tort liability have resulted, including those contained (among very much else) in the Building Safety Act 2022 (UK) (BSA 2022), which first require brief explanation. However this chapter's primary focus is a provision far from novel: the dormant section 38 ('Civil Liability') of the Building Act 1984, providing for the actionability of loss-causing breach of the Building Regulations. The UK government has said it intends finally to bring section 38 into force.

[1] J Levin, *Tort Wars* (Cambridge, Cambridge University Press, 2008).

[2] See eg A Beever and C Rickett, 'Interpretive Legal Theory and the Academic Lawyer' (2005) 68 *MLR* 320; R Stevens, *Torts and Rights* (Oxford, Oxford University Press, 2007).

[3] TT Arvind and J Steele (eds), *Tort Law and the Legislature: Common Law, Statute and the Dynamics of Legal Change* (Oxford, Hart Publishing, 2013).

[4] See D Nolan, 'Defective Premises and Economic Loss: A Problem Best Left to Legislation?', this volume, ch 6, esp section III.

Although its main focus is not tort liability, the BSA 2022 extends the Defective Premises Act 1972 (DPA 1972) to cover renovation work on existing buildings (it previously applied only to *initial* construction):[5] flammable cladding and insulation materials have frequently been installed in 'improvement' works (as retrofitted at Grenfell in 2015–16, on the tower originally built in 1972–74). More striking is the lengthy extension of limitation periods for claims under the DPA 1972 (and, when it comes into force, section 38 of the Building Act 1984).[6] The change has expressly retrospective effect for the DPA 1972.[7] Indeed, while limitation periods are in future extended to 15 years, the period is extended for fully *30 years* for claims that accrued prior to the commencement of the BSA 2022's relevant section.

The BSA 2022 also creates new liabilities for those who supply 'construction products' that fail to comply with statutory requirements, leading to a building that is 'unfit for habitation'.[8] Again there is a 15-year limitation period.[9] However for *cladding* products only, there is also retrospective liability for non-compliance 'at any time before the coming into force of this section'.[10] The limitation period for claims about cladding is again extended to 30 years where 'the right of action accrued before the commencement date'.[11] To quote from the Explanatory Notes published with the 2022 Act, unsafe cladding products have caused 'particular problems' of 'historical fire safety defects',[12] the government asserting:

> There is evidence that the past actions of manufacturers and sellers of cladding products have contributed to the creation of these defects and the resultant fire safety risks.[13]

The 2022 Act also introduces 'remediation contribution orders'.[14] Their aim is to allocate the cost of expensive renovation works to developers (and landlords), removing the financial burden from tenants. But the statutory remedy does not depend on a 'tort' involving breach of statutory duty. Indeed, the point is to redistribute the costs 'fairly', quite apart from private law liabilities in tort, under the relevant lease, or otherwise. Of these remediation contribution orders, Edwin Johnson J recently commented:

> Parliament has decided that, irrespective of fault, it is fair for those with the broadest shoulders to bear unprecedented financial burdens. To that end the 2022 Act … provides for wholesale intervention in and beyond normal contractual relationships

[5] Defective Premises Act 1972 (DPA 1972), s 1; cf *Jenson v Faux* [2011] EWCA Civ 423, [2011] 1 WLR 3038 (holding that conversion of loft and cellar into additional living space was not 'work for or in connection with the provision of a [new] dwelling'; cf now BSA 2022, s 134 (inserting new s 2A into the DPA 1972).

[6] BSA 2022, s 135(1) (inserting new s 4B, Limitation Act 1980).

[7] ibid s 135(3) (subject to protection of a defendant's European Convention rights: s 135(5)).

[8] ibid s 148.

[9] ibid s 150 (inserting a new s 10B(1), Limitation Act 1980).

[10] ibid s 149(2).

[11] Limitation Act 1980, s 10B(2) (cf saving of ECHR rights in BSA 2022, s 149(9)).

[12] Explanatory Notes to the BSA 2022, paras 1239–40.

[13] ibid para 1241.

[14] BSA 2022, s 124.

> in order to transfer the potentially ruinous cost of remediation from individual leaseholders to landlords, and to distribute it between landlords and developers and their associates according to criteria which Parliament has decided are necessary and fair.[15]

Note that developers' 'associates' include parent companies of a thinly capitalised developer.[16] Remediation contribution orders cut through the usual rules of limited liability within corporate groups:

> The obvious purpose behind [these] association provisions is to ensure that [wealthy parent companies] … cannot evade responsibility for meeting the cost of remedying the relevant defects by hiding behind the separate personality of the development company.[17]

As Bright and McFarlane comment, the BSA 2022 has 'jettisoned' several 'axioms of private law (even including such basic ideas as legal personality)' to advance Parliament's policy goal (ie to provide effective remedies for leaseholders suffering loss through no fault of their own).[18]

Among this raft of policy-driven changes is the government's intention to bring into force section 38 of the Building Act 1984. Section 38 makes breaches of the Building Regulations actionable in damages.[19] That provision has been on the statute book, but never brought into force, ever since the Health and Safety at Work etc Act 1974 (section 71). In its initial post-Grenfell reform proposals (2020) the government had proposed *repealing* section 38 'without ever bringing it into force', since there had been no support for its commencement in the public consultation on 'Building a Safer Future'.[20] But, after criticism that its proposals did not go far enough to protect leaseholders against the cost of remediation, the government reversed its position. In 2021 it announced that section 38 would now be commenced to provide 'compensation … for physical damage caused by a breach of building regulations'.[21] Thus, in addition to the Regulations' enforcement by local authority building control departments, and criminal sanctions,[22] breaching the Building Regulations will trigger liability in damages.

This chapter analyses section 38's belated 'activation', following consideration of the nature and instrumental uses of statutory torts. The most striking difference from the common law, perhaps, is the openly political debate about the creation

[15] *Triathlon Homes LLP v Stratford Village Development Partnership* [2024] UKFTT 26 (PC) [75] ('*Triathlon Homes*'). As was noted in the Introduction to this volume (p 2), the Court of Appeal heard an appeal in this case in March 2025.

[16] D Sawtell, 'Rationalising Associate Liability Under the Building Safety Act 2022', this volume, ch 8, 230.

[17] *Triathlon Homes* [2024] UKFTT 26 [266].

[18] S Bright and B McFarlane, 'Private Law Failings and Policy Development Following the Grenfell Tower Fire' in J Gardner et al (eds), *Politics, Policy and Private Law*, vol I: *Tort, Property and Equity* (Oxford, Hart Publishing, 2023) 150.

[19] Building Regulations 2010, SI 2214/2010 ('Building Regulations').

[20] Explanatory Notes to the Building Safety Bill 2020, para 892.

[21] Ministry of Housing, Communities and Local Government, *Building Safety Bill: Government Response to Pre-legislative Scrutiny by the Select Committee* (Cmd 473, 2021) para 23.

[22] Building Act 1984, s 35.

of a new statutory tort (or repeal of an old one). Aside from the legislation on defective cladding and construction, high-profile recent examples in the United Kingdom include (i) the repeal of actionability of workplace health and safety regulations,[23] and (ii) making actionable higher education institutions' obligation to secure freedom of speech.[24] Both controversial reforms are examined later in the chapter. (By contrast, section 38 has attracted less debate, and one can only speculate why it was for so long held dormant, and whether even now it will actually be brought into force). Such debates are often strongly instrumental in flavour. Would the putative tort improve compensation for a deserving group of victims at the cost of a suitable set of defendants? Alternatively, or additionally, would it improve enforcement of a public duty by enlisting tort claimants as 'private enforcers'? Might the enforcers need the additional incentive of gain-based, exemplary or other supra-compensatory remedies? Conversely, would private enforcement be open to abuse, or cut across the enforcement priorities of expert regulators? The open discussion of policy in parliamentary debates stands in marked, refreshing contrast to common law adjudication. Perhaps influenced by fashionable rights-based theories hostile to incorporation of public-interest concerns into tort, English courts have recently sought to mute reliance on policy concerns in favour of emphasising precedent and doctrinal 'principle'.[25]

Rights-based theories tend (as noted) to ignore statutory torts. Theorists of this school may deny that they are properly 'torts' at all. Making a general, undirected public duty actionable by individuals is, on this view, incoherent, in the absence of the individual claimant having a *right* that correlates to the public duty. Worse still would be to add remedies unrelated to the individual claimant's loss (ie the harm to the right invaded) as an expedient to stimulate enforcement of a public duty.[26] Statutory actions with such features might be seen as structural impossibilities, or even perversions of tort law's private, interpersonal, bilateral nature.

One possible response is to query why we should assume as true a certain theory of corrective justice as the starting point, and use it to deny that some statutory claims are 'torts'. Could the statutory examples not, conversely, pose a problem for a narrow insistence on corrective justice, if it is unable to explain legal institutions with a strong resemblance to paradigm common law torts? Whether statutory claims are properly 'torts' is not an abstract or academic question alone. Since statutes are rarely complete and exhaustive codes, courts must necessarily

[23] Enterprise and Regulatory Reform Act 2013, s 69.

[24] Higher Education (Freedom of Speech) Act 2023, s 4.

[25] Consider *Robinson v Chief Constable of West Yorkshire* [2018] UKSC 4, [2018] AC 736 (discussed by J Morgan, 'Nonfeasance and the End of Policy? Reflections on the Revolution in Public Authority Liability' (2019) 35 *Journal of Professional Negligence* 32).

[26] EJ Weinrib, *The Idea of Private Law* (Oxford, Oxford University Press, 2012) 48:

> The plaintiff's function in initiating a lawsuit is [according to economic analysis of law] not to secure redress for wrongful injury but to claim a bounty for prosecuting inefficient economic activity. Economic analysis thus submerges the private nature of tort law in a public law of economic regulation … [and] effaces its characteristic features.

interpret them against the law's background regime of concepts and principles.[27] Is the correct categorisation as 'tort' or not? As will be seen, the question is pressing given how often difficulties arise about statutory actions' scope and meaning. Parliament is given to silence over fundamental issues such as the kinds of loss that are recoverable. (Section 38 is itself a clear example of such inconclusive drafting.) The interpreting court tends to reach for 'tort' to find the answers. The reasons for doing so include concerns for systemic consistency, familiarity with and (excessive?) attachment to established common law principles, and a pragmatic reading-across of tortious rules in the absence of any other indication from the statute. On one view then, 'statutory torts' certainly are tortious, irrespective of the role of public policy in their genesis, their justification, and sometimes their basic structures. But the miscellany, diversity and inconsistency that prevails across the swathe of statutory torts means that assimilating them into one single coherent theory, based on corrective justice or otherwise, may not be possible. Parliaments of many eras have enacted different statutory claims, using different statutory formulations, for very different reasons.

II. Are 'Statutory Torts' Really Torts?

Parliament can do anything, according to the traditional Diceyan conception of legally unlimited sovereignty.[28] It can certainly mandate compensation for individuals who suffer loss through breach of some pre-existing, but hitherto non-actionable, statutory duty. Parliament could even provide for enforcement of statutory duties by private action without any need to show loss, allocating the penalty for infringement to the successful enforcer as an incentivising 'bounty'. (Of one such archaic provision, in the Lord's Day Observance Act 1780, Rowlatt J observed (in 1931) that Parliament had 'enlisted the motive of [the enforcer's] private greed to ensure that the offender shall be made to smart for his offence'.[29]) Equally, Parliament might remove previous actionability, as in the Common Informers Act 1951 (repealing the provisions that Rowlatt J had, with evident reluctance, applied).

But are these statutory actions *torts*, properly so-called? Does it matter?

This chapter suggests that it certainly does matter. Not only for conceptual or taxonomic tidiness (to the extent that that matters at all); rather, because much of

[27] As true for (eg) criminal law as for tort. See *Sweet v Parsley* [1970] AC 132, 162 (Lord Diplock):

> [O]nly too frequently the actual words used by Parliament to define the prohibited conduct are in themselves descriptive only of a physical act and bear no connotation as to any particular state of mind on the part of the person who does the act. Nevertheless, the mere fact that Parliament has made the conduct a criminal offence gives rise to some implication about the mental element of the conduct proscribed.

[28] cf *City of London v Wood* (1602) 12 Mod 669, 688; 88 ER 1592 (Holt CJ): 'an Act of Parliament can do no wrong, though it may do several things that look pretty odd'.

[29] *Orpen v Haymarket Capitol Ltd* [1931] All ER 360 (KB) 361.

the detailed law governing statutory claims derives from the surrounding common law rules, principles and concepts. The conclusion that a statutory claim is a *tort* – more usually an assumption than an explicit conclusion – therefore answers important questions about its nature (for example, procedure, defences, remedies). Parliament could, in theory, exhaustively define all these connected questions. In practice this happens rarely, and existing legal concepts fill the gaps, if only *faute de mieux*. It follows that whether a statutory claim is a 'tort' matters a great deal.

Unfortunately, then, there is great controversy on this classificatory question. In an ideal world, the legislature (or, rather, Parliamentary Counsel) would address the question explicitly and clarify whether statutory claims are torts, or anyway to be treated as such. But usually Parliament fails to do so. In their leading work on statutory torts, Stanton et al note how difficult it is to state 'what is a tort', save by resorting to conventional or historical definitions.[30] The problem is acute. Sometimes Parliament expressly states that a given duty is to be actionable as '(the tort of) breach of statutory duty'. In other provisions, Parliament simply makes damages available for a given breach. Are the latter necessarily 'torts'?[31] Stanton et al deplore the lack of statutory guidance, and any consistent approach to drafting. This legislative ambiguity means we cannot avoid theoretical debates about the definition of 'tort' by statutory fiat.

Some theories suggest that many statutory actions are, in fact, *not* true torts. Compensating those who suffer loss from breach of 'undirected' statutory duties,[32] owed to the public as a whole, cannot rest on the breach of any *right* of the claimant's. (As arguably is true of the building regulations, which have been authoritatively held a '*public health* measure' and therefore not actionable by individual housing developers seeking protection against economic loss.)[33] As far as tort law is concerned, such claims without violation of rights would involve

[30] K Stanton et al, *Statutory Torts* (London, Sweet & Maxwell, 2003) ch 1.

[31] cf *The Owners – Strata Plan No 84674 v Pafburn Pty Ltd* [2023] NSWCA 301, (2023) 113 NSWLR 105 ('*OSP 84674*'): '[the] inevitable conclusion … is that a cause of action for a breach of a duty imposed by a statute invokes liability in tort' (Basten JA at [81]; Ward P agreed and Adamson JA found similarly on this point at [12]). On appeal (*Pafburn Pty Ltd v The Owners – Strata Plan No 84674* [2024] HCA 49), the High Court was not required to consider whether the relevant statutory liability was a 'tort'. However, noting that the Civil Liability Act 2002 (NSW) did not define 'tort', the majority (Gageler CJ, Gleeson, Jagot and Beech-Jones JJ at [21]) stated that the word therefore held its 'common law meaning':

> 'Tort' is a concept of significant elasticity and indeterminacy which extends to any form of wrong which attracts a remedy in civil law and not within another recognised class of actionable wrongs (such as breach of contract or breach of trust).

[32] Bright and McFarlane (n 18) 138–40.

[33] *Governors of the Peabody Donation Fund v Sir Lindsay Parkinson & Co* [1985] AC 210 (HL) 241. Lord Keith (declining to recognise liability under the London Government Act 1963) said the Act's purpose

> is not to safeguard building developers against economic loss resulting from their failure to comply with approved plans. It is in my opinion to safeguard the occupiers of houses built in the local authority's area, and also members of the public generally, against dangers to their health which may arise from defective drainage installations. The provisions are public health measures.

damnum absque iniuria (merely a factual loss, in the absence of a legal wrong to the claimant) – a logical impossibility. There might be *liability*,[34] but not a 'tort' which requires breach of a duty *owed to the claimant*. For example, under Lord Campbell's Act, persons financially dependent on a breadwinner whose death results from a tort can bring compensation claims for their lost dependency.[35] But it is the *breadwinner* who had the right not to be killed. The statute *exceptionally* allows the dependents to enforce a right belonging to another. Outside the bounds of such a statute, however, on ordinary and fundamental principles a party who foreseeably suffers loss consequent on injury to *another's* (personal or property) rights suffers classic *damnum absque iniuria*.[36] It is surely a fortiori when *nobody* has a right correlating to an 'undirected' *public* duty.

Debates about public nuisance parallel those around statutory 'torts'. In public nuisance, an individual who suffers particularly significant loss ('special damage') from interference with interests of the general public has a claim for damages. Orthodoxy classifies this as a 'tort' claim. However, its dual nature is an anomaly. Public nuisance connotes *both* a common law crime (essentially a rag-bag of 'regulatory' or 'public welfare' offences predating the modern regulatory state)[37] *and also* ('unusually') a tort.[38] But some scholars object that a *tort* (an action for the enforcement of *private rights*) cannot coherently derive from the *crime* of public nuisance which consists of duties to the *public at large*.[39] As Stevens explains, the 'tort' of public nuisance offends the doctrine of privity: *only* those to whom a duty is owed can enforce it; *only* those who bear rights have standing to enforce them.[40]

Perhaps, though, *certain* public nuisance claims can coherently be classified as 'torts'. Neyers argues that public nuisance can be 'reconceptualised' as properly tortious in two situations only: claims involving rights to use the highway (and navigable rivers) and rights to fish in tidal waters, these being rights that are conferred *both* on the public at large *and on individuals*.[41] A broader application of a similar strategy is Dagan and Dorfman's recent argument that all have (or should have) private rights as individuals to use and enjoy public spaces – eg public parks.[42] The authors insist that these are *private* rights 'on the same model of

[34] A Robertson, 'Justifying Liabilities and Duties' in S Degeling, M Crawford and N Tiverios (eds), *Justifying Private Rights* (Oxford, Hart Publishing, 2020).

[35] Fatal Accidents Act 1976, s 1.

[36] *Leigh and Sillavan Ltd v Aliakmon Shipping Co Ltd* [1986] AC 785 (HL); *West Bromwich Albion FC v Al Safty* [2006] EWCA Civ 1299; *Paul v Royal Wolverhampton NHS Trust* [2024] UKSC 1, [2024] 2 WLR 417 [2]-[3].

[37] JR Spencer, 'Public Nuisance: A Critical Examination' [1989] *CLJ* 55, 59. In *R v Rimmington* [2005] UKHL 63 [31] ('*Rimmington*'), Lord Bingham endorsed Spencer's argument for abolishing the common law crime, as superseded by modern regulatory legislation – but it was a decision for Parliament.

[38] *Rimmington* [2005] UKHL 63 [7] (Lord Bingham).

[39] JW Neyers, 'Reconceptualising the Tort of Public Nuisance' [2017] *CLJ* 87, 88–92.

[40] R Stevens, *Torts and Rights* (Oxford, Oxford University Press, 2007) 186ff.

[41] See also A Ripstein, 'Public and Private in the Tort of Public Nuisance' in A Robertson and JW Neyers (eds), *Private Law and the State* (Oxford, Hart Publishing, 2024).

[42] H Dagan and A Dorfman, 'Public Nuisance for Private Persons' (2024) 74 *University of Toronto Law Journal* 198, 211.

rights that figures prominently in the law of torts' – they simply relate to the *public sphere*.[43] But even a broad definition of these 'private rights to use and enjoy public spaces' cannot encompass swathes of public nuisance. Neither its 'social regulator' role in the premodern state, nor its burgeoning use (in the United States) to tackle contemporary problems such as gun crime, opiate addiction or climate change,[44] plausibly involve 'private rights'.[45]

Do rights-based arguments constrain the legislative freedom to create new torts? First, even granting the premise, it could be suggested that, whenever Parliament makes an existing public statutory duty actionable at the suit of individuals,[46] by definition this creates *private* rights to enjoy the relevant public good. Such a 'deeming' process avoids, or perhaps denies, the debate about the true scope of the tort of public nuisance. Arguably, such unconcern with tort theory is Parliament's prerogative. As Bright and McFarlane accurately note, rights-based accounts of tort seem to be directed primarily, perhaps exclusively, to courts developing the common law.[47] Take the supposed prohibition on courts considering policy concerns about the public interest.[48] It seems most unlikely that this would extend, or *could* extend, constitutionally speaking, to *parliamentary* reform of tort liability.[49]

Equally, might not Parliament choose to treat *any* breach of duty as actionable, even in the absence of a correlative right? Donal Nolan, in this collection, offers a positive appraisal of the DPA 1972, by sharp contrast with builders' fluctuating liability for pure economic loss in judicially developed common law negligence.[50] Nolan has, however, argued elsewhere that it is a 'conceptual impossibility' to have a *right* not to suffer economic loss[51] – hence his chapter's commendation for the conceptual premise underlying *Murphy v Brentwood District Council*.[52] But Nolan accepts that Parliament may nevertheless ordain *liability* for economic loss.[53] The DPA 1972 itself may be consistent with principle. Nolan has argued that voluntary assumption of responsibility, the main exception to the pure economic loss 'rule', has 'at least as much in common with contract law' as with tortious negligence.[54]

[43] ibid 212.

[44] cf RA Epstein, 'The Private Law Connections to Public Nuisance Law: Some Realism About Today's Intellectual Nominalism' (2022) 17 *Journal of Law, Economics & Policy* 282, 286 criticising the 'enormous and unprincipled expansion' of public nuisance.

[45] Compare *Ashby v White* (1703) 2 Ld Raym 938 (vindication of right to vote in parliamentary election) with RC Boldt and DG Gifford, 'Interference with the Democratic Process as Public Nuisance' (2025) 84 *Maryland Law Review* (forthcoming).

[46] Compare Education (No 2) Act 1986, s 43 (universities' obligation to secure freedom of speech); and Higher Education (Freedom of Speech) Act 2023, s 4 (civil claims by individuals who 'sustain loss' from breach of the re-enacted duty).

[47] Bright and McFarlane (n 18) 137.

[48] Stevens, *Torts and Rights* (n 40) 309–10.

[49] ibid 331: 'The legislature can create any rights it chooses, for any purpose'.

[50] Nolan (n 4).

[51] D Nolan, 'Rights, Damage and Loss' (2017) 37 *OJLS* 255.

[52] *Murphy v Brentwood District Council* [1991] 1 AC 398 (HL) ('*Murphy*').

[53] Nolan (n 51) 266 (citing eg Financial Services and Markets Act 2000, s 150).

[54] ibid 268.

This suggests a principled basis for the DPA 1972. As many commentators note, it creates a statutory hybrid between contract and tort.[55]

Some argue that, despite its expansion by the BSA 2022, DPA 1972 liability is still too limited. Philip Britton suggests that Parliament's recent expansion of the DPA 1972 was a 'quick fix' that failed to consider the advantages of a broad new statutory duty of care on '*all* those who play a role in commissioning, building or enabling non-compliant residential construction'.[56] That wider approach, seen in recent Australian legislation,[57] could (comments Britton) 'appropriately incentivise … acceptable build quality'.[58] It may be noted that the New South Wales Court of Appeal had no doubt that the broad statutory duties under that state's Design and Building Practitioners Act 2020 sound in 'tort' (for the purposes of apportionment under the Civil Liability Act 2002); in part, as extensions of existing duties, rather than 'novel' or 'freestanding' ones.[59] But, more generally, the Court rejected the view that 'tort' means *common law* rather than statutory duties: this was 'fundamentally wrong'.[60] That narrow definition of 'tort' was implausible given that common law and statute form a 'complex entangled' system, through a 'symbiotic' relationship.[61]

In some departments of the law, statutory liability can go far beyond the DPA 1972. Notably, English criminal procedure contains a quite general, and significant, exception to the rights-based definition. Since the 1970s criminal courts have been able to make 'victim compensation orders' as part of their sentencing powers.[62] Such orders can be made even when the convicted person has no civil liability in tort.[63] Spencer notes the 'striking' difference in philosophy:

> For the criminal courts, that those convicted of criminal offences should automatically be liable to compensate those who suffer loss as a result of them seems obvious. For the civil courts, by contrast, it does not seem obvious at all.[64]

To state the point again, the fundamental *damnum absque iniuria* objection prevents the generalisation of tort liability for *all* breaches of criminal or other public duties.[65] If losses resulting from breach of statutory duty would not *at common law* give rise to a claim (ie not 'personal injury, injury to property or economic loss'), it is a powerful indication that Parliament did not intend the

[55] See, further, the main text to nn 204-207 below.

[56] P Britton, 'The Building Safety Bill: Better Redress for Homeowners? Part 1' (Housing After Grenfell, 22 December 2021) https://www.law.ox.ac.uk/housing-after-grenfell/blog/2021/12/building-safety-bill-better-redress-homeowners-part-1 (original emphasis).

[57] See, eg, M Bell et al, 'Construction Regulatory Reform: Where to From Here?' (2022) 39 *International Construction Law Review* 144.

[58] Britton (n 56).

[59] *OSP 84674* [2023] NSWCA 301 [76] (see also n 31 above). On those duties, see, further, n 89 below.

[60] ibid [82].

[61] ibid [87].

[62] Powers of Criminal Courts Act 1973, s 35(1); Powers of Criminal Courts (Sentencing) Act 2000, s 130(1)(a).

[63] *R v Chappell* (1985) 80 Cr App R 31.

[64] JR Spencer, 'Civil Liability for Crimes' in M Dyson (ed), *Unravelling Tort and Crime* (Cambridge, Cambridge University Press, 2014) 308.

[65] cf the position in France (ibid 309).

provision to be actionable in tort.[66] Moreover, courts lean heavily against holding general public statutory duties actionable, in accordance with the 'normal judicial reluctance to permit individual enforcement of obligations owed to the public'.[67]

Some reject the premise of the rights-based critique. 'Functionalist' accounts identify a number of purposes that tort law might seek to advance, whether singly or in combination. The protection of rights is only one of its possible functions. This affronts corrective justice theorists such as Beever, criticising the functionalist vision of tort as the common law's 'Swiss Army knife'.[68] Such functionalist accounts identify plural ambitions for common law doctrines.[69] Still less, on that view, is the *legislature* confined by the logic of corrective justice. As Zubrzycki comments, legislatures are not required to 'create statutes that track some theoretician's view of the common law of torts'.[70] But, as explored below, Zubrzycki nevertheless doubts that every statutory regime with 'superficial' resemblance deserves the label of 'tort'.

As pointed out already, labelling matters. Let us accept that Parliament may legislate for unusual, anomalous or even 'impossible' liabilities. In practice, all are prone to be treated as 'tort' nevertheless. The advantage is to 'import' all the elaborate learning on the subject[71] – to fill the gaps that almost any statute, however detailed, is bound to contain.

Only rarely does Parliament create a complete and exhaustive new code to govern all issues that may inevitably arise. Parliament does not legislate into a vacuum – as those drafting legislation appreciate. Cane comments that, although Parliament could (in theory) legislate entirely novel departures, in practice both propriety and expediency require legislation consistent with existing legal institutions, concepts and values.[72] This is certainly the starting point, and one strongly presumed. As Atiyah observed, '[v]ery few statutes are self constrained instruments'; instead they become 'part of a very large body of law even though not one word is said about these things in the Act itself'.[73] As Lord Burrows remarks (with his experience of legislating, as a Law Commissioner), it is hard to see how statutes could be drafted without presupposing the background of existing legal principles.[74]

[66] *Pickering v Liverpool Daily Post* [1991] 2 AC 370 (HL) 420 (Lord Bridge).

[67] Stanton et al (n 30) 40.

[68] A Beever, *Rediscovering the Law of Negligence* (Oxford, Hart Publishing, 2007) 197.

[69] G Calabresi, 'The Complexity of Torts – The Case of Punitive Damages' in MS Madden (ed), *Exploring Tort Law* (Cambridge, Cambridge University Press, 2005).

[70] C Zubrzycki, 'Tort(?) Arms Races: Abortion and Beyond' (2024) 73 *DePaul Law Review* 705, 714.

[71] But contrast SF Sperino, 'The Tort Label' (2015) 66 *Florida Law Review* 1051, arguing that the 'organizational label' has weak explanatory power for statutory liabilities (specifically US discrimination law) because 'the idea of a general tort law is a fallacy' (at 1080); thus, common law 'tort' has no uniform, generally-accepted core meaning.

[72] P Cane, 'Taking Disagreement Seriously: Courts, Legislatures and the Reform of Tort Law' (2005) 25 *OJLS* 393. See further M Krygier, 'The Traditionality of Statutes' (1988) 1 *Ratio Juris* 20.

[73] PS Atiyah, 'Common Law and Statute Law' (1985) 48 *MLR* 1, 2.

[74] A Burrows, 'The Relationship between Common Law and Statute in the Law of Obligations' (2012) 128 *LQR* 232; A Burrows, 'Preservation, Removal and Freezing of the Common Law by Statute' in TT Arvind and J Steele (eds), *Contract Law and the Legislature: Autonomy, Expectations, and the*

Statutory 'torts' are an excellent example of the crucial role played by background concepts. Common law tort principles persist even in areas governed by legislation. As noted, some statutes deem duties actionable in terms 'as breach of statutory duty'. This formulation seems staggeringly inept. There is no single unified 'tort of breach of statutory duty' with a standardised set of incidents.[75] Even within the large case law on industrial safety statutes, it is 'not at all clear that the policies which apply [there] should be transferred by analogy to fundamentally different subjects'.[76] Not least since, even within the same field of industrial safety, differently worded provisions attract divergent interpretations. Different statutory duties are, in short, actionable to different extents. Liability may diverge on the standard of conduct constituting breach,[77] the defences available to liability[78] and the interests protected (ie what constitutes 'actionable damage'). All too often, Parliament simply leaves the courts to answer such 'fundamental questions'.[79]

Considering statutory torts involving environmental damage, Stanton et al state it is 'virtually impossible to discern a general theory which justifies and links these torts', which have emerged 'ad hoc': 'The rationale for the decision to create civil liability in addition to regulating an activity and imposing criminal penalties for conduct is usually unclear.'[80] The authors note that when Parliament fails to define 'damage' (ie precisely which interests are protected), '[i]t is all too easy for established thinking to be borrowed from negligence to fill the gap'.[81] A clear example is the judicial refusal to compensate 'relational pure economic loss' in oil pollution cases. On ordinary tortious principles, such loss was presumed unrecoverable unless Parliament had made it

> abundantly clear that the old and widely accepted principles governing and limiting the liability of wrongdoers for damages in reparation for delict … were to be departed from in this special case of contamination by oil spilled from a vessel at sea.[82]

It was held insufficient that the statute expressly imposed liability 'for *any* damage caused'[83] because such 'a distinct change in the law would have been made

Making of Legal Doctrine (Oxford, Hart Publishing, 2020): 'almost every statute depends on the survival or preservation of some of the common law' (at 17).

[75] Stanton et al (n 30) 8: (the technique is therefore 'unhelpful and liable to cause difficulties').

[76] ibid.

[77] For detail, see ibid ch 8 ('Defining the Obligation').

[78] ibid ch 9 ('Defences and Restrictions on Liability').

[79] ibid 9. For a counterpoint to this view, see Nolan (n 4) 171–2.

[80] Stanton et al (n 30) 536. An observation true, perhaps, for the entire patchwork of statutory torts (and cf Sperino (n 71) for scepticism about the unity of *common law* 'tort').

[81] ibid 551. (Cf Ripstein (n 41) 278 n 11, querying Spencer's critique of public nuisance (n 37) 'on the grounds that [public nuisance] conflicts with what [Spencer] takes to be general tort principles, by which he simply means negligence law').

[82] *Landcatch Ltd v International Oil Pollution Compensation Fund* 1999 SLT 1208, 1223 (Lord McCluskey) ('*Landcatch*').

[83] Merchant Shipping (Oil Pollution) Act 1971, s 1(1) (emphasis added) (cf now Merchant Shipping Act 1995, ss 156(3)(a) and 170).

unambiguous and explicit'.[84] Therefore the pursuer, a supplier of salmon smolt (ie juvenile fish), could not claim for loss of business following oil pollution off Shetland (where most of its salmon-farming customers were located) because the smolt themselves (raised on the unpolluted Scottish mainland) had been physically unharmed.

For pragmatic reasons, statutory actions such as that under section 38 of the Building Act 1984 are likely be treated as 'tort' claims. Whether this is desirable as a matter of principle divides opinion. Lord Burrows advocates strongly the integration of statutory and common law sources of private law. Application of general principles enhances 'consistency' between torts (etc), irrespective of their legal basis. That is undoubtedly an important advantage. As a general matter of statutory interpretation, statutory words and concepts should be read consistently with the extant law. The context for interpretation of a novel provision includes the pre-existing statute book, and the common law. Those who draft statutes are aware, of course, of the need to use language consistently with any pre-existing legal meanings.[85] If, when creating a statutory tort the legislature ordains an action for 'loss' – a word otherwise left undefined – courts sensibly presume, as their starting point, that 'loss' has the meaning it bears in tort law generally (and tort remains largely a common law field).[86] This assists consistency and predictability.

The aim is to read a statute consistently with all other rules of law, whether statutory or judge-made, to produce where possible a coherent system of laws.[87] Lord McCluskey was therefore correct to observe in the *Landcatch* case that '[t]he words in a statute are not freshly minted in a new currency whose value is unknown'; on the contrary, a word like 'loss' has an established 'essence and patina' – it has so often been used in statutes, and considered in common law cases, that it acquires 'an aura, a lawyers' baggage'.[88] Parliament presumptively uses such a term of art in its established sense.[89] (Being sovereign, Parliament could certainly choose to depart from settled understandings, yet if it 'decides to rob [words] of their familiar meaning … it would not and could not do so by stealth. It would hardly do so by deliberately creating a semantic mystery, with clues buried in various parts of the statute'.[90])

[84] *Landcatch* 1999 SLT 1208, 1223 (Lord McCluskey).

[85] For this reason, it is dangerous to suppose that statutory language should have the ordinary, everyday meaning that a layperson ignorant of the law would assign: FAR Bennion, *Understanding Common Law Legislation: Drafting and Interpretation* (Oxford, Oxford University Press, 2001) ch 7. Sir Edward Coke (preface to the third volume of *Reports*, 1602) defended the continued use of Law-French to deter altogether reading by 'the unlearned' (ie lay people), who were otherwise prone to 'suck out errors'.

[86] cf *OSP 84674* [2023] NSWCA 301 [87]: common law and statutory torts are 'symbiotic' and 'entangled'.

[87] See further Lord Sales, 'Exploring the Interface Between the Common Law of Tort and Statute Law' [2024] *Journal of Personal Injury Law* 3.

[88] *Landcatch* 1999 SLT 1208, 1123–24.

[89] Indeed, it may expressly say so: Design and Building Practitioners Act 2020 (NSW), s 37(3): plaintiff 'entitled to damages for the breach of the duty *as if the duty were* a duty established by the common law' (emphasis added).

[90] *Landcatch* 1999 SLT 1208, 1124.

More contestable is Burrows's claim that common law rules are (more?) 'carefully crafted' and so 'likely to be both principled and practically workable'.[91] This might entail a narrow and suspicious approach to statutory language, routinely reading it down to preserve common law rules.[92] But a presumption against altering the common law has long been obsolete as a general canon of statutory construction (albeit with important constitutional exceptions such as the 'principle of legality' and a suspicion of clauses ousting judicial review). In the modern 'age of statutes', courts have long had to accept legislation as a 'guest to be welcomed' in the 'house of the common law', not some 'alien intruder'.[93] Thus, while existing concepts and understandings are the correct starting point for statutory interpretation, they must not be insisted upon or carried too far.[94] Stanton et al therefore question the Court's strong adherence to 'old and widely accepted' common law principles denying the recovery of economic loss in *Landcatch*. It was not 'conducive to a reasoned discussion of the policy reasons which led to the [International Oil Pollution] Convention', with the Court of Session indeed 'rebuffing' counsel's reference to the policies justifying wide and strict environmental liability.[95]

Nolan is also critical of the persistence of common law doctrine in statutory fields.[96] Rosen notes that private law legislation tends to be sporadic, and that which exists is typically left to specialist lawyers within the legislature, as a 'technical' matter.[97] Moreover, when interpreted and applied by the courts, private law statutes are so completely 'suffused with traditional principles and categories' that their meaning is the effective product of 'dual authorship [by] democratic legislature and professional courts'. What Lord Burrows praises as 'consistency', Rosen therefore deems a failure of democratic scrutiny. Legislative interventions typically 'leave unexamined a core set of general private law principles' (expounded by the judiciary alone). Nevertheless, sometimes the legislature does manage to infuse

[91] Burrows (n 74) (2012) 128 *LQR* 232, 243.

[92] Burrows (ibid 239) queries whether courts have been too ready to hold that statutory schemes impliedly exclude the 'carefully developed evolutionary system' of common law (specifically restitution of social security payments under Social Security Administration Act 1992, s 71; cf *Child Poverty Action Group v Secretary of State for Work and Pensions* [2010] UKSC 54, [2011] 2 AC 15 [14] (Lord Brown): 'common law restitution claims are, at the best of times, far from straightforward. … It seems to me inconceivable that Parliament would have contemplated leaving the suggested common law restitutionary route … [available] alongside the carefully prescribed scheme of recovery set out in the statute').

[93] H Stone, 'The Common Law in the United States' (1936) 50 *Harvard Law Review* 4, 15.

[94] cf SF Sperino, 'Statutory Proximate Cause' (2013) 88 *Notre Dame Law Review* 1199, 1222:

> Many statutes expressly abrogate common law understandings of legal rights and obligations. Indeed, some statutes radically upset traditional common law duties. It is odd that these statutes would be read in tandem with common law [tort concepts].

[95] Stanton et al (n 30) 551.

[96] Nolan (n 4), esp section VI.

[97] A Rosen, 'The Role of Democracy in Private Law' in PB Miller and J Oberdiek (eds), *Oxford Studies in Private Law Theory* (Oxford, Oxford University Press, 2023) vol II, 214: 'private law legislation often remains a professional affair rather than meaningfully democratic'.

interpersonal relationships with 'broader social considerations', which Rosen welcomes for 'add[ing] to the tapestry of modern private law'.[98]

In conclusion, it seems that Parliament can and does create statutory torts that are only questionably 'torts' according to rights-based tort theory – and for overtly instrumental reasons too. The courts' pronounced tendency to assimilate statutory claims with the rest of (common law) tort principles promotes consistency, albeit some commentators question whether a determination to 'preserve' the common law could sometimes thwart the statute's purpose. Potentially also, this assimilation violates the conceptual purity of tort law by treating as 'torts' claims that are not based on breaches of private rights.

Perhaps, however, such examples are sufficiently unusual that the core of tort remains intact. Bacharis argues that there is a 'spectrum' within tort law, ranging from the paradigm of interpersonal wrongs through to the *private* enforcement of *public* duties ('a peculiar public-private mix').[99] Such 'enforcement' actions are a hybrid, using the basic form of a tort claim but often with modification to its 'essentially relational' structure on such important matters as standing, procedure and remedies. (Some examples are considered below). The point of Bacharis's 'continuum' approach is that these actions have considerable continuity with torts based on private rights, but significant differences too. It would be erroneous either to lump all these together as undifferentiated 'torts',[100] *or* to classify enforcement actions as simply 'not torts' on a stark binary divide. More generally, John Gardner emphasises the varying degrees of (strict or loose) relational 'correlativity' within tort law, suggesting that 'hyper-relationism' should be understood as an *overreaction* to the 'relationality eliminators' of (eg) economic analysis of law.[101] The debate, Gardner fears, has been excessively polarised.[102]

Stevens, however, characteristically emphasises the rights-based distinction. Torts protect private rights as a matter of interpersonal morality, whereas criminal law makes things wrongful as a matter of wider public interest.[103] There is, admittedly, a significant overlap within many long-established common law wrongs (eg battery, which is both a tort and a crime),[104] but by no means total coincidence. Stevens identifies trespass to land, breach of confidence, breach of contract, and

[98] ibid 238.

[99] G Bacharis, 'A Spectrum of Actions for Wrongs: From Tort Law to Pure Enforcement' in Robertson and Neyers (n 41) 258.

[100] ibid 273 'undue application of general private law norms might … lead to systemic mistakes'.

[101] J Gardner, *From Personal Life to Private Law* (Oxford, Oxford University Press, 2018) ch 1.

[102] ibid 57 ('Fanaticism breeds fanaticism').

[103] R Stevens, 'Private Rights and Public Wrongs' in M Dyson (ed), *Unravelling Tort and Crime* (Cambridge, Cambridge University Press, 2014).

[104] G Lamond, 'What is a Crime?' (2007) 27 *OJLS* 609, 618 ('core forms of criminality have underlying civil wrongs – wrongful death underlying murder, assault underlying offences against the person, and conversion underlying the law of theft').

(since 2009) libel,[105] as private law wrongs that are *not* criminalised.[106] Moreover, the constant stream of new statutory offences has not been mirrored by a flood of statutory *torts*. In Stevens's view this is because

> the number of private rights we have that the law should recognise is very restrictive. Once we have listed bodily safety, freedom of movement, reputation, and personal property the list is almost complete. The kind of conduct that the legislature might want to regulate that is not potentially wrongful to anyone else is much broader.[107]

Whatever freedom the legislature has to create 'regulatory offences' according to its view of public policy,[108] in Stevens's view it should not treat them as *interpersonal* wrongs. (Might the lack of a word for the equivalent of 'criminalisation' show how uncommon the process is? 'Tortifying'?)

III. Instrumental Uses of Statutory Torts: Compensation and Enforcement

Parliament could make statutory public duties actionable for various reasons beyond the creation and vindication of interpersonal rights (accepting that that may be the core concern of *common law* tort). Widening entitlements to compensation, and strengthening the enforcement of the duty, are two obvious instrumental concerns.

Novel, express actionability can compensate parties who would not otherwise have claims in tort, by extending to *loss* that would otherwise be outside the category of protected interests.[109] Or a statutory tort could impose duties on a wider set of *parties* that would otherwise not be liable.[110] Or it could impose *more stringent* duties, making breach easier to prove and increasing the prospect for recovering compensation. (It is trite law that a claimant need prove only breach of the statutory duty (whatever it is) 'simpliciter' – ie need not prove a *culpable* breach – to recover damages, *if* the statutory duty is an actionable one.[111])

Thus presented, this seems a matter of straightforwardly distributive political choices. Who should pay how much to whom? That depends on the competing claims of the claimant group and the defendant group to be protected against loss, and shielded from liability, respectively. Such distributive choices are implicit in all

[105] Coroners and Justice Act 2009, s 73.

[106] cf Lamond (n 104) 619 ('many areas of intentional [civil] wrongdoing, such as trespass and breach of contract' are *not* criminal).

[107] Stevens (n 103) 144.

[108] ibid 142: 'only the legislature that has the legitimacy and practical competence to create them'.

[109] Consider, for example, damages for economic loss caused by omissions from company prospectus or stock market listing particulars: Financial Services and Markets Act 2000, s 90(1)(b)(ii).

[110] Local authority building inspectors owe no duties to home-owners in negligence, in contract or under the DPA 1972; but could be liable under the Building Act 1984, s 38.

[111] *X v Bedfordshire County Council* [1995] 2 AC 633 (HL) 731–35 (Lord Browne-Wilkinson).

tort adjudication too,[112] but courts do not and probably should not consider this explicitly – although distributive effects are one reason why common law liabilities evolve only gradually, whereas statutory torts could well break entirely new ground. Parliament might conversely decide to *remove* actionability for essentially distributive reasons. A striking recent example was repealing the actionability of statutory health and safety duties by section 69 of the Enterprise and Regulatory Reform Act 2013. This reversal of very long-standing legal policy,[113] now requiring injured employees to prove negligence by an employer rather than breach simpliciter of the relevant statutory duty, was in Spencer's view 'remarkably wrong-headed'.[114] As he comments, the winners from the reform are employers' *insurers* – at the expense of injured workers who will find it harder to recover compensation.

It is, hopefully, not too cynical to suggest that, when loss flows from breaches of duties by *governmental* bodies, it is unlikely that Parliament will impose new or more extensive liabilities. Successive UK governments have proved notoriously unreceptive to suggestions that public authority liability be extended.[115] The English courts are almost certainly correct to hold, unvaryingly, that Parliament did *not intend* broad duties on public authorities to sound in damages, unless the legislation expressly says otherwise.

The legislature also has other compensatory options available to it, should it decide that loss-bearing parties ought to be relieved. Unlike common law courts, for which tort is the only game in town, the legislature could create or extend a statutory compensation scheme, the social security system, some scheme of compulsory private insurance, or otherwise ordain compensation without tort liability. For 'claimants' such mechanisms may be preferable, given the daunting cost of litigation. For the government rather less so. Assuming that the cost would fall on the taxpayer (as with social security), governments are understandably reluctant to provide public compensation for *every* victim of misfortune. When the cry that 'something must be done' is too loud to be ignored, the government might find it politically expedient to saddle private parties with new liabilities, rather than setting up a publicly funded compensation scheme. Pertinently, that informs part of the strategy for distributing the gigantic cumulative costs of cladding remediation following the Grenfell disaster.[116] We have noted the BSA 2022's extension of the DPA 1972, and imposition of new construction product liabilities and the far-reaching remediation contribution orders. Furthermore, outside the law altogether, the government successfully exerted pressure on large construction

[112] eg Cane (n 72) 415–16.
[113] cf *Groves v Lord Wimbourne* [1898] 2 QB 402 (CA).
[114] Spencer (n 64) 306.
[115] See eg Law Commission, *Administrative Redress: Public Bodies and the Citizen* (Law Com No 322, 2010) para 1.3: 'This project was notable in that the key stakeholder – Government – was firmly opposed to our proposed reforms' (which the Law Commission accordingly withdrew).
[116] See NJ McBride, 'Private Law in the Ruins', this volume, ch 10, 263. Note some costs are borne by the government (ie for replacing cladding on buildings above 11 metres tall (initially taller than 18 metres)): Building Safety Fund and Cladding Safety Fund.

firms to 'agree' to remediation of fire-safety defects in buildings over 11 metres tall, constructed between 1992 and 2022 (and to reimburse public funds spent on such remediation).[117]

Parliament could also deem a statutory duty actionable as an *enforcement* strategy. Tort places enforcement in *individual* hands. That may valuably reinforce the activities of public enforcement bodies (regulators, prosecutors, police). Individuals typically claim to recover compensation for loss (as just discussed). They have direct financial incentives to claim – harnessing this incentive may counteract underenforcement of a given statutory duty.[118]

What of duties whose breach may cause only diffuse harm to general public interests, or no tangible harm whatever? If the legislature is to channel the enforcement potential of tort claims here, it would need to think beyond 'compensation'. Legislation could provide that the individual claimant may, if successful, recover the defendant's profits from breaching the statute, or could authorise exemplary damages, or permit the claimant to keep all or part of a statutory fine. Supracompensatory awards have been known from ancient times (eg multiple damages, the multiplier varying according to ease of stealing different kinds of property).[119] They are, however, impossible to reconcile with a theory of tort based on compensation for invading the claimant's private rights.[120] They are often criticised as a 'windfall' for the claimant. That is a tendentious word. The whole point would be to create a reward or 'bounty' of sufficient size to motivate private enforcement.

Indeed, the very purpose of disgorgement or punitive remedies is to deter breach. Exemplary damages are sensitive both to the degree of the defendant's culpability, and the likelihood of their being pursued for the conduct (namely, a higher award of exemplary damages where the level of enforcement is low, to ensure that the 'tort does not pay'). By contrast, standard compensation is assessed purely by the measure of the claimant's loss. The internal logic is entirely different. However, Parliament does not often use these techniques in practice.[121] Absenting express statutory provision, the courts perpetuate tort's central concern with compensating loss.

Statutory torts might *reinforce* the work of a regulator by basing individual claims on a regulator's favourable finding. Competition law provides an

[117] Bright and McFarlane (n 18) 131. As of October 2024, 54 major housebuilders had entered the Developer Remediation Contract with the Secretary of State.

[118] This concern underlay the legislation making universities' duties to promote freedom of speech actionable through 'civil claims': Higher Education (Freedom of Speech) Act 2023, s 4.

[119] F Parisi et al, 'Deterrence of Wrongdoing in Ancient Law' in G Dari-Mattiacci and DP Kehoe (eds), *Roman Law and Economics Volume II: Exchange, Ownership, and Disputes* (Oxford, Oxford University Press, 2020).

[120] A Beever, 'The Structure of Aggravated and Exemplary Damages' (2003) 23 *OJLS* 87; cf Calabresi (n 69).

[121] cf (exceptionally) Crime and Courts Act 2013, s 34: exemplary damages against media defendants which do not join official press regulator; and (disgorgement) Housing Act 1988, ss 27(4)(a), 28(1): damages assessed by increase in value of landlord's property following tenant's wrongful eviction.

excellent example.[122] While the European Union treaties did not provide for individual enforcement of their competition law provisions (prohibiting cartels and abuse of dominant market position), the Court of Justice of the European Union recognised a right to claim compensation for anticompetitive behaviour:

> [S]uch a right strengthens the working of the [European] Community competition rules and discourages agreements or practices, which are frequently covert, which are liable to restrict or distort competition. From that point of view, actions for damages … can make a significant contribution to the maintenance of effective competition in the Community.[123]

(Such 'follow-on actions' after a regulatory finding of breach were incorporated into domestic UK competition law by the Enterprise Act 2002.)

As noted, however, courts are less keen to develop *supra* compensatory remedies. In the leading English case *Devenish Nutrition Ltd v Sanofi-Aventis SA* the claimant (an animal-feed manufacturer) argued that it had been overcharged for certain raw materials by the defendants, which (the European Commission had found) operated an illegal price-fixing cartel.[124] However, Devenish had passed on the higher costs to its own customers, arguably therefore suffering no loss itself (ie it was the 'downstream' consumers who ultimately bore the cost of the cartel's illegal price maintenance). Given these difficulties in proving *loss*, Devenish claimed exemplary and gain-based damages. It failed on both counts, even though Arden LJ accepted that gains-based awards could further enhance private claims' 'complementary' effect on public enforcement of competition law.[125] Likewise for Longmore LJ, the nub of the claimant's case was that gains-based remedies would provide 'an incentive for the eradication' of cartels (which were 'a notorious evil'); but in his view, that was not a step for the *courts*.[126]

The *Devenish* decision has been criticised for leaving competition law rules underenforced. Virgo and Odudu note that if recognised, *gains-based* awards would 'encourage private parties to deploy additional resources to the task of identifying anti-competitive conduct to the benefit of the community'.[127] Courts ordering disgorgement of a cartel's profits would 'encourage private parties to serve the important public function of monitoring compliance with competition law' – with 'much wider public significance' than simply 'vindicating private law rights'.

The suggestion, then, is that, although compensation claims do complement the work of competition regulators, a wider suite of remedies would serve that policy better. Yet it is possible to go too far. Duplication of the regulator's

[122] See also eg Telecommunications Act 1984, s 18.

[123] Case C-453/99 *Courage Ltd v Crehan* [2001] ECR I-06297 [27]. See further N Dunne, 'Antitrust and the Making of European Tort Law' (2016) 36 *OJLS* 366; K Barker, 'Modelling Public and Private Enforcement: The Rationality of Hybridity' (2018) 37 *University of Queensland Law Journal* 9.

[124] *Devenish Nutrition Ltd v Sanofi-Aventis SA* [2008] EWCA Civ 1086; [2009] Ch 390.

[125] ibid [94]–[96], [102].

[126] ibid [149].

[127] GJ Virgo and O Odudu, 'Remedies for Breach of Statutory Duty' [2009] *CLJ* 32, 34.

functions could be unnecessary, or positively unjust. At first instance in *Devenish*, Lewison J dismissed the exemplary damages claim.[128] Even though the defendant's conduct was (on the pleadings) a clear example of intentional wrongdoing within the 'second category' in *Rookes v Barnard* (ie being deliberately calculated to make a profit in excess of liability to pay compensation),[129] Lewison J nevertheless declined to award exemplary damages. The European Commission had already fined the defendants in *Devenish* for their participation in the cartel. Those fines obviously had a deterrent effect and it was unnecessary to invoke tort law's deterrent remedy too. It would, moreover, violate the double-jeopardy principle, punishing the defendant twice over for the same wrong.

Conversely, the legislature might decide that actionability of a statutory duty would result in *overenforcement*. This concern informed the reversal of statutory health and safety duties' previous actionability, by the Enterprise and Regulatory Reform Act 2013, noted above. That significant change formed part of the general deregulation agenda of the UK's coalition government (2010–15). The government argued that strict liability created an overdeterrent effect and wished to reassure businesses that, as long as they acted like responsible employers (ie discharged their common law duty of reasonable care to their employees), they would not face liability. This policy has received much criticism. If the problem was not so much the state of the law but employers' overfearful *perceptions* of it, would better education not be a more suitable response?[130] Why remove actionability of *all* the health and safety duties, rather than removing claims based on *strict* duties only? The sweeping reversal of actionability went further than the government's own expert reviewer, Professor Löfstedt, had recommended.[131]

The government pointed out that the statutory duties would still be enforced by the Health and Safety Executive (HSE). Critics wondered whether the HSE had the resources to enforce the law in the large number of cases which would no longer attract claims in tort.[132] In its own Enforcement Policy Statement (2015), the HSE reserves prosecution for serious or persistent breaches of the law.[133] A retired Supreme Court judge described his experience of strict, actionable duties' positive effects on workplace safety.[134]

[128] *Devenish Nutrition Ltd v Sanofi-Aventis SA* [2007] EWHC 2394 (Ch); [2009] Ch 390 [40]–[52]. The decision on exemplary damages was not challenged in the Court of Appeal.

[129] *Rookes v Barnard* [1964] AC 1129 (HL) 1206.

[130] HL Deb 6 Mar 2013, vol 743, col 1521 (Lord McKenzie): 'perception seems a very flimsy structure on which to make such a fundamental change to the law'.

[131] Department for Work and Pensions, *Reclaiming Health and Safety for All: An Independent Review of Health and Safety Legislation* (Cmd 8219, 2011); cf HC Deb 16 Apr 2013, vol 561, col 228 (Chuka Umunna MP).

[132] HL Deb, 14 Jan 2013, vol 742, col GC161 (Baroness Donaghy): 'The All-Party Parliamentary Group on Occupational Safety and Health is very concerned that this [Bill] will have a negative effect on preventing injuries in the workplace, as compensation claims have always helped to drive forward improvements to help to ensure that such incidents are not repeated.'

[133] 'Enforcement Policy Statement' (Health and Safety Executive, 2015) https://www.hse.gov.uk/pubns/hse41.pdf, [1.4].

[134] HL Deb, 6 Mar 2013, vol 743, col 1513–14 (Lord Brown of Eaton-under-Heywood).

The government, and ultimately Parliament, was unmoved by these objections. Such debates about actionability, either its extension or withdrawal, turn on empirical claims about the effectiveness of enforcement (or more worryingly but perhaps typically, on quasi-empirical speculation).[135] Ultimately the resolution of such debates involves political judgement about how stringently statutory duties should be enforced – and by whom.

As noted, competition law compensation claims 'follow on' from a regulatory finding of anticompetitive conduct. Not every statutory duty is enforced by a dedicated regulator.[136] Even when a regulator exists, private claims could be permitted in parallel with, or as an alternative to, regulatory enforcement. This interrelationship proved controversial in parliamentary debates on what became the Higher Education (Freedom of Speech) Act 2023. In brief, the 2023 Act re-enacts universities' duties to 'secure freedom of speech'[137] and extends such duties to student unions.[138] Controversially, and most relevant for this chapter, the Act makes breaches of those duties actionable in damages.[139] (The Act also makes provision for enforcement action by the higher educational regulator, the Office for Students.[140])

The novel statutory tort was vigorously contested during the Bill's passage through Parliament. Critics feared that it would undermine the regulatory work of the Office for Students. Enforcement requires assessment of what 'reasonably practicable' steps higher education institutions should take when 'securing freedom of speech within the law'.[141] Opponents of the legislation argued it would be better to entrust that delicate question of 'practicability' to the regulator's expertise exclusively,[142] ie preferable to leaving such difficult questions to an ordinary civil court, adjudicating claims for breach of statutory duty.

The then Conservative government, as promoter of the 2023 Bill, successfully insisted on retention of the new tort (albeit conceding that the 'relevant [Office for Students] complaints scheme' must be exhausted *before* a civil claim for damages can be brought).[143] The government argued that its aim was not to supplant the role of the regulator. Rather, the statutory tort was a 'back-stop' – an alternative route for individuals dissatisfied by the regulator's handling of their complaint. In

[135] cf J Morgan, 'Policy Reasoning in Tort Law: The Courts, the Law Commission and the Critics' (2009) 125 *LQR* 215.

[136] Prior to the creation of the Office for Students (Higher Education and Research Act 2017), no higher education regulator existed to enforce (eg) Education (No 2) Act 1986, s 43 (duty to secure freedom of speech).

[137] Higher Education (Freedom of Speech) Act 2023, ss 1 and 2; cf Education (No 2) Act 1986, s 43.

[138] Higher Education (Freedom of Speech) Act 2023, s 3.

[139] ibid, s 4.

[140] ibid, ss 5–8.

[141] Higher Education and Research Act 2017, ss A1(1) and A1(2) (as inserted).

[142] Note also Higher Education (Freedom of Speech) Act 2023, s 10 creating a new Director for Freedom of Speech and Academic Freedom to 'oversee' the Office for Students' 'free speech functions'.

[143] Higher Education and Research Act 2017, s A7(3) (as inserted); cf saving for 'civil proceedings … for an injunction only' in s A7(5)).

effect, an indirect appeal to the ordinary courts. As for why this might be thought necessary, there is the well-known criticism that, when regulators are selected for their experience of the relevant sector, and work closely in harmony with those being regulated, there is a danger of 'regulatory capture'.[144] In the present context, that is, the Office for Students might defer unduly to universities' own judgements about what steps are 'practicable'. That would entail an insufficiently robust protection for freedom of speech. (Similar concerns justify the (vestigial) power for private individuals to initiate criminal prosecutions: as a safeguard against certain crimes being overlooked or 'under-prosecuted' by the state authorities, inadvertently or otherwise.)[145]

The 2023 Act caused concern in higher education circles.[146] The prospect of compensation claims against universities, colleges and their student unions certainly focused attention on the underlying statutory duties to promote freedom of speech (which date from 1986). Whether there is really a censorship 'problem' to be addressed divides opinion along strongly party-political lines.[147] Indeed, the incoming Labour government of 2024 prioritised halting the Act's imminent commencement on assuming office.[148]

Despite these heated disagreements, the statutory tort's potential either to do harm, or do good, might have been exaggerated. Responding to Lord Etherton's concerns that the 2023 Bill's original tort clause did not require loss to be proved (and so might create a tort actionable per se),[149] the then government amended it to state that the breach must cause the individual claimant 'to sustain loss'. Perhaps then realising the restrictive implications, the government inserted another (contentious) amendment, clarifying that '"loss" means loss of any kind

[144] Several peers who spoke against the tort (advocating, instead, regulation by the Office for Students exclusively) were themselves masters of Oxford and Cambridge colleges! cf HL Deb 21 March 2023, vol 828, col 1695 (Lord Moore of Etchingham).

[145] cf *Gouriet* v *Union of Post Office Workers* [1978] AC 435 (HL) 477: private prosecutions 'a valuable constitutional safeguard against inertia or partiality on the part of authority' (Lord Wilberforce).

[146] cf GJ Virgo, 'Private Law and Public Universities' (Obligations Conference, Alberta, July 2023).

[147] See also eg HL Deb 28 June 2022, vol 823, col 624–26 (University of Cambridge exemplifies censoriousness) (Lord Moore of Etchingham).

[148] The relevant provisions were to come into force on 1 August 2024, under the Commencement order made by the then (Conservative) education minister on 25 April 2024: The Higher Education (Freedom of Speech) Act 2023 (Commencement No 2) Regulations 2024, SI 566/2024. Universities duly scrambled to adopt new Codes of Practice on Freedom of Speech (cf Higher Education and Research Act 2017, s A2 (as inserted)). (This chapter's author laboured over a code for Corpus Christi College, Cambridge.) After the general election of 4 July 2024, the new (Labour) Secretary of State for Education stopped the provisions from coming into force on 1 August by repealing the earlier Commencement order on 25 July 2024: The Higher Education (Freedom of Speech) Act 2023 (Commencement No 2) (Revocation) Regulations 2024, SI 824/2024. The minister stated this was 'to consider options, including [the 2023 Act's] repeal. I am aware of concerns that the Act would be burdensome on providers [of higher education] and on the OfS [Office for Students]' (HCWS26). The Government subsequently announced that, while it remained committed to freedom of speech in universities, '[u]nnecessary elements of the [2023] Act which risk leaving universities vulnerable to disproportionate costs for legal disputes will be scrapped, including the statutory tort' (Press Release, Department for Education, London, January 2025).

[149] HL Deb 21 March 2023, vol 828, col 1686.

(pecuniary or non-pecuniary)'.[150] Although material damage could sometimes flow from violations of free speech (eg dismissal from employment), more often 'loss' would be intangible. Quite how a court would *quantify*, in damages, the disappointment of a student unable to hear a 'cancelled' speaker would have been interesting to see. The levels of any such awards would surely be modest. Because it appears the tort may not now be brought into force,[151] we will never find out.

Freedom-of-speech 'crusaders' might not have needed much financial incentive to enforce universities' free-speech duties. Although it widened the definition of 'loss', the then government seems not to have contemplated introducing *exemplary* damages as a further incentive because that loss will typically be diffuse, absent or difficult to prove. As universities would (one hopes) rarely breach their free-speech obligations with the requisite 'contumelious disregard of rights' (to justify exemplary damages at common law),[152] perhaps the government prudently declined to introduce such a provocative clause when the *loss-based* statutory tort had already proven divisive.

Of course, it would have been possible to go further still. Another controversial, recent development in US law squarely aims to incentivise individual enforcement of 'public' law. A 2021 Texas statute provides that *any person* may bring a damages claim against anyone (eg a pregnant woman, medical professional) involved with procuring an abortion 'after detection of an unborn child's heartbeat' to recover damages deemed to be no less than US$10,000.[153] (The legislature's tactic was to weaponize *private* enforcement when, prior to *Dobbs v Jackson Women's Health Organization*,[154] enforcement of anti-abortion laws by *public officials* risked being held unconstitutional.)[155] The US$10,000 'damages' award is, of course, 'untethered from' and unrelated to any loss suffered by the enforcing plaintiff, and so it 'cannot be understood as reparatory'.[156] It is purely a bounty. It reinforces the (presumably) strong moral objections that enforcers have to women seeking abortions. The Texan enforcement mechanism could prove extremely effective, enlisting (as was said in a different context) 'private persons acting, if you please, under the strong stimulus of personal ill will or the hope of gain'.[157]

Yet enforcement of laws premised on individual self-interest is deliberately opposed to all the precepts of *public* law enforcement. It would be quite improper for a public prosecutor to be influenced by self-interest, least of all the 'hope of gain'.

[150] Higher Education and Research Act 2017, s A7(2) (as inserted).

[151] cf n 149 above.

[152] *Whitfield v De Lauret & Co* (1920) 29 CLR 71 (HCA), 77 (Knox CJ).

[153] The Texas Heartbeat Act, Senate Bill 8 (2021).

[154] (2022) 597 US 215, (2022) 142 S Ct 2228 ('*Dobbs*').

[155] The Supreme Court accordingly dismissed a challenge to the constitutionality of the Texas statute, prior to *Dobbs*: see *Whole Woman's Health v Jackson* (2021) 142 S Ct 522.

[156] J Wall, 'The Margins of Private Law: SB-8 and the Private Enforcement of Abortion Law' in K Falconer, K Barker and A Fell (eds), *Life and Death in Private Law* (Oxford, Hart Publishing, 2024) 60; Zubrzycki (n 70) 718: 'authorizing universal enforcement for a morality crime, rather than implementing a broad but genuine notion of harm to private individuals'.

[157] *United States v Griswold* (1885) 24 F 361 (USDC Or), 366 (Deady J) ('*Griswold*').

History shows that leaving law-enforcement to individuals, motivated by profit, leads to numerous abuses.[158] Individuals have no reason, unlike a disinterested public enforcement official, to condone minor or technical breaches.[159] Worse, the 'bounty hunter' might positively encourage breaches of law, entrapping violators to widen their haul. Other abuses include aggressive tactics, extorting payments to drop claims and collusive litigation. As Wall notes, the legal system usually insists on safeguards (eg 'state-sponsored fact-finding, consistent and impartial prosecution') when curtailing liberty according to the 'open-ended list of values that the state is responsible for promoting'.[160] When private individuals choose to enforce their *own* rights through a tort action by contrast, they are given absolute discretion, allowed to act on financial incentives in bringing and compromising claims (as is common in practice), and so on.[161] For Wall, therefore, the Texas Heartbeat Act miscategorises as a tort (with these procedural consequences) what is in fact enforcement of a public duty ('a task that is entirely foreign to private law').[162]

There are particular objections to using tort to enforce morally-contentious public duties. Beck argues:

> Self-interested informers wielding law enforcement powers tend to inflame pre-existing social conflicts. As accounts of unwarranted enforcement actions and abusive litigation tactics circulate, the public tends to lose respect for laws subject to popular enforcement, particularly in contexts where opinions were already divided on the underlying legislative mandates.[163]

Zubrzycki similarly argues that the Texan abortion statute risks increasing social tensions, by 'disconcertingly' enlisting private law to police the US 'culture wars'. Using tort as the enforcement vehicle 'personalizes' such questions, encouraging society to view them as 'violations [not] of community rules, but as personal affronts'.[164] A dissenting judgment in the landmark *Dobbs* case deplored the Texas law's intention to 'turn neighbor against neighbor, enlisting fellow citizens in the effort to root out anyone who tries to get an abortion'.[165] Thus, while appealing to private interest may be 'one of the least expensive and most effective means'

[158] R Beck, 'Popular Enforcement of Controversial Legislation' (2022) 57 *Wake Forest Law Review* 553, 568 (discussing, inter alia, the Lord's Day Observance Act 1780, cf *Orpen v Haymarket Capitol Ltd* [1931] All ER 360 (KB)); cf MS Greve, 'Private Enforcement of Environmental Law' (1990) 65 *Tulane Law Review* 339 (non-financial incentives and 'ideological' campaigning groups).

[159] *Hughes Aircraft Co v United States, ex rel Schumer* (1997) 520 US 939, 949 (Thomas J): private enforcers 'are motivated primarily by prospects of monetary reward rather than the public good … [and] thus less likely than is the Government to forgo an action arguably based on a mere technical noncompliance'.

[160] Wall (n 156) 63.

[161] cf Kristelia García, 'Selective enforcement' (2025) 113 *Georgetown Law Journal* (forthcoming) (analysis of private rights-holders' 'heterogenous' choices whether to enforce copyright).

[162] Wall (n 156) 64.

[163] Beck (n 158) 562.

[164] Zubrzycki (n 70) 729–30.

[165] *Dobbs* (2022) 597 US 215, (2022) 142 S Ct 2228, 2318 (Breyer, Sotomayor and Kagan JJ).

of law enforcement,[166] it may also create social disruption. 'Decoupling' damages from the actual loss suffered by the claimant (including also multipliers, or caps, on compensation) is a regulatory strategy that can be used to stimulate or inhibit litigation, to produce optimal levels of enforcement.[167] Of course, however, it highlights such a 'tort's' distance from the paradigmatic enforcement of private rights. Critics of the Higher Education (Freedom of Speech) Act 2023 may reflect that, however unwelcome the (attempted) 'tortification' of this politically contentious question, the UK Parliament did not go as far as Texas.

IV. Actionable Building Regulations: A Statutory Tort Reanimated

As noted already, provision for the actionability of the Building Regulations has been on the UK statute book for 50 years, but not brought into force. Section 38(1)(a) of the Building Act 1984 provides: 'breach of a duty imposed by building regulations, so far as it causes damage, is actionable, except in so far as the regulations provide otherwise'.[168] The Building Regulations 2010 themselves are complex. In broad outline, they require those carrying out building work to do so 'in a workmanlike manner' and 'with adequate and proper materials',[169] as well as complying with a host of detailed requirements on construction quality.[170] Non-compliance with the Building Regulations is an offence.[171] Section 38, if and when commenced, would also 'tortify' such breaches.

The rationale for section 38's original enactment, in 1974, is unclear.[172] Still more unclear is why it was never brought into effect (nor has it yet, at time of writing). The mystery is long-standing. Relatively early in the period of limbo,[173] Spencer uncovered (with assistance from the Member of Parliament for Cambridge) that its commencement had initially been postponed pending the outcome of the 1970s Royal Commission on Personal Injuries (an odd position, as Spencer commented, given how infrequently *defective construction* claims concern *personal injuries*). Following the Pearson Royal Commission's report in 1978, the government gave unilluminating answers to further inquiries by the MP for Cambridge. Spencer deemed the failure to bring the provisions into force a constitutional abuse, effectively a suspension of statutory laws – as denied to the Crown by the Bill of

[166] *Griswold* (1885) 24 F 361, 366.

[167] eg A Mitchell Polinsky, 'Detrebling versus Decoupling Antitrust Damages: Lessons from the Theory of Enforcement' (1986) 74 *Georgetown Law Journal* 1231.

[168] cf s 38(1)(b) of the Building Act 1984 (enabling the insertion of 'prescribed defence' into the Building Regulations).

[169] Building Regulations 2010, reg 7(1).

[170] ibid sch 1.

[171] Building Act 1984, s 35.

[172] Health and Safety at Work etc Act 1974, s 71.

[173] JR Spencer, 'When Is a Law not a Law?' (1981) *New Law Journal* 644.

Rights 1689. In Spencer's view, an Act of Parliament's commencement provisions are meant only to allow preparation by enforcement bodies, and sufficient notice to the public, before a complex law is brought into force.

> Parliament does not intend to give the civil service a power of indefinite veto over any proposal in the Act which the civil service, let alone 'other bodies' to whose lobbying it is receptive, think not in the national interest.[174]

Whatever reasons dissuaded ministers from bringing the actionability clause into force between 1974 and Spencer's critique of 1981, it was re-enacted as section 38 of the Building Act 1984. That has never been brought into force either. As Britton and Bell suggest in their leading work: 'In 1984 it could reasonably be assumed that liability at common law in contract or tort, as in *Dutton* and *Anns*,[175] would do the same – perhaps an even better – job.'[176] While a sensible conjecture, this leaves unclear why the apparently otiose provision should have been re-enacted in 1984 (given the then extensive common law liability in negligence). Moreover, as Britton and Bell go on to say, the overruling of those leading cases in 1991 by *Murphy*[177] 'should have triggered a rethink'.[178] There is no sign that this happened. The 1984 Act tort remained pointedly uncommenced, despite the fall of *Anns v Merton*. It is tempting to endorse Arden's 'cynical' speculation that this claimant-friendly provision was successfully resisted by 'counter-lobbying from a construction industry which does not want those most affected by its failures to be able to hold it to account'.[179]

This chapter's introduction notes the stated intention finally to bring section 38 into force (a reversal of the then government's initial post-Grenfell policy).[180] However at time of writing, the statutory claim has still not been commenced. In the absence of any statement about this by the government, one can only speculate further. Today we can, probably, discount Arden's suggestion about 'counter-lobbying from the construction industry'. Post-Grenfell political reality saw the government determined that the builders and suppliers responsible for unsafe cladding (etc) should bear much of the cost of remediation.[181] Could the government's apparent reluctance stem, instead, from the potential liability that may fall on *public* bodies too? Their position seems, characteristically, uncertain.

But the risk of extensive public authority liability is amply demonstrated by an earlier phase of the common law's approach to defective buildings. Notoriously

[174] ibid. On duties to consider bringing a statute into force, cf now *R v Home Secretary, ex parte Fire Brigades Union* [1995] 2 AC 513 (HL).

[175] *Dutton v Bognor Regis Urban District Council* [1972] 1 QB 373 (CA); *Anns v Merton London Borough Council* [1978] AC 728 (HL).

[176] P Britton and M Bell, *Residential Construction Law* 2nd edn (Oxford, Hart Publishing, 2025) 319 fn 288.

[177] [1991] 1 AC 398 (HL). See, further, Nolan (n 4) section IIIA.

[178] Britton and Bell (n 176) 319 fn 288.

[179] A Arden, 'Grenfell Tower: The Greatest Failure' (2017) 20 *Journal of Housing Law* 97, 102.

[180] As also noted, Parliament has enacted a new 'special time limit' of 15 years to bring claims (inter alia) under Building Act 1984, s 38: Limitation Act 1980 s 4B(3)(b) (as inserted).

[181] cf *Triathlon Homes* [2024] UKFTT 26 [75].

during the *Dutton–Anns* era, as much (if not much more) negligence liability fell on local authority building inspectors than on the builders that were, surely, more directly to blame for shoddy construction. Stapleton points out that when primary wrongdoers are impecunious or uninsured, the result can be overdeterrence of 'peripheral parties' (in particular public authorities, frequently the 'last person standing').[182] However, the *Anns* liability of the 1980s did not arise directly from breach of statutory duty by local authority inspectors, instead being a (dubious) *common law* duty to take care that builders complied with their statutory obligations. The Building Regulations still primarily impose duties on builders, etc. However, authorised inspectors also have duties to certify those builders' compliance.

At their core, the Building Regulations state that 'building work' must comply with a detailed catalogue of requirements.[183] A new Part 2A of the Regulations, inserted in 2023,[184] now lists 'dutyholders' (eg designers, contractors and clients), their required 'competences', and their duties (heavily qualified for *domestic* clients); and there is a general duty that '[a]ny person carrying out any building work must ensure the work … [is] in compliance with all relevant requirements.'[185] The stated aim of this 2023 reform was to 'provide accountability and clarity of roles and responsibilities of those involved in the procurement, design and undertaking of building work, and the duties which will apply to them.'[186] Following responses to public consultation, the government decided not to implement an earlier proposal that designers should have a 'strict liability duty' to ensure 'compliance with all relevant building regulations.'[187]

There is no mention in the new Part 2A of 'competences' and 'duties' of local authority building inspectors. Nevertheless, building control authorities have specific duties to approve plans, inspect works carried out, and (for example) to issue completion certificates 'where they are satisfied, after taking all reasonable steps … [that] the relevant provisions have been complied with in relation to the building.'[188] When (or if) section 38 of the Building Act 1984 is finally brought into force, it would appear that inspectors' breach of such inspection/certification duties under the Building Regulations would also be actionable (as much as the 'primary' duties of builders, etc), 'so far as it [the breach of the duty] causes damage' (section 38(1)(a)).

[182] J Stapleton, 'Duty of Care: Peripheral Parties and Alternative Opportunities for Deterrence' (1995) 111 *LQR* 30.
[183] Building Regulations 2010, reg 4(1).
[184] Building Regulations etc (Amendment) (England) Regulations 2023, reg 6.
[185] Building Regulations 2010, reg 11J(1).
[186] Explanatory Memorandum to the Building Regulations etc (Amendment) (England) Regulations 2023, para 7.6. Note: no stated intention to clarify *liability* in anticipation of the commencement of Building Act 1984, s 38.
[187] ibid, para 10.4.
[188] Building Regulations 2010, reg 17(1).

Under the DPA 1972, building inspectors certifying compliance with the Building Regulations have been held *not* to 'take on work' in the relevant sense, so falling outside DPA 1972 liability.[189] Interestingly, however, at first instance Waksman J invoked section 38 of the Building Act 1984 as one supporting reason for that construction. Albeit not yet in force,

> [section 38] is some indication that as far as the building regulations are concerned, *including for approved inspectors*, it is contemplated that there would be a separate free-standing regime for any civil liability.[190]

This was only an obiter comment about a provision that was not in question (since not, of course, in force). But it reveals an assumption that section 38 was intended to make 'approved inspectors' liable, as well as builders and designers.

Is it possible that the government had not appreciated the potential for section 38 to revive the heavy financial burden that fell on local authorities in the *Dutton–Anns* era, before negligence liability was curtailed in *Murphy*? It certainly appears to have misunderstood the equivalent statutory Scottish tort (or delict). Section 51 of the Building (Scotland) Act 2003 has been in force since 2005, and makes the Building Regulations actionable. Apparently, however, no claims have been brought under that provision. The absence of claims in Scotland was one reason cited by the UK government for its initial proposal (later reversed) to repeal altogether the equivalent section of the Building Act 1984 (ie on the ground of redundancy).[191] Perhaps the UK government was persuaded to change its mind by reasoning that to commence section 38 would *appear* to do something more to improve claimants' legal position, while producing little change in practice. If so, the UK government miscalculated because the Scottish scheme is sufficiently different that it cannot be used to make confident predictions about actionability of the Building Regulations in England. Britton and Bell point out why the statutory Scottish tort remains unused (despite the absence of any equivalent to the DPA 1972 in Scots law): in Scotland, statute places 'the fall-back duty of compliance with "the building code" on the homeowner – the would-be pursuer'.[192] That is not true in England.[193]

It therefore appears that, although building control inspectors have been omitted from 2023's inserted catalogue of Building Regulations 'dutyholders', they could be liable if failures to discharge their statutory inspection duties caused loss. The fact that Scottish local authorities have not seen such a revival of *Anns*-style liabilities turns on the different scheme of obligations in Scotland. It may be that the government has belatedly realised the potential for serious damage to local

[189] *The Lessees and Management Company of Heron's Court v Heronslea Ltd* [2019] EWCA Civ 1423, [2019] 1 WLR 5849. The fourth defendant was an approved building control inspector.
[190] *The Lessees and Management Company of Heron's Court v Heronslea Ltd* [2018] EWHC 3309 (TCC), [2019] BLR 401 [36] (emphasis added).
[191] Explanatory Notes to the Building Safety Bill 2020, para 892.
[192] Britton and Bell (n 176) 354.
[193] See now Building Regulations 2010, reg 11C.

authority budgets during a prolonged crisis in the public finances. In which case, its continuing reluctance will also spare *builders* from liability under section 38 when the real aim is to protect public authorities. (If that is correct, section 38 could be amended so as to apply explicitly only to builders, etc, and not public authorities; but the (unexplained) non-commencement of the existing section is the path of least resistance.)

While understandable as a matter of *Realpolitik*, if this explains the reluctance to bring section 38 into force it is regrettable. Holding local authorities liable would encourage their proper enforcement of the Building Regulations. It would also, of course, provide a realistic, solvent target for building-owners to recover compensation. A public authority carve-out would, in short, contradict both strands of post-Grenfell government policy. It would limit remedies for owners of defective buildings and undermine incentives to maintain high standards of construction.

Assuming it ever is brought into force, what losses would fall within section 38's scope? This too is not entirely clear. Stanton et al question what they describe as the 'common assumption' that section 38 liability 'extends to claims for those kinds of defects in property which are nowadays classified as a species of pure economic loss'.[194] They give two reasons for suggesting that the 1984 Act has a narrower purpose, being confined to building *safety*, which would be reflected in the damages recoverable. First, that section 38 re-enacted a provision originally contained in the Health and Safety at Work etc Act 1974. Stanton et al view this initial statutory 'home' as evidence of Parliament's original concern with safety. Thus, only personal injuries caused by collapsing buildings (or, possibly, remediation of dangerous structures) would be within the section. With respect, however, the argument about statutory origin is a weak one. Part III of the 1974 Act, entitled 'Building Regulations', has little to do with the rest of the Act. The buildings provisions were, Spencer reports, tacked on following the lapse of an earlier separate Bill on that specific topic (1974 was an unsettled parliamentary year, given two general elections).[195] Perhaps building regulation is the famous 'etcetera' in the 1974 Act's short title? Secondly, Stanton et al cite the House of Lords decision in *Peabody* holding that the Building Regulations' purpose is to ensure *safe* buildings, rather than to protect the *economic* interests of property developers (and owners).[196] If that view of the Regulations were maintained if/when section 38 is brought into force, substandard construction, in breach of Building Regulations without being *unsafe* (eg poorly insulated, thus expensive to heat), would not result in liability.

Section 38's wording is inconclusive. Subsection (4) states: '"damage" includes the death of, or injury to, any person (including any disease and any impairment

[194] Stanton et al (n 30) 427.

[195] JR Spencer, 'The Defective Premises Act – Defective Law and Defective Law Reform: Part II' [1975] *CLJ* 48, 56.

[196] *Governors of the Peabody Donation Fund v Sir Lindsay Parkinson & Co Ltd* [1985] AC 210 (HL). cf *Murphy* [1991] 1 AC 398, 490 (Lord Oliver): 'nothing in the statutory provisions [Public Health Acts and the Building Regulations] even suggest that the purpose of the statute was to protect owners of buildings from economic loss'.

of a person's physical or mental condition)'. This could be viewed as confirming the legislative focus on safety and personal injuries. However, an explicitly incomplete definition ('includes …') obviously cannot be exhaustive, or indeed conclusive. Notably, a backbench amendment to the 2022 Building Safety Bill proposed inserting words into section 38(4) of the Building Act 1984 explicitly to *include* 'economic loss'.[197] The 'probing amendment' was not seriously debated or pressed to a division.[198] The government moved no amendments in response to clarify the scope of section 38. Indeed, its contemporary 2022 'factsheet' on building redress (withdrawn after the BSA 2022's enactment) stated of the Building Act 1984: 'Purely financial loss is not covered by section 38, although it is in scope of a [DPA 1972] claim.'[199] Again, none of this can be conclusive. The proposed 'economic loss' amendment to section 38(4) would have been consistent either with mere *clarification* of the 1984 Act (making explicit what is currently unstated), or with its substantive *extension*. It is unfortunate that the legislative opportunity to resolve the uncertainty was missed. It is particularly regrettable when the new liabilities for non-compliant building products and cladding explicitly impose obligations 'to pay damages to a person with a relevant interest in relation to the relevant building for personal injury, damage to property *or economic loss* suffered by that person'.[200] The express inclusion of 'economic loss' in the BSA 2022 could be contrasted with its omission from the Building Act 1984. Again, however, this is not decisive.

As noted earlier in this chapter, leaving central concepts of statutory torts undefined is a lamentable tradition. It has been suggested that even the DPA 1972 left the nature of recoverable loss ambiguous. In a contemporary appraisal, Spencer identified a 'serious obscurity' in the DPA 1972's drafting: the failure to specify whether it extends to purely economic loss.[201] Spencer accepted that the Law Commission had clearly intended to cover economic loss, in the Report that led to the DPA 1972.[202] An entire section of the Report addressed the remedy for *poor-quality* buildings (ie those less suitable or less valuable), as opposed to positively *unsafe*. The remedy for this would, naturally, be the cost of repairing the defects of quality – which is 'economic loss'. The Law Commission's goal was contract-type liability but without the restrictions of privity, so that claims could be brought both *by* subsequent purchasers of houses, and *against* subcontractors, etc.[203]

[197] HC Deb 19 January 2022, vol 707, col 370: new cl 11(2) – see also cl 12.

[198] ibid col 389: withdrawn clauses were 'specific technical amendments to give the Government examples of how we could fix the problem' (Stephen McPartland MP).

[199] Department for Levelling Up, Housing & Communities and Ministry of Housing, Communities & Local Government, 'Redress: Factsheet' (UK Government, 5 April 2022) https://www.gov.uk/government/publications/building-safety-bill-factsheets/redress-factsheet#building-act-1984-section-38.

[200] BSA 2022 ss 148(6) and 149(6) (emphasis added).

[201] JR Spencer, 'The Defective Premises Act – Defective Law and Defective Law Reform' [1974] *CLJ* 307, 319–20.

[202] Law Commission, *Civil Liability of Vendors and Lessors for Defective Premises* (Law Com No 40,1970).

[203] ibid 3–9.

While it might be thought implicit in this 'contract-extension' philosophy that pure economic loss should be recoverable, Spencer thought there was room for doubt. The DPA 1972 schema was neither straightforwardly contractual (so that economic loss would naturally be recoverable),[204] nor entirely tortious (raising the debatable 'bar' on economic loss),[205] but sat somewhere between the two ('a sort of hermaphrodite', Spencer commented). Given that the Law Commission's Report was not at that time admissible as an aid to judicial construction, Spencer criticised the drafter's failure to address economic loss explicitly as a 'bad mistake' that could trigger expensive litigation, risking a narrow construction of the Act that would 'wreck [the Law Commission's] intentions'.

Stanton et al noted in 2003 there was still no positive authority on point.[206] However, the Law Commission's Report could surely now be used to discern the intention of the DPA 1972. The Court of Appeal recently waved aside defendants' objections that the claimant must still own the defective buildings in order to claim under the Act, expressly noting 'an equivalence between the measure of loss for breach of contract and the applicable measure under the DPA'.[207] Assuming that this (Spencer's preferred construction) is followed in future, it could lend further weight to the view that section 38 of the Building Act 1984 does *not* extend to economic loss. For, as Spencer reasoned, if the 1984 Act claim (and its identical predecessor in the Health and Safety at Work etc Act 1974) always included economic loss, 'it makes section 1 of the DPA 1972 largely redundant'.[208]

V. Conclusion

In *Murphy*, overruling *Anns*, the House of Lords insisted that whether local authorities should 'insure' building owners against shoddy workmanship was, whatever its social-policy attractions, a question for the legislature and not the courts. In particular, their Lordships held that, since the legislature had already intervened with the DPA 1972, a statutory 'consumer protection' regime against poor construction, the common law could not properly go further. There is much to be said for this division of labour, given the difficulties the courts had found in confining *Anns* liability within sensible limits.[209] Professor Nolan's

[204] Bright and McFarlane (n 18) 137 note that the non-excludability of DPA 1972 liability sits uneasily with its supposedly contractual (voluntary) nature.

[205] For contemporaneous doubts: *Dutton v Bognor Regis Urban District Council* [1972] 1 QB 373 (CA).

[206] Stanton et al (n 30) 429.

[207] *URS Corp Ltd v BDW Trading Ltd* [2023] EWCA Civ 772, [2024] 2 WLR 181, [2024] KB 827, [2023] BLR 437 [192] (Coulson LJ). The UK Supreme Court heard an appeal against this decision in December 2024 (decision awaited at time of writing).

[208] Spencer (n 195) 48.

[209] *Murphy* [1991] 1 AC 398, 457 (Lord Mackay LC): *Anns* required distinctions 'which have no justification on any reasonable principle and can only be described as capricious', but it would be inconsistent with DPA 1972 'to remove altogether the qualifications on the [*Anns*] cause of action'.

chapter describes how difficulties over negligence liability for defective construction have troubled judges across the common law world.[210] He hails the DPA 1972 as a superior solution.

Statute may create torts that the common law cannot. But legislation is not necessarily a panacea. Much depends on the detail. The distinctiveness of statute should not be exaggerated when background (ie common law) concepts and principles help give meaning to statutory torts. At the very least, judicially developed concepts act as an important gap-filler. Moreover, statutes tend to become assimilated back into the common law to some degree, ultimately perhaps to produce 'statute-based common law'.[211]

The Law Lords in *Murphy* placed the ball firmly back in Parliament's court. But Parliament does not always perform its role as law-giver. Statutory claims can face various restrictions. These may be a matter of conscious design. On enactment, for example, the DPA 1972 applied only to *initial* construction of dwellings (extended to later building work by the BSA 2022); the DPA's section 2 also empowered the government to approve the National Housebuilders' Association's warranty, which it did until 1979. Crucially, this 'warranty' (despite its limited nature) excluded the statutory liability entirely, during those years of approval.[212] Other limitations may be inadvertent. We have seen how environmental statutes have been interpreted to exclude 'relational' economic loss because it is outwith common law concepts with which Parliament is presumed to legislate consistently. The failure to define 'loss' in the DPA 1972 has also been criticised.

Although it seems reasonably clear (with respect to Spencer's critique) that the DPA 1972 *does* compensate pure economic loss, the same cannot be said of section 38 of the 1984 Act. After half a century's dormancy it is (apparently) to be brought to life. But when it finally awakes, like Sleeping Beauty, what will section 38 mean? Which parties will be liable and with respect of what kind of loss? We can no longer take the detached perspective of Stanton et al, who viewed section 38's scope as an interesting but entirely academic question since it 'seems almost certain that this piece of consumer protection will never be operative'.[213] In *Murphy*, the courts insisted that protection against shoddy construction was Parliament's responsibility. Given the impetus of the Grenfell disaster, Parliament has spoken at last. But what its words mean still remains unclear.

[210] Nolan (n 4), esp section III.

[211] Burrows (n 74) (2012) 128 *LQR* 232, 240: 'in some areas the weight of judicial decisions is such that it is easy to forget that one is [not] dealing with … pure common law'.

[212] Spencer (n 201) 320–322 (s 2 'watered down' the DPA 1972 'as a sop to builders and architects', leaving the section 1 duty 'all dressed up … with nowhere to go').

[213] Stanton et al (n 30) 427.

8

Rationalising Associate Liability under the Building Safety Act 2022

DAVID SAWTELL*

I. Introduction

The cost of remediating a multi-occupancy residential building with fire safety defects is often extremely high, far beyond the means of ordinary homeowners. The existing private law remedies previously available to secure compensation from culpable parties, such as developers, designers or builders, have been partial and limited, leading to a narrow pool of defendants who often cannot satisfy any judgment. The UK government's different building safety funds in respect of cladding remediation have helped towards the cost, but there is very little appetite for a solution that sees the state paying most of the cost of the remediation of buildings with fire safety defects, whether in England and Wales or elsewhere.

One of the obvious practical problems for residential leaseholders is identifying a solvent defendant against whom they have a cause of action in law. The UK government has targeted the developers of projects with significant construction defects to pay for the cost of remediating them. The developer of a project, however, may well have been a special-purpose vehicle, since dissolved, or be significantly undercapitalised. The profits of the development could easily have been paid to holding companies who used subsidiaries to undertake developments, or to other forms of corporate groups or structures.

Part 5 of the United Kingdom's Building Safety Act 2022 (BSA 2022) creates a new concept of associate liability to address these problems. The first standout feature of this regime is that claimants or applicants for a building liability order or remediation contribution order are now able to pursue remedies against the

* I am extremely grateful to Peter Underwood for his comments and advice in respect of an early draft of this chapter, as well as to those attending the sessions of the symposium both in Oxford and in Melbourne in 2023 for their insightful comments. I also sincerely thank the editors for their helpful comments and suggestions. All errors remain my own.

'associates' of parties with primary liability,[1] regardless of whether or not such associates are vicariously liable for the acts of the parties with primary liability, and regardless of whether such associates had any fault or causative involvement in the design or construction of the defective building. The second important feature of associate liability under the BSA 2022 is that liability is imposed retrospectively, rather than only prospectively. Before 2022, the owners of corporate groups, investors and other potential associates were unaware that their entity structures would be vulnerable to claims arising from the actions of legally independent parties.

This chapter will demonstrate how the scheme of associate liability under the BSA 2022 does not fit existing private law structures or justifications for imposing liability on parties who do not have primary liability for acts or omissions. Instead, the new regime of associate liability adopts a form of collective liability for corporate groups that have been involved in the development or construction of defective homes. The test of associate liability does not, however, require any examination of the way in which the corporate group is composed or the degree of control exercised over the wrongdoer, while the only control mechanism is a broad and open-textured test of whether it is 'just and equitable' to impose liability, without any legislative steer as to what satisfies this test.

This chapter argues that the test for associate liability, rather than merely being an extension of private law liability, represents a significant rupture with the conventional understanding of private law and instead reflects a political objective rather than any juridical rationale for imposing liability. It is indicative of a policy decision to reallocate the cost of remediation of a particular class of buildings rendered unsafe from leaseholders and the government to a class of parties who are portrayed as having profited from these afflicted building developments. It should, therefore, be compared to other exceptional instances where extensions of liability to entities related to the original tortfeasor have been advocated, such as product liability or environmental torts. The fact that liability can be imposed on an associated entity in the absence of any fault or culpability at all, at the instigation of a party that was not in a recognised private law relationship with either the original wrongdoer or the defendant, makes it extremely difficult to reconcile with our conventional understanding of the structure of private law. This can only be explained by reference to policy considerations. As a consequence, when deciding whether it is just and equitable to make a building liability order or a remediation contribution order, a court or tribunal should explicitly take into account those policy considerations, and should consider how those considerations have been given effect in existing areas of private law.

[1] Building liability orders were created by the Building Safety Act 2022 (BSA 2022), s 130. Such an order provides that the liability of a corporate body is also the liability of another, associated, body corporate. Remediation contribution orders were created by the BSA 2022, s 124. Such an order requires a specified body or partnership to make payments towards the costs of remedying building safety defects; as well as landlords and developers, associated parties of landlords and developers can be made subject to such an order. These orders are discussed in section IV of this chapter.

Section II of this chapter will outline how corporate groups and associated entities are used in residential property development. Section III looks at how the use of such investment structures can hamper a homeowner's ability to secure meaningful or adequate compensation for the cost of remediation through accepted construction law. Section IV sets out the scheme for associate liability under the BSA 2022. Section V compares this scheme to other private law systems, including accessory liability, vicarious liability and arguments in favour of enterprise liability in company law. Section VI considers the policy of associate liability, both from the perspective of the homeowner and the government, but also that of the developer and the investor. Section VII uses the decision of the First Tier Tribunal in *Triathlon Homes LLP v Stratford Village Development Partnership* as a case study of how the associate liability scheme has been applied in the context of the complicated investment structure for residential development that came out of the athletes' village for the London 2012 Olympic Games.[2] Section VIII then critically compares the BSA 2022 to developments in Victoria, Australia, where a different approach has been adopted to attributing liability for building defects to parties other than the primary wrongdoer.

II. The Use of Associated Entities and Corporate Groups in Residential Developments

It is impossible to generalise the different vehicles or structures used since the 1990s for the purpose of residential property development. There are, however, a number of general legal points that have shaped the forms of investment structures deployed.

The starting point is that real property, as an investment, has several distinct features that affect the structures used for investment and development. First, a building, as a physical asset, is subject to deterioration, hence requiring regular management and maintenance.[3] As a consequence, a residential property development requires ongoing management. Secondly, it is very difficult to diversify a property portfolio based on individual buildings. Each of those developments carries its own, specific, risks, such as construction cost overruns, construction defects or market forces.[4] Direct investment in a property development therefore represents only one of the forms in which property investment takes place. Investors in property development often consider investment strategies that both

[2] *Triathlon Homes LLP v Stratford Village Development Partnership* [2024] UKFTT 26 (PC) ('*Triathlon*'). As was noted in the Introduction to this volume (p 2), the Court of Appeal heard an appeal in this case in March 2025.

[3] D Hartzell and AE Baum, *Real Estate Investment: Strategies, Structures, Decisions*, 2nd edn (Chichester, Wiley, 2021) 12.

[4] ibid 16.

spread the risk of a single development, and cauterise that risk (if it eventuates) from the assets in the rest of their investment portfolio.

It is therefore common for limited companies, and less so for limited liability partnerships, to be used as vehicles for property investment. A limited company is a distinct entity with its own legal personality. Absent the limited company being a sham or one of the exceptions discussed below, it is not possible to attribute the debts and liabilities of that entity to the company's members, even if there is only one shareholder.[5] Limited liability allows an investor to accept taking on a higher-risk venture without being exposed to financial ruin.[6] Limited liability also allows for more efficient diversification. A property investor can minimise risk by owning a diversified portfolio of assets, while reducing the cost of raising capital by mitigating the risk of a non-diversified holding.[7] As noted by Frank Easterbrook and Daniel Fischel, '[b]ecause limited liability increases the probability that there will be insufficient assets to pay creditors' claims, shareholders of a firm reap all of the benefits of risky activities but do not bear all of the costs'. Instead, any remaining costs (such as unsatisfied tort claims) are typically borne by creditors (including involuntary creditors, such as tort claimants).[8]

One common model of a vertically integrated corporate group structure sees one limited company acquire land, another undertake construction and a third provide construction and management services (such as design and the supply of materials).[9] It is far from being the only kind of structure that has been in use, however. An investment structure can also involve a number of parties so as to allow for a larger number of investors and other participants to become involved in the investment. Some of those parties may well only have an interest in, and exercise control over, financial aspects of the development, delegating design and construction decisions to more experienced and qualified project participants. In those circumstances, the other participants in the project may well defer to that party's expertise, and expect them to make any decisions in respect of design, specification and quality control. This has none of the hallmarks of a single enterprise, as opposed to a project involving a disparate group of participants.

The practical and conceptual difficulties with entity-based liability have long been flagged. Adolf Berle identified how an enterprise could be operated through a larger group of corporations controlled by a central holding company. He argued for the recognition of the enterprise in law.[10] Douglas Brodie identified enterprise liability as a potential basis for the explanation of vicarious liability, as

[5] *Salomon v A Salomon and Co Ltd* [1897] AC 22 (HL).
[6] A Muscat, *The Liability of the Holding Company for the Debts of its Insolvent Subsidiaries* (Oxford, Routledge, 1996) 268.
[7] FH Easterbrook and DR Fischel, 'Limited Liability and the Corporation' (1985) 52 *University of Chicago Law Review* 89, 96.
[8] ibid 103–04.
[9] Muscat (n 6) 392.
[10] AA Berle Jr, 'The Theory of Enterprise Entity' (1947) 47 *Columbia Law Review* 343.

well as providing a theoretical platform for its future reform and development.[11] Enterprise liability is often justified on the basis of control. There is, however, no obvious test for control that academic scholarship has coalesced around. Meredith Dearborn advocates recognition of enterprise liability based on the economic fact of the enterprise, referring to functional integration and subsidiary purpose.[12] Brodie identified the concept of enterprise risk as a core anterior concept to enterprise liability.[13] Ewan McGaughey has argued that enterprise law should be acknowledged as a coherent subject, instead of artificially segregating corporate, labour, competition or insolvency law, and shielding each of them from public policy.[14] The recognition of the importance of the enterprise, however, has not so far led to a widely acknowledged test for enterprise liability.

Arguments that English law should recognise enterprise liability have so far fallen on mostly barren ground. In *Adams v Cape Industries Plc*, it was made clear that group companies ought to be treated as separate entities with their own legal obligations.[15] The notion of enterprise liability was robustly rejected. Although there had been some limited cases in which the 'corporate veil' was pierced,[16] this has more recently been strictly limited to cases where the arrangement was a mere façade or sham: it has been considered to be perfectly acceptable to use corporate group structures to ensure that legal liability only fell on one part of a corporate group.[17] As Lord Sumption noted in *Prest v Petrodel*, subject to limited exceptions (such as misapplication of a company's assets or wrongful or fraudulent trading), 'the separate corporate identity of a company is a fact of legal life that all courts are required to recognise and respect, whatever jurisdiction they are exercising.'[18] 'Piercing the corporate veil', in English law, can only be done in very limited and extreme circumstances; it has essentially fallen out of favour with most courts and commentators.[19]

The common law test for vicarious liability, as well, makes no explicit reference to enterprise liability, beyond a recognition that it comprises an underlying policy consideration. In *BXB v Trustees of the Barry Congregation of Jehovah's Witnesses*,

[11] D Brodie, *Enterprise Liability and the Common Law* (Cambridge, Cambridge University Press, 2010) 181.

[12] M Dearborn, 'Enterprise Liability: Reviewing and Revitalizing Liability for Corporate Groups' (2009) 97 *California Law Review* 195, 247–60.

[13] Brodie (n 11) ch 3.

[14] E McGaughey, *Principles of Enterprise Law: The Economic Constitution and Human Rights* (Cambridge, Cambridge University Press, 2022) 686.

[15] *Adams v Cape Industries Plc* [1990] Ch 433 (EWCA).

[16] See eg *DHN Food Distributors Ltd v Tower Hamlets London Borough Council* [1976] 1 WLR 852 (EWCA), where the corporate veil was pierced for the benefit of the parent company for the purpose of compensation for compulsory purchase of the subsidiary's assets.

[17] *Adams v Cape Industries Plc* [1990] Ch 433, 544 in a judgment of the whole court.

[18] *Prest v Petrodel* [2013] UKSC 34, [2013] 2 AC 415 [155]. For one example where this threshold was crossed, see *Re A Company* [1985] BCLC 333, where findings were made that intricate trust structures were simply devices to conceal the assets of the first defendant and his relatives.

[19] M Petrin and B Choudhury, 'Group Company Liability' (2018) 19 *European Business Organization Law Review* 771.

Lord Burrows did not consider it to be an aspect of the two-stage test of (1) the relationship between the defendant and the tortfeasor, and (2) the link between the commission of the tort and that relationship, but instead only deployed the 'policy' of enterprise liability or risk as a 'final check'.[20]

There are some, very limited, exceptions to the *Salomon* principle. As Lord Collins of Mapesbury JSC identified in *Enviroco Ltd v Farstad Supply A/S*, there are a number of situations in which company law takes account of groups of companies.[21] The EU Accounting Directive required larger corporate undertakings to prepare consolidated group accounts and management reports. This was transposed into UK law in what is now section 1162 of the Companies Act 2006. Corporate groups are also taken into account for the purposes of the control of transactions between a company and its directors or the purchasing of a company's own shares. This reflects the recommendations of the Report of the Company Law Amendment Committee, led by Wilfred Greene MR, that led to the Companies Act 1928 and the Companies Act 1929.[22] In successive Companies Acts, therefore, voluntary creditors are protected by enhanced disclosure requirements, while the members of the company are protected from dealings within the company group. Under the Pensions Act 2004, the Pensions Regulator has the power to issue a contribution notice stating that the target is under a liability to pay a sum specified to the trustees of a pension scheme. Such a notice, however, can only be issued when the target company has been at fault in some way.

A form of extended liability for manufacturers which exposed their commercial products to market was created by the EU product liability regime through the Product Liability Directive. In the UK, this was implemented in the Consumer Protection Act 1987. By section 2 of that Act, where damage is caused wholly or partly by a defect in a product, then the producer and the supplier are liable for the damage. For example, in *O'Byrne v Aventis Pasteur SA*, the Supreme Court held that the UK distributor of a drug was the proper defendant to proceedings.[23] In that case, the UK distributor was a wholly owned subsidiary of the French manufacturer. The Supreme Court did not consider this, however, to be decisive on its own; it was one of a number of factors pointing to the product being put into circulation by the supplier at the behest of its parent.[24]

It is possible to compare the developer of a defective residential block to the manufacturer of a defective product intended for consumer consumption. On this argument, in both cases, it is the developer or the manufacturer who has introduced the defective physical item (whether a physical structure or a chattel) into a market where members of its intended client base have considerably less power.

[20] *BXB v Trustees of the Barry Congregation of Jehovah's Witnesses* [2023] UKSC 15, [2024] AC 567 [58], [82] ('*BXB*'). This is discussed further in section V of this chapter.

[21] *Enviroco Ltd v Farstad Supply A/S* [2011] UKSC 16, [2011] 1 WLR 921 [16].

[22] Company Law Amendment Committee, *Report of the Company Law Amendment Committee* (Cmd 2657, 1926).

[23] *O'Byrne v Aventis Pasteur SA* [2010] UKSC 23, [2010] 4 All ER 1 [36].

[24] ibid [28]–[36].

The analogy, however, is not a perfect one. For example, it is the contractor, and not necessarily the developer, which has actually brought the building into being. Furthermore, the actual reasoning in *O'Byrne v Aventis Pasteur SA* points away from a parent company to a developer being attributed with its liability merely because of the corporate relationship: instead, the nature of the relationship and, in particular, the extent of control over the subsidiary must be considered.

III. Paying for Remediation

The difficulties that residential leaseholders face when seeking judicial remedies in respect of the cost of the remediation of defective buildings, especially multi-occupancy buildings, are now well documented.[25] This section will set those difficulties against the context of the different investment structures introduced above.

The freehold of a multi-occupancy building may well be vested in a limited company or be owned by way of a trust of land by two limited companies, with the residential leasehold interests demised either out of the freehold or an intermediate headlease. The value of the freehold may be very limited, with its only economic value being the ground rents reserved (and, possibly, any profits made in respect of the management of the building). Instead, the value of the development is realised on the sale of the long leasehold interests. The freeholder may well own no other assets apart from the freehold interest itself. The limited company or companies holding the freehold may well have been a subsidiary or subsidiaries of a larger corporate group structure. The contractor (which might itself be associated with that group structure) may have contracted with a special-purpose vehicle for the purpose of the development; the shareholding in that vehicle may have been held by the corporate group.

The standard framework in private law of common law claim rights and corresponding duties, supplemented by a cautious and limited Defective Premises Act 1972, has in reality left many domestic property owners without practical redress for defective buildings. If a residential leaseholder purchased their apartment off-plan, there may be express terms in their sale agreement with the developer as to the quality of the construction (including specification, workmanship and fitness for purpose). This developer, however, may have been a special-purpose vehicle, which is either dissolved on practical completion of the development or which does not possess the assets to satisfy any judgment. In *Rendlesham Estates Plc v Barr Ltd*, for example, the developer, City Wall Limited, was reliant on financing from the Royal Bank of Scotland and possessed very limited resources of its own; it ultimately went into administration, rendering the value of any contractual claim by the leaseholders who purchased their interests

[25] P Britton and M Bell, *Residential Construction Law* 2nd edn (Oxford, Hart Publishing, 2025).

off-plan from them effectively worthless; instead, those leaseholders brought claims under the Defective Premises Act 1972 against the contractor.[26] As Susan Bright and Ben McFarlane have argued, whatever the doctrinal merits of limiting claims in tort by defining claims for the cost of remediation as economic loss for which the contractor did not owe a duty of care to the subsequent owners of a building,[27] the resulting inability for leaseholders to recover in tort has had harsh consequences for purchasers of domestic property.[28]

One of the planks in the argument for opposing associate liability is the argument that a creditor chooses who to contract with, such as by lending money or by entering into a building contract. It could be argued that residential leaseholders who have chosen to purchase an interest in land in respect of a particular building should not be treated as involuntary creditors. This argument, however, carries little weight in the particular circumstances that leaseholders of defective blocks find themselves in. Firstly, before 2017, there was very limited general awareness of fire safety risks caused by combustible cladding and other dangerous external wall build-ups. Furthermore, it is almost impossible for an individual leaseholder purchaser to carry out their own investigation of the safety features of a multi-occupancy block. They are very largely reliant on information provided by others, the competency of the designer and builder, and the diligence of the project consultancy team and the building inspector. The residential leaseholder's choice, therefore, was not informed and independent.[29] Finally, Muscat is correct to note that there is a distinction between a creditor who voluntarily extends credit, and those whose claims did not relate at all to the extension of credit, with the leaseholder falling into the second camp.[30] A residential leaseholder may well have limited market options when choosing an apartment or flat and have little knowledge of the original developer or builder of their property (especially if they are not the original purchaser, but a subsequent owner), further increasing the dissimilarity with a truly voluntary creditor.

The result of the typical forms of real estate investment structures, therefore, was that they were effective in preventing liability from attaching to the ultimate beneficiaries of the profits of defective developments. The cost of remediating such defective buildings fell on underresourced freeholders and, through their service charge obligations, residential leaseholders. Claims by leaseholders in negligence, contract and under the Defective Premises Act 1972 were deflected away from the entities that had actually received the profits from the developments in the first place. This was a normal, and accepted, business practice. Furthermore, besides

[26] *Rendlesham Estates Plc v Barr Ltd* [2014] EWHC 3968 (TCC), 157 ConLR 147 [2], [8]–[10].

[27] *Murphy v Brentwood District Council* [1991] 1 AC 398 (HL).

[28] S Bright and B McFarlane, 'Private Law Failings and Policy Development Following the Grenfell Tower Fire' in J Gardner et al (eds), *Politics, Policy and Private Law*, vol I: *Tort, Property and Equity* (Oxford, Hart Publishing, 2023) 134.

[29] Applying the test in Dearborn (n 12) 205 as to the distinction between a voluntary and an involuntary creditor.

[30] Muscat (n 6) 184.

the government, there was no source of financing for the cost of remediation except for residential leaseholders, an outcome that was politically unacceptable.

IV. The Scheme of the Building Safety Act 2022

There was no formal consultation in respect of Part 5 of the BSA 2022. Through a number of announcements by the government introducing the legislation, it is possible to identify the justification advanced for the need for new remedies and forms of liability to overcome the problems set out above. The Explanatory Notes to the BSA 2022 refer to the practice of using a thinly capitalised subsidiary company to manage a development which is then wound up once it has been completed. Existing English private law structures were considered 'insufficient' to address the consequences of this conduct.[31] The overall scheme of associate liability under sections 121, 124, 130 and 131 of the BSA 2022 is to cut through the parent–subsidiary barrier, so that the corporate group is made liable for building safety defects in the developments it has been responsible for.

A. Building Liability Orders

Section 130 of the BSA 2022 creates a new remedy, styled a 'building liability order'. By section 130(1), the High Court can make such an order if it considers it 'just and equitable'. By section 130(2), a building liability order is an order that provides that the 'relevant liability' of a body corporate which is the 'original body' relating to a specified building is also a liability of a 'specified body corporate' or joint and several liability of two or more specified bodies corporate. A building liability order, therefore, springs from the liability of an original body corporate, even if it has been dissolved before or is dissolved after the making of the order.[32] Only a liability that is incurred under the Defective Premises Act 1972 or, if it is brought into force, section 38 of the Building Act 1984; or a liability incurred as a result of a 'building safety risk', which is a risk to the safety of people in or about a building arising from the spread of fire or structural failure, can be the subject of an order.[33] Section 130 does not limit the class of applicants to homeowners, and on its face it can be relied upon by parties which are liable for construction defects such as developers or builders against associates of other liable parties. In a multi-party construction dispute as to the cost of remediation, therefore, section 130 will be a powerful tool even if no residential homeowners are involved.

[31] Explanatory Notes to the BSA 2022, paras 1072–74.
[32] BSA 2022, s 130(5).
[33] See also J Morgan, 'Tort as a Tool of Government Policy: Section 38 of the Building Act 1984: Sleeping Beauty Awakes?', this volume, ch 7.

By section 130(4), a body corporate may be specified under section 130 if it is, or has at any time in the relevant period been, associated with the original body, where the relevant period is defined as starting with the beginning of the carrying out of the works in relation to which the relevant liability was incurred, and ending with the making of the order. Liability will, therefore, be imposed retrospectively for defects to existing buildings, and not just future ones.[34]

B. Remediation Contribution Orders

Section 124 of the BSA 2022 allows the First Tier Tribunal to make a 'remediation contribution order' in relation to a relevant building: again, the safety-valve test is whether 'it is just and equitable' to make the order. A remediation contribution order is an order requiring a specified body corporate or partnership to make payments to a 'specified person' for the 'purpose of meeting costs incurred (or to be incurred) in remedying relevant defects in respect of a relevant building'.[35] Section 124 specifies a number of potential applicants, including the Secretary of State, the local authority, a person with a legal or equitable interest in the building (which would include a leaseholder but probably not a management company) and any other person specified in secondary legislation.[36] The new jurisdiction, therefore, extends beyond parties who may be conceivably in some kind of private law relationship with each other. There is a considerable overlap with the public law power of a local authority to serve an improvement notice on the owner of a hazardous building under the Housing Act 2004. The persons who may be specified as a paying party under a remediation contribution order are: (a) 'a landlord under a lease of the relevant building or any part of it'; (b) 'a person who was such a landlord at the qualifying time' (ie 14 February 2022); (c) 'a developer in relation to the relevant building'; or (d) 'a person associated with a person within any of paragraphs (a) to (c)'.[37]

C. Associates

The test for whether a party is an associate is set out in section 131 in respect of building liability orders and in section 121 in respect of remediation contribution orders. Although there are some differences between the two sections, for reasons which are not obvious, they are sufficiently similar to be considered together.

[34] BSA 2022, s 130(6).
[35] ibid s 124(2).
[36] ibid s 124(5).
[37] ibid s 124(3). A relevant building is defined by s 117(2), which limits it to buildings: (a) 'at least 11 metres high' or (b) 'at least five storeys'.

Both sections make reference to a test of 'control'. All of the cases in section 131 make express reference to control: section 131(1) states that a body corporate (A) is associated with another body corporate (B) if (a) one of them controls the other, or (b) a third body corporate controls both of them. The cases in which a body corporate is regarded as controlling another are set out in subsections (2)–(4). When it comes to section 121, subsections (2)–(4) do not refer expressly to 'control', although practically they necessarily involve de jure control; subsection (5) then states that a body corporate is also associated with another body corporate if (a) at any time in the relevant period a person was a director of both of them, or (b) at the qualifying time, one of them controlled the other or a third body corporate controlled both of them. Subsections (6)–(8) then set out the cases where a body corporate is regarded as controlling another body corporate. It is unclear why a different reference to control was used in these two sections.

Different forms of legal entity are addressed in the detailed provisions of the sections. For example, both section 121(6) and section 131(2) refer to the case where one body corporate controls another by possessing (or being entitled to acquire) at least half of the issued share capital of the other company; being able to exercise at least half of the votes in general meetings; or being entitled to at least half of the distributed income, or at least half of the assets of the other in a winding up. Similarly, with limited-liability partnerships, sections 121(7) and 131(3) provide that a body corporate controls a limited liability partnership if it holds a majority of the voting rights; is a member of the other and has a right to appoint or remove a majority of the other members; or is a member and controls alone or pursuant to an agreement with other members a majority of the voting rights. The definitions in respect of capital and voting rights, therefore, refer to either majority control or majority profit share. Both sections 121 and 131 also import a concept of de facto (as opposed to de jure) control which is similar to section 1162(4) of the Companies Act 2006. Under section 121(8) and section 131(4), a body corporate X controls body corporate Y if X has the power, directly or indirectly, to secure that the affairs of Y are conducted in accordance with X's wishes.

D. The Missing Test of Culpability

What is missing from these provisions is any assessment of culpability or causative potency in respect of the original wrongdoing on the part of the potential associates, or the degree of connection between the enterprise that the wrongdoer was involved in and the respondent to the application. Instead, liability can be imposed on an associate without any contribution or connectedness to the primary breach of duty. There is nothing in the regime that requires the court or the tribunal to carry out any analysis of culpability. While the express wording of the scheme refers to a test of 'control', this is not a reference to involvement in the acts or omissions leading to the construction defects. A party that acquires a majority shareholding or even de facto control long after practical completion may find itself liable as an associate (subject to the 'just and equitable' safety valve). Furthermore, simply because a party can exercise control, does not mean that it did, or that it had any culpability for the defects in the development. On the other hand, not all parties that had meaningful control over the development and its design fall within the scope of associate liability. Purely financial investors who had oversight over the project, such as funders who employed their own surveyors, and contractual joint venturers fall outside its purview. The test of control in sections 121 and 131, being limited for the most part to either de jure or de facto control, is simultaneously too wide and too narrow, and does not seek to determine causative contribution or degree of involvement. The only way that any assessment of culpability could be imported into any analysis is through the safety-valve test of whether it is 'just and equitable' to make an order.

V. Comparisons with Other Private Law Systems

It is the absence of the need to establish causative potency, moral culpability or connectedness with the wrongdoer's enterprise, whether by way of direct involvement in the breach of duty or a relationship of close control over the party primarily liable, that sets the regime for associate liability under the BSA 2022 apart from other private law regimes for secondary liability. For accessory liability to be established, a claimant must first prove a primary wrong, before going on to show that the accessory 'did something wrong in relation to the primary wrong' (the conduct element) and 'was at fault in some way' (the mental element).[38] As Paul Davies has noted, '[t]he moral core of accessory liability is best respected by imposing liability only upon those who are culpable'.[39] By reference to accessory liability regimes in the criminal law, common law and equity, he demonstrates that there must be some link between the act of the accessory and the violation of the claimant's rights through the primary wrong.[40] These requirements are absent from associate liability.

At first blush, a more promising analogue is vicarious liability. To make out vicarious liability, a two-stage test must be satisfied. Firstly, a sufficient relationship between the defendant and the tortfeasor must be established. Secondly, a close connection between the wrongful conduct and the acts that the tortfeasor was authorised to do must be demonstrated, so that it can fairly and properly be regarded as done by the tortfeasor while acting in the course of the tortfeasor's employment or quasi-employment. By contrast with accessory liability, once these two elements are proven, liability is strict without any further need to examine the

[38] PS Davies, *Accessory Liability* (London, Hart Publishing, 2015) 1.
[39] ibid 4.
[40] ibid 21.

defendant's culpability.[41] Enterprise risk or enterprise liability has been cited as an underlying justification for the doctrine as part of the fair allocation of costs of an enterprise undertaking business: as Brodie noted, '[i]nvoking enterprise liability as a justification for vicarious liability … has a considerable pedigree'.[42] As Warren Swain observed, however, enterprise liability has 'waxed and waned' in popularity, and it has proven difficult to identify a unifying justification for the doctrine that academic and judicial opinion can coalesce around.[43]

Critically, however, the doctrine of vicarious liability depends on a close nexus between the wrongdoer, the wrong and the defendant. In the course of advocating enterprise liability as a rationale for vicarious liability, Brodie acknowledges that his justification of liability on the basis of the risk that an enterprise creates requires an analysis of the extent of the connection between the wrong in question and the enterprise.[44] Until the 'just and equitable' stage, the BSA 2022 does not require any analysis of the connection between the wrongdoing and the entity that is the respondent to the application. Furthermore, even if enterprise risk is one possible rationale for vicarious liability, it does not by itself set the limits on when such liability is imposed. While a number of recent decisions in the Supreme Court have referred to the risks created by an enterprise in the course of its business as being at least part of an underlying justification for the imposition of vicarious liability, it has not become a part of the legal test.[45] If vicarious liability, as a form of private law strict liability, is advanced as a potential analogue for associate liability, then that analogy also imports a requirement to examine closely the connection between the defendant and the wrongdoing, introducing fairness as part of the just and equitable test.[46]

[41] *Lister v Hesley Hall* [2002] 1 AC 215 (HL); *BXB* (n 20).

[42] Brodie (n 11) 6; D Brodie, 'Enterprise Liability: Justifying Vicarious Liability' (2007) 27 *OJLS* 493. See also the discussion in A Gray, *Vicarious Liability: Critique and Reform* (London, Hart Publishing, 2019) ch 5, as well as his criticism of the theory in the following chapter. Gray's chapters were cited by Lord Burrows in *BXB* (n 20) [2023] UKSC 15 [47].

[43] W Swain, 'Vicarious Liability, a Pailful of Slops and Other Hazards' in K Barker and R Grantham (eds), *Apportionment in Private Law* (Oxford, Hart Publishing, 2018), ch 4, 110; see also W Swain, 'A Historical Examination of Vicarious Liability: A "Veritable Upas Tree"?' (2019) 78 *Cambridge Law Journal* 640.

[44] Brodie (n 11) ch 3, citing *Bazley v Curry* (1999) 174 DLR (4th) 45, 62.

[45] See eg *Cox v Ministry of Justice* [2016] UKSC 10, [2016] AC 660 [21]–[24] (Lord Reed); *Armes v Nottinghamshire County Council* [2018] AC 355 [53]–[60] (Lord Reed); *Mohamud v Wm Morrison Supermarkets plc* [2016] UKSC 11, [2016] AC 677 [10], [40], [55] (Lord Toulson); but see also *Various Claimants v Wm Morrison Supermarkets plc* [2020] UKSC 12, [2020] AC 989 [26], where Lord Reed stated that the close-connection test did not require an examination of social justice, but should be decided 'by orthodox common law reasoning'; *Various Claimants v Barclays Bank plc* [2020] UKSC 13, [2020] AC 973 [27] (Baroness Hale), where it was doubted whether this added anything to the legal test, 'Where it is clear that the tortfeasor is carrying on his own independent business'; and *BXB* (n 20).

[46] S Smith, *Rights, Wrongs and Injustices* (Oxford, Oxford University Press, 2018) 267–68 and fn 132 identifies fairness as a rationale for various liability:

> If you have engaged someone to work on your behalf, it is fair to attribute their actions to you when they are engaged in that work. It follows that, if the employee's actions are tortious, the liability for the tort is fairly attributed to the employer.

From this, the author submits, if an associate has not been a part of the enterprise risk, then it is not fair to impose liability.

Witting proposes a justification of organisational deterrence in imposing vicarious liability on corporate groups.[47] A justification based on deterrence, however, is not engaged by the retrospective effective of the associate liability scheme under the BSA 2022. Whereas it is possible to see how investors, concerned with whether they could be visited with the consequences of building safety defects, would modify their behaviour to ensure that their developments were safer in the future, this does not justify the retrospective imposition of liability. As set out in the scenario, many investors reposed their trust in construction professionals and experienced developers and left the relevant fire safety details to them.

Instead, the scheme of associate liability in the BSA 2022 imposes a form of enterprise, as opposed to entity, liability in company law. The fact that the regime, on its face, ignores the question of actual control or culpability, as opposed to the potential for control through shareholding or membership, makes it a very stark form of enterprise liability that has previously failed to gain traction among scholars. Berle's argument for enterprise liability based on the profits received from a subsidiary – 'you profit, you pay' enterprise liability – has not been accepted either academically or, until now, in doctrinal law.[48] Writing in 2018, before the BSA 2022 was enacted, in the context of veil piercing, Witting stated that, 'there appears to be little justification for a principle of extended liability directed solely at controlling shareholders'.[49] As Witting observes, while equity ownership may provide a parent company with the ability to exercise control over its subsidiaries, this should not be equated with the actual exercise of that control. Although the parent company may exercise general strategic control, they may well leave detailed operational control to the subsidiary.[50] He goes on to argue that the simple fact that one company owns the majority of the shares in a subsidiary or that it shares directors should not compromise its separate legal personality or provide a basis for overlapping liability.[51] It might well be that the architects of the regime precisely intended to postpone all discussion of culpability, connectedness and, indeed, fairness to the 'just and equitable' stage. If that is right, then they failed to give any kind of lodestone or steer to the court or tribunal in how to gauge the application of that test, and the policy of the BSA 2022 should not be divined purely from the very wide range of potentially liable parties.

The other obvious way in which the BSA 2022 departs from conventional private law structures is its imposition of retrospective liability. Muscat has said

[47] CA Witting, 'Modelling Organisational Vicarious Liability' (2019) 39 *Legal Studies* 694. Note, however, that deterrence as a justification for vicarious liability was rejected in *Armes v Nottinghamshire County Council* [2017] UKSC 60, [2018] 1 AC 355 [67] (Lord Reed); cf *BXB* (n 20) [2023] UKSC 15 [47].

[48] Dearborn (n 12) 200.

[49] CA Witting, *Liability of Corporate Groups and Networks* (Cambridge, Cambridge University Press, 2018) 2.

[50] ibid 48.

[51] ibid 67.

that certainty is a virtue; '[i]n commercial law, it is lifeblood': it allows investors to organise their affairs, engage in long-term planning, and assess risks.[52] Contracting parties and investors were entitled to deal with the various entities as separate legal persons, rather than as constituent parts of a corporate group. When parties set up investment structures for residential property development, they relied upon the English law position that was restated in *Adams v Cape Industries Plc* and *Prest v Petrodel* that separate entities in a group structure would not be made liable for breaches of contract or statutory duty of other entities save where these were voluntarily assumed by the defendant (by contract, suretyship or assumption of responsibility) or in extreme circumstances such as where the entities were being used as part of a sham.

VI. Rationale and Public Policy

The most obvious justification for the new scheme is that it allows for the cost of remediation to be borne by those parties which profited from the initial development. In effect, the applicant is allowed to swim back up the profit waterfall, without having to scrutinise blameworthiness or even involvement. The way in which this is implemented, however, is crude. It is only possible to follow control through majority control or holdings. Some investors will be left without liability, especially where they are minority stakeholders. In any case, the statutory regime does not refer explicitly to tracing the development profits. There are a number of other divergences from this rationale in the scheme's detail. The associate of the landlord of a relevant building on 14 February 2022 may be made liable to a remediation contribution order, even if neither that landlord nor the associate had any role in the development but had acquired their interest some time after practical completion. The scheme does not, therefore, reflect 'you profit, you pay'.

In reality, the scheme reflects a policy of changing the starting position for who bears the burden of the cost of remediation. It transfers the cost of remediation from leaseholders, the state (in the form of funds set up to remediate defective buildings, such as the Building Safety Fund),[53] and an initial, small, group of primarily liable entities, towards a pool of defendants who qualify for membership by virtue of exercising majority control over parties who had some degree of involvement in the building at some point since the works began. It is therefore

[52] Muscat (n 6) 146.

[53] The Ministry of Housing, Communities and Local Government (formerly the Department for Levelling Up, Housing and Communities) has sought to use the status of the Secretary of State as a prescribed 'interested person' who has standing to bring applications for remediation contribution orders by virtue of regulation 2(1) of the Building Safety (Leaseholder Protections) (Information etc) (England) Regulations 2022 to pursue a number of parties and their associates for the cost of remediating buildings that was incurred through government funds. See, for example, the application for a remediation contribution order against Yianis Group in respect of developments at Canary Wharfside: T Howard, 'Docklands Test Case for Cladding Bill' *The Times* (29 March 2024).

a crude form of enterprise liability, which does not take into account the actual degree of control exercised, connection of the defendant to the enterprise risk, culpability or blameworthiness, save through the broad and currently unstructured test of whether it is 'just and equitable' to impose liability. It is also assumed in the structure of associate liability that the holding companies and other entities that become liable for the liabilities of other entities will themselves have sufficient resources to meet these claims. In fact, these associate bodies may themselves be unable to respond to claims, with the profits of the original development having long since been paid out.

The other major problem with the new scheme is that the risk profile of property investment has been changed with retrospective effect. Lenders, investors and others dealing with a single entity in a corporate structure (such as a holding company) reasonably dealt with it without having undue concern to the possibility of liabilities arising from separate companies. As Lord Wilberforce acknowledged in *Ford & Carter v Midland Bank Ltd*: 'When creditors become involved, as they do in the present case, the separate legal existence of the constituent companies of the group has to be respected.'[54] In the past, liability has been imposed on a purely behavioural basis, looking at whether there is a contractual nexus (including suretyship) or a common law or statutory duty of care; it has not been imposed purely on the grounds of status or control save in very narrow circumstances. Creditors and investors in parties who have subsequently turned out to be associates and hence potentially liable for very large costs had no way of identifying these liabilities, or even knowing that they should have inquired about them.

In the author's view, given the problems with the test for associateship in sections 121 and 131, the 'just and equitable' threshold for making either a remediation contribution order or a building liability order should play a very important role in ensuring that such orders are only made against parties which have contributed materially to the existence of construction defects or which had an involvement in the overall enterprise responsible for them. Beyond an unreasoned desire to shift liability on to parties with greater means, regardless of culpability, knowledge or a nexus with the original wrongdoer, it is very difficult to justify making such orders against investors or members who acquired their interest in the primary obligor after completion of the defective building works and who had no way of finding out about the earlier defective developments that obligor had been involved in. Likewise, there are likely to be associates who were investors in the original development, but who had no meaningful involvement in or control over the design or construction decisions that led to the fire safety defects. Application of the 'just and equitable' test should, it is submitted, import questions of control, knowledge and connectedness by analogy with existing private law approaches to accessorial and vicarious liability. It is open to the courts to require either some degree of culpability on the part of the associate (by analogy

[54] *Ford & Carter v Midland Bank Ltd* (1979) 129 *New Law Journal* 543 (HL), 544 (Lord Wilberforce).

with accessory liability), or a sufficiently close connection between the enterprise risk created by the overall enterprise and the defendant so that it is just and fair that liability is imposed (by analogy with vicarious liability). As the next section of this chapter sets out, however, an early case has rejected this approach.

VII. Case Study: Associate Liability for the London Olympic Village

In January 2024, the First Tier Tribunal in England handed down a much-anticipated judgment in respect of an application for a remediation contribution order in *Triathlon Homes LLP v Stratford Village Development Partnership.*[55] Although it was not the first such order made, the profile of the dispute as well as its value (with an order being made for nearly £18 million), together with the complexity of the dispute, makes it an important case study.

The development in question was the former athletes' village for the London 2012 Olympic Games, which accommodated over 17,000 athletes and officials. Following the Olympic Games, the athletes' village was converted into a large permanent residential estate, including affordable housing, and is now known as East Village. The developer for this project was Stratford Village Development Partnership (SVDP).

SVDP had been incorporated by the Olympic Delivery Authority for the sole purpose of funding and developing the Olympic Village, and then converted the accommodation into residential dwellings. In 2014, following this 'retrofitting', its entire shareholding was sold to QDD Athletes Village UK Limited.[56] This entity was a wholly owned subsidiary of QDD Limited, which in turn was owned by QDD Holdco Limited. QDD Holdco, in turn, was owned by two entities, domiciled in Jersey and the British Virgin Islands. In 2016, an additional jointly owned subsidiary, East Village London LLP, was interposed above QDD Holdco. In 2018, Get Living plc replaced East Village London LLP as the parent of SVDP.[57] Get Living itself did not exist as a corporate entity until 2018. It had been established as a real estate investment trust (REIT). REITs are internationally recognised; conceived by the US Real Estate Investment Trust Act in 1960, the structure has been internationally accepted as a method of diversifying property holdings.[58] This (very simplified) thumb sketch illustrates the intricate complexity of the web of corporate vehicles sometimes utilised in property investment.

[55] *Triathlon* (n 2).
[56] ibid [140]–[141].
[57] ibid [142]–[147].
[58] See D Brounen and S de Koning, '50 Years of Real Estate Investment Trusts: An International Examination of the Rise and Performance of REITs' (2012) 20 *Journal of Real Estate Literature* 197. The UK regime was introduced by the Finance Act 2006.

Following the Grenfell Tower disaster, fire safety detects were identified in Plot N26, one of the constituent parts of East Village, in November 2020. These included the presence of combustible insulation and breather membranes in the cladding used in the blocks, as well as inadequate firestopping and combustible timber decking in the external balconies.[59] The total cost of the remediation was estimated to be in excess of £24.5 million (to which the Building Safety Fund, a government fund for remediating high-rise residential buildings rendered unsafe by fire safety defects, had already contributed almost £20 million).[60] The Tribunal accepted that none of QDD Limited, Triathlon or Get Living had knowledge of any risks associated with the cladding in the development, nor did they have an opportunity to affect the specification.[61]

Some of the leases in the block were owned by Triathlon Homes LLP; others were owned by subsidiaries of Get Living. The repair and maintenance of the East Village was the responsibility of East Village Management Limited (EVML). This company was jointly owned by Triathlon and Get Living. It was named as a respondent to the application, so that it could be the beneficiary of the order itself.

Triathlon, the applicant, made its application both in respect of the future costs of remediating the buildings, but also the past costs it had paid through the service charges under its leases. This raised the question of whether section 124 of the BSA 2022, which creates the remediation contribution order regime, has retrospective effect, allowing for an order to be made in respect of costs incurred before the Act came into force. The provision of the BSA 2022 retrospectively extending the limitation period for claims under section 1 of the Defective Premises Act 1972, section 135 of the BSA 2022, is clear on its face that it has this effect.[62] Given the lack of similar clarity in relation to section 124, the respondents in the *Triathlon* case argued that section 124 should not be interpreted to have retrospective effect, or alternatively, that if it could, then it would not be just and equitable to impose retrospective liability.

The tribunal in the *Triathlon* case reviewed the leading House of Lords decision in *L'Office Cherifien des Phosphates Unitramp SA v Yamashita-Shinnihon Steamship Co Ltd (The Boucraa)*.[63] By reference to substantial authority, Lord Mustill restated the rule that, unless the contrary intention appears, an enactment is presumed not to be intended to have a retrospective operation, with the limited exception of procedural matters.[64] The Upper Tribunal in the slightly earlier case

[59] *Triathlon* (n 2) [2024] UKFTT 26 [10].

[60] ibid [12], [214].

[61] ibid [165]–[174], [250].

[62] Section 135(3) states that '[t]he amendment made by subsection (1) in relation to an action by virtue of section 1 of the Defective Premises Act 1972 is to be treated as always having been in force'. This was considered by the Court of Appeal in *URS Corporation Limited v BDW Trading Limited* [2023] EWCA Civ 772, [2024] 2 WLR 181 [155]–[172] (Coulson LJ).

[63] *L'Office Cherifien des Phosphates Unitramp SA v Yamashita-Shinnihon Steamship Co Ltd* [1994] 1 AC 486 (HL).

[64] ibid 524. See eg *Wright v Hale* (1860) 6 H&N 227, 158 ER 94 (Exch) 42, 230, 95 (Pollock CB): 'There is a considerable difference between new enactments which affect vested rights and those which merely affect the procedure in Courts of justice.'

of *Adriatic Land 5 Ltd v Long Leaseholders at Hippersley Point*, which considered the leaseholder protection regime in Schedule 8 of the BSA 2022, had considered that paragraph 9 of that schedule did have retrospective effect, hence preventing a landlord from recovering, through the service charge, costs of professional services relating to relevant defects it had incurred before the Act came into force.[65] In that case, Edwin Johnson J, President of the Upper Tribunal, was persuaded by the words of the Explanatory Notes to the Act that this was a 'one-off intervention designed to deal with the current serious problems with historical building safety defects in medium- and high-rise buildings',[66] holding that '[w]hat might be seen as unfair results are, it seems to me, simply a reflection of life in the new world of the 2022 Act'.[67] In that case, therefore, policy trumped fairness to the landlord.

When it came to interpreting section 124 in the *Triathlon* case, the Tribunal was again impressed by the argument that policy considerations should lead to a provision having retrospective effect: 'it is consistent with the purpose and structure of Part 5 that the radical protection it extends to leaseholders should not be restricted by precise distinctions of time'.[68] It was also considered to be inconceivable that Parliament would intend that individual leaseholders would be treated differently depending on whether or not their building had been remediated before or after the Act came into force.[69] This point, however, ignores the fact that all prospective legislative change alters the law from a certain date, so that otherwise identical cases are treated differently. Again, this conclusion appears to have been driven by policy reasons.

The Tribunal then went on to consider whether it would be 'just and equitable' to make a remediation contribution order. Both parties advanced an array of arguments pointing towards and away from making an order. Ultimately, the Tribunal concluded that an order should be made against both SVDP and Get Living. Its assessment of the different factors displays the importance of policy factors in their decision.

(1) The Tribunal gave no weight to the changes in the ownership of SVDP and Get Living. In particular, the Tribunal considered that QDD Athletes Village UK Limited chose to take on SVDP including any latent and consequential liability: 'Each willingly assumed the risks associated with their investment.'[70] This conclusion ignores the fact that no party could have known (let alone willingly assumed) the risk that Parliament would legislate to retrospectively

[65] *Adriatic Land 5 Ltd v Long Leaseholders at Hippersley Point* [2023] UKUT 271 (LC) ('*Adriatic Land 5 Ltd*'). The Court of Appeal signalled its intention to hear an appeal in this case sequentially with that in *Triathlon* (n 2): [2024] EWCA Civ 1381.

[66] ibid [155], referring to the Explanatory Notes to the BSA 2022, para 957. This paragraph of the notes, however, refers to s 120 of the BSA 2022, while para 1759, which does specifically refer to para 9 of sch 8, contemplates a distinction between costs incurred before and after the Act came into force.

[67] *Adriatic Land 5 Ltd* (n 65) [2023] UKUT 271 [158].

[68] *Triathlon* (n 2) [75].

[69] ibid [76]–[78].

[70] ibid [250]–[253].

impose liabilities on the developer. Any legal structures (such as warranties or indemnities) that the investors would have considered at the time of acquisition could not possibly have taken this into account.

(2) While it was noted that SVDP had third-party rights against the relevant contractors and consultants, it was not considered that the ability (or inability) to pass on liability to another party should be given much weight.[71] The Tribunal referred expressly to Parliament's intent that an application for a remediation contribution order should 'provide a route to securing funding' without being forced to wait for the outcome of complex litigation. It was not considered unfair that Triathlon could bypass the parties' network of contractual provisions and obtain a remedy directly from Get Living.[72]

(3) It was, however, considered to be a more important factor that SVDP was the developer of East Village. The Tribunal considered expressly that the policy of the BSA 2022 was to impose primary responsibility for the cost of remediation on the original developer. If it was just and equitable to make an order against SVDP, it would also be just and equitable to make an order against Get Living, on which SVDP depended for financial support. It was considered that the purpose behind the associate provisions in the Act was to ensure that wealthy parent companies could not evade liability behind thinly capitalised or insolvent development entities.[73]

(4) Making an order would reduce the burden on the Building Safety Fund: it was considered 'difficult to identify a clear and convincing reason why it would be just and equitable to allow the best part of £20 million to remain in Get Living's bank account, earning interest or being put to account for its benefit, rather than being returned to the Building Safety Fund where it could be used to remediate other buildings'.[74] The fact that the public purse had, in fact, benefited from the sale of the development and had assisted Triathlon's purchase of its interest was discounted.[75]

The Tribunal, therefore, gave no weight to Get Living's lack of culpability or involvement in the original development. Further, its conclusion that Get Living assumed the risk of liability ignores the fact that, in 2018, no one could have foreseen that future legislation would have retrospectively imposed SVDP's liability on it by ignoring Get Living's separate corporate identity. The unguarded references to Get Living 'retaining' £20 million which the Building Safety Fund had contributed towards the cost of remediation, a sum which the Tribunal did not attribute to direct profits from the development, demonstrate that the policy consideration of moving

[71] ibid [256].
[72] ibid [258]–[263].
[73] ibid [265]–[266].
[74] ibid [270]. It was held that Get Living had not identified a reason 'why it would be just and equitable to allow Get Living to retain the best part of £20m, rather than this sum going to the Building Safety Fund' [277].
[75] ibid [274].

liability from leaseholders (including corporate leaseholders, such as Triathlon) and the public purse on to developers and investors was the ultimate steer to 'just and equitable'. Private law considerations of culpability or even knowledge were ignored. No thought was given to considering what proportion of Get Living's profits were attributable to this single development in the context of a highly diversified portfolio and mixed fund.[76] Instead, the decision in *Triathlon* reflects a policy of transferring the cost of remediation to parties who fall within the net of associate liability without any consideration for traditional private law considerations.

Since *Triathlon* was decided by the Tribunal, another substantial application for remediation contribution orders has been determined. In *Grey GR Limited Partnership v Edgewater (Stevenage) Limited and others*, the First Tier Tribunal made remediation contribution orders against 76 respondents in respect of the cost of remediating the 16-storey Vista Tower in Stevenage.[77] The Tribunal in that case placed particular weight on the strength of the connections between the individuals behind the original developer and each respondent.[78] At the same time, it was careful to avoid making orders against genuinely independent external investors.[79] The Tribunal did not, however, set out to establish any broader guiding principles as to the just and equitable test.

VIII. The Experience of Victoria, Australia

Sadly, the Grenfell Tower disaster was not a unique incident. The way in which the government in the Australian state of Victoria responded to its own cladding crisis affords an informative comparison. On 14 November 2014, nearly three years before the Grenfell Tower fire, the Lacrosse building in Melbourne suffered a catastrophic fire. A cigarette butt left smouldering in a cigarette tray led to a conflagration that spread to the top of a high-rise building within a matter of minutes. More than 400 residents had to be evacuated. Proceedings in the Victorian Civil and Administrative Tribunal,[80] and the subsequent appeal to the Victorian Court of Appeal,[81] established that a number of parties in the construction supply chain had been at fault in the decisions that led to the installation of highly combustible aluminium composite panels.[82] It quickly became apparent that, as in England

[76] The same approach that equity adopts in respect of a mixed fund and explained in *Foskett v McKeown* [2001] 1 AC 102 (HL) 131–33 (Lord Millet) could have been adopted.

[77] (2025) CAM/26UH/HYI/2023/0003 UKFTT (PC). See also S Degeling and J Gardner, 'Procedural Challenges and Opportunities for Leaseholders', this volume, ch 9, section II.B.

[78] ibid [349]–[368].

[79] ibid [372].

[80] *Owners Corporation No 1 of PS613436T v LU Simon Builders Pty Ltd* [2019] VCAT 286.

[81] *Tanah Merah Vic Pty Ltd v Owners Corporation No 1 of PS631436T* [2021] VSCA 72.

[82] The proceedings are discussed by D Sawtell and D Maxwell, 'The Lacrosse Apartment Fire: Liability for Using Grenfell Style Cladding' (Housing After Grenfell, 29 March 2019) https://www.law.ox.ac.uk/housing-after-grenfell/blog/2019/03/lacrosse-apartment-fire-liability-using-grenfell-style-cladding, in

and Wales, numerous buildings across Australia suffered from similar fire safety defects, with combustible cladding being identified on over 3,400 residential apartment buildings, with a cost of rectification estimated in 2019 to be A$6.2 billion.[83]

Prefiguring the BSA 2022, a number of jurisdictions enacted legislative responses to facilitate financial recovery for the cost of remediation through judicial remedies. The Victorian government introduced the Cladding Safety Victoria Act 2020 (Vic) which, amongst a raft of other provisions, affected entity liability in relation to building safety. This new regime serves as an important comparator to the associate liability model in the BSA 2022. Where the Victorian government pays towards the cost of cladding rectification works, the Crown is afforded a subrogated claim in respect of the defective construction.[84] By section 137F(3) of the Building Act 1993 (Vic), if this subrogated claim is exercisable against an entity that is not an individual, then it is enforceable both against the entity and the people who were its officers at the time of the act or omission that gave rise to the right or remedy. An officer who is the subject of a claim, however, can raise a defence by proving that the act or commission by the entity occurred without the knowledge or consent of that officer.[85]

Unlike the regime in the BSA 2022, therefore, the target for the new action in Victoria is the persons (legal or natural) who acted as the directing force for the entity in question. Liability can only be imposed on those in post at the time of the act or omission; it does not extend to subsequently appointed persons. Critically, the focus is on culpability: an officer who can demonstrate that they did not know, or did not agree, to the act or omission in question, has a defence to liability. This is in contrast to the BSA 2022, where Get Living's lack of culpability in respect of the original construction of the development was held, on the facts of the *Triathlon* case, to be irrelevant to the question of whether it was just and equitable for an associate to be the subject of an order.

The new Victorian regime was considered in 2023 by the County Court of Victoria in *Owners Corporation 1 Plan No PS 707553K v Shangri-La Construction Pty Ltd*.[86] The construction company, Shangri-La, fitted combustible cladding to a multi-apartment residential development. The owners' corporation entered into a funding arrangement with Cladding Safety Victoria for the building's remediation. The State of Victoria brought a subrogated claim against the construction

respect of the first-instance decision, and D Sawtell and D Maxwell 'The Lacrosse Apartment Fire: Obtaining Justice for Dangerous Cladding' (Housing After Grenfell, 18 April 2021) https://www.law.ox.ac.uk/housing-after-grenfell/blog/2021/04/lacrosse-apartment-fire-obtaining-justice-dangerous-cladding, in respect of the appeal.

[83] Construction, Forestry, Maritime Employees Union, 'Shaky Foundations: The National Construction Crisis' (CFMEU, 2019) https://www.cfmmeu.org.au/sites/www.cfmmeu.org.au/files/uploads/CFMEU-Shaky-Foundations-FINAL.pdf, 1.

[84] Cladding Safety Victoria Act 2020 (Vic) s 54, substituting a new s 137F(1)–(2), (9A) and new definitions (in sub-s (10)) into the Building Act 1993 (Vic).

[85] Building Act 1993 (Vic) s 137F(4).

[86] *Owners Corporation 1 Plan No PS 707553K v Shangri-La Construction Pty Ltd* [2023] VCC 1473.

company and its director. The company went into liquidation. The director admitted knowing that the cladding was combustible, but denied knowing that its use was problematic.[87] Counsel for the director argued that an analogy should be drawn between liability under section 137B and the High Court of Australia's interpretation of section 75B of the (now superseded) Trade Practices Act 1974 (Cth), which had extended liability from a corporation which has engaged in misleading or deceptive conduct to persons who had 'aided, abetted, counselled or procured the contravention'.[88] That Court had held that knowledge of the falsity of the representations was required under that section 75B action; knowledge merely that the representations had been made was not enough.[89] The Court in *Shangri-La*, however, distinguished this line of authority, holding that this principle did not apply to liability under section 137B of the Building Act 1993 (Vic), because knowledge was an element of the defence, and not of the primary cause of action.[90] Moreover, MacNamara J expressed concerns that to allow directors and managers of building companies – a class 'whom on the face of it Parliament seemed to seek to subject to liability for the cladding fiasco' – to escape liability by showing that they had relied upon experts (such as fire engineers) would render section 137B a 'mere *brutum fulmen*' (empty threat).[91] Ultimately, therefore, the director was held personally liable on policy grounds.[92]

The decision was appealed to Victorian Court of Appeal, under the case name *Naqebullah v State of Victoria*.[93] The retrospective effect of the legislation in imposing liabilities on an entity's officers was confirmed, in part because the mischief that the provisions were designed to tackle arose from past installation and use.[94] As for the degree of knowledge required, it was confirmed that it did not matter that the applicant did not know that the cladding was problematic.[95] The Court identified that different liability regimes (such as vicarious liability) require different states of knowledge:

> Each circumstance in which the liability of the principal actor is extended to associated parties raises difficult issues of policy informed by notions of responsibility and culpability.[96]

[87] ibid [105]–[108].

[88] This is now found in *Competition and Consumer Act 2010* (Cth), sch 2, s 2(1) ('*Australian Consumer Law*').

[89] *Yorke v Lucas* (1985) 158 CLR 661 (HCA).

[90] *Owners Corporation 1 Plan No PS 707553K v Shangri-La Construction Pty Ltd* [2023] VCC 1473 [134].

[91] ibid [139].

[92] ibid [139]–[140]. Further detailed guidance as to the scope of the subrogation scheme was provided by the Victorian Court of Appeal following its hearing of a special case referred to it by the County Court of Victoria: *State of Victoria v LU Simon Builders Pty Ltd* [2025] VSCA 52.

[93] [2024] VSCA 307.

[94] ibid [52].

[95] ibid [68].

[96] ibid [71].

To require the officer to be 'knowingly concerned' in the contravention would tend to defeat the purpose of a provision which was intended to address dangers arising from building products which had been installed without due appreciation of their unsuitability.[97] The appellate decision, therefore, expressly acknowledged the importance of policy in identifying the correct limits to extensions of liability.

There are significant differences between the *Shangri-La* case and the regime in Victoria, and the BSA 2022. The Victorian liability regime is driven by responsibility. While it does not precisely coincide with a Hohfeldian analysis of claim rights and corresponding duties, it still links together two parties and one activity, albeit through the lens of a subrogated claim.[98] Furthermore, liability is not absolute, with knowledge continuing to play a role (albeit as a defence, and following *Shangri-La*, permitting liability without requiring knowledge of the default itself). The BSA 2022 model of associate liability, however, is driven by the entity structure, with no regard for responsibility. There is no need to establish fault on the part of the respondent, or even a correlative claim right and duty.

IX. Conclusion

Weinrib identified that private law concerns an action by a plaintiff against a defendant that retroactively affirms the correlative rights and duties of the parties, with an entitlement to damages for the violation of those rights or the breach of those duties.[99] These features do not stand as surrogates for 'independently justifiable collective purposes', but are 'the juridical markers of the immediate connection between the parties'. The structure of associate liability, the retrospectivity of its application and the approach of the courts so far to the test of 'just and equitable', fall a long way away from this approach. Liability may be imposed on entities that potentially had no involvement at all in the events giving rise to a liability, without an examination of the degree of connectedness between the associate and the enterprise risk that the original wrongdoer was a part of. The Tribunal in *Triathlon* jettisoned any analysis of culpability or the extent of the nexus between the original wrongdoer and the respondent, and instead applied the test of 'just and equitable' to transfer the cost of remediation from leaseholders and the public purse to an associate who happened to exercise control over the developer or the landlord at the time of the order.

Bright and McFarlane demonstrate that the BSA 2022 signals a recognition by the legislature that there are overriding policy grounds for departing from

[97] ibid [75].

[98] WN Hohfeld, 'Some Fundamental Legal Conceptions as Applied in Judicial Reasoning' (1913) 23 *Yale Law Journal* 16; (1917) 26 *Yale Law Journal* 710; J Finnis, 'Some Professorial Fallacies about Rights' (1972) 4 *Adelaide Law Review* 377; R Stevens, 'When and Why does Unjustified Enrichment Justify the Recognition of Proprietary Rights?' (2012) 92 *Boston University Law Review* 919.

[99] EJ Weinrib, *The Idea of Private Law* (Oxford, Oxford University Press, 1995) 8–10.

private law in order to provide more effective remedies for leaseholders in buildings with significant fire safety defects.[100] The scheme of associate liability under the BSA 2022 reflects a public policy ambition to transfer the cost of remediating historic construction defects from residential leaseholders and government building safety funds to those parties which profited from the initial development. It is, however, a crude instrument. It adopts a highly simplistic form of enterprise, as opposed to entity, liability. It also does not reflect 'you profit, you pay' liability because it excludes potential beneficiaries of developments from its scheme while imposing liability on parties that only acquired their interest in the primary obligor after the development was completed and any profits were distributed. It is certainly not a regime that encourages further dense urban development with initial funding from a diverse range of sources.

As a consequence of the potential for this regime to impose liability on unwitting and uninvolved parties, it is submitted that the test of 'just and equitable', carrying with it an element of judicial discretion, should be applied in such a way as to ensure that only those parties that had either (1) meaningful control and knowledge (and hence culpability) or (2) a sufficiently close connection with the overall enterprise giving rise to the defects such that it would be fair for liability to be imposed, should be made liable. The reasoning in *Triathlon* as to what are relevant and irrelevant considerations for the test of whether it is just and equitable to impose associate liability should therefore be rejected in favour of more established private law considerations.

Private law can, and does, take into account policy considerations, but through a rigorous and careful examination of the connection between the original wrong, wrongdoer and the defendant, even where liability is ultimately strict. Such an approach will allow for a more predictable, and more principled, application of the test of 'just and equitable'.

[100] Bright and McFarlane (n 28) 150.

9

Procedural Challenges and Opportunities for Leaseholders

SIMONE DEGELING AND JODI GARDNER*

I. Introduction

There is a wealth of literature on the social, economic and legal impacts of the 2017 Grenfell fire. The horror of 72 men, women and children losing their lives in a wealthy, developed country with a strong and detailed legal regime resulted in a media and political campaign. One of the most important aims of this campaign was to ensure that people living in buildings with fire safety defects could have the defects remediated. There were multiple barriers to this aim. First, the existing law did not easily provide avenues for redress for leaseholders.[1] Additionally, there were other barriers, many of which reflected the standard difficulties of complex litigation – including costs, knowledge imbalance, emotional burden and significant delays. A novel legal process was therefore necessary to provide a means of remedying or removing building defects. The Building Safety Act 2022 (BSA 2022)[2]

* We are grateful for the research assistance of Alexander Breckenridge and Jack McKenzie, alongside the comments of David Sawtell, Jillaine Seymour and the editors on an earlier draft. All errors are our own.

[1] For discussion of the hurdles faced by negligence claims for defective premises, especially in the light of the House of Lords decision in *Murphy v Brentwood District Council* [1991] 1 AC 398 ('*Murphy*'), see D Nolan, 'Defective Premises and Economic Loss: A Problem Best Left to Legislation?', this volume, ch 6. The position in *Murphy* was subsequently confirmed in *Robinson v PE Jones (Contractors) Ltd* [2011] EWCA Civ 9, [2011] 3 WLR 815 (CA). Finally, the Defective Premises Act 1972 (DPA 1972) included a statutory duty (s 1) to 'build dwellings properly'. Landlords and others who build or construct a building have a duty (s 1) to use proper materials, do the work in a proper manner and make sure the building is fit for human habitation on completion which was owed to the person ordering the construction of the dwelling (s 1(a)) and 'every person who [subsequently] acquires an interest (whether legal or equitable) in the dwelling' (s 1(b)). However, prior to amendment by the BSA 2022 (inserting DPA 1972, s 2A), this duty was owed only in relation to the creation of a new dwelling. It was not engaged when further work was done on an existing dwelling.

[2] See generally J Charlson, 'Legal Framework' in J Charlson and N Dimka (eds), *Lessons from Grenfell Tower: The New Building Safety Regime* (London, Routledge, 2024) 45; D Sawtell and S Jones, 'Opening the Floodgates? Potential Parties to Claims under the Building Safety Act 2022' (Society of Construction Law (UK), May 2023); and in this volume, F Bettini and M Cappelletti, 'Tackling Building Safety through Private Law: A Comparative Analysis' (ch 2); J Morgan, 'Tort as a Tool of Government Policy: Section 38 of the Building Act 1984: Sleeping Beauty Awakes?' (ch 7); D Sawtell,

was enacted, giving leaseholders[3] in relevant buildings[4] the right to apply to the First Tier Tribunal (FTT) for remedial orders in respect of relevant defects.

This collection provides a valuable and important analysis of many of the legal issues associated with existing and new substantive rights in relation to building safety and defective premises, focusing on the Grenfell tragedy and beyond. Our chapter considers a different segment of the puzzle: the civil procedure aspects of these new substantive rights created under the BSA 2022.[5] Specifically, our analysis focuses on the civil procedures that attend Remediation Orders[6] by which the FTT may require a landlord[7] to remedy a relevant defect[8] within a specified time frame, and Remediation Contribution Orders,[9] which permit the FTT, if it considers it 'just and equitable',[10] to order a landlord or other party[11] to make payments to a specified person for the purposes of meeting costs incurred, or to be incurred, in remedying defects.[12]

Civil procedures are rules which enable courts and tribunals to deal with disputes and enable parties to vindicate their rights. They are the enabling rules which allow for the transformation of our legal substantive rights into enforceable orders and decisions of courts and tribunals. The BSA 2022 is designed to respond to a collective harm. Fire safety issues or structural faults may systematically be present throughout a building or may be concentrated in only one part. Either way, the integrity of the whole building depends on the soundness of the parts. For example, the cladding on my balcony may be defective but if a fire erupts there it will potentially impact the whole building. Given that the harm is collective, what civil procedures are available to permit leaseholders collectively to enforce their substantive rights under BSA 2022 sections 123 and 124?

'Rationalising Associate Liability under the Building Safety Act 2022' (ch 8). Further changes to the BSA 2022 are expected be enacted via the Leasehold and Freehold Reform Act 2024. This chapter does not consider those changes.

[3] Anyone with a legal or equitable interest; BSA 2022, ss 123(2), 123(5)(d), 124(1), 124(5)(e). Per BSA 2022, ss 123(5) and 124(5), the Building Safety Regulator, the local authority, a fire and rescue authority and any other prescribed 'interested person' may also apply.

[4] Including a commercial tenant if the building is mixed use.

[5] The BSA 2022 enacted a suite of reforms which, in addition to Remediation Orders (s 123) and Remediation Contribution Orders (s 124) mentioned above, includes Building Liability Orders (s 130) such that if it is 'just and equitable' to do so (s 130(1)) the FTT may hold the original developer responsible for the damage or defect regarding liability under the DPA 1972 or as a result of a 'building safety risk' (ss 130(3) and 130(6)). Limitation periods for claims under the DPA 1972 were also extended. Where the cause of action accrued before 28 June 2022, a claimant now has 30 years to sue under the DPA 1972 (BSA 2022, s 135, inserting Limitation Act 1980, s 4B). For new dwellings completed on or after 28 June 2022 and any refurbishment or remedial work on existing buildings completed after that date, the limitation period is 15 years (BSA 2022, s 135, inserting Limitation Act 1980, s 4B). This chapter does not consider these limitation period reforms nor Building Liability Orders (s 130): as to these, see Bettini and Cappelletti (n 2) section II.B and Sawtell (n 2).

[6] BSA 2022, s 123.

[7] BSA 2022, s 123(3), 'relevant landlord' means 'a landlord under a lease of the building or any part of it who is required, under the lease or by virtue of the lease or an enactment, to repair or maintain anything in relation to the relevant defect'.

[8] BSA 2022, s 120(2).

[9] BSA 2022, s 124.

[10] BSA 2022, s 124(1).

[11] BSA 2022, s 124(3), which is defined to include the landlord (s 124(3)(a)–(b)), the developer (s 124(3)(c)) or a person associated with either of them (s 124(3)(d)).

[12] BSA 2022, s 124(2).

Proceedings before the FTT are governed by its own rules of procedure: the First Tier Tribunal Rules.[13] Inter alia, these provide mechanisms for collective enforcement of rights to seek orders under sections 123 and 124. For example, via the joinder of additional parties and cases,[14] for the consolidation of cases raising common issues,[15] for lead cases[16] to be brought, and for other interested persons,[17] such as public bodies and officials, to seek orders. However, there is arguably a disconnect between the object of the reforms in permitting remediation of defective buildings and the ability of leaseholders to enforce any orders obtained. As discussed in section II of this chapter, depending on the procedure employed, the ability to enforce is not universal. We suggest that adding representative actions to the options for collective enforcement may further tackle some of the procedural challenges and provide an additional avenue for collective action that will enhance access to justice for people stuck in defective and potentially fatal buildings.

Another significant barrier to leaseholders bringing an action is cost. The usual pattern in civil litigation is that costs 'follow the event', which means that the losing party is liable to pay the winner's legal costs. However, the FTT is a costs-neutral jurisdiction for sections 123 and 124 matters. As a result, the losing party (or indeed any party) can only[18] be required to pay costs if 'a person has acted unreasonably in bringing, defending, or conducting proceedings'[19] or if there are wasted costs.[20] This means that in general a leaseholder will be required to pay their own costs and there appears to be no mechanism in place by which the burden of costs may be shared amongst those who take the benefit of any orders obtained.[21] The level of these costs will depend on the facts and in larger building developments with complex defects, requiring expert evidence and legal counsel, costs may easily mount. Related to the issue of cost is information asymmetry.

[13] Tribunal Procedure (First Tier Tribunal) (Property Chamber) Rules 2013, SI 2013/1169 ('FTT Rules').

[14] FTT Rules, rr 10(1) and 10(2).

[15] FTT Rules, r 6(3)(b).

[16] FTT Rules, r 23.

[17] BSA 2022, ss 123(2), 123(5), s 124(1) and 124(5).

[18] There are other circumstances in which the FTT may make a costs order; neither applies to s 123 or 124 matters.

[19] FTT Rules, r 13(1)(b).

[20] FTT Rules, r 13(1)(a). '[W]asted costs' are defined in the Tribunals, Courts and Enforcement Act 2007, s 29(5) (TCEA).

[21] However, separately from these civil procedure rules, the landlord may be able to pass on their costs to leaseholders through the service charge provisions of the lease itself. To avoid potential injustice to leaseholders where their action has been successful they can apply to the FTT for an order under s 20C of the Landlord and Tenant Act 1985 (LTA) which prevents the landlord doing this. The case law is complex and not discussed here. The FTT or other tribunal is empowered to make such order in relation to service charges as it considers 'just and equitable' (LTA s 20C(3)). Per *Plantation Wharf Managemwent v Fairman* [2019] UKUT 236 (LC) ('*Plantation*') [53]–[56] (Judge Stuart Bridge), apart from the respondent(s), s 20C orders bind only the named applicant(s) and any tenant that is named or otherwise identified. Further changes have been introduced to prevent passing on legal and professional costs incurred by the landlord in relation to relevant defects by BSA 2022 sch 8. For a guide to the steps applying sch 8 see the Appendix to *Lehner v Lant Street Management Company* [2024] UKUT 0135 (LC). Furthermore, leaseholders who establish that they have been incorrectly charged for remediation as service charges may be eligible for an order under s 124. See eg *Batish v Inspired Sutton Limited* [2023] UKFTT Case Reference LON/00BF/HYi/2022/0002 (PC) ('*Batish*').

As will be highlighted in section II, the 'relevant landlord' against whom an order may be made includes a developer, whom it may be expected will either have a better understanding or have ready experts to hand who both know and understand the information relevant to the dispute. Even a cursory examination of the decisions of the FTT in section 123 matters, and the schedules of specified defects and required remediations, indicates that a degree of expertise is required to understand the technical nature of the defects and the required solutions. This information gap places additional burdens on leaseholder applicants. We therefore tentatively suggest that in appropriate cases the FTT be empowered to make orders requiring contributions from other leaseholders to leaseholder applicant's costs.

This chapter proceeds as follows. Section II outlines the orders under BSA 2022 sections 123 and 124. Section III provides an overview of procedure in the FTT (III.A), and discusses the addition of parties and consolidation of claims (III.B), the lead case procedure (III.C), claims by other interested persons (III.D) and other group procedures (III.E), specifically representative actions. Section IV concludes and reinforces the important role of civil procedure in legal reforms and access to justice.

II. Building Safety Act 2022 Orders

A. Overview

The law regarding remediation under the BSA 2022 is exceptionally technical and complicated. The table below briefly summarises the facts and circumstances engaging Remediation Orders and Remediation Contribution Orders under the BSA 2022.

	Remediation Order (section 123)	**Remediation Contribution Order (section 124)**
Summary of order	Order by the FTT requiring a landlord ('relevant landlord')[22] to remedy specified building defects within a nominated time period.[23] A landlord who has paid or is liable to pay for the cost or remediation can recover[24] that cost or a contribution towards it from other landlords of the same building where the amount is not recoverable as a service charge from the tenants.	Order by the FTT requiring an identified body corporate or partnership to make payments to a person for the purposes of meeting the costs incurred or to be incurred in remedying specified building defects.[25]

(continued)

[22] BSA 2022, ss 123(3) and (4).

[23] BSA 2022 s 123(2). Only the FTT is competent to make an order under s 123 or 124. This means that the Upper Tribunal cannot make an order under s 123 or 124 (except in its appellate capacity). See generally *Triathlon Homes LLP v Stratford Village Development Partnership* [2024] UKFTT 26 (PC) ('*Triathlon*') [48]–[49] (Johnson J and Martin Rodgers KC).

[24] Building Safety (Leaseholder Protections) (Information etc) (England) Regulations 2022, SI 859/2022 ('Leaseholder Protection Regulations') regs 3, 4 and 5, enacted pursuant to BSA 2022, s 123(1).

[25] BSA 2022, s 124(2).

(Continued)

	Remediation Order (section 123)	**Remediation Contribution Order (section 124)**
Which buildings does this regime apply to ('relevant buildings')?[26]	A self-contained building, or a self-contained part of a building, in England, that contains at least two dwellings and (a) is at least 11 metres high or (b) has at least five storeys.[27]	
Which defects in these buildings are covered ('relevant defects')?[28]	A defect arising: (a) as a result of anything done or not done in connection with works relating to the construction or conversion of the building for residential use, or works themselves done to remedy an existing defect;[29] (b) where the defect causes a risk to the safety of people in or about the building arising from the spread of fire or the collapse of the building or any part of it;[30] and (c) the works were completed between 28 June 1992 and 28 June 2022[31] (for original construction) or are works commenced after 28 June 2022, such as refurbishments or works themselves intended to correct an original defect, subject to 15-year prospective limitation period.[32]	
When may the FTT make an order?	The FTT holds a power and a discretion to make or not to make the order. The FTT's power is engaged where the circumstances meet the requirements for a Remediation Order set out in section 123.[33]	The FTT holds a power and a discretion to make or not to make the order, this discretion to be exercised if the FTT considers it 'just and equitable' to do so.[34]

(continued)

[26] BSA 2022, s 117.

[27] See definition of 'self-contained' in BSA 2022 ss 117(4) and 117(5). There are also certain exclusions from 'relevant building' if the freehold is leaseholder owned, or on commonhold land, or leaseholders have exercised specified rights under the Landlord and Tenant Act 1987 (first refusal or compulsory acquisition) or under the Leasehold Reform, Housing and Urban Development Act 1993 (collective enfranchisement).

[28] BSA 2022, s 120(2) ('relevant defect').

[29] BSA 2022, ss 120(2) ('relevant defect') and 120(3) ('relevant works').

[30] BSA 2022, ss 120(2) ('relevant defect') and 120(5) ('building safety risk'). The date for determining whether there is a building safety risk is the date of the hearing, applying the state of knowledge of building materials as at that date: see *Waite v Kedai Ltd* [2023] UKFTT Case Reference LON/ooAY/HYI/2022/0005&0016 (PC) ('*Waite*') [75] (Judge Timothy Powell and Mrs Helen Bowers MIRCS).

[31] BSA 2022, s 135, inserting Limitation Act 1980, s 4B. 28 June 2022 is the expiration of the 30-year retrospective limitation period under DPA 1972, s 1 (claim in relation to original construction defect).

[32] BSA 2022, s 135, inserting Limitation Act 1980, s 4B. DPA 1972, s 2A (claim in relation to work carried on by a business to a dwelling, including refurbishment and remediation). See also *Triathlon* (n 23).

[33] *Secretary of State for Levelling Up Housing and Communities v Grey GR Limited Partnership* [2024] UKFTT Case Reference CHI/ooHN/2023/0008(1) (PC) ('*Chocolate Box*') [204]–[207] (Judge J Dobson, Mrs J Coupe, Mr J Stead).

[34] BSA 2022, s 124(1).

(Continued)

<table>
<tr><th></th><th>Remediation Order (section 123)</th><th>Remediation Contribution Order (section 124)</th></tr>
<tr><td></td><td>The FTT's power is permissive. It holds a broad discretion whether or not to exercise this power and on what terms.[35] As to when this discretion should be exercised, no criteria are given in the BSA 2022 or the Leaseholder Protection Regulations.[36] Rather, the FTT itself will determine the factors relevant or irrelevant to the exercise of its discretion and the relative significance of those factors.[37]

The FTT will make a remediation order when it considers it just and fair to do so.[38] This is a balancing exercise to be undertaken against the background purpose of the BSA 2022, which is to ensure building defects are remediated and the safety of occupiers is protected.[39]</td><td></td></tr>
<tr><td>Who may apply for an order ('interested person')?[40]</td><td colspan="2">(a) the Building Safety Regulator;
(b) the local authority for the area in which the building is situated;
(c) a fire and rescue authority for the area in which the building is situated;
(d) a person with a legal or equitable interest in the building or any part of it (this therefore includes a leaseholder); and
(e) any other person prescribed by regulation as an 'interested person'.

In England, for a section 123 order, an 'interested person' includes the Secretary of State[41] and for a section 124 order it similarly includes the Secretary of State[42] as well as the Homes and Communities Agency (and the named manager, body corporate or management company ('RTM company'[43])) in relation to the relevant building.[44]</td></tr>
</table>

(continued)

[35] *Secretary of State for Levelling Up, Housing and Communities v Grey GR Limited Partnership* [2024] UKFTT Case Reference CAM/26UH/HYI/2022/0004 (PC) ('*Grey*').

[36] *Chocolate Box* (n 33) [211] (Judge J Dobson, Mrs J Coupe, Mr J Stead).

[37] ibid [212] and [227] (Judge J Dobson, Mrs J Coupe, Mr J Stead).

[38] In *Chocolate Box*, the FTT in interpreting s 123 held that, whilst direct application of the 'just and equitable' standard found in ss 124 and 130 is not what Parliament intended [221], the approach of the FTT in exercising its discretion 'cannot be far from that' [225] in the sense that 'equitable essentially means fair … [and] … the test cannot be far from justice and fairness' [225].

[39] ibid [227] (Judge J Dobson, Mrs J Coupe, Mr J Stead).

[40] BSA 2022, ss 123(5) and 124(5).

[41] Leaseholder Protection Regulations, reg 2(1).

[42] BSA 2022, s 124(5)(a).

[43] As defined in the Commonhold and Leasehold Reform Act 2002, ss 71–74.

[44] Leaseholder Protection Regulations, reg 2A.

(Continued)

	Remediation Order (section 123)	**Remediation Contribution Order (section 124)**
Who are the FTT's orders directed to?	A landlord ('relevant landlord') under a lease of the building or any part of it who is required by that lease or another enactment to repair or maintain anything relating to the defect.[45] A landlord for this purpose includes a person who is party to a lease otherwise than as a landlord or tenant.[46] For example, a management company in a tripartite lease.	A 'specified body corporate or partnership'[47] which is defined to mean: (a) a landlord under a lease of the relevant building or any part of it; (b) a person who was such a landlord[48] at the beginning of 14 February 2022;[49] (c) a developer in relation to the building;[50] or (d) a person associated with any of the above.[51]
Who is bound by the order?	The parties to the application. Subject to the addition of parties and consolidation of cases and, in relation to common or related issues, the lead case procedure discussed below.	

B. Remediation Orders

As a factual matter, the defects being remedied via section 123 orders are all those that meet the statutory definition of 'relevant defect' outlined above. However, it is important to realise that the subject of any one application may comprise a composite list of defects for the relevant building. Different parts of the same building may suffer different defects, but it is not necessary that all leaseholders experience the consequences of the *same building defect* to be joined in a single section 123 application.[52] Per that definition, these defects will be items going to

[45] BSA 2022, s 123(3).
[46] BSA 2022, s 123(4).
[47] BSA 2022, s 124(2).
[48] BSA 2022, s 124(3)(b).
[49] This is the 'qualifying time' per BSA 2022, s 119(2)(d).
[50] BSA 2022, s 124(3)(c). Developer is defined in BSA 2022, s 124(5) to mean 'a person who undertook or commissioned the construction or conversion of the building or part of it, with a view to granting or disposing of interests in that building or parts of it'.
[51] BSA 2022, s 124(3)(d).
[52] Moreover, given the generous standing requirements, the applicant may not have suffered any defect at all as they may be an 'interested person', for example, a local authority, Secretary of State, etc.

the structural safety or risk of fire or spread of fire in the building as a whole, but need not directly impact every leaseholder in the building equally or at all.

This is shown by the facts of *Grey*.[53] The Secretary of State for Levelling Up successfully applied for a section 123 order against the freehold owner of Vista Tower, a 16-storey residential block with 73 residential flats. The Schedule to the section 123 order in the report of the FTT's decision records the scope of works required by the order. The combustible items were on the east, south and west elevations of the building but not the north elevation. Further, balcony/terrace remediation was needed on the east elevation but not the south or west. Thus, individual leaseholders may not necessarily have had cladding on the exterior of their residential unit affected or may not have had a balcony requiring repair. On the facts of *Grey*, it was the Secretary of State who brought the application,[54] but if the leaseholders or any one of them had made the application all would have benefited from the orders and all had a community of interest in the safety and integrity of the building as a whole.

Once the elements of relevant defect and building are engaged, an interested person may apply for a section 123 order against a relevant landlord. The burden of proof lies on the applicant to establish a 'coherent, initial case that there [are relevant defects that cause a building safety risk] … that would entitle [the FTT] to make a remediation order'.[55] On the applicant establishing their prima facie case for a remediation order, the FTT holds the power to make the requested order and a discretion to decide whether or not to exercise that power and on what terms.

So, what is the nature of this power and discretion? In *Grey*[56] it was common ground between the parties that Vista Tower was a 'relevant building', the Secretary of State was an 'interested person' and the respondent was a 'relevant landlord' with no intervening leases or landlords.[57] None of the leaseholders were parties to the proceedings.[58] After a protracted process of case management hearings, the parties ultimately agreed on the specification of the relevant defects and required remedial works. The question of the nature of the FTT's discretion arose because by the time of the FTT's decision, the respondent had already entered into a contract for the remedial works (to which the Secretary of State for Levelling Up, Housing and Communities was not a party), and contractors had commenced on-site working to the specifications agreed in the case management conferences. The respondent argued that, in these circumstances, an order under section 123 was otiose and could potentially cause administrative delay and confusion, adding a further layer of supervision to an existing contractual supervisory arrangement. Moreover, a

[53] *Grey* (n 35) [1].
[54] As permitted under Leaseholder Protection Regulations, reg 2(1).
[55] *Waite* (n 30) [80] (Judge Timothy Powell and Mrs Helen Bowers MIRCS).
[56] *Grey* (n 35).
[57] ibid [42] (Judge Wayte and Judge Wyatt).
[58] ibid [55] (Judge Wayte and Judge Wyatt).

section 123 order could also result in further sanction, such as contempt of court, should the deadline for completion under the section 123 order not be met.[59]

The FTT rejected these arguments, holding on the facts that an order should be made. The power to make a section 123 order is a sui generis power given to ensure compliance with remediation obligations for 'life-threatening building safety defects in tall residential buildings' and therefore 'different considerations apply' to those discussed when ordering specific performance.[60] The focus of the BSA 2022 was identified as 'leaseholder protection',[61] and, consistent with this objective, the FTT's discretion as to the exercise of its power and the terms of that exercise should be 'practically focussed on ensuring the defects are remedied in a responsible fashion'.[62] Thus, the fact of delay by one or both parties was not on these facts persuasive,[63] and allegations of a 'political motivation' for making the application was held not to be relevant to the exercise of discretion.[64] However, the issue of the extant contract for remediation by the respondent and third party builders clearly *was* significant. The FTT acknowledged that if making the section 123 order would inhibit the completion of that contract, this would be a factor weighing against the exercise of discretion.[65] Further, on the facts of this case, the terms of the remediation order were required to accommodate these contractual arrangements, such that the order was subject to the terms of these arrangements and any extensions of time provided by them.[66] It '[was] not a fault-based order, or a case where an order should set short deadlines and expect active interventions to put pressure on a defaulting landlord'.[67]

The purpose of the order in *Grey* was said to be as a 'backstop'[68] for leaseholders, the FTT emphasising that they were not parties to the works contracts. However, the leaseholders were not parties to the proceedings either, so it is not clear how a section 123 order would have provided a backstop for anyone other than the Secretary for State. As discussed in section IV below, this lack of privity to the proceedings is arguably an obstacle to leaseholders' ability directly to enforce the terms of the remediation order. A section 123 order (other than one ordering payment of a sum) is enforceable with the permission of the County Court in the same way as an order of that court.[69] Thus, for example, breach of a

[59] ibid [107]–[109] (Judge Wayte and Judge Wyatt). The respondent and a construction company were parties to the works contract. The respondent also entered into a grant funding agreement with the Department of Levelling Up, Housing and Communities and Homes England: [56].

[60] ibid [121] (Judge Wayte and Judge Wyatt). See also *Chocolate Box* (n 33) [218] (Judge J Dobson, Mrs J Coupe and Mr J Stead).

[61] *Grey* (n 35) [130] (Judge Wayte and Judge Wyatt).

[62] ibid [122] (Judge Wayte and Judge Wyatt).

[63] ibid [123] (Judge Wayte and Judge Wyatt).

[64] ibid [128] (Judge Wayte and Judge Wyatt).

[65] ibid [130] (Judge Wayte and Judge Wyatt).

[66] ibid.

[67] ibid.

[68] ibid.

[69] BSA 2022, s 123(7) and see also TCEA, s 27. cf *Termhouse (Clarendon Court) Management Ltd v Al-Bailhaa* [2021] EWCA Civ 1881, [2022] 1 WLR 1529 [31] (Newey LJ with whom Nugee LJ and

section 123 order is punishable as contempt of court,[70] but may only be enforced by a party to the proceedings.

C. Remediation Contribution Orders under BSA 2022 Section 124

A section 124 order may be made if it is 'just and equitable' to do so. But what does this mean? Some guidance is given in *Triathlon*.[71] Five buildings, originally developed by Stratford Village Development Partnership (SVDP) as part of the accommodation for the 2012 London Olympic Games, required remediation to remove combustible aluminium cladding, inadequate firestopping, the use of combustible material on exterior balconies and other fire-related defects.[72] Each building contained town houses, maisonettes or retail units at the lower levels, and flats on the upper levels.[73] At the time of the application Triathlon Homes held the long leasehold on 129 residences with the rest ultimately being held on long leasehold by Get Living plc. Get Living also owned the original developer, SVDP, although did not at the time the development was being undertaken. SVDP itself was the beneficial owner of the freehold. The management company responsible for the repair and maintenance of the common parts of the complex was East Village Management Ltd (EVML), a vehicle jointly owned by Get Living and Triathlon. Evidence indicated that £16.03 million had been expended or would be expended by EVML in remediation costs, representing Triathlon's share of the remediation cost.[74] Triathlon successfully applied for a section 124 order against SVDP as the original developer and Get Living (SVDP's parent), arguing that the amounts paid by EVML (jointly owned by Triathlon and Get Living) on account of remediation ought to be reflected in a section 124 order requiring payment by SVDP and Get Living to EVML.[75]

It was uncontentious that the statutory elements of 'relevant defects' in a 'relevant building' were satisfied, that Triathlon was an 'interested person' with standing to apply for an order, and that SVDP and Get Living were a 'specified body corporate or partnership' capable of bearing responsibility under the section.[76] The FTT

Francis LJ agreed [36]–[37]), considering the parallel example of s 176C of the Commonhold and Leasehold Reform Act 2002. Civil Procedure Rules 1998 (CPR) r 70.5 applies to these enforcement proceedings in the County Court.

[70] *Grey* (n 35) [107]. See *Webster v Southwark London Borough Council* [1983] QB 698.

[71] *Triathlon* (n 23); cf Sawtell (n 2), section VII. As was noted in the Introduction to this volume (p 2), the Court of Appeal heard an appeal in this case in March 2025.

[72] *Triathlon* (n 23) [9]–[10] (Edwin Johnson J and Martin Rodger KC).

[73] ibid [4] (Edwin Johnson J and Martin Rodger KC).

[74] ibid [249] (Edwin Johnson J and Martin Rodger KC).

[75] ibid [292] (Edwin Johnson J and Martin Rodger KC) making an order pursuant to s 124 for 'the respondents to make payment of … £16,031,244.53 to EVML'.

[76] ibid [37], [124], [236], [266] (Edwin Johnson J and Martin Rodger KC).

confirmed that section 124 offers a novel remedy which is 'non-fault based'[77] and in respect of which an applicant's entitlement to commence proceedings or obtain an order does not depend on any other claims or potential claims in relation to relevant defects being determined.[78] Further, it is not possible to contract out of the section 124 regime.[79] The FTT identified that the policy of the BSA 2022 is that primary responsibility for the costs of remediation are intended to fall to the original developer, and others who have a liability to contribute to the cost may similarly pass on this cost to the developer.[80]

On the question of what circumstances would render it 'just and equitable' to make the order, the principal factor relied on by Triathlon in favour of a contribution from SVDP was that SVDP was the developer and was therefore ultimately responsible for the relevant defects.[81] This factor was significant in the FTT's reasons.[82] Furthermore, the fact that SVDP depended on Get Living for financial support justified the order against Get Living.[83] The FTT held as irrelevant that the remediation works were being funded by the Building Safety Fund[84] or indeed that the respondent may be able to pass on the burden of the order to a third party,[85] although the FTT noted its discretion to fashion the terms of any section 124 order, including imposing conditions that will make the order 'just and equitable'.[86] This may, for example, require the recipient to repay to the party subject to the order any amounts also recouped by the recipient from third parties.

The other significant factor considered by the FTT was timing. The Tribunal confirmed that section 124 orders are available in respect of remediation costs incurred before commencement of the BSA 2022 on 28 June 2022. On the independent question of whether it would be 'just and equitable' to make an order in respect of these costs, the FTT held that the mere fact that some of the remediation costs were incurred before 28 June 2022 was not 'a sufficient reason or a contributory reason' to conclude that it would not be just and equitable to make a section 124 order in respect of those costs.[87]

Section 124 orders are orders for the payment of a sum and are not merely declaratory.[88] This is shown by section 124(2) which defines a remediation contribution order as 'an order requiring [the respondent] to make a payment'. Similarly,

[77] ibid [261] (Edwin Johnson J and Martin Rodger KC).
[78] ibid [261] and [279] (Edwin Johnson J and Martin Rodger KC).
[79] ibid [262] (Edwin Johnson J and Martin Rodger KC).
[80] ibid [265] (Edwin Johnson J and Martin Rodger KC).
[81] ibid [241] (Edwin Johnson J and Martin Rodger KC).
[82] ibid [265] (Edwin Johnson J and Martin Rodger KC).
[83] ibid [266] (Edwin Johnson J and Martin Rodger KC).
[84] ibid [273] (Edwin Johnson J and Martin Rodger KC).
[85] ibid [256] (Edwin Johnson J and Martin Rodger KC).
[86] ibid [249] (Edwin Johnson J and Martin Rodger KC).
[87] ibid [290] (Edwin Johnson J and Martin Rodger KC).
[88] cf *Termhouse (Clarendon Court) Management Ltd v Al-Bailhaa* [2021] EWCA Civ 1881, [2022] 1 WLR 1529, [24]–[26] and [31]–[35] (Newey LJ with whom Nugee LJ and Francis LJ agreed: [36]–[37]) where s 27A of the LTA was construed to be merely 'declaratory in nature' [33]. The FTT's role was held to be to 'decide what service charges can be charged rather than what the tenant owes' [24].

see the decision in *Triathlon*, where the FTT made orders for various parties to 'make payment'.[89] In consequence, section 124 orders are recoverable as if they were payable under an order of the County Court.[90]

III. Available Civil Procedures

Orders under sections 123 and 124 require a procedural apparatus to bring these entitlements to life. A claimant's ability to exercise these statutory claims rests on a body of civil procedure, itself informed by principles of justice, including that there should be wide access to the court system and the relief available in courts to vindicate rights[91] and that undue delay should be minimised as far as possible.[92] The high costs of legal action, both to litigants and society as a whole, is also a factor.[93]

There is a significant body of literature highlighting the many benefits, and multiple challenges of collective enforcement, including the controversial use of litigation funding.[94] It lies beyond this discussion to canvass all relevant arguments other than to note that, as a general matter, costs are one motivation behind the courts and tribunals exercising active case management and that different civil procedures treat costs differently. This is likely to be a factor in the calculus for claimants and their lawyers in choosing the procedural means through which their claim will be exercised. It is also important to recognise that, when developing novel causes of action and remedies, it is crucial to consider the procedures available to enliven these causes of action.

In the context of an application for orders under section 123 and/or 124, collective procedures are of interest given the likely collective nature of the harm sought to be addressed. The circumstances and facts of these cases will typically be characterised by multiple parties with the same or similar claims or, at least, the same

Section 27A(1) concerned applications 'for a determination whether a service charge *is payable*' (emphasis added). It was therefore not susceptible to TCEA, s 27.

[89] *Triathlon* (n 23) [292] (Edwin Johnson J and Martin Rodger KC).

[90] TCEA, s 27, engaging CPR 70.5.

[91] See N Andrews, *Principles of Civil Procedure* (London, Sweet & Maxwell, 1994) 29; A Zuckerman, *Zuckerman on Civil Procedure: Principles & Practice*, 4th edn (London, Sweet & Maxwell, 2021) [1.27]–[1.28].

[92] Andrews (n 91) 30.

[93] Zuckerman (n 91) [1.29]–[1.33].

[94] See eg R Mulheron, *The Class Action in Common Law Legal Systems: A Comparative Perspective* (Oxford, Hart Publishing, 2004); S Degeling and M Legg, 'Undue Influence, Litigation Funding and Book Building in Group Proceedings' (2023) 42 *Civil Justice Quarterly* 247; S Degeling and M Legg, 'Fiduciaries and Funders: Litigation Funders in Australian Class Actions' (2017) 36 *Civil Justice Quarterly* 244–64; N Chamberlain, 'Class Actions in New Zealand: An Empirical Study' (2018) 24 *New Zealand Business Law Quarterly* 132; B Lammon, 'An Empirical Study of Class-Action Appeals' (2022) 22 *Journal of Appellate Practice & Process* 283; S Degeling, J Gardner and J McGeechan, 'Small Claims, Big Challenges: Collective Enforcement of Consumer Claims' in J Gardner & I Ramsay (eds), *Landmark Cases of Consumer Law* (Oxford, Hart Publishing, 2024) 387.

or similar questions of law or fact on which determination of their application will rest. Further, these litigants may not have the funds to bring their own individual application, or the cost of litigation may be disproportionate to the value of their individual claim. A collective procedure permits efficient use of judicial, societal and parties' resources by permitting the same issue to be dealt with in one go, allowing a pooling or sharing of risk of the costs of litigation, and also offering the prospect of consistency of outcome and parity of treatment for similar claims and for a common defendant. Alternatively, actions brought by 'interested parties' or so-called 'regulator actions' by public authorities such as those brought by the local authority, the relevant Secretary of State, or fire and rescue services may be relevant. The discussion in this section considers the various collective procedures and other interested party actions provided for in the FTT Rules and those which could be incorporated into the FTT procedures for section 123 and 124 claims.

A. Procedures in the FTT

The FTT is created by statute[95] and has the powers, functions and jurisdiction conferred by that or other relevant statutes. As a general matter, the FTT's decisions do 'not bind anyone except the parties to the case being decided',[96] and, in relation specifically to sections 123 and 124, the power is to make orders requiring the payment of money or requiring defects to be remedied. These sections do not empower the FTT to make declarations as to title or other orders in rem which might have third-party effects. Moreover, the FTT does not have to follow its own prior decisions, although previous decisions 'command appropriate respect'.[97] However, it is acknowledged that 'there are dangers in paying too close a regard to previous decisions … [as] it can elevate issues of fact into issues of law or principle'.[98] That said, FTT decisions are not entirely inert as regards other parties and proceedings. As discussed further below, the FTT's own rules contemplate lead cases and the joinder or consolidation of cases, and a decision of the FTT may bind the parties via issue estoppel in any subsequent attempt at litigating the issues.[99]

As has been said, proceedings before the FTT are governed by the FTT Rules and are not subject[100] to the Civil Procedure Rules 1998 (CPR).[101] The overriding

[95] TCEA, s 3.

[96] *Hampshire County Council v JP* [2009] UKUT 239 (AAC) [15] (the Tribunal). The remit of the FTT under ss 123 and 124 does not include the powers to make orders in rem.

[97] *Chocolate Box* (n 33) [35] (Judge J Dobson, Mrs J Coupe, Mr J Stead). Note, however, the specific effect of decisions on common or related issues of fact and FTT Rules 23 and 24 discussed below.

[98] *London Borough of Camden v The Information Commissioner & YV* [2012] UKUT 190 (AAC) [20] (Judge Edward Jacobs).

[99] *Inhenagwa v Onyeneho* [2017] EWHC 1971 (Ch) [40]ff (Morgan J).

[100] *The Commissioner for Her Majesty's Revenue and Customs v McCarthy & Stone (Developments) Limited* [2014] UKUT 0196 (TCC) [43] (Judge Greg Sinfield).

[101] SI 3132/1998.

objective of the FTT Rules is to enable the FTT to deal with cases 'fairly and justly'[102] such that the Tribunal must deal with cases in a manner proportionate to their complexity and available resources, avoiding unnecessary formality and seeking flexibility in the proceedings, ensuring so far as practicable that parties can participate in the proceedings, using the expertise of the FTT and avoiding delay so far as is compatible with proper consideration of the matters before it.[103] Furthermore, the FTT has broad case-management powers and may regulate its own procedure.[104] In exercising any power under the FTT Rules or interpreting any rule or practice direction, the FTT must seek to give effect to the above overriding objective of dealing with cases 'fairly and justly'.[105]

B. Addition of Parties and Consolidation of Cases

Given that a decision of the FTT binds only the parties, it is unsurprising that those applications which have already been brought under sections 123 and 124 include examples where the recorded applicants include a (potentially lengthy) list of named leaseholders who are all individually parties to the action.[106] Consistently with the principle of res judicata, it is the policy of the law to ensure that all necessary parties are before the court or tribunal to ensure that matters in dispute may be 'completely and finally determined'.[107] The FTT is empowered to add, substitute or remove any party as applicant or respondent and to give any consequential directions.[108] Further, the FTT may consolidate or hear together two or more proceedings or parts of proceedings raising common issues.[109] A leaseholder who is not a party may therefore apply to be added as a party[110] if they have a sufficient interest in the proceeding, and presumably any party may apply for the addition of any additional non-party (eg a landlord or developer) as

[102] FTT Rules, r 3(1).

[103] FTT Rules, rr 3(2)(a)–(e). In terms of the evidence used by the FTT in ss 123 and 124 cases, consistently with this mandate, decision-making is 'not constrained by formal burdens of proof.' Rather, although an 'evidence-based exercise', inspection reports, expert evidence and the experience and observations of the FTT's members, including at site inspections, are important. See *Waite* (n 30) [81] (Judge Timothy Powell and Mrs Helen Bowers MIRCS).

[104] FTT Rules, r 6(1), subject to the TCEA and any other enactment.

[105] FTT Rules, r 3(3).

[106] See, eg, in relation to s 124: *Batish* (n 21). In relation to s 123: *Waite* (n 30) (the record does not identify the '(3) other leaseholders' who are parties); *Wyatt v WN Enterprises Ltd* [2024] UKFTT Case Reference LON/ooBA/HYI/2023/0017 (PC), listing eight additional leaseholders as applicants; *Di Bari v Avon Ground Rents Ltd* [2024] UKFTT Case Reference LON/00AP/HYI/2022/0017 (PC) ('*Di Bari*'); *Mistry v Wallace Estates Ltd* [2024] UKFTT Case Reference LON/ooAH/HYI/2022/0012 (PC) ('*Mistry*').

[107] Zuckerman (n 91) [13.1].

[108] FTT Rules, rr 10(1) and 10(2).

[109] FTT Rules, r 6(3)(b).

[110] FTT Rules, r 10(3).

applicant or respondent.[111] The effect of this procedure is, therefore, to increase the list of parties to the action, whether as applicant or respondent.

The advantage of adding a party or consolidating cases is obviously that it binds more parties to the FTT's determination and orders. This is advantageous for the respondent because it avoids death by a thousand cuts, and avoids wasting time and resources, both for the parties and the FTT.[112] However, it does not dispose of any right to apply for an order by a leaseholder who is *not* ultimately a party.[113] Thus, a non-party leaseholder could not rely on the FTT's ruling. That leaseholder would still be required to bring their own action for an order under section 123. It is unclear what approach the FTT would take to any such application. Further, this procedure appears to be cost heavy because each party incurs costs.

C. Lead Case Procedure

If two or more cases have commenced where the FTT has not yet made a decision disposing of the proceedings and the cases give rise to common or related issues, the FTT may direct that one or more of these cases be specified as a 'lead case' and stay the other cases (the 'related cases').[114] The FTT will then make a decision in the lead case on the 'common or related issues' that binds all parties in the related cases on the common or related issues.[115] The FTT must then give directions in the cases that are stayed providing for their disposal or further directions in those cases.[116] In addition to the related cases (which have been stayed), a 'subsequent application' may be brought where a decision has been given in a lead case, relying on the prior determination of the common or related issues. The FTT similarly need not determine the common or related issues in any subsequent case but instead may rely on its earlier decision.[117]

Much therefore turns on the characterisation of 'common or related issues'. At the date of writing, there are few, if any, cases which have been decided by the

[111] FTT Rules, rr 10(1) and 10(2).

[112] There are also consequences for FTT s 20C LTA orders in relation to service charges, including where landlord legal costs are attempted to be passed onto leaseholders. An application by leaseholders for relief is similarly only capable of binding (apart from the respondent(s)), the named applicant(s) and any tenant that is named or otherwise identified: *Plantation* [2019] UKUT 236 (LC) [53]–[56] (Judge Stuart Bridge) discussed in n 21 above. See eg *Di Bari* (n 106) [2] (Judge Martyński).

[113] Unless, for example, the case is also designated a 'lead case' per FTT Rules, r 23 and then the subsequent leaseholder is bound on the common issues by FTT Rules, r 24.

[114] FTT Rules, r 23. Note that, independently of r 23, the FTT may under r 6(3)(b) 'consolidate or hear together two sets of proceedings or parts of proceedings raising common issues, or treat a case as a lead case (whether under rule 23 or otherwise)'.

[115] FTT Rules, r 23(5)(b). Per r 23(5)(a) the FTT must send a copy of its determination in the lead cases to all parties in the related cases and these parties have 28 days to apply to the FTT for a direction that the lead case is not binding on them (r 23(6)).

[116] FTT Rules, r 23(7).

[117] FTT Rules, r 24(3)(a), subject to the respondent's right to object.

FTT using the lead-case procedure.[118] The ultimate test of this procedure will be whether 'common or related issues' may encompass an issue common to various applications for section 123 or 124 orders, where that issue is not part (or, at least, is not only part), for example, of the application for the same order against the same landlord in respect of the same defects in the same building. An example of such an issue may be as to the meaning of 'just and equitable' in section 124(1) if that were engaged on the facts of various different applications before the FTT. We argue that this question would similarly be a sufficiently 'common or related issue' satisfying FTT Rules rule 23(1).

On the question of enforcement, as explained above, subject to a right to object, the stayed cases are all bound by the outcome in the lead case and any subsequent cases on the common or related issues are bound by the FTT's decision in relation to those issues.[119] Thus, the lead case procedure does offer a means of access to section 123 and 124 orders. It provides privity to the order, permitting direct enforcement by leaseholders and gives subsequent leaseholders the protection of an earlier successful application whilst also offering efficiencies to the respondent and the FTT. The only question remains that of costs. It appears that the burden of litigation is borne by the lead applicant. The others free ride.

D. Other Interested Persons

The BSA 2022 provides that an action may be commenced by an 'interested person' which, as outlined above, opens the door to various public officers and bodies bringing actions. For example, in *Grey*,[120] the applicant was the Secretary of State for Levelling Up, Housing and Communities.[121] Whilst the possibility of this type of action has obvious benefits for leaseholders in that they do not directly bear the costs of bringing the action, the question of enforcement arises. Returning to the basal principle that only parties to the decision may enforce it, an individual leaseholder presumably is not able directly to enforce a section 123 or 124 order obtained by an interested person. Their only redress would be in the political sphere, putting pressure on that body or officer, or, alternatively, to seek orders requiring the interested person to enforce the section 123 or 124 order, which would amount to seeking orders compelling the commencement of enforcement proceedings in the County Court.[122] It is unclear what the basis of an application

[118] Research has located none. In *Di Bari* (n 106) and *Mistry* (n 106), the applicant is labelled the 'lead applicant' but it does not seem that this refers to the lead case procedure. Rather these cases are examples of multiple applicants.

[119] FTT Rules, r 24(3)(b).

[120] *Grey* (n 35).

[121] See also *Chocolate Box* (n 33). In *Waite* (n 30) the London Borough of Lambeth applied to be an interested person but was not active in the carriage of the proceedings, [21] (Judge Timothy Powell and Mrs Helen Bowers MIRCS).

[122] Recall that s 123 and s 124 orders are not directly enforceable in the FTT.

for these orders would be. The only other conceptual possibility, canvassed briefly below in section III.E, is that the interested person themselves brings the action for a section 123 or 124 order as a representative in a representative action, which would offer the possibility of direct enforcement by leaseholders with the consent of the relevant court or tribunal.

E. Other Group Procedures

The other procedural possibilities for collective redress include representative actions, class actions and group litigation orders. Class actions and group litigation orders do not apply to applications for section 123 and 124 orders and will not further be discussed.[123] By contrast, we argue that representative actions may be of utility for leaseholders in this context and should be added to the available procedures supporting applications for section 123 and 124 orders. In a representative action the applicant is the party of record who brings an application on behalf of those represented who are not parties to the action but are bound by any subsequent decision. Those represented may only enforce any judgment obtained in the proceedings with leave of the court. The procedure rests on the identification of the relevant group holding a common interest in having an issue determined, whose members are described but not individually identified.

The foundation for bringing the representative action into applications for orders under sections 123 and 124 is the 'overriding objective' which is to enable the FTT to deal with cases 'fairly and justly',[124] including 'ensuring, so far as practicable, that the parties are able to participate fully in the proceedings'.[125] Relying on the FTT's power to regulate its own procedure,[126] we argue that this mandate for justice would be served by permitting a form of representative action in these applications. The question is, where would the FTT draw the procedure from? There are two potential sources, neither of which binds the FTT. However, arguably they both supply models for the rule which could be enacted within the FTT Rules.

The first is the representative action which exists in CPR 19.8.[127] As has been said, this does not directly assist us in the FTT because the CPR does not apply to proceedings in the FTT. The second is the 'old rule in the Court of Chancery' which was by the Judicature Acts extended to the new High Court of

[123] Class actions are only available for claims under s 47A of the Competition Act 1998 and therefore are not engaged in s 123 and s 124 cases. Group litigation orders are available under CPR 19.22 for the case management of claims which give rise to common or related issues of fact or law. However, as already observed, proceedings in the FTT are not governed by the CPR.

[124] FTT Rules, r 3(1).

[125] FTT Rules, r 3(2)(c).

[126] FTT Rules, r 6(1).

[127] Previously this was numbered 19.6. As of 6 April 2023, renumbered 19.8 by The Civil Procedure (Amendment) Rules 2023, r 12(9).

Justice[128] and formed the basis for the modern form of the rule in CPR 19.8.[129] As a tribunal created by statute, the FTT has no inherent jurisdiction[130] and thus the Chancery procedure is similarly not directly applicable.[131] This Chancery rule was that, whilst the default position was that all interested parties in a suit were required to be before the court so that a 'final end' might be reached, where the parties 'were so numerous that you could never "come at justice" … the [default position] … was not allowed to stand in the way'.[132] Instead, '[g]iven a common interest, and a common grievance, a representative suit was in order if the relief sought was in its nature beneficial to all whom the plaintiff proposed to represent'.[133] In light of the general familiarity with CPR 19.8, this may be preferred for practical reasons.

So, what then are the general features of CPR 19.8, and why might representative actions assist leaseholders? CPR 19.8 provides that, where more than one person has the same interest in a claim, one of them may represent all who have that interest.[134] Subject to meeting the 'same interest' requirements of CPR 19.8, a person may constitute themselves as a representative without the permission of the court and the consent of those represented is similarly not required.[135] Unless the court otherwise directs, any decision or judgment given in a claim in which a party is acting as representative is binding on all of those represented on the common issues.[136] One of those represented may with the permission of the court apply to enforce the judgment against the respondent(s).[137] The primary benefit for leaseholders of this procedure is therefore that they are able to enforce orders obtained by the representative without themselves bringing an application for

[128] *Duke of Bedford v Ellis* [1901] AC 1 ('*Ellis*') 8 (Lord Macnaghten). See also the discussion in *Lloyd v Google LLC* [2021] UKSC 50, [2022] AC 1217 ('*Google*') [34]–[39] (Lord Leggatt JSC with whom Lord Reed PSC, Lady Arden, Lord Sales and Lord Burrows JJSC agreed). The history of the chancery procedure is discussed in D Meyerowitz-Katz, 'Fiduciary Duties of Representative Parties: Conflicting Case Law and Conflicting Interests' (2022) 96 *Australian Law Journal* 185; J Sorabji, 'The Hidden Class Action in English Civil Procedure' (2009) 28 *Civil Justice Quarterly* 498; S Yeazell, 'From Group Litigation to Class Action Part I: The Industrialization of Group Litigation' (1980) 27 *UCLA Law Review* 514.

[129] Most recently, in *Google*, the UK Supreme Court has observed 'a welcome revival of the spirit of flexibility [referring to CPR 19.8 cases] which characterised the old case law': *Google* [2021] UKSC 50, [2022] AC 1217 [48] (Lord Leggatt JSC with whom Lord Reed PSC, Lady Arden, Lord Sales and Lord Burrows JJSC agreed)).

[130] TCEA, s 3.

[131] cf *Burwood Council v Ralan Burwood Pty Ltd (No 2)* [2014] NSWCA 179, [18], [21]–[26] (Sackville AJA).

[132] *Ellis* [1901] AC 1, 8 (Lord Macnaghten).

[133] ibid. See also *Campbells Cash and Carry Pty Ltd v Fostif Pty Ltd* [2006] HCA 41, (2006) 229 CLR 386 [43] (Gummow, Hayne and Crennan JJ).

[134] CPR 19.8(1). On representative actions generally, see J Seymour, 'Representative Procedures and the Future of Multi-Party Actions' (1999) 62 *MLR* 564.

[135] *Independiente Ltd v Music Trading On-Line (HK) Ltd* [2003] EWHC 470 (Ch) [32] (Morritt VC). The Court may, however, direct that a person *not* act as a representative: CPR 19.8(3).

[136] CPR 19.8(4)(a).

[137] CPR 19.8(4)(b). The rule also permits the court to enforce a judgment or order *against* other non-parties, for example, those who are not named in the s 123 order.

an order under section 123 or 124. This contrasts with the lead case procedure which is only engaged where 'two or more cases have commenced … [in cases giving rise] … to common or related issues'.[138] Similarly, a lead case may impact a subsequent case, assuming 'a subsequent application is made … [including] any of the common or related issues'.[139] Moreover, in cases such as *Grey*, where the applicant was the Secretary of State, a CPR 19.8 type procedure provides a genuine backstop for leaseholders because it would permit them, even though not parties to the action, and subject to the court's permission, directly to enforce any order obtained by the applicant.

The crucial issue is, therefore, whether the 'same interest' requirement is met. Courts have historically taken a relatively restrictive approach to this question, being reluctant to find the same interest where, for example, different defences apply to the claims of those represented. This argument rests on the view that, by pursuit of the action as a representative proceeding, the respondent may be denied the opportunity to raise separate defences against individual members of the group.[140] However, whether the existence of separate defences undermines 'same interest' for the purposes of CPR 19.8 is contested.[141] It remains to be seen the extent to which individual defences or arguments against liability would arise on the specific facts of section 123 and 124 applications. For example, in section 124(1), application of the criteria 'just and equitable' across a complex corporate structure may open the door to individual arguments against liability and, in section 123(2), variations in the profiles of the members of the represented group introduce similar arguments.

Modern authority advocates a more flexible approach to CPR 19.8 actions, emphasising that, so long as those represented do not have *conflicting interests*, they might be said to hold the same interest.[142] There is thus a distinction between conflicting interests, which will defeat any possibility of a representative action, and 'cases where there are merely divergent interests, in that an issue arises or may well arise in relation to the claims of (or against) some class members but not others'.[143] So long as the representative party, in advancing the case with respect to the common issues on behalf of the group, does not prejudice

[138] FTT Rules, r 23(1).

[139] FTT Rules, r 24(1).

[140] *London Association for Protection of Trade v Greenlands Ltd* [1916] 2 AC 15 (HL) 39 (Lord Waddington).

[141] As Seymour (n 134) 572 argues, in many instances, interpreting 'same interest' in this way would 'effectively limit … the availability of the procedure to those cases where the group represented is defined only in terms of the elements of the claim brought'. Thus, to use the risk that defences might be denied against some in the group as a test of whether there is the 'same interest' limits membership of the group represented to those in which a CPR 19.8 action would not be required in the first place, as 'proof of membership of the group, [would] in effect, prove … the claim'.

[142] *Google* [2021] UKSC 50, [2022] AC 1217 [71] (Lord Leggatt JSC with whom Lord Reed PSC, Lady Arden, Lord Sales and Lord Burrows JJSC agreed).

[143] ibid [72] (Lord Leggatt JSC with whom Lord Reed PSC, Lady Arden, Lord Sales and Lord Burrows JJSC agreed).

the position of those represented,[144] there is 'no reason of principle why all should not be represented by the same person'.[145] In outlining this approach, the UK Supreme Court in *Lloyd v Google* highlighted that a court may, for example, adopt a bifurcated process where issues such as damages quantification require individual assessment. Thus, common issues of law or fact are determined via the representative procedure, leaving any issues requiring individual determination to be dealt with at a subsequent stage of the proceeding.[146] The presence of these individual issues will not defeat the availability of the representative procedure. It remains an open question the extent to which the bifurcated approach outlined in *Google* resolves any possible role for separate defences or arguments against liability as defeating the availability of a CPR 19.8 type action. Specifically, it is conceivable that per section 124(1) an order may be 'just and equitable' against one respondent, but not another, in respect of the same defect, depending on the granular application of section 124(1) to the facts. The broad discretion given to the FTT to make a section 123 order when it is just and fair[147] opens the door to a similar analysis, taking into account potential variations in the profiles of those represented. However, we argue that, following *Google*, this should not prevent the FTT from making section 123 or 124 orders to the extent that a subsequent stage of the procedure could be employed separately to deal with any non-common issues.

The other barrier to 'same interest' might potentially lie in *Rendlesham Estates plc v Barr*.[148] However, for the reasons outlined next, we argue that *Rendlesham* presents no obstacle to a representative action for section 123 and 124 applications. In *Rendlesham* a representative claimant unsuccessfully attempted to claim damages under DPA 1972 section 1(1) (building not 'fit for habitation when completed') for the cost of remedial works to the common or structural parts of a multi-residence building on behalf of all owners of apartments, including owners who were not party to the proceedings. The Court relied on *Emerald Supplies Ltd v British Airways plc*[149] in holding that a representative action could not proceed as proof of damage was an essential element to determining 'unfitness for habitation' and therefore that 'no two owners [had] the same interest'.[150] However, in *Google* the Supreme Court expressly held *Rendlesham* was 'wrong'[151] to conclude

[144] ibid (Lord Leggatt JSC with whom Lord Reed PSC, Lady Arden, Lord Sales and Lord Burrows JJSC agreed).

[145] ibid [72] (Lord Leggatt JSC with whom Lord Reed PSC, Lady Arden, Lord Sales and Lord Burrows JJSC agreed).

[146] ibid [81] (Lord Leggatt JSC with whom Lord Reed PSC, Lady Arden, Lord Sales and Lord Burrows JJSC agreed).

[147] *Chocolate Box* (n 33) [225]–[227] (Judge J Dobson, Mrs J Coupe, Mr J Stead).

[148] *Rendlesham Estates plc v Barr* [2014] EWHC 3968, [2015] 1 WLR 3663 (TCC) ('*Rendlesham*').

[149] *Emerald Supplies Ltd v British Airways plc* [2010] EWCA Civ 1284, [2011] Ch 345 (CA) ('*Emerald*').

[150] *Rendlesham* [2014] EWHC 3968, [2015] 1 WLR 3663 [88] (Edwards-Stuart J).

[151] *Google* [2021] UKSC 50, [2022] AC 1217 [58] (Lord Leggatt JSC with whom Lord Reed PSC, Lady Arden, Lord Sales and Lord Burrows JJSC agreed).

from *Emerald* that 'if damage is an ingredient of the cause of action a representative claim could not be maintained'.[152] Moreover, the particular facts and statutory context of *Rendlesham* limit its applicability to section 123 and 124 applications. Liability under the DPA 1972 depended on the unfitness of habitation of a 'dwelling' and each apartment constituted a distinct dwelling, the fitness for habitation of which had to be considered separately. Thus, in *Rendlesham*, the Court extended the duty under DPA 1972 section 1 to work carried out on the common parts 'for in or connection with the provision of a dwelling'.[153] In contrast, an application under section 123 or 124 does not depend on each claimant establishing such a breach of a duty, as the liability of the defendant rather arises from there being a 'relevant defect' in a 'relevant building'. Moreover, in *Millharbour Management Ltd and Others v Weston Homes Ltd*,[154] a DPA 1972 case decided before, but not referred to in, *Rendlesham*, a representative action was permitted, with the 'same interest' being established.[155]

Returning to section 123 and section 124 applications, we submit that an 'interested person' such as the Secretary of State holds the 'same interest' as a leaseholder for the purposes of a CPR 19.8 type action.[156] The fact that the Secretary of State has no interest as a resident or leaseholder, and therefore *diverges* from the interest of leaseholders does not derogate from this entitlement. Crucially, the interests of the Secretary of State and the leaseholders are not in *conflict* with respect to the common issues. Therefore, we argue that those who apply as an 'interested person' may do so as a representative under a CPR 19.8 type action, permitting those represented to apply for permission directly to enforce any order obtained.

Further, a CPR 19.8 type action may also have benefits for other leaseholders who themselves commence a representative action for section 123 or 124 orders. As explained above, a leaseholder who commences an application which is designated a lead case appears to have no recourse for costs against the other leaseholders in stayed or subsequent cases who may take the benefit of any orders obtained in the lead case. Rather, the other leaseholders free ride. However, in a representative action the court may, if it is in the 'interests of justice to do so', make an order requiring those represented to contribute to the representative's costs[157] and similarly to give leave for this order to be enforced against those

[152] *Rendlesham* [2014] EWHC 3968, [2015] 1 WLR 3663 [90] (Edwards-Stuart J).

[153] ibid [82] (Edwards-Stuart J).

[154] *Millharbour Management Ltd v Weston Homes Ltd* [2011] EWHC 661, [2011] 3 All ER 1027 (TCC).

[155] ibid [30] (Akenhead J).

[156] Indeed, this interest is itself conferred and confirmed by BSA 2022 ss 123(5) and 124(5) and the Leaseholder Protection Regulations.

[157] See eg *Chandra v Mayor* [2016] EWHC 2636, [2017] 1 WLR 729 [9] (Judge Purle QC). cf *Google* [2021] UKSC 50, [2022] AC 1217 [79] (Lord Leggatt JSC with whom Lord Reed PSC, Lady Arden, Lord Sales and Lord Burrows JJSC agreed).

represented.[158] Even taking the point that the FTT is a costs neutral jurisdiction for section 123 and 124 matters, it may be argued that permitting a form of representative action in the FTT Rules for these applications should also carry the ability to order contributions to the applicants costs, at least where the representative is another leaseholder.

IV. Conclusion

The impact of the events on 14 June 2017 provided a stark and painful lesson that no country is safe from defective premises, and that if buildings are not constructed and maintained in a safe manner, there can be fatal consequences. The unsafe cladding on the Grenfell Tower was not unique. As at the end of December 2024 (more than seven years since the Grenfell fire), there were at least 3,539 residential buildings in England 11 metres and over with unsafe cladding which had not been fully remediated,[159] and there are numerous other serious fire safety defects (such as missing cavity barriers) for which there are no data. This is a national scandal.

Despite the additional powers of sections 123 and 124 of the BSA 2022, there are many barriers preventing remediation. This chapter addressed one of the challenges, the civil procedure difficulties. An analysis of the procedural aspects of remediation orders and remediation contribution orders under the BSA 2022 highlights two key points. The first is costs. Whilst the existing procedures, namely, the addition of parties or consolidation of cases, the lead case procedure and actions by 'other interested parties', do provide various means for parties to be joined and for selected other applicants to take the benefit of a decision in a case giving rise to common or related issues, there appears to be little provision for those who take the benefit of these orders also to *share the burden* of obtaining this relief. Even appreciating that the FTT is an accessible jurisdiction that is 'costs neutral', the overriding objective of the FTT to deal with cases 'fairly and justly'[160] suggests that some contribution to costs between those who take the benefit of the orders is called for. The second is the important role that civil procedure has in the recognition of novel causes of actions and the privity of parties to any orders obtained. Orders must be capable of enforcement. As shown by the discussion of

[158] CPR 19.8(4)(b). Alternatively, a leaseholder may attempt the (perhaps ambitious) argument that its costs of litigation in obtaining the relevant s 124 order was itself a 'cost … incurred or to be incurred in remedying relevant defects' within the meaning of s 124(2) and thus include this amount in the remediation contribution order itself, to be paid by the respondent.

[159] Ministry of Housing, Communities & Local Government, 'Building Safety Remediation: Monthly Data Release – December 2024' (UK Government, 23 January 2025) https://www.gov.uk/government/publications/building-safety-remediation-monthly-data-release-december-2024; further, the remit of BSA 2022 ss 123 and 124 is not limited to unsafe 'cladding' but instead turns on the presence of 'relevant defects' per s 120(2). The number of 'relevant buildings' with 'relevant defects' which may be covered by these orders is therefore potentially astronomic.

[160] FTT Rules, r 3(1).

the 'other interested person' action, there is an enforcement gap because those who are intended factually to take the benefit of an order are not parties. A representative action is one procedural means of addressing this issue.[161] More generally, attention to the procedural aspect of the defective building regime is required to ensure that the substantive rights intended to be conferred are capable of enforcement and will make it significantly easier for all residents to live in a safe and habitable home.

[161] Alternatively, the BSA 2022 or associated regulations require amendment to permit leaseholders the ability directly to enforce orders obtained by an 'interested person'.

10

Private Law in the Ruins

NICHOLAS J McBRIDE*

The title of this chapter is an adaptation of Walker Percy's *Love in the Ruins*, which aptly summed up the source of the building safety crisis with which this book seeks to grapple:

> Don't tell me the USA went down the drain because of Leftism, Knotheadism, apostasy, pornography, polarization, etcetera etcetera. All these things may have happened, but what finally tore it was that things stopped working and nobody wanted to be a repairman.[1]

In this chapter I will argue four things.

First, the Grenfell Tower fire and the response to that fire almost perfectly manifest and exposed fundamental problems and disorders that afflict, and are destined to doom, modern Western, liberal societies ('MWLs', for short).

Second, these problems and disorders mean that private law is unable to achieve its ambition of helping to promote the flourishing of its subjects while maintaining its legitimacy.

Third, given this, it may be no surprise that at this particular juncture in history many academics prefer to think of private law not as seeking to promote anyone's flourishing, but as serving much more limited goals – such as the promotion of economic efficiency, or protecting people's independence as human beings – that can be achieved, at least in part, despite the problems and disorders that afflict MWLs.

Fourth, we should reject these consoling accounts of private law and honestly confront what (if anything) can be done for private law so that it can fulfil its vocation once more.

I. How the West was Lost

The decline and fall of all civilisations is usually marked by a defining event that both symbolises its collapse and encapsulates in microcosm the reasons for that

* Fellow, Pembroke College, Cambridge.

[1] W Percy, *Love in the Ruins* (London, Eyre & Spottiswoode, 1971) 62–63.

collapse. In MWLs those defining events have usually been associated (for some reason) with *fire*. The United States, has experienced three fires that may be seen as such defining events of collapse: the first two in 2023, in East Palestine, Ohio and in Lahaina, Hawaii; the third in 2025, in the Pacific Palisades. France's defining event was the destruction by fire of the roof and famous spire of Paris's Notre-Dame Cathedral in 2019. And the event in the United Kingdom that may be seen definitively as marking its collapse as a civilisation was, of course, the Grenfell Tower fire in 2017. Almost every factor that has played a leading role in the decline of the UK as a nation came together on 14 June 2017 to gut Grenfell Tower and kill 72 of its inhabitants; they would then go on to dictate the government response to that tragedy. Those factors are: national bankruptcy, corporate fraud, missing virtues, degraded language, and misplaced trust in authority figures.

A. National Bankruptcy

In Ernest Hemingway's novel *The Sun Also Rises* an ex-soldier called Mike is asked how he went bankrupt: 'Two ways,' Mike said. 'Gradually and then suddenly.'[2] For a very long time, the UK has been in the 'gradual' phase of becoming bankrupt, and with the national debt of £2.5 trillion now exceeding the UK's GDP (£2.4 trillion) we may be entering the 'suddenly' stage. With a budget deficit of £131 billion in 2023–24 (on top of a deficit of £137 billion in 2022–23), and no prospect of the UK government ever achieving a surplus of income over expenditure for a sustained period, the national debt will only become unsustainably larger. The same grim picture applies to local government as well, which is collectively £120 billion in debt.[3] There are obvious limits to how much further into debt local authorities can go, with the result that a recent survey by the Local Government Association revealed that one in five local authorities expect in the near future to issue a section 114 notice, declaring that its expenditure 'in a financial year is likely to exceed the resources (including sums borrowed) available to it to meet that expenditure'.[4]

The primary consequences of the UK's effective bankruptcy are twofold. First, UK politics ceases to be recognisably democratic, as the bond market possesses the power to dictate what political priorities any UK government will pursue and, indeed (as the fall of Liz Truss revealed), who will be prime minister.[5] Second,

[2] E Hemingway, *The Sun Also Rises* (New York, Charles Scribner's Sons, 1926) ch 13.

[3] 'See How Much Your Council Owes as Local Authority Debts Hit £122bn' (In Your Area, 21 January 2024) https://www.inyourarea.co.uk/news/council-debt-hits-122bn-check-your-local-authority-with-our-interactive-map.

[4] 'Section 114 Fear for Almost 1 in 5 Council Leaders and Chief Executives After Cashless Autumn Statement' (Local Government Association, 6 December 2023) www.local.gov.uk/about/news/section-114-fear-almost-1-5-council-leaders-and-chief-executives-after-cashless-autumn. The notice title refers to Local Government Finance Act 1988, s 114(3).

[5] The power of bond markets over governments with out-of-control finances has long been recognised. A sell-off of US government bonds in 1993–94 triggered a U-turn in the US government's economic policy, and led to its achieving surpluses in its finances from 1997 to 2001. James Carville,

lacking the wherewithal to absorb economic shocks such as Covid-19, the UK's economy is now extremely fragile. When such shocks occur, the UK government is faced with the unpalatable choice between allowing the shock to tip the economy into depression and courting the risk of hyper-inflation by printing money to mitigate the effects of the shock.

The UK's national bankruptcy is a major reason for the Grenfell Tower fire, and the government's response to it. As Peter Apps's brilliant *Show Me The Bodies: How We Let Grenfell Happen*[6] makes clear, Grenfell Tower – and thousands of high-rise buildings like it – would not have been allowed to be clad with ACM (aluminium composite material) had the UK government not pursued a deregulatory agenda from 2010 onwards. This agenda was intended to boost economic growth and the government finances by seeking:

> [A]ny and all ways it could find to reduce what it referred to as 'burdens on business'. Amid a belief that a recovery in new housebuilding – that had plummeted to historic lows during the recession which followed the banking crisis – was crucial to the economic recovery, the residential construction industry was placed at the heart of this drive.[7]

Nor would there have been the same financial pressure to use cheaper materials such as ACM in refurbishing Grenfell Tower had it not been for the fact that 'the Treasury had imposed a cap on council borrowing for the simple reason that it would appear on the national balance sheet'; thus, '[t]he refurbishment would be done on a shoestring [and] costs would be squeezed to make it fit'.[8]

Once the Grenfell Tower fire made it clear that the UK government's deregulatory drive and attempts to cut public spending had amounted to a false economy (to put it mildly), the UK's national bankruptcy also made entirely predictable the government's response to the need to remediate thousands of high-rise buildings clad in ACM and similar materials. The government would not pay because it could not pay – and so the bill for remedying the government's error was almost entirely laid by the government at the door of the building industry and the freeholders of the buildings needing remediation (who would then pass the bill onto their leaseholders).

Hence private law grotesqueries like section 123 of the Building Safety Act 2022 (allowing 'interested persons' to go to court to obtain a 'remediation order' against the freeholder of an at-risk building); section 124 (allowing 'remediation contribution orders' to be made in relation to a particular building against the building's

adviser to then President Clinton, remarked at the time: 'I used to think that if there was reincarnation, I wanted to come back as the President or the Pope or a .400 baseball hitter. But now I would like to come back as the bond market. You can intimidate everybody': D Wessel and TT Vogel Jr, 'Arcane World of Bonds is Guide and Beacon to a Populist President' *Wall Street Journal* (25 February 1993) A1.

[6] P Apps, *Show Me the Bodies: How We Let Grenfell Happen* (London, Oneworld Publications, 2022); cited pagination is from the e-book version.

[7] ibid 57.

[8] ibid 136.

landlords and developers and their associates when it would be 'just and equitable to do so'); sections 126–129 (allowing the Secretary of State for Housing to create regulations[9] that have the effect of forcing building contractors to sign up to a 'contract' under which they undertake to cover the costs of remediating at-risk buildings by threatening that if they do not, they will not be regarded as 'responsible' contractors and consequently not allowed to bid for construction work in the future); and section 130 (allowing the High Court to make 'a building liability order if it considers it just and equitable to do so' against a company that is 'associated' with another company that is liable in respect of an at-risk building).[10]

B. Corporate Fraud

Within the market order that for so long underpinned the material prosperity of the West, there are only two ways of making money: (i) producing useful goods and services for other people; (ii) deceiving other people into thinking that the goods and services you are producing are useful. Markets only work to produce prosperity if activity (i) is maximised, and activity (ii) is minimised. However, governments that pursue deregulatory agendas allow activity (ii) to proliferate, and moreover temptations to engage in activity (ii) are increased as (a) the supply of workable ideas for producing useful goods and services dries up; and (b) more entrants to particular markets cut the profit margins available for producing actually useful goods and services. So deregulation + (a) + (b) will trigger an explosion of fraud, with the result that markets no longer operate in the West as engines of prosperity, but as instruments of its downfall. The above equation accounts for the growth of fraud as a major force in the financial services industry and the pharmaceutical sector.

It also seems to account for how high-rise buildings like Grenfell Tower ended up being clad with 'solid petrol'[11] in the form of ACM. As Apps explains, the fire safety risk associated with the cladding panels used on Grenfell 'was discovered in 2004. They could have been taken off the market then. But no one then was willing to risk corporate profits for basic fire safety.'[12] Because the panels had a core of (highly flammable) pure polyethylene (PE) between two aluminium plates, they were 'around £2 to £3 cheaper per square metre, which gave it an edge when construction firms tried to squeeze every penny out of their costs.'[13] Internal emails

[9] Now created: the Building Safety (Responsible Actors Scheme and Prohibitions) Regulations 2023, SI 2023/753.

[10] See also, in this volume, F Bettini and M Cappelletti, 'Tackling Building Safety through Private Law: A Comparative Analysis' (ch 2) and D Sawtell, 'Rationalising Associate Liability under the Building Safety Act 2022' (ch 8).

[11] Apps (n 6) 25, 87.

[12] ibid 87.

[13] ibid 89.

and reports showing awareness that the panels became extremely flammable when bent into an 'L shape' 'cassette' so that they could be hung neatly on the outside of a building also sought to conceal this information from the outside world: 'This shortfall [in safety] … is something we have to keep VERY CONFIDENTIAL!!!!'[14] And there was no compunction about using such flammable materials in jurisdictions – such as the UK – where building regulations could be interpreted as allowing them to be used: 'For the moment, even if we know that PE material in cassette has a bad behaviour exposed to fire, we can still work with national regulations who [*sic*] are not as restrictive.'[15]

The same story appears to have been played out in respect of the similarly highly flammable plastic insulation – polyisocyanurate and phenolic – that lay underneath the ACM cladding on the walls of Grenfell Tower. Both types of insulation were sold as achieving a 'Class 0' rating, making them suitable for use on high-rise towers, triggering the following 2012 text exchange between those selling phenolic: 'Doesn't actually get Class 0 when we test the whole product tho. LOL!' 'WHAT. We lied?' 'All we do is lie in here.'[16] Questioned on whether phenolic was actually safe to use in a high-rise building, one manager observed 'I think [they] are getting me confused with someone who gives a damn. I'm trying to think of a way out of this one, imagine a fire running up this tower!!!!!!!!!!!!'[17] The same manager's response to phenolic's being certificated by an independent building safety body as 'a material of limited combustibility' that was 'suitable for use' in parts of a building 'more than 18m above the ground' was 'FANBLOODYTASTIC'.[18] When asked how the safety body's representative had come to such a baffling conclusion, the manager's response was, 'We threw every bit of fire test data we could at him, we probably blocked his server. … We didn't even have to get any real ale down him!'[19]

C. Missing Virtues

If we were asked to describe the character of the just-mentioned manager, the word 'irresponsible' would probably come first to mind. He is 'irresponsible' in the sense of *showing no awareness that he might later be asked to account for the impact of his actions*. The same lack of responsibility is shown by the safety regulators who allowed the impression to be created that ACM was safe to use on high-rise buildings by giving ACM a 'Class 0' rating. Having created that impression in the

[14] *Grenfell Tower Inquiry: Phase 2 Report: Report of the Public Inquiry into the Fire at Grenfell Tower on 14 June 2017* (HC 19, 2024) ('*GTI Phase 2 Report*') [20.7].
[15] ibid [20.24].
[16] Apps (n 6) 122 (text correspondence between two employees of Kingspan, sellers of phenolic).
[17] *GTI Phase 2 Report* (n 14) [22.94].
[18] ibid [22.95].
[19] ibid [22.97].

minds of builders and architects, they insisted that this was not their fault. The fact that they had issued vague guidance that 'filler material' should be of 'limited combustibility'[20] was meant to rule out the use of ACM and there was therefore nothing they needed to do to correct the impression that ACM was safe to use on high-rise buildings.[21]

A different kind of irresponsibility was shown on the night of the Grenfell Tower fire. The virtue that too many lacked that night was *a willingness to take responsibility with the result that one might later obtain credit for, or be blamed for, the impact of one's actions*. The guidance to residents of Grenfell Tower to 'stay put' in their flats and wait to be rescued by firefighters was finally abandoned at 2.47 am on 14 June 2017, nearly two hours after the fire started.[22] Around that time, 116 people were still in the tower, and 72 of them would die.

Despite the extensive consideration given to the matter in the Grenfell Tower Inquiry, it remains unclear how many of those 72 could have been saved had the guidance to 'stay put' been abandoned earlier, and callers to the emergency control centre told to get out of the tower if they possibly could – but it is clear some could have been saved.[23] That they were not was due to a number of factors, including (i) the lack of a television in the control centre that would have shown call handlers the scale of the fire in the tower and avoided them telling panicked callers such things as 'The fire is actually on the fourth floor but it's obviously creating a lot of smoke';[24] and (ii) the unwillingness/inability of those in charge of the fire services on the scene to abandon the 'stay put' policy and order call handlers to tell residents to get out of the tower if they could.

(i) was due to the fact that: 'The control room was equipped with a large plasma screen television, which would normally have had rolling 24-hour news footage, but it was not working. A smaller set was not turned on.'[25] No one took the responsibility of simply turning on the only available television set. As for (ii), at around 2 am, three different fire officers were in successive command on the ground at Grenfell Tower, and despite the first feeling 'helpless' and the third 'shocked' at the sight of the fire, none took the responsibility at that point of lifting

[20] ibid esp ch 23.

[21] Apps (n 6) 43, quoting a February 2015 email from civil servant Brian Martin regarding a fire in a tower in Dubai: 'There are provisions in the building regulations designed to prevent this kind of problem. So this shouldn't be a problem in the UK. There are, of course, no guarantees.' In a subsequent January 2016 email (regarding another fire in a hotel in Dubai) Martin would take the same position, observing of ACM that 'when it gets exposed to a fire the aluminium melts away and exposes the polyethylene core. Whoosh!' but reassuring that under UK building regulations requiring that 'filler material' be of 'limited combustibility … [t]he polyethylene core of [ACM] would be regarded as filler material so should not be used over 18m'. See also Evidence to Grenfell Tower Inquiry, email from Brian Martin to Bob Ledsome (4 January 2016) (CLG10007889) 1.

[22] *Grenfell Tower Inquiry: Phase 1 Report: Report of the Public Inquiry into the Fire at Grenfell Tower on 14 June 2017* (HC 49-III, 2019) [15.49].

[23] See, especially, *GTI Phase 2 Report* (n 14) pt 8.

[24] Apps (n 6) 121.

[25] ibid 120.

the stay put advice – that would take a further 45 minutes.[26] At least one victim of the fire might have survived had one of the officers in charge taken the responsibility of abandoning the 'stay put' policy at 2 am. Apps reported:

> [T]he words of a father describing the loss of his five-year-old son. He said his son would have lived if they had not been told – by a firefighter who reached them at 2 am – to stay put in the flat. 'Every single minute from that day, I'm thinking: what if we had not waited? What if that fireman at around 2 am has taken us out instead of telling us to wait and shut the door? What if? And this "what if" makes my head and heart explode with pain and anger, and my heart is shredded.'[27]

A third kind of irresponsibility is *an unwillingness to accept justified blame for the impact of one's actions*. In the aftermath of the Grenfell Tower fire, this third kind of irresponsibility has resulted in

> corporations and public bodies … [giving] carefully constructed statements, full of vapid expressions of sympathy and detailed explanations of why their company is not to blame for what happened at the tower. The [Grenfell Tower Inquiry]'s own barrister has described the attitudes as 'a merry-go-round of buck passing'.[28]

Underpinning these three kinds of irresponsibility is the absence of the cardinal virtue of *courage*. (Courage is a cardinal virtue in that someone who lacks courage will find it hard to possess any of the other virtues.) It takes courage to accept blame for the impact of one's actions, or to take the risk of incurring such blame by taking responsibility for dealing with a problem, or to court unemployment by standing up to the demands of your paymasters and following the dictates of your conscience instead (which conscience *will* hold you accountable for the impact of your actions). Courage is the virtue that MWLs principally lack, and that lack of courage contributed both to the tragedy at Grenfell Tower and the response to it.

D. Degraded Language

Apps concludes his history of the Grenfell Tower fire by observing that:

> The world that gave us the Grenfell Tower fire looks irredeemably dishonest. It is a story of corporate structures that allowed human beings to abandon their conscience and sense of agency and to think only about sales and profit margins. Government institutions placed ideology above human lives at every turn.[29]

The dishonesty that gave rise to the Grenfell Tower fire was facilitated by, and reflected in, the English language being degraded. As George Orwell observed in 1946, 'The great enemy of clear language is insincerity. When there is a gap

[26] ibid 100.
[27] ibid 239.
[28] ibid 240.
[29] ibid 243.

between one's real and one's declared aims, one turns as it were instinctively to long words and exhausted idioms, like a cuttlefish squirting out ink.'[30]

The background to, and the response to, the Grenfell Tower fire provide many examples of how language has been degraded to conceal fraud, or to give the appearance that problems were being handled when they were actually being waved away. We have already seen one: the use of the ambiguous term 'filler material' to give the impression that use of ACM was restricted, when few in the building industry had in fact received that message. Another example is the marketing material for K15, one of the types of insulation that was used behind the cladding on Grenfell Tower, which *begins*:

> In the past, erroneously, the relative environmental sustainability of insulation materials has been compared on the basis of embodied energy and ozone depletion potential. It is now recognised that a much wider basket of embodied environmental impacts (including those caused by their embodied energy), rather than embodied energy alone, is the only credible tool of comparison …
>
> For buildings designed to today's Building Regulations energy use standards it is now also known that the embodied environmental impacts of all the materials and labour used to create a building are insignificant in comparison with the lifetime operational environmental impacts of that building and so are of very limited importance. Since it is operational energy use that creates the vast majority of operational environmental impact, saving energy by specifying the lowest U-values possible is the most environmentally sustainable action to take.[31]

As Orwell observed, language 'becomes ugly and inaccurate because our thoughts are foolish, but the slovenliness of our language makes it easier for us to have foolish thoughts'.[32]

Orwell went on to condemn in particular the political language of his time, arguing that it was 'designed to make lies sound truthful … and to give an appearance of solidity to pure wind'.[33] Not much has changed in the almost 80 years since he wrote that. Here is the government minister introducing the Bill that became the Building Safety Act 2022:

> Today marks the next significant step on our path to a robust but proportionate building safety regime that delivers high standards of safety for people's homes, particularly those that are high rise, while providing reassurance to leaseholders, residents and the market that the vast majority of homes in this country are safe. In February, I announced our five-point plan to support leaseholders and address building safety issues: a plan to remove unsafe cladding where it is necessary and proportionate to do so; to provide certainty to leaseholders in the significant minority of buildings that require works; to

[30] G Orwell, *Orwell and Politics* (London, Penguin, 2020), originally published as G Orwell, 'Politics and the English Language' *Horizon* (1946).

[31] Evidence to Grenfell Tower Inquiry, Kingspan Insulation Solutions, 'Kooltherm K15 Rainscreen Board: Insulation for Use Behind Rainscreen Cladding Systems' (Brochure, June 2006) (KIN00005371).

[32] Orwell (n 30) 398.

[33] ibid 410.

> make industry pay its fair share for its failures and poor practices and ensure a change in the broader culture and attitude of the industry to quality and safety; to create a world-class building safety regime; and to inject confidence and certainty into this part of the housing market, which has been suffering from market failure, with significant detrimental effects for many homeowners across the land.[34]

Just as with the marketing material, this opening statement is larded with ready-made phrases that show the statement does not reflect any genuine, worthwhile thinking by the government. Instead, the minister's 'words, like cavalry horses answering the bugle, group themselves automatically into the familiar dreary pattern'[35] that is designed to convey the impression that something effective is being done about a problem affecting thousands of people. 'Majorities' are always 'vast' (as they are in the marketing material); plans are always 'five-point plans' (not two points or six points or 20 points) when they are not 'five-year plans'; people will always be made to pay their 'fair share' (never an 'unfair share' or no share at all); the government will always act in a 'proportionate' way, but that 'proportionate' way will also be 'robust' and result in the production of something 'world-class' (when the number of things in the UK that are genuinely world-class can be counted on the fingers of one hand). Just as with 'embodied energy' and 'embodied environmental impact' in the marketing material, the phrase 'market failure' is used merely because it sounds impressive, and not because 'market failure' (an economic term, with a moral meaning) properly describes what is happening when thousands of people find that their flats are unmarketable.

A serious country would not allow its companies or elected representatives to use language in this kind of hackneyed and manipulative fashion. But the UK is no longer a serious country.

E. Misplaced Trust in Authority Figures

The same government minister cited above was asked in the same debate, over the second reading of the Building Safety Bill, whether, in order to be marketable, flats in buildings less than 18 metres tall would need fire certificates (EWS1 forms) for their external walls. He responded:

> The expert advice that I commissioned has concluded that there is no systemic risk to life from purpose-built flats in this country and in particular – this was the question that I asked of the experts – from those flats that are low and medium-rise, meaning those of 11 to 18 metres. The experts' advice, following on from that, is that they do not see a need for lenders to ask for EWS1 forms in the ordinary course of business. … They do not conclude – as one would not expect them to do – that all buildings below 18 metres are safe. One can never say that, and there will be buildings that need

[34] HC Deb 21 July 2021, vol 699, col 1016.
[35] Orwell (n 30) 407.

> remediation below that level, but because there is no systemic risk and the number of buildings is likely to be very small, it is not appropriate, in their opinion, which the Government have accepted, that lenders and other parties in the market should act as if there was a widespread and systemic issue.[36]

As well as providing another fine example of what the Scots would call 'havering', this statement illustrates a fifth factor that has helped to doom MWLs, which is placing unjustified trust in authority figures.[37] Someone who holds themselves out as an authority figure necessarily claims that we will do better following their guidance or instruction in a particular matter than we would if we made up our own mind in relation to that matter.[38] Placing one's trust in an authority figure is justified if and only if that claim is justified.

The complexity of MWLs, and in particular their technological sophistication, means that one is forced on a daily basis to put one's trust in authority figures – there is simply no practical alternative when you are confronted at every turn with issues and problems that you cannot be expected to understand with any degree of expertise.[39] For example, our minister could not be expected to know whether the use of flammable cladding and insulation poses a big problem for buildings that are less than 18 metres tall. So he has to consult (unnamed) experts on the issue who hold themselves out as authority figures on that issue. And having consulted, the minister can then hold himself as an authority figure for banks and building societies – which are as ignorant as the minister on this issue – and reassure them that all is well on that front.

This chain of authority works well insofar as the claims to authority made by the authority figures in the chain are justified. However, those claims will tend to be unjustified if the authority figure in question is (a) incompetent or (b) self-serving in the guidance or instruction that they provide.[40] Unfortunately, as an authority figure the minister in our example seems to be self-serving. Note that he asked his experts to assess whether there is a systemic *risk to life* from flammable materials being used on the outside of buildings less than 18 metres high. This should be irrelevant to lenders, who want to know whether a *flat* that they are proposing to lend someone money to buy is liable to suffer *fire damage* as a result

[36] HC Deb 21 July 2021, vol 699, col 1027.

[37] For a striking and recent example of the damage done by misplaced trust in authority figures, witness the incompetent/corrupt performance of the US Food and Drug Administration in regulating the use of opioid pain-killers: A Kolodny, 'How FDA Failures Contributed to the Opioid Crisis' (2020) 22 *AMA Journal of Ethics* 743. Between 1999 and 2022, almost 275,000 Americans died of overdosing on prescription opioid medications. This is over four times the number of American soldiers who died in the Vietnam War (another example of the horrendous toll that misplaced trust in authority figures has exacted on the West: see D Halberstam, *The Best and the Brightest* (New York, Random House, 1972)).

[38] J Raz, *The Morality of Freedom* (Oxford, Oxford University Press, 1986) ch 3.

[39] See eg Arthur C Clarke's 'third law': 'Any sufficiently advanced technology is indistinguishable from magic' (AC Clarke, 'Clarke's Third Law on UFO's' (1968) 159 *Science* 255, 255).

[40] For arguments that the managerial class will almost always be incompetent to achieve the results that they are supposed experts at achieving, see NJ McBride, *The Humanity of Private Law, Part II: Evaluation* (Oxford, Hart Publishing, 2020) 102.

of the condition of its external walls. So the minister's assurance that, based on his experts' advice, lenders need not seek external wall fire certificates in relation to the purchase of flats in buildings less than 18 metres high makes no sense. As for the minister's experts, they also seem to be self-serving, telling the minister whatever they know the minister wants to hear: it is hard to imagine that anyone could provide reassurance as to the risk to life from buildings less than 18 metres high going up in flames without undertaking a nationwide, building-by-building survey. In both cases, our authority figures seem to be simply saying whatever they can say to revive the housing market for flats, and there is no basis for thinking that lenders will do better if they go along with what those kinds of authority figures say instead of making their own judgement.

In this case, going along with what authority figures such as the minister and his experts say may be unjustified but will probably turn out to be harmless. It is likely that lenders grossly overreacted to the Grenfell Tower fire by demanding ESW1 forms in relation to all flat purchases (another example of the West's endemic lack of courage) and reversing that policy will not result in lenders losing their shirts. But, on the night of the Grenfell Tower fire, some people will have lost their lives because of the trust they put in the fire services and call handlers when they were advised that the best thing they could do was to 'stay put' in their flats. The claims to authority made by the emergency services in giving that advice were unjustified – because of the incompetence of those services on the night – and people would have done far better to disregard the advice they were given and get out of the tower as quickly as possible.[41]

Moreover, the formulation of the 'stay put' policy itself involved a claim to authority – that people generally would do better following that policy than making up their own mind what to do when they became aware of a fire in a block of flats in which they were staying. Was that claim justified? Apps reports that the policy was based on 'incompetence at all levels' in interpreting statistics about the spread of fire within blocks of flats, and 'a misguided fear of a panicked evacuation, which is particularly prevalent within the fire service'.[42] He also points to various self-serving considerations that underlay the adoption of the 'stay put' policy:

> [It] is an enormously convenient policy and were we to acknowledge it needed to change, many implications would follow. … All told, it is simply easier and cheaper to stick with stay put – and to close eyes and ears to the evidence that our total reliance on it may be misplaced.[43]

[41] See, eg the 'family of five on the seventeenth floor' of Grenfell Tower who 'first phoned 999 at 1.29 am' and were 'told repeatedly and unambiguously [then and in subsequent calls] that help was coming and that the safest option was to stay put. … Further calls were made at 3.09 am and 3.18 am, and the family were told to "make a run for it" but could not leave due to the smoke. "I could have got out a long time ago, we could have but they said, 'Stay in the flat, stay in the flat,'" said the father in [the last] call. The family was never reached. All five of them died. It is estimated they could have fled up until 2.45 am and survived': Apps (n 6) 130.

[42] ibid 195.

[43] ibid 196.

II. The Irrelevance of Private Law

I have elsewhere chided Ben McFarlane for his optimism in stating that, so far as the common law is concerned, 'dusk never comes' and that we are destined 'always to be dazzled by the eternal sunshine of the common law'.[44] My view was and is that: 'This confidence is misplaced. Everything that has a beginning can have an end as well, and it is possible for the common law to sicken and become decadent.'[45] I went on to observe that:

> The midnight of the common law is marked by its irrelevance. People generally come to perceive the common law as remote and uncaring, and irrelevant to their daily life. As a result, 'justice for all' ceases to be a government priority. Justice once again becomes a local affair, with those who can afford it relying on arbitration and other alternative forms of dispute resolution to protect their interests, while those who cannot are left to fend for themselves.[46]

My claim in this section is that precisely the same factors that have undone MWLs – national bankruptcy, corporate fraud, a lack of virtue, abuses of language, and misplaced trust in authority figures – and that came together to bring about the Grenfell Tower fire have also effectively rendered private law an irrelevance in the national life of the UK.

The UK's national bankruptcy means that the government legal aid budget has been cut to the bone,[47] and under the Legal Aid, Sentencing and Punishment of Offenders Act 2012, most civil cases do not qualify for legal aid. Ministers and civil servants working in the Ministry of Justice and under the cosh of the Treasury have become suckers for any and every idea for cutting the costs of running the justice system, no matter how damaging the effects on private law's effectiveness. Examples: increasing fees for accessing the courts;[48] using AI to resolve private law disputes;[49] and allowing judges to decide private law cases without hearing arguments from the parties to the case in court.[50]

The effect of all this is that English private law provides a Rolls-Royce service for commercial litigants, and the equivalent of an Austin Allegro for ordinary people. Anecdotes from judges and barristers about the civil divisions of the Royal

[44] B McFarlane, 'Understanding Equitable Estoppel' (2013) 66 *Current Legal Problems* 267, 304–305.

[45] NJ McBride, *The Humanity of Private Law, Part I: Explanation* (Oxford, Hart Publishing, 2019) 252.

[46] ibid 253.

[47] The depressing tale has been well told by Frederick Wilmot-Smith: see his articles 'Necessity or Ideology?' (2014) 36 *London Review of Books*; 'Court Cuts' (2015) 37 *London Review of Books*; and 'Justice eBay Style' (2019) 41 *London Review of Books*.

[48] The Court Fees (Miscellaneous Amendments) Order 2021, SI 2021/985.

[49] Online Dispute Resolution Advisory Group, 'Online Dispute Resolution for Low Value Civil Claims' (Civil Justice Council, February 2015).

[50] See *Practice Direction 51ZC: The Small Claims Determination Pilot*, https://www.justice.gov.uk/courts/procedure-rules/civil/rules/part51/practice-direction-51zc-the-small-claims-paper-determination-pilot. I am indebted to Frederick Wilmot-Smith for having drawn this pilot scheme to my attention.

Courts of Justice being 'quiet' indicate that the right balance has not been struck: the price for their services has been set too high for demand to match supply. A look at the neutral case citations for EWCA Civ cases on Westlaw confirms this impression. In 2018, 2,962 cases were given an EWCA Civ citation. In 2019, that number was down to 2,291. After the courts got back to normal post-Covid in 2022, the downward trend continued: in 2022, 1,717 cases were given an EWCA Civ citation; in 2023, it was 1,566; and in 2024, it was 1,603.

The state has abandoned ordinary people – in terms of allowing them to access the benefits of the best English private law has to offer them[51] – at precisely the time when they need private law the most, in order to protect them from the general wave of corporate fraud and personal and institutional lack of virtue (in particular, irresponsibility) that characterises the West in its twilight years. It might be thought that the recent (May 2023) £150 million settlement of the civil claims arising out of the Grenfell Tower fire shows that private law is still capable of protecting ordinary people against the effects of fraud and irresponsibility[52] – but that is very much the exception that proves the rule: the national attention given to the Grenfell Tower fire meant that the estates of those who died in the fire, and the survivors, would not lack for high-quality representation. Lower-level cases are far more likely to fall by the wayside.

For example, landlord freeholders of many high-rise buildings that are both clad in combustible ACM and lack any centralised fire alarm system responded to the Grenfell Tower fire by instituting 'waking watches' where someone (often smoking cigarettes!) would be employed to stay up all night in the building watching out for fires, and in the event of a fire would alert the residents. It was acknowledged by the government in Parliament that these 'waking watch' schemes were 'being used excessively [and] can be rip-offs'.[53] But the only leaseholders who would be able and willing to pursue a civil case against their freeholder to recover the fees they had been unjustifiably made to pay under their service charge for a 'waking watch' in their building would be the very rich or very desperate.[54]

[51] Of course, some protection is offered ordinary people through their being able to access tribunals to hear their cases – but the first-tier tribunals will only hear cases relating to a variety of topics, such as tax or property disputes (including, now, remedial orders under the Building Safety Act 2022: see S Degeling and J Gardner, 'Procedural Challenges and Opportunities for Leaseholders', this volume, ch 9) or claims against the government in relation to decisions on education, healthcare and immigration. There is no first-tier tribunal with authority to hear ordinary people's general private law claims.

[52] Media reports providing the figures cited here include Brian Farmer, 'Judge Approves £150 Million Settlement of Grenfell Compensation Claims' *The Independent* (2 May 2023).

[53] HC Deb 21 July 2021, vol 699, col 1020.

[54] Judicial deference to authority figures meant that challenges to these charges were initially waved away: see eg *FirstPort Property Services Ltd v Tenants* [2018] UKFTT Case Reference LON/ooAH/LSC/2017/0435 (PC). There seems to have been only one successful challenge to a 'waking watch' charge, and that turned on a technicality to do with the freeholder's failure to do a proper fire risk assessment: *Radcliffe Investment Properties Ltd v Meeson* [2023] UKUT 209 (LC). Interestingly, given the argument in the text, 'Meeson' is Nigel Meeson KC, who was one of the leaseholders bringing the claim and who represented those leaseholders (who held the leasehold on 79 out of 96 flats in a development in Manchester) in court. It is hard to imagine those leaseholders would have gone to court without having as one of their number an expert lawyer who was willing (presumably) to represent them pro bono.

Part of the lack of confidence that ordinary people are likely to feel in terms of taking advantage of private law is due to the language in which it tends nowadays to be expressed, which language perfectly exemplifies Orwell's observation (quoted above) that, '[w]hen there is a gap between one's real and one's declared aims, one turns as it were instinctively to long words and exhausted idioms'.[55] There is a strong modern-day preference for framing private law in similarly general, vague terms. So: claimants will be recognised as having rights against a defendant if it would be 'fair, just and reasonable' for them to do so,[56] or if the defendant has been 'unjustly enriched at the claimant's expense',[57] or if there exists a relationship of 'trust and confidence' between the parties.[58] The 'non-core' terms of a contract between a 'consumer' and a 'trader' will be liable to be adjusted if they are 'unfair' in that they cause 'a significant imbalance in the parties' rights and obligations under the contract to the detriment of the consumer'.[59] Claimants are recognised as enjoying certain 'human rights' against 'public bodies', but those rights may be qualified as 'is necessary in a democratic society in the interests of public safety, for the protection of public order, health and morals, or for the protection of the rights and freedoms of others'.[60]

The 'declared aim' underpinning this kind of language is to encourage the parties in a private law case – in particular, the losing party – to think that the courts are simply giving effect to what the law says in deciding the case. But the 'real aim', which accounts for the preference for such vague language, is to give the judiciary a great deal of latitude in deciding a case so that they can give effect to what Lord Goff called the judge's 'educated reflex to facts'[61] in making their decision. However, the vagueness of the language in which private law is currently framed means that parties to a private law case can have no real assurance as to what the outcome of their case will be. As a result, going to law becomes an unjustifiable gamble for anyone without the kind of wealth that allows them to afford to make a habit of visiting casinos.

Our fifth factor that has helped to undermine MWLs is a misplaced trust in authority figures. This same factor blunts private law's effectiveness in that should someone seek to use private law to challenge the actions or determinations of an authority figure, the judges will often side with the authority figure against their challenger.[62] Such challenges are normally the stuff of public law, and some indication of the judicial deference to authority figures in the context of the Grenfell

[55] See n 30.

[56] *Cox v Ministry of Justice* [2016] UKSC 10, [2016] AC 660 [42]; *Robinson v Chief Constable of West Yorkshire* [2018] UKSC 4, [2018] AC 736 [27].

[57] *Banque Financière de la Cité v Parc (Battersea) Ltd* [1999] 1 AC 221 (HL) 226–27.

[58] *FHR European Ventures LLP v Cedar Capital Partners LLC* [2014] UKSC 45, [2015] AC 250 [5].

[59] Consumer Rights Act 2015, s 62.

[60] Human Rights Act 1998.

[61] Lord Goff, 'The Future of the Common Law' (1997) 46 *ICLQ* 745, 754.

[62] For examples of the courts' deference to authority figures in the medical context, see *Bell v Tavistock and Portman NHS Foundation Trust* [2021] EWCA Civ 1363 (deferring to doctors' judgements on whether a child is *Gillick* competent to consent to life-changing surgery); and *A NHS Trust v ST* [2023]

Tower fire is provided by *Rennie v Secretary of State for the Home Department*.[63] In that case, the Court declined to review the Home Secretary's failure to implement Sir Martin Moore-Bick's recommendation – arising out of the Phase 1 of his inquiry into the Grenfell Tower fire – that the owner and manager of every high-rise residential block of flats be required to prepare personal emergency evacuation plans (PEEPs) for those who would not be able to leave the block of flats without assistance in the event of a fire breaking out.

In light of this, it is probably just as well that the civil claims arising out of the Grenfell Tower fire were settled, as the judiciary might well have found that the government had no case to answer in respect of claims against government officials for their failures leading to the Grenfell Tower fire. As it is, the government's reported contribution of £25 million to the £150 million settlement – 17 per cent – surely does not properly reflect the contribution of public bodies and officials to the outbreak of the fire.

III. Private Law's Goals

How far should we be concerned at these trends, that render private law an irrelevance for many people? To answer this question, we need to distinguish two different kinds of explanations of private law. The first sees it as seeking to achieve a goal that cannot be achieved at all if private law is as irrelevant as it is today. Call this kind of goal a 'G goal', with a capital 'G'. The second sees it as seeking to achieve a goal that can still be achieved *in part* even if private law is as irrelevant as it is today for most people. Call this kind of goal a 'g goal', with a small 'g'.

On my view, private law pursues a G goal. I argue that private law seeks to promote the flourishing of its subjects while maintaining the conditions of its being regarded as legitimate.[64] A private law that is irrelevant as private law is today for many people cannot achieve that goal. While it may still be able to promote the flourishing of some of its subjects,[65] it cannot do so in a way that would be regarded as legitimate.[66] A private law that gives the impression that it exists for the benefit of a wealthy few, while amounting to nothing more than a 'sounding brass or tinkling cymbal'[67] for the rest is, almost by definition, illegitimate.

EWCOP 40 (ruling (at [93]) that a patient lacked capacity to make decisions about her medical treatment because she did not believe what her doctors were telling her).

[63] *Rennie v Secretary of State for the Home Department* [2023] EWHC 1794 (Admin).

[64] This is my essential thesis in McBride (n 45).

[65] Although, if the arguments in ibid, 97–107, are correct, not even this is likely to be true: a political community that is not geared towards promoting the flourishing of *all* of its members will tend not to be able to promote the flourishing of *any* of its members.

[66] ibid 200–02.

[67] *Simpson v Attorney-General (Baigent's Case)* [1994] 3 NZLR 667 (HC) 693 (Hardie Boys J, quoting 1 Corinthians 13:1).

By contrast, the most popular accounts of private law see it as pursuing a g goal: they simply disagree over what that g goal is. On an economic account of private law, the g goal is maximising wealth by creating incentives against the wasteful destruction of wealth and assurances promoting the creation and transfer of wealth. The trends described in the previous section no doubt mean that g goal is not achieved to as great an extent as could be the case, but the g goal is still achieved in part among those with the means to take advantage of private law.

Similarly, on a Kantian account of private law, the g goal is upholding the independence of each person to decide for themselves what will happen to the means that belong to them, free from anyone else dominating them and usurping their powers of control over those means. The irrelevance of private law to ordinary people means that this g goal is not realised for many people: those who lack the means to enforce their rights and so, in practice, have to submit to being controlled by others. However, the g goal is still achieved in part – again among those with the means to take advantage of private law. Their independence from being dominated by others is secured by the full panoply of rights that private law affords everyone, and the remedies that are made available when those rights are violated.

On the more popular g goal accounts of private law, such as the economic or Kantian accounts, the irrelevance of private law is a matter of obvious regret. Enhancing private law's ability to achieve its g goal should be regarded as a public priority – but no more important than other public priorities such as properly funding education or defence or welfare schemes. In contrast, on my G goal account of private law, the irrelevance of private law *must* be remedied if there is to be any point in having our system of private law *at all*. A G goal theorist would rage against the dying of the light that private law used to shed on our civilisation.

Seen in this way, the g goal accounts of private law seem to perform the same sort of function that James Burnham thought liberal ideologies did in relation to the decline of the West. Burnham argued that liberal ideologies reconciled people in the West to the factors that were sowing the seeds of the West's long-term destruction. For example, so what if the government is spending far more than it is able to recoup by way of taxation? It has no choice but to do this if we are to live in a society where everyone can think they are free and equal. So what if deregulation and market competition is triggering an explosion in corporate fraud? That's something we have to live with as deregulation and competitive markets are essential to our prosperity. So what if there is a marked decline in the peoples of the West being endowed with certain basic virtues, like a sense of responsibility and the courage to live up to those responsibilities? It's no business of the state to teach people to be virtuous. So what if language is decaying so that it no longer promotes thought but enables manipulation? Everyone has a right to freedom of speech. So what if society is being dragged down by people's putting misplaced trust in those claiming authority over them? That's why we have democracy and elections.[68]

[68] J Burnham, *The Suicide of the West* (New York, John Day Co, 1964) chs 1, 16.

In the same way, I would suggest, g goal accounts of private law reconcile us to the fact of private law's irrelevance to the lives of most ordinary people by allowing us to think that there is still some point in our system of private law even despite that irrelevance. Of course, this does not establish that my G goal account of private law is superior to its g goal rivals.[69] But it does suggest that: (a) those who adopt a g goal account of private law should consider whether the popularity of such accounts rests in part on their 'convenience' (to borrow a word from Apps) in that they allow us to live with the increasing irrelevance of private law and do not force us into rebelling against that status quo; and (b) those who do wish to challenge the status quo by fighting to improve such things as access to justice should acknowledge that putting such a high priority on securing access to justice only really makes sense if a G goal account of private law is correct, and explicitly base their fight on such an account.

IV. Can Private Law Come Back?

Assuming for the purposes of this chapter that my G goal account of private law – as existing to promote the flourishing of its subjects while maintaining its legitimacy – is superior to its g goal rivals, is there any hope that private law might be rehabilitated so that it can once more perform its G goal function?

Some hope might be provided by looking back to the condition of England when the private law that we are all familiar with got its start. That was in 1350, when England – like the rest of Europe – was facing up to the consequences of the Black Death, which killed *at least* a third of the populations it affected between 1347 and 1351. This would be the equivalent of a plague killing at least 22 million people in the UK today over the course of four years. (In contrast, Covid-19 killed, *at most*, a hundredth of that number – as of January 2023, just over 200,000.)[70] The effect of the Black Death was to radically destabilise English society. As Robert Palmer explains in his brilliantly researched *English Law in the Age of the Black Death*,[71] the response of Edward III and his advisers was to use law, and private law in particular, to pull the various sections of society together and put them on a virtual war footing, insisting that the upper orders do their part to contribute to the public welfare, while forcing ordinary people – through the 1351 Statute of Labourers – to go to work, and radically expanding the range of private law causes of action in order to provide remedies against those who proved (perhaps

[69] My book-length vindication of that claim is McBride (n 45).

[70] 'Cumulative Number of Coronavirus (COVID-19) Deaths in the United Kingdom (UK) (as of 13 January 2023)' *Statista* (30 November 2023) https://www.statista.com/statistics/1109595/coronavirus-mortality-in-the-uk/.

[71] R Palmer, *English Law in the Age of the Black Death 1348–1381: A Transformation of Governance and Law* (Chapel Hill, NC, University of North Carolina Press, 1993).

inevitably, given the loss of skilled labour caused by the Black Death) incompetent at their jobs.[72]

This response transformed the English social and legal order. Before 1350, law was used almost exclusively – and in a purely reactive manner – to address problems arising out of the operation of feudal chains of exploitation, where those in one stratum of society would feed off those in the strata below them. After 1350, law was set down the path of operating 'as an assertive instrument of social control' with the result that 'the king's government became responsible for the running of the whole [of] society'.[73] As an instrument of social control, law was directed initially at preserving 'as far as possible the status quo'[74] but evolved eventually – in line with my G goal account of private law – into seeking to create and maintain a social order that exists for the benefit of all of the members of that order.[75]

It is that path that the law, and private law in particular, has now strayed from and it is the whole point of this book to see how private law can get back on that path, at least in the field of promoting building safety. But for that to happen, there would need to exist what existed in 1350: a top-to-bottom determination to get our social order back on track in the face of disaster. While undoubtedly present in the symposia giving rise to this book, this determination is sadly lacking both in society as a whole and in the upper echelons of governments and economic life in the West. Instead, the race for the lifeboats has begun among those who can read the signs of the times.

In anticipation of impending disaster, billionaires have been buying up farms and estates in remote areas of the United States and New Zealand where they can ride out the storm, while seeking advice from psychologists as to how to persuade their minions not to kill them and take over after the balloon goes up.[76] Politics seems no longer to be concerned with fostering (and debating over the nature of) the common good but has become vapid and narcissistic in the same way that politics in the Roman Republic did before the Republic fell.[77] Serious and credible allegations have been made of corruption among Western politicians and their acolytes of a degree that most right-thinking people are still unwilling to entertain, so disturbing are the implications of those allegations.[78] The best guess as to what

[72] See eg ibid 213: '*Assumpsit*, thus allied with the Statute of Labourers, was part of a considered and controlled government policy of coercing working people to work well. The law became overtly and explicitly a governmental tool to control society, to preserve traditional society in the wake of the Black Death by regulating performance in occupations.'

[73] ibid 5.

[74] ibid.

[75] See McBride (n 45) 251–52 for an explanation of how that evolution might have occurred.

[76] D Rushkoff, *Survival of the Richest: Escape Fantasies of the Tech Billionaires* (London, Scribe UK, 2022).

[77] For a brilliant and wonderfully accessible account of the fall of the Republic, see R Harris, *The Cicero Trilogy* (London, Hutchinson, 2021) (also published under the separate titles, *Imperium*, *Lustrum* and *Dictator*). The parallels with the modern-day state of politics (particularly in the United States) are distressingly obvious.

[78] P Schweizer, *Profiles in Corruption: Abuse of Power by America's Progressive Elite* (New York, Harper Collins, 2020); T Burgis, *Kleptopia: How Dirty Money Is Conquering the World* (London,

is waiting for those of us without the means, or pull, to obtain a lifeboat to escape what is coming is a return to a pre-1350 existence: living in a neo-feudalist order that has given up all ambitions of fostering people's flourishing but again allows those on top to extract rents from those below them.[79]

I am not hopeful, then, that private law can *at this time* make a comeback and again contribute to the welfare of ordinary people in the way that other contributors to this book might hope that it can. I emphasise the words 'at this time' because of course private law can come back as a force in the life of the nation. But it can only do so, as I have said, if there exists a general national determination to return to living in a social order that seeks to foster the flourishing of all its members, with private law playing its proper and legitimate part in creating and maintaining that social order. I see no evidence that such a determination exists at the moment. It seems that such a determination will only emerge out of our undergoing the terrible hardships involved in being reminded, over and over again, what the consequences are of *not* living in such an order – with the Grenfell Tower fire being one such consequence.

One day we will learn our lesson, but it seems that we still have much to go through, and much to endure, before we do. But when we do, private law will rise again as a force in our daily life.

William Collins, 2020); P Schweizer, *Secret Empires: How the American Political Class Hides Corruption and Enriches Family and Friends* (New York, Harper Collins, 2018).

[79] Y Varoufakis, *Technofeudalism: What Killed Capitalism* (London, Bodley Head, 2023); J Kotkin, *The Coming of Neo-feudalism* (New York, Encounter Books, 2020). At the end of McBride (n 40), at 189–93, I predicted that neo-feudalism would be the result of a politics that had given up on fostering human flourishing; and that life akin to living in the Soviet Union or Mao's China would be the result of a politics centred on inauthentic models of human flourishing such as the Possessions Model that dominates in the West or the Service Model that is popular among those (particularly in Generation Z) who have rejected the Possessions Model. I warned that our only hope of avoiding disaster was the adoption of a politics based on the authentic, Journey Model, of human flourishing advocated for in the book.

INDEX

www.ingramcontent.com/pod-product-compliance
Ingram Content Group UK Ltd.
Pitfield, Milton Keynes, MK11 3LW, UK
UKHW020845290926
15470UKWH00004B/1561

9 781509 976607